EARLY STUART IRISH WARRANTS, 1623–1639

EARLY STUART IRISH WARRANTS, 1623–1639

The Falkland and Wentworth Administrations

Edited by

MARK EMPEY

IRISH MANUSCRIPTS COMMISSION

2015

Published by
Irish Manuscripts Commission
45 Merrion Square
Dublin 2
Ireland
www.irishmanuscripts.ie

ISBN 978-978-1-906865-56-6

Images used in the design of the dust jacket include a portrait entitled *Thomas Wentworth, 1st earl of Strafford, with Sir Philip Mainwaring, 1639–1640* by Anthony van Dyck courtesy of the Trustees of the Rt Hon. Olive, Countess Fitzwilliam's Chattels Settlement, by permission of Lady Juliet Tadgell, and a warrant for breaking prison (DDCR/7/1/1/1) courtesy of East Riding Archives and Local Studies Service.

Typeset by Carole Lynch in Adobe Garamond
Printing arranged by O'Sullivan Print
Index prepared by Julitta Clancy

CONTENTS

ACKNOWLEDGEMENTS

As with any project of this nature, permission to consult and publish manuscripts is entirely dependent on the goodwill and co-operation of those who preserve them. I am grateful to the Rare Books and Manuscript Department at the Bodleian Library; the East Riding Archives and Local Studies Service in Beverley, in particular the former archives manager, Ian Mason, and the collections officer, Joanna Larter; and finally, the Keeper of Marsh's Library, Jason McElligott, and the librarian, Maria O'Shea.

I would also like to thank Mary O'Dowd who first suggested that I bring the Irish warrants at Beverley to the attention of the Irish Manuscripts Commission. Likewise David Edwards recommended that I include the warrants in the Bodleian Library. His advice throughout this project is deeply appreciated. John McCafferty and Raymond Gillespie have been, and remain, a constant source of support and encouragement for which I will always be thankful. Brendan Scott went beyond the call of duty to offer his help on several queries. I will be forever indebted to Bríd McGrath. She was incredibly generous in sharing her research and gave up much of her free time to assist me on a number of occasions. Special thanks must go to my father, Adrian, who regularly trawled through the 2,600 pages of his 1924 edition of *Webster's New International Dictionary* in an effort to find the meaning of archaic words. Who knew it was more than just a doorstop?

Finally, this work would never have come to fruition without the help and guidance I received from James McGuire and Cathy Hayes of the Irish Manuscripts Commission. They are an editor's dream: efficient, supportive and unfailingly enthusiastic. It has been a great pleasure and honour to work with them

ABBREVIATIONS

BL	British Library
DIB	*Dictionary of Irish Biography* (9 vols, Cambridge, 2009; www.dib.cambridge.org)
Cotton, *Fasti*	Henry Cotton, *Fasti ecclesiae Hibernicae: the succession of the prelates and members of the cathedral bodies of Ireland* (5 vols, Dublin, 1848)
HMC	Historical Manuscripts Commission
Hughes, *Patentee officers*	James L. J. Hughes (ed.), *Patentee officers in Ireland, 1173–1826* (IMC, Dublin, 1960)
IMC	Irish Manuscripts Commission
Lib. mun. pub. Hib.	John Lodge (ed.), *Liber munerum publicorum Hiberniae or The Establishments of Ireland* (2 vols, London, 1852)
McGrath	Bríd McGrath, 'A biographical dictionary of the membership of the Irish House of Commons, 1640–1641' (Ph.D. thesis, University of Dublin, 1997)
MS/MSS	manuscript/manuscripts
ODNB	*Oxford Dictionary of National Biography* (60 vols, Oxford, 2004; www.oxforddnb.com)
TCD	Trinity College Dublin

INTRODUCTION

In its modern context a warrant is usually associated with the apprehension of an individual or group of people suspected of an offence. Its function and purpose, however, extends much further. The definition of a warrant in the *Oxford English Dictionary* is 'a document conveying authority or security', or more specifically, 'a writing issued by the sovereign, an officer of state, or an administrative body, authorising those to whom it is addressed to perform some act.' Authorisations of this kind could take various forms including licences, attachments and protections. The process of a warrant in the seventeenth century, however, is difficult to ascertain. The *Calendar of chancery warrants* shows that from the reign of Edward I onwards it was the ordinary practice of the English chancery court to file the various warrants that it received from the king or others.[1] The vast majority of these led to the issue of more formal instruments under the Great Seal. The absence of this kind of record for Ireland means that only some tentative comments can be made about the procedure involved in issuing a warrant in the circumstances of the early seventeenth century. The documents in this collection consist of a heterogeneous assortment of executive warrants, which may have resulted in more formal commissions under a seal. Volume four of the Wentworth Woodhouse Muniments at Sheffield City Library, for example, contains warrants directed to the lord deputy and council from Whitehall.[2] These were ordered on the back of private petitions sent to the king by an individual or group who sought to bypass the Irish administration — something which Wentworth was very keen to stop when he took office. The majority of the petitions that are cited in these warrants, however, were addressed to Dublin Castle, but in cases where there is no reference to a petition it remains unclear what action lay behind the order.[3] For the most part they were directed by the viceroy although they could also come from the privy council when the viceroy was not in residence.

Warrants are an invaluable source for the study of Irish history, no more so than in the early Stuart period. Dated between 1623 and 1639, this collection of more than 600 warrants ranges across a broad spectrum of political, religious, social, cultural, economic, military and administrative affairs during the viceroyalties of Viscount

1 *Calendar of chancery warrants preserved in the Public Record Office* [vol. I], A.D. 1244–1326 (HMC, London, 1927).

2 A number of these, furthermore, correlate with warrants issued by the Irish administration in this volume.

3 References are made to a 'petition book' or 'book of petitions' in the warrants. There appears to be no petition book extant for the period under consideration in this collection. However, BL, Harleian MS 4297 contains petitions for ecclesiastical matters for the early years of Wentworth's administration and there is a petition book for 1637 and 1638 (BL, Harleian MS 430).

Falkland (1622–9) and Sir Thomas Wentworth (1632–40).[4] They also afford insights into the interim government (1629–33) of the lords justices Loftus and Cork.[5] The importance of these warrants is that they shed significant light on the function of government while simultaneously they provide fascinating accounts of the activities of groups and individuals. Of added interest in this collection is the fact that every county is included and all levels of society are represented, ranging from nobility and bishops to bricklayers, brewers, divers and shoemakers. Thus the warrants not only show the efficiency of the instruments of government; they also reveal how far the administration's authority stretched.[6]

There are a number of aspects that feature regularly. For example, a sizeable proportion relates to political or ecclesiastical appointments. These could take the form of senior positions such as vice-treasurer or bishop, but they also include local offices like sheriff and curate. There is a notable emphasis on transporting goods, especially horses, hawks, pipestaves and oats, as well as soldiers. More importantly, the warrants reflect an improving economy. Wentworth's eagerness to strengthen trading links with Spain is noticeable but the evidence also points to an expanding domestic economy. This is reinforced by the government's sanctioning of several markets and fairs across the country. Local events of this kind were obvious meeting points for members of the public, whose political, religious or ethnic backgrounds differed markedly. Indeed, these warrants demonstrate a high degree of interaction between the various social groups in Ireland. This is most evident when examining legal disputes where natives and settlers frequently resorted to the courts to resolve their differences.[7] Above all, the warrants capture routine events that tend to be overlooked in correspondence or other state documents. Orders for the detention of rebels, malefactors and burglars, containing information about the crime committed, feature prominently in this collection. In addition, there are a number of references to begging passes for individuals who have encountered misfortune as well as orders that provide temporary protection for people in financial arrears. Merchants notably sought respite in situations where they lost their goods as a result of inclement weather or piracy. Protections could also extend to people who inherited debts of their deceased spouses. References to cultural activities make for equally interesting reading. Rope dancers and stage players, for example, were licenced to travel the country thereby giving a revealing insight into the appeal of, and appetite for, the theatre and theatrics among members of the public.

The warrants are transcribed from four sets of manuscripts. Over half of them derive

4 Henry Cary (*c.* 1576–1633), 1st Viscount Falkland (see *DIB*); Thomas Wentworth (1593–1641), created 1st earl of Strafford, 1640; lord deputy, 1632–40; lord lieutenant, 1640–41 (see *DIB*).

5 Adam Loftus (1568?–1643), 1st Viscount Loftus of Ely (see *DIB*); Richard Boyle (1566–1643), 1st earl of Cork (see *DIB*).

6 There are other collections of Irish warrants in the early Stuart period. Carte MSS 61 and 62 in the Bodleian Library, Oxford, contain warrants issued by Sir Arthur Chichester, lord deputy of Ireland, 1605–16 (see *DIB*). Additional warrants issued between 1604 and 1618 can be found in HMC, *Report on the manuscripts of the late Reginald Rawdon Hastings, esq.* (4 vols, London, 1928–47), iv, 18–53. Volume four of the Wentworth Woodhouse Muniments (Strafford Papers) in Sheffield City Library also contain copies of warrants between 1632 and 1638, but these were issued from Whitehall.

7 See Raymond Gillespie, *Seventeenth-century Ireland* (Dublin, 2006), pp 50–51.

from MS Eng. Hist. C. 304 in the Bodleian Library at Oxford, covering the period between September 1633 and January 1635. There are in excess of two hundred warrants from the recently discovered Calverley-Rudston papers housed in the East Riding Archives and Local Studies Service at Beverley in Yorkshire. Regrettably, few dates are recorded. References to individuals in initials suggest that the collection is a contemporary copy of originals that were issued from Dublin Castle. Nonetheless, it is possible to date the warrants between June 1634 and approximately 1637 on the basis of the internal evidence. The remaining two sets of manuscripts are from Marsh's Library, Dublin. There are thirty three warrants from MS Z3.2.6 which span between the years 1623 and 1638, while MS Z4.2.1 contains just the solitary warrant from 1639. Interestingly, there are only two duplicates with minor variations: a warrant to Richard Gething for the office of collector of the composition rents in Munster (warrant numbers 28 and 113), and a warrant for the fair of Doneraile to Sir William St Leger (warrant numbers 29 and 104). But rather curisouly the warrant to Gething has conflicting dates. The Marsh's Library copy is dated 6 November 1633 while the Bodelian Library version is 2 December 1633. There reasons for this are unclear.

Very little is known about how the warrants ended up in private ownership. According to Mary Clapinson and T. D. Rogers, the Bodleian set was once part of Phillipps MS 3612 when it was bought at an auction in Sotherby's on 6 June 1898. The manuscript was then donated to the Bodleian Library by F. J. Varley fifty years later.[8] The warrants are just one of four collections bound in MS Eng. Hist. C. 304 that also include material relating to English and Dutch history in the seventeenth and eighteenth centuries. Furthermore, the original pagination marked on the top right hand corner begins at f. 35 (now f. 448r), indicating that some documents are missing, and there are eight folios torn out after f. 538v which went unnoticed when the folios were renumbered. What became of the first thirty four folios is a mystery, but it is tempting to suggest that they were warrants issued shortly after Wentworth's arrival in Ireland at the end of July 1633.

The provenance of the two guard books in Marsh's Library is equally unclear. MS Z.3.2.6 is a miscellaneous collection of material chiefly relating to the seventeenth and early eighteenth centuries, while MS Z.4.2.1 primarily concerns court proceedings and adminstrative affairs in the early Stuart and Cromwellian period.[9] The thirty three warrants in the former manuscript are book-ended by documents relating to the eighteenth century. Moreover, they appear to have been bound with the intention of compiling all seventeenth-century material together. As a result, some chronological inconsistancies are present.

The history of the warrants in the Calverley-Rudston papers at East Riding Archives and Local Studies Service is easier to trace. They formed part of a collection relating to the Rudston family of Hayton. Until 1997 they were in the possession of the

8 Mary Clapinson and T. D. Rogers (eds), *Summary catalogue of post medieval western MSS in the Bodleian Library, Oxford* (3 vols, Oxford, 1991), i, 227. See also Brian C. Donovan and David Edwards, *British sources for Irish history, 1485–1641: a guide to manuscripts in local, regional and specialised repositories in England, Scotland and Wales* (IMC, Dublin, 1997), p. 217.

9 *Catalogue of the manuscripts remaining in Marsh's Library, Dublin*, comp. John Russell, ed. Newport J. D. White (Dublin, 1913), pp 46–54, 69–71.

family's decendents, then residing in Australia, when the East Riding Archives and Local Studies Service was contacted about preserving the papers.[10] They are generally in excellent condition. Only 24 out of the manuscript's 239 pages are either missing or badly torn. Consequently nineteen warrants are incomplete but for the most part there is sufficient information to understand the content and order being given. Quite how the warrants ended up in Yorkshire, however, is not clear. The fact that they are contemporary copies of the originals may be a factor. Yet other than the first page, which refers to Wentworth granting Captain William Rudston full command of 150 foot soldiers in the East Riding in June 1634, the remaining warrants all relate to Ireland.[11] The Rudstons, moreover, had no ties with the Dublin administration other than the fact that Wentworth jointly held the office of lord president of the Council of the North and chief governor of Ireland from 1633 until his execution in 1641.[12]

The structure of the warrants follows an almost invariable format. There is a margin of approximately two and a half centimeters from the left. The Bodleian set and the Calverley-Rudston papers both have the title of the warrant in the margins. This does not apply to the Marsh's Library collection. Instead a summary of the warrant is provided at the top of the page in a late seventeenth- or early eighteenth-century hand.

EDITORIAL CONVENTIONS

Modern spelling and punctuation have been adopted and contractions silently expanded for ease of reading. Personal names have also been modernised where possible. Folio or page transitions are indicated in bold in square brackets, interlineal insertions are marked by caret symbols and marginalia indicated in angle brackets. Where words are crossed out and/or illegible this is indicated by [ ]; confident suggested readings of missing words are included within square brackets.

The initials of individuals mentioned in the Calverley-Rudston papers are retained in the text; where possible and with a degree of certainty individuals have been identified in footnotes. For those that remain unidentified researchers can consult a range of key texts, such as John Lodge (ed.), *Liber munerum publicorum Hiberniae or The Establishments of Ireland* (2 vols, London, 1852), Walter Metcalfe, *A book of knights* (London, 1885), James L. Hughes (ed.), *Patentee officers in Ireland, 1173–1826* (IMC, Dublin, 1960), *Calendar of the State Papers relating to Ireland, of the reign of Charles I* (London, 1901), and J. T. Gilbert, *Calendar of ancient records of Dublin* (18 vols, Dublin, 1892).

10 The editor would like to thank the collections officer at the East Riding Archives and Local Studies Service, Ms Joanna Larter, for providing him with information about the Calverley-Rudston papers.

11 For an overview of the Irish warrants in the Calverley-Rudston papers see Mark Empey, 'Irish warrants – hidden treasures from the East (Riding)' in *History Ireland*, vol. 21, issue 1 (2013), pp 20–21.

12 Mark Empey, 'Paving the way to prerogative: the politics of Sir Thomas Wentworth, *c.* 1614–1635 (PhD thesis, University College Dublin, 2009).

WARRANTS NO. 1–34

OCTOBER 1623–JANUARY 1638

MARSH'S LIBRARY, MS Z3.2.6

1. [f. 61] 1623: LORD DEPUTY FALKLAND'S WARRANT FOR A COMMISSION TO ENQUIRE ABOUT WASTES IN THE WOODS IN THE TERRITORY OF RANELAGH, COUNTY WICKLOW[1] [22 OCTOBER 1623]

By the lord deputy

Falkland

Whereas the lands in the territory of Ranelagh in the county of Wicklow are by office found to belong to the king's majesty and we are informed that since the finding of the said office much waste and spoil hath been made of the woods and timber thereon growing to the great loss of his Majesty's behalf, these are therefore to will and require you to draw up a commission in due form directed to our trusty and well beloved Sir William Brabazon, knight, Sir William Parsons, knight and baronet,[2] Master of the Court of Wards and Liveries and surveyor general of his highness's kingdom of Ireland, John Brereton, esquire, his Majesty's sergeant at law, Sir Henry Bealing, knight,[3] Edward Bolton, esquire,[4] ~~solicitor~~ his Majesty's solicitor general, Captain Dennis Dale, Calcott Chambré, esquire,[5] Robert Pont, clerk, or to any three of them whereof Sir William Brabazon, knight, Sir William Parsons, knight and baronet, John Brereton, esquire, his Majesty's sergeant at law, or Edward Bolton, esquire, his Majesty's solicitor general, to be always one; to enquire as well by view as by the oaths of good and lawful men of the same county by whom such waste hath been committed, when and to what value. And the same to be returnable with as much expedition as may be [ ] X X X X X X X X X X X X X X X X X X X X,[6] for doing whereof this shall be your warrant. Given at his Majesty's Castle of Dublin the 22nd day of October 1623.

To his Majesty's learned Council or any of them.

J. Veele[7]

2. [f. 62] 1624: A LICENCE FOR GEORGE FORTE & MATTHEW MORRIS TO TAN & DRESS LEATHER IN MARYBOROUGH & THE LIBERTY THEREOF [1 JULY 1624]

By the lord deputy

Falkland

These are to will and require you presently upon sight hereof to draw up a fiant in due form of law containing a license unto George Forte and Mathew Morris during

1 The headings of warrants 1–34 are written in a different (later, probably eighteenth-century) hand from that of the secretary.

2 William Parsons (1570?–1650), later lord justice of Ireland (see *DIB*).

3 Sir Henry Bealing (or Bellings) (*c.* 1603–77), father of the lawywer and historian, Richard Bellings (see under Richard Bellings, *DIB*).

4 Edward Bolton (1592–1659), solicitor general of Ireland (see *DIB*).

5 Calcott Chambré, d. 1635.

6 This is how it appears in the manuscript and there is no obvious explanation.

7 John Veele, Irish secretary of state.

their natural lives and the longer liver of them and their several assigns (having been brought up as apprentices in the trade of tanning), by themselves or there [*sic*] servants or apprentices, to tan and dress leather at the town or fort of Maryborough, ^or the liberties thereof^ in the Queen's County; with a prohibition to all others not to tan or dress leather within the said town or liberties other then such as have been authorized heretofore by Sir Henry Sidney, knight,[8] sometimes lord deputy of this kingdom, or by some other succeeding lord deputy by letters patents under the great seal of this kingdom, upon such pains and penalties as in the statutes made in the eleventh year of his Majesty's reign of the late Queen Elizabeth entitled an act for the limitation of places for tanning, and set down and provided with a *Non obstante* of the statute and all such other clauses as in grants of like nature are usual; and inserting a *proviso* that the several patentees shall from time to time keep and bring up to the trade of tanning one, two or more apprentices; and another *proviso* for the observing of all such instructions as shall be contained in a schedule to their letters patents of licence to be annexed. And for so doing this shall be your sufficient warrant. Given at his Majesty's Castle of Dublin the first of July 1624.

To our well beloved, his Majesty's attorney and solicitor general, or either of them (as shall appertain).

J. Veele

3. [f. 63] 1625: WARRANT FOR A COMMISSION TO SIR EDWARD VILLIERS, LORD PRESIDENT OF MUNSTER & OTHERS TO ADMINISTER THE OATH OF SUPREMACY [27 MAY 1625]

By the lord deputy

Falkland

Whereas by the statute of 2 Eliz: it was among other things enacted that all and every officer and minister having her highness's fee or wages within this kingdom of Ireland should take and receive a corporal oath upon the Evangelist before such person or persons as should please her highness, her heirs or successors, or the lord deputy or other chief governor or governors of this kingdom, to name and assign according to the effect expressed in the said statute, these are therefore to will and require you forthwith to draw up a fiant in due form of a commission directed to our right trusty and right well beloved Sir Edward Villiers, knight,[9] lord president of Munster, or in his absence to the vice president here, and to Henry, earl of Thomond,[10] Richard, earl of Cork, Dominick, Lord Viscount Kinsale,[11] and to our trusty and well beloved the justices of assize for that province for the time being, and Sir Richard Aldworth, knight,[12] provost marshal of the said province, or to any two or more of

8 Henry Sidney (1529–86), lord deputy of Ireland (see *DIB*).

9 Edward Villiers (*c.* 1585–1626), government official and administrator (see *ODNB*).

10 Henry O'Brien (d. 1639), 5th earl of Thomond (see *DIB*).

11 Dominick Sarsfield (d. 1636), 1st Viscount Sarsfield of Kilmallock, and Viscount Kinsale (see *DIB*).

12 Richard Aldworth (d. 1629), provost marshal of Munster and army officer (see *DIB*).

them, hereby giving them full power and authority to call before them from time to time all and every officer and officers of all and every city or town corporate within the liberties of the said province and all other person or persons whatsoever within the said province, which by the said statute ought to take the said oath, and them and every of them to require to take their said corporal oath to his Majesty, his heirs and successors, in such manner as by the said statute is expressed and according to the power and authority given by commission in his behalf by his late Majesty unto the Lord Viscount Wilmot,[13] lord president of Connacht, which is to be initiated ^by you^ in the whole substance hereof *mutatis mutandis*. And for so doing this shall be your [ ] warrant. Given at his Majesty's Castle of Dublin, the 27th of May 1625.

To our well beloved, his Majesty's attorney and solicitor general, or to either of them.

J. Veele

4. [f. 64] 1625[/6]: WARRANT FOR APPOINTING ~~WILLIAM HILTON~~ THE KING'S ATTORNEY FOR THE PROVINCE OF CONNACHT [27 FEBRUARY 1626]

By the lord deputy

Falkland

Whereas by the death of Walter Archer, late attorney of the province of Connacht, that place is now become void and in our gift and disposal, these are therefore to will and require you presently upon sight hereof to draw up a fiant [ ] in due form of law containing a grant of the said office of king's attorney unto ~~their~~ our well beloved William Hilton, councillor at law,[14] with the yearly stipend or fee thereunto belonging from the day of the death of the said Archer together with all such other fees, profits, perquisites and commodities whatsoever to the same belonging or in anywise appertaining in as large, ample, and beneficial manner as the said Archer, or any other formerly held or enjoyed the same, inserting therein all such other clauses as in like grants are usual. And the same fair[ly] engrossed in parchment to send us under your hand to be further passed as appertaineth. And for so doing this shall be your warrant. Given at his Majesty's Castle of Dublin, 27 February 1625[/6].

To our trusty and well beloved, his Majesty's attorney and solicitor general, or either of them.

Nich. Whyte[15]

[13] Charles Wilmot (1570/1–1643/4), 1st Viscount Wilmot of Athlone (see *DIB*).

[14] William Hilton, lawyer and judge of the prerogative court.

[15] Nicholas Whyte, MP for Kildare in 1634 (see McGrath).

5. [f. 65] 1625[/6]: A WARRANT FOR APPOINTING SAMUEL MAYART[16] 2ND JUDGE OF THE COMMON PLEAS [16 JANUARY 1626]

By the lord deputy

Falkland

These are to will and require you forthwith to draw up a fiant in due form of law containing a grant of the office or place of second judge of his Majesty's Court of Common Pleas in this kingdom unto Samuel Maynart [*sic*], esquire, to have, hold and enjoy the same together with all fees, profits, advantages, emoluments, privileges, & immunities whatsoever ^thereunto belonging^ from the death of Sir Gerald Lowther, knight,[17] during pleasure in as large, ample and beneficial manner as the said Sir Garret Lowther[18] or any other supplying that place have heretofore held and enjoyed the same according to the purport of his Majesty's letters in that behalf unto us of the 21st of July last, a copy whereof for your better instruction we have herewith sent you. And the same fair[ly] engrossed in parchment under your hand to send unto us to be further passed as appertaineth. And for so doing this shall be a sufficient warrant. Given at his Majesty's Castle of Dublin the xvith day of January 1625[/6].

To our well beloved, his Majesty's attorney and solicitor general, or either of them.

Jo. Veele

6. [f. 66r] 1625: A WARRANT FOR THE APPOINTMENT OF SIR EDWARD VILLIERS, LORD PRESIDENT OF MUNSTER, IN THE PLACE OF THE EARL OF THOMOND, DECEASED [24 MAY 1625]

By the lord deputy

Falkland

Whereas the king's most excellent majesty that now is taking into his gracious princely knowledge and observation the good part, valour and discretion of Sir Edward Villiers, knight, hath thought good in his princely wisdom to make choice of him to succeed the earl of Thomond,[19] deceased, late president of the province of Munster in this realm in the government of that province and to that end hath been pleased by his highness's letters unto us directed, dated at Westminster the sixth day of this present month of May, to require us with the advice of some of his highness's learned Council here to make forth unto the said Sir Edward Villiers such letters patents, commissions, warrants and instructions for the exercising and enjoying of the office of lord president of Munster with all authority, privileges, immunities and pre-eminence thereunto in anywise appertaining and in his large, ample and beneficial manner to all intents and purposes as Sir Henry Brunkard, the Lord Danvers,[20] the earl of Thomond, or any other president of Munster or of the province of Connacht in this realm, have had

16 Samuel Mayart (1587–*c.* 1647), lawyer (see *DIB*).

17 Gerard (Garret) Lowther (d. 1624), justice of the common pleas in Ireland (see *DIB*).

18 Gerald Lowther (1590–1660), lawyer and judge (see *DIB*).

19 Donough O'Brien (d. 1624), 4th earl of Thomond (see *DIB*).

20 Henry Danvers (1573–1644), earl of Danby (see *DIB*).

and enjoyed the place of president with all fees, commodities, entertainments and allowance whatsoever belonging or formerly allowed to his highness's president of that province or to any of them, to have hold, exercise and enjoy the said office of president of Munster in such sort as the same hath been held and exercised by the said former president or any of them together with all the said [**f. 66v**] fees and allowances from and immediately after the day of the death of the said earl of Thomond. These are therefore to will and require you presently upon sight hereof to draw up a fiant in due form of law containing a grant from his Majesty unto the said Sir Edward Villiers of the said office of lord president of the province of Munster with all authorities, privileges, pre-eminence, sureties, fees, commodities, entertainments and allowance whatsoever heretofore allowed to the president of that province or to any of them, to have, hold, exercise and enjoy the said office of president of Munster unto the said Sir Edward Villiers according to the tenor of his Majesty's said letters, the copy whereof for your better instruction we herewith send unto you to press and also to draw up in due form of law the fiant of all such commissions unto the said Sir Edward Villiers as have been heretofore granted either unto the said late earl of Thomond, lord president of Munster, or to any other lord president of that province. And the same ~~to send unto us~~ fair[ly] engrossed in parchment under your hand to send unto us to be further passed as shall appertain; for doing whereof this shall be your warrant. Given at his Majesty's Castle of Dublin the 24th day of May 1625.

To our well beloved, his Majesty's attorney and solicitor general, or to either of them.

J. Veele

7. [f. 67] ATTORNEY OF CONNACHT TO WALTER ARCHER, 1625 [27 SEPTEMBER 1625]

By the lord deputy

Falkland

Whereas by the death of Damian Peck, late attorney of the province of Connacht, that place is now void and in his Majesty's gift and disposition, these are therefore to will and require you presently upon sight hereof to draw up a fiant in due form of law containing a grant of the said office of attorney of the said province of Connacht unto our well beloved Walter Archer of the town of Kilkenny, esquire, to have and to hold the said office of attorney of that province unto him the said Walter Archer together with ~~the fees~~ the yearly stipend belonging unto the said office ^unto the said Walter^ from the day of the death of the said Damian Peck with all fees, profits, perquisites, ~~and~~ commodities, privileges, pre-eminences and authorities whatsoever unto the same belonging or in anywise appertaining in as large, ample and beneficial manner as the said Damian Peck formerly held or enjoyed or of right ought to have holden or enjoyed the said office, inserting therein all such other clauses as in like grants are usual. And the same fair[ly] engrossed in parchment to send us under your hand. And for so doing this shall be your warrant. Given at Kilbeggan this 27th of September 1625.

To our trusty and well beloved, his Majesty's attorney ^and solicitor^ general, or either of them.

Richard Grace

8. [f. 68] GRANT TO JOHN KENNEDY, REMEMBRANCER OF THE EXCHEQUER, 1625[21] [21 AUGUST 1625]

By the lord deputy

Falkland

These are to will and require you privately upon sight hereof to draw forth a fiant of a grant in due form of law unto Robert Kennedy and John Kennedy, esquires, of the office of remembrancer of his Majesty's Court of Exchequer within this realm of Ireland otherwise called the office of chief remembrancer of his highness's said Court of Exchequer with all stipends, fees, perquisites, gifts, grants, rights, privileges and other appurtenances whatsoever to the said office any way incident, belonging or appertaining in as large, ample and beneficial manner and form as the said office was at any time heretofore granted unto Henry Draicott, esquire, John Thomas, esquire, Roger Manwaring, gent, Richard Colman, gent, or Sir James Carroll, knight,[22] by the name of James Carroll, esquire, or any other whatsoever, to have, hold, exercise and enjoy the said office with appurtenances by the said Robert Kennedy and John Kennedy during their natural lives and the life of the longer liver of them or by their sufficient deputy or deputies. And for your so doing this shall be your sufficient warrant. Given at his Majesty's Castle of Dublin 21 August 1625.

To our well beloved, his Majesty's attorney and solicitor general, or either of them.

John Veele

9. [f. 69] 1626: WARRANT FOR APPOINTING HENRY HART[E] & FRANCIS BURGESS USHERS OF THE COURT OF WARDS [10 JUNE 1626]

By the lord deputy

Falkland

These are to will & require you forthwith to ~~draw~~ draw up a fiant in due form of law containing a grant to be made unto Henry Harte & Francis Burgess, gent, of the office or place of usher of his highness's Court of Wards in this kingdom as the same is now established, to have and to hold the said office during good behaviour with all the rights, fees & perquisites thereunto belonging or appertaining in as large & ample manner as the same is now enjoyed or was therefore granted to Mathew Mainwaring, esquire. And the same fair[ly] engrossed in parchment under your hand to send unto us to be further passed as appertaineth. And for so doing this shall be your warrant. Given at his Majesty's Castle of Dublin the xth of June 1626.

21 See also warrant no. 410, 20 May 1634, for appointment of William Bramhall as chief remembrancer of the exchequer following 'manifold misdeanours and abuses committed by' Robert Kennedy.

22 James Carroll (d. 1639), landowner and state official (see *DIB*).

To our well beloved, his Majesty's attorney & solicitor general, or either of them.
John Veele

10. [f. 70] 1626: A WARRANT FOR RENEWING THE COMMISSION TO DANIEL MOLYNEUX[23] OF THE OFFICE OF ULSTER KING AT ARMS [3 NOVEMBER 1626]

By the lord deputy

Falkland

Whereas we think fit and expedient that the commission should be renewed which was granted to Daniel Molyneux, Ulster King of Arms and principal herald through this realm, the last day of February in the fourth year of his late Majesty's reign for conferring with the nobility and gentry of this realm in matters of arms, descents and pedigrees, and reforming of such abuses as shall occur in his visitation and travel as are prop[er] and incident to his place of King of Arms as by the said commission (which we herewith all have sent you) more at large appeareth, these are therefore to will & require you to draw up a fiant in due form according to the tenure and form of the said former commission adding only a clause for executing the same by the said Ulster himself or by his sufficient deputy or deputies. And the same fairly engrossed in parchment under your hand to send unto us to be further passed as appertaineth. And for so doing this shall be your warrant. Given at his Majesty's Castle of Dublin the third of November 1626.

To our well beloved, his Majesty's attorney & solicitor general, or either of them.
John Veele

11. [f. 71] 1626: A WARRANT FOR APPOINTING SIR RICHARD ALDWORTH, PROVOST MARSHAL OF MUNSTER, TO ACT AS VICE-PRESIDENT IN THE PLACE OF SIR EDWARD VILLIERS FOR A TIME [30 JUNE 1626]

By the lord deputy

Falkland

Forasmuch as our right trusty and well beloved Sir Edward Villiers, knight, lord president of the province of Munster, is to make his present repair unto the court in England about his Majesty's important affairs and hath by our allowance & consent made choice of Sir Richard Aldworth, knight, provost marshal of that province & one of his Majesty's Privy Council of this kingdom, to be vice president there during his lordship's absence, these are therefore to will & require you forthwith to draw up a fiant in due form containing not only a grant of a license for his lordship to repair into England & then to reside for the space of three months after the day of his departure out of this kingdom, but also of full power & authority for the said Sir Richard Aldworth during his lordship's absence to be vice president of that province & to govern & rule the same & his Majesty's subjects there resident, and to order all

[23] Daniel Molyneux (1568–1632), herald (see *DIB*).

the civil causes & affairs of the state & all other matters & business which concern the martial & public government of that province, with the advice & consent of the Council there already established as fully and effectually to all intents and purposes as if his lordship were personally present, inserting therein all such clauses as in grants of like nature are usual. And the same fair[ly] engrossed in parchment under your hand to send unto us to be further passed as appertaineth. And for so doing this shall be your warrant. Given at his Majesty's Castle of Dublin the xxxth of June 1626.

To our well beloved, his Majesty's attorney & solicitor general, or either of them.

John Veele

12. [f. 74] 1627: A WARRANT FOR A COMMISSION TO SIR WILLIAM ST LEGER[24] & TO RAISE FORCES BOTH HORSE & FOOT IN MUNSTER [8 APRIL 1627]

By the lord deputy

Falkland

These are to will and require you forthwith to draw up a fiant of a commission to be granted unto Sir William St Leger, knight, lord president of the province of Munster, & in his absence to his vice president for the time being and to the Privy Council & others or any two or more of them whereof the said Sir William or his vice president to be always one, to raise, levy, muster & survey the forces as well of horse & foot within the said province and then to employ against rebels or otherwise in defence of the ~~province~~ ^said province^ as occasion shall require, and to them shall be thought meet according to a commission of this kind issued unto Sir Edward Villiers, knight, late lord president of the said province. And the same fair[ly] engrossed in parchment under your hand to send unto us to be further passed as apptaineth. And for so doing this shall be your warrant. Given at his Majesty's Castle of Dublin the viiith of April 1627.

To our well beloved, his Majesty's attorney & solicitor general, or either of them.

John Veele

<for raising of horses ~~& foot~~>

13. [f. 75] 1627: A WARRANT FOR A COMMISSION TO THE LORD PRESIDENT & OTHERS TO TAKE ON THEM THE CIVIL GOVERNMENT OF THE PROVINCE OF MUNSTER [8 APRIL 1627]

By the lord deputy

Falkland

These are to will and require you forthwith to draw up a fiant of a commission unto Sir William St Leger, knight, lord president of the province of Munster, and in his absence to his vice president and to the Privy Council & others or any two or more of them whereof the said Sir William St Leger, and in his absence his vice president, to be only of the quorum for the civil government of the province of Munster according

24 William St Leger (*c.* 1580–1642), solider and politican (see *DIB*).

to such articles & instructions as have been heretofore or hereafter shall be given from his Majesty or the Council of England, or by the lord deputy or chief governor or governors & Council, have according to a commission in this kind issued unto Sir Edward Villiers, knight, late lord president of the said province. And the same fairly engrossed in parchment under your hand to send unto us to be further passed as apptaineth. And for so doing this shall be your warrant. Given at his Majesty's Castle of Dublin the viiith April 1627.

To our well beloved, his Majesty's attorney & solicitor general, or either of them.

John Veele

<For the civil government according to articles & instructions from the Board>

14. [f. 76] 1627: A WARRANT OF THE LORD DEPUTY FOR ENFORCING SIR WILLIAM ST LEGER, LORD PRESIDENT OF MUNSTER, & OTHERS TO ADMINISTER THE OATHS [8 APRIL 1627]

By the lord deputy

Falkland

Whereas by the statute of 2 Eliz: it was amongst other things erected that all & every officer and minister having his highness's fee or wages within this kingdom of Ireland should take and receive a corporal oath upon the Evangelist before such person or persons as should please her highness, her heirs or successors, or the lord deputy or other chief governor or governors of this kingdom, to name and assign according to the effect expressed in the said statute, these are therefore to will & require you forthwith to draw up a fiant in due form of law containing a grant of full power and authority unto our right trusty & well beloved Sir William St Leger, knight, lord president of Munster, or in his absence to the vice president there, & Henry earl of Thomond, Richard earl of Cork, Dominick Lord Viscount of Kinsale & to our trusty & well beloved the lords justices of assize for that province for the time being, & Sir Richard Aldworth, knight, provost marshal of the said province, or any two or more of them, to call before them from time to time all & every officer and officers of all and every city or town corporate within the limits of the said province and all other person or persons whatsoever within the said province, which by the said statute ought to take the said oath & them & every of them to require to take the said corporal oath to his Majesty, his heirs & successors, in such manner as by the said statute is expressed and according to the power and authority given in this behalf by his late Majesty unto the Lord Viscount Wilmot, lord president of Connacht. And the same fair[ly] engrossed in parchment under your hand to send unto us to be further passed as apptaineth. And for so doing this shall be your warrant. Given at his Majesty's Castle of Dublin the viiith of April 1627.

To our well beloved, his Majesty's attorney and solicitor general, or either of them.

John Veele

<president of Munster &c. to administer the oath>

15. [f. 77] 1627: LORD DEPUTY'S WARRANT FOR A COMMISSION TO SIR WILLIAM ST LEGER, LORD PRESIDENT OF MUNSTER, & THE PRIVY COUNCIL FOR THE CIVIL GOVERNMENT OF SAID PROVINCE [8 APRIL 1627]

By the lord deputy

Falkland

These are to will & require you forthwith to draw up a fiant of a commission unto Sir William St Leger, knight, lord president of the province of Munster, and to the Privy Council and others (whereof the said lord president and in his absence the vice president to be of the quorum) for the civil government of the said province according to a former commission of this nature issued unto Sir Edward Villiers, knight, late lord president there. And the same fair[ly] engrossed in parchment under your hand to send unto us to be further passed as apptaineth. And for so doing this shall be your warrant. Given at his Majesty's Castle of Dublin the viiith of April 1627.

To our well beloved, his Majesty's attorney & solicitor general, or either of them.

John Veele

16. [f. 78] LORD DEPUTY'S WARRANT TO THE LORD PRESIDENT OF MUNSTER OR VICE PRESIDENT IN THE ABSENCE OF THE LORD DEPUTY TO LEAD FORTH THE ARMY TO PARLEY &C. [8 APRIL 1627]

By the lord deputy

Falkland

These are to will and require you forthwith to draw up a fiant in due form containing a grant of a commission to Sir William St Leger, knight, lord president of the province of Munster, and in his absence to the vice president of the said province for the time being of chief leader of his Majesty's army and of all the forces, which now are or hereafter shall be within that province in our absence or the absence of any other lord deputy, chief governor or governors of this kingdom, and also power and authority to plea with rebels and traitors and their adherents, maintainers, aiders and abettors in the said province and to give safe conduct and protection to every such offender for such times as they, the said lord president and vice president or either of them, shall think meet. And the same fair[ly] engrossed in parchment under your hand to send unto us to be further passed as apptaineth. And for so doing this shall be your warrant. Given at his Majesty's Castle of Dublin the viiith of April 1627.

To our well beloved, his Majesty's attorney and solicitor general, or either of them.

John Veele

<leading the forces in absence of the lord deputy>

17. [f. 79] 1628: TO ENQUIRE ABOUT MALCOLM DROMMOND'S[25] LANDS IN THE BARONY OF STRABANE [23 NOVEMBER 1628]

By the lord deputy

Falkland

These are to will and require you to draw forth the form of a commission according to law to be directed unto Sir John Cunningham, knight, Stephen Allen, esquire, his Majesty's attorney for the province of Ulster, Hugh Mitchell, James Stewart, William Hamilton, Hugh Hamilton, esquires, James Galbraith,[26] Nicholas Coombe and Edward Tarleton,[27] or any three or more of them, thereby authorizing the said commissioners to enquire by the oaths of good and lawful men of the county of Tyrone whether the small proportion of Ballimagoregh in the barony of Strabane in the said county now in the possession of Malcolm Drommond, esquire, or of his assigns or undertenants or any part thereof hath been aliened or let unto any person or persons being mere Irish and to whom or to any other person or persons which (within the space of one year before such demise or alienation) have not taken the Oath of Supremacy within six months after such alienation or demise; and further to enquire what lands or tenements (lying within the said proportion or hereunto were adjoining and get no parcel of the same) have been occupied and enjoyed by the said Malcolm Drommond or by any other under whose right he claimeth without any lawful grant or title derived from his Majesty or any of his noble progenitors; and further giving authority to the said commissioners to distinguish and set forth by metes and bounds one full fourth part of the said proportion to be let to the mere Irish at the will and pleasure of the said Malcolm if he shall desire the same according to his Majesty's late instructions to us in that behalf directed. And the same fair[ly] engrossed under your hand to send us to be further passed as appertaineth; for doing whereof this shall be a sufficient warrant. Given at his Majesty's Castle of Dublin 23 November 1628.

To our trusty and well beloved, his Majesty's attorney and solicitor general, or either of them.

H. d'Launc

<Malcolm Drommond undertaker>

18. [f. 80] 1628: WARRANT FOR A COMMISSION ABOUT ALEX CUNNINGHAM'S LANDS IN THE BARONY OF RAPHOE [30 NOVEMBER 1628]

By the lord deputy

Falkland

These are to will and require you to draw forth the form of a commission according to law to be directed ^to^ Sir John Cunningham, knight, John Hamilton,[28] Malcolm

25 Malcolm Drommond (Drummond), inherited lands following the death of his brother, Sir Johm Drummond. Letters patent of denization were issued to Malcolm and also a grant to him, his heirs and assigns, of the small proportion of Ballymagoiegh on 29 May 1629. See George Hill, *An historical account of the plantation in Ulster at the commencement of the seventeenth century, 1608–1620* (Belfast, 1877), p. 532, 232n.

26 James Galbraith (d. 1649–54), MP for Strabane (see McGrath).

27 Edward Tarleton (d. after 1666), MP for Killybegs (see McGrath).

28 John Hamilton (1613–after 1650), MP for Bangor (see McGrath).

Drom[m]ond, and William Cunningham, esquires, James Galbraith, and Edward Tarleton, gent, or any two or more of them, thereby authorizing these commissioners to enquire by the oaths of good and lawful men of the county of Donegal whether the two quarters of land known by the several names of Drumloghran and Carcoman, being parcel of the small proportion of Portlagh in the barony of Raphoe within the said county now in the possession of Alexander Cunningham, gent, his assigns or undertenants, or any part thereof hath been aliened or let unto any person or persons being mere Irish and to whom or to any other person or persons which (within the space of one year before such demise or alienation) have not taken the Oath of Supremacy within six months after such alienation or demise; and further to enquire what lands or tenements have been occupied and enjoyed by the said Alexander Cunningham or by any other under whose right he claimeth without any lawful grant or title, and further giving authority to the said commissioners to distinguish and set forth by metes and bounds one full fourth part of the said two quarters to be let to the mere Irish at the will and pleasure ~~of~~ of the said Alexander Cunningham if he shall desire the same, according to his Majesty's instructions to us in that behalf directed. And the same engrossed under your hand to send us to be further passed as apptaineth. And for so doing this shall be your warrant. Given at his Majesty's Castle of Dublin *ultimo die Novembris* 1628.

To our trusty and well beloved, his Majesty's attorney and solicitor general, or either of them.

H. d'Launc

19. [f. 81] 1628: WARRANT FOR A COMMISSION TO ENQUIRE ABOUT WILLIAM BAILIE'S[29] LANDS IN THE COUNTY CAVAN [4 DECEMBER 1628]

Falkland

These are to will and require you to draw forth the form of a commission according to the law to be directed to John Hamilton, esquire, Stephan Allen, esquire, Richard Ashe, gent,[30] Robert Allen, gent, James Mooreherd, clerk, or any two or more of them, to enquire by the oaths of good and lawful men of the county of Cavan whether the small proportion of Toneregie consisting of a thousand acres of land more or less granted by former letters patents to William Bailie, gent, lying within the barony of Clanchie[31] and county of Cavan aforesaid or any part thereof hath been at any time since the grant thereof made to the said William alienated or set unto any person or persons being mere Irish ^and to whom^ or to any other person or persons which within the space of one year before such demise or alienation hath not taken the Oath of Supremacy nor within six months after such alienation or demise; and further to enquire the particular ancient known name or names, quantity or quantities of all and every the particular polls, gallons, pottles and parcels of land, tenements and premises belonging to the said

29 William Bailie of Finnylton (Finlaystown), Renfrewshire, granted denization in 1610 and received 1,000 acres in Cavan in 1611 (see McGrath, under Robert Baylie, MP for Cavan).

30 Richard Ashe (or Ash) (1609?–1659?), MP for Belturbet (see *DIB*).

31 Clankee.

small proportion and now held and possessed by the said William, or his assigns or by his or their undertenants; and further to limit, bound, distinguish and lay out the same by certain meres, metes and bounds; and likewise further to enquire what concealed lands, tenements and hereditaments are lying and being within the said proportion, or are thereunto near adjoining, and yet no parcel of the same that have been claimed, occupied or enjoyed by the said William Bailie, or by his assigns or by any other, under whose right he claimeth without any lawful grant or title thereof derived from his Majesty or any of his noble progenitors; and further likewise to distinguish and set forth by like name or names, meres and bounds, limits and divisions of parcels, one full fourth part of the said proportion and lands to be let unto the mere Irish at the will and pleasure of the said William Bailie, his heirs and assigns, and also to enquire and lay down in particular what performance of building and plantation the said William Bailie or his assigns hath made upon the said proportion since the grant of the said patent. And likewise to enquire of such other matter and things as in the discretion of the said commissioners shall be thought fitting to be enquired of and agreeable to his Majesty's late instructions concerning the undertakers of Ulster unto us in that behalf directed; and the same fair[ly] engrossed under your hand to send us to be further proceeded in as appertaineth. And for the same this shall be your sufficient warrant. Given at his Majesty's Castle of Dublin the fourth day [of] December *anno domini* 1628.

To our trusty and well beloved, his Majesty's attorney and solicitor general, or either of them.

H. d'Launc

<William Bailie, undertaker>

20. [f. 82] 1628: CAVEAT OF LORD DEPUTY FALKLAND AGAINST PASSING A GRANT TO THE EARL OF CORK OF THE ABBEY LANDS &C. OF THE MANOR OF DUNGARVAN [13 OCTOBER 1628]

By the lord deputy

Falkland

His Majesty's learned Council surveyors & auditors – a caveat that no lands be past to the earl of Cork or others of the manor of Dungarvan &c.

These are to will & require you & every of you to be specially careful that no fiant or patent be drawn up or permitted to be past unto the now earl of Cork or to any other person or persons of any part of the manors, abbey lands, tenements or hereditaments mentioned in the schedule herewith sent you, or of the manor of Dungarvan in the county of Waterford, until his Majesty's pleasure therein be further signified unto you by us, who have been required by his highness's letters of the 16th of August last to give you & every of you this charge of the performance, whereof you & every of you are not to fail at your perils. Given at his Majesty's Castle of Dublin the xiiith day of October 1628.

To our trusty & well beloved, his Majesty's learned Council, surveyor & auditor general & to every of them.

John Veele

21. [f. 83] 1628: WARRANT FOR A COMMISSION ABOUT SIR JOHN CUNNINGHAM'S WARRANT LANDS IN COUNTY DONEGAL [20 NOVEMBER 1628]

By the lord deputy

Falkland

These are to will and require you to draw forth the form of a commission according to law to be directed unto Andrew, lord bishop of Raphoe,[32] William Simpell, John Hamilton, esquires, Anthony Stewart, gent, and James Cunningham, esquire, or any two or more of them, thereby authorizing the said commissioners to enquire by the oaths of good and lawful men of the county of Donegal whether the small proportion of Ardee, the small proportion of Dacastrowes, and the quarter of land of Dunmoir[33] within the barony of Raphoe and county aforesaid, or either or any of them now in the possession of Sir John Cunningham, knight, or of his assigns or undertenants or any part thereof hath been alienated or let unto any person or persons being mere Irish and to whom or to any other person or persons (which within the space of one year before such demise or alienation) have not taken the Oath of Supremacy within six months after such alienation or demise; and further to enquire what lands or tenements (lying within the said proportions or hereunto were adjoining and yet no parcel of the same) have been occupied and enjoyed by the said Sir John Cunningham, or by any other under whose right he claimeth without any lawful grant or title derived from his Majesty or any of his noble progenitor[s]; and further giving authority to the said commissioners to distinguish and set forth by metes and bounds one full fourth part of the said proportion to be let to the mere Irish at the will and pleasure of the said ^Sir^ John Cunningham if he shall desire the same according to his Majesty's last instructions to [be] in that behalf directed. And the same fair[ly] engrossed under your hand to send us to be further passed as appertaineth. And for so doing this shall be your warrant. Given at his Majesty's Castle of Dublin 20th November 1628.

To our trusty and well beloved, his Majesty's attorney and solicitor general and [to] either of them.

H. d'Launc

22. [f. 84] 1628: COMMISSION TO ENQUIRE ABOUT THE LANDS OF SIR HENRY PEIRCE[34] IN THE COUNTY CAVAN[35] [5 DECEMBER 1628]

By the lord deputy

Falkland

These are to will and require you to draw forth the form of a commission according unto the law directed unto Sir James Crage,[36] knight, Stephen Allen, esquire, attorney of Ulster, James Stanyhurste, esquire, Robert Whitehead, esquire, and James Morehead,

32 Andrew Knox (1559–1633), bishop of Raphoe (see *DIB*).

33 Dunmore.

34 Henry Peirce (Peirs/Pierce/Piers) (d. 1638), administrator (see *DIB*).

35 Page is slightly torn at the edges.

36 James Crage (Craig), prominent Ulster landholder.

clerk, or any two or more of them. Th[ese are to direct] them or any two or more of them to enquire by the oaths of good ... men of the county of Cavan whether the great proportion of Kinneghals ... containing 2,000 acres of land more or less and the final proportion of Cashel containing 1,000 acres of land more or less lying within the said county of Cavan and granted by former letters patents unto Esmy, Lord Aubigney,[37] and now held and possessed by Sir Henry Peirce, knight and baronet, and his assigns and undertenants, or any part thereof hath been alienated or let unto any person or persons being mere Irish or to any other person or persons which within the space of one year before such demise or alienation have not taken the Oath of Supremacy nor within six months after such alienation or demise; and further to enquire of the particular name or names of every pole, pottle or parcel of land belonging unto the said proportions or either of them and possessed by the said Sir Henry Peirce or his assigns and the same to bound, meet and set out. And likewise to enquire what lands, tenements and hereditaments are within the said proportions or near thereunto adjoining and get no parcel thereof, and have been and are claimed, occupied, possessed or enjoyed as concealment or otherwise by the sa[id] Sir Henry Peirce or by his assigns or by any other without any lawful grant or title thereof unto him or them derived from his Majesty nor any of his noble progenitors; and further also giving power and authority unto said commissioners or any two or more of them to distinguish and set forth by meres and bounds one full fourth part of the said proportion respectively according unto the first survey thereof to be set to the mere Irish at the will and pleasure of the said Sir Henry Peirce and his assigns; and likewise to enquire of what performance of buildings and plantation towns and English inhabitants are within the said proportion respectively and further to enquire of such other matters and things as in the discretion of the said commissioners shall be thought fitting to be enquired of and agreeable unto his Majesty's late instructions concerning the undertakers of Ulster unto us in that behalf directed. And the same fair[ly] written under your hand to send us to be further proceeded in as appertaineth. And for the same shall be your sufficient warrant. Given at his Majesty's Castle of Dublin the fifth day of December *anno domini* 1628.

To our trusty and well beloved, his Majesty's attorney and solicitor general, or either of them.

H. d'Launc

23. [f. 85] 1628: ANOTHER COMMISSION TO ENQUIRE ABOUT THE LANDS IN THE BARONY & PARISH OF OMEY, COUNTY TYRONE [5 FEBRUARY 1629]

By the lord deputy

Falkland

These are to will and require you to draw forth the form of a commission according to law to be directed to Sir William Cole, knight,[38] Bryan Maguire, esquire, Thomas

[37] Esmé Stuart (1579?–1624), Lord Aubigney (Augbigny) and 1st duke of Lennox (see *ODNB*).

[38] William Cole (1571?–1653), English soldier and planter (see *DIB*).

Perkins, esquire,[39] Edward Archdale, William Ancketill,[40] William Hamilton and Bartholomew Richmond, esquires, and Edward Tarleton, gent, or any two or more of them, thereby authorizing the said commissioners to enquire by the oaths of good and lawful men of the county of Tyrone whether the small proportions of Cloghnamore and Gravetaghe lying and being within the barony of Omey in the said county of Tyrone now in the possession of the right honourable Ferdinando, Lord Hastings,[41] or his assigns or undertenants, or any part or parcel thereof or the sessioghs of land of Eddermore, Creaghduff *alias* Dakill, Gortnefane, Edenreagh, Lislawchill, Algolan, Aghamore, Aiskerbagh, Skraie, Lisalin, Coolkreaghagh, Roskawy, Edenreaghy, Gortferie *alias* Gortarey, Lisnanoagh, Casshelnegore, Cananaire, Creevie and Lurgaboy, Corhully, Tunellackan, Towreagh, Learbegg, Learmore, Langhill, Skeart, Gannenaghan, Downew *alias* Lisdewneigh, Cloghogale, Tawnaghavannan, Golaneboy, Trientorilly *alias* Mollaghinbriny, Leckatonncall, Careghowgan, Cooleneherney, Sessioghkeale, Aghnemeolagh, Mollaghduff, Kilrin, Killmannaghan, Edeneing and Tawnaghcarragh, Lisdeleloughora, Gortnecreigh, Gortgariff, Agheleigh, ~~Chathaghlaghare *alias* Claraghlegherne~~, Tullyard, Collowe *alias* Mollane and Lanebaragh, Leighfresh, Nebraskagh *alias* Brackhahy, Dowse, Ballyneddan, Charrakaskin, and Mullaghnecoltier or the townland of Claraghloghan *alias* Claraghloghine, Bovicketalle, Lisnebyaher *alias* Lisnebyhen, Drombaharly *alias* Clonferkogye, Dromsheall and Coolekeragh, Drossoge in Downe, Syogelly *alias* Gortnecolagh and Kilmore, or the half balliboe of Carana *alias* Careny, or the half sessiagh of land called Sifin lying & being within the said barony of Omey and county of Tyrone also in the possession of the said Lord Hastings, or his assigns or undertenants, or any part or parcel thereof have or hath been let or alienated to any person or persons being mere Irish and to whom or to any other person or persons which within one year before or six months after such alienation or demise have not taken the Oath of Supremacy; and further to enquire what lands or tenements lying within or near adjoining to the said proportions or lands and therewith occupied have been enjoyed by the said Lord Hastings, or by any other under whose right he claimeth without any lawful grant or title derived from his Majesty or any of his noble progenitors; and further giving authority to the good commissioners to distinguish and set forth by metes & bounds one full fourth part of all the same proportions & land to be let to the mere Irish at the will & pleasure of the said Lord Hastings if he shall desire the same; and likewise ^as well of the bounds of the parish of Urney and if it be fit to divide the same how much of the said parish lieth within the said proportions & whether there be therein a chapel how far it is from the said parish church as^ to enquire of all other things which by virtue of his Majesty's late letter & instructions in this behalf to us directed may be enquired of. And the same fair[ly] engrossed under your hand to send us to be further passed as appertaineth. And for

39 Thomas Perkins, one of the original corporators of the borough for the county of Donegal (see Aidan Clarke, *Prelude to Restoration in Ireland* (Cambridge, 1999), p. 186).

40 William Ancketill, sheriff of Tyrone in 1635 (see Clarke, *op. cit.,* p. 184n).

41 Ferdinando Hastings (1609–56), 6th earl of Huntingdon.

your so doing this shall be your warrant. Given at his Majesty's Castle of Dublin the fifth day of February *anno domini* 1628.

To our trusty and well beloved, his Majesty's attorney and solicitor general, or either of them.

H. d'Launc

<Lord Hastings's undertaker>

24. [f. 87] 1628: LORD DEPUTY FALKLAND'S COMMISSION TO ENQUIRE ABOUT THE LETTING OUT THE LANDS OF THE GREAT PROPORTION OF TENTONAGH IN THE BARONY OF CLOGHER & CO. TYRONE [16 DECEMBER 1628]

By the lord deputy

Falkland

These are to will and require you to draw forth the form of a commission according to law to be directed to Sir Daniel Leigh, knight & baronet,[42] Sir Henry Titchbourne, knight,[43] Stephen Allen, esquire, his Majesty's attorney for Ulster, Hamlett Moore, William Anctell and Thomas Perkins, esquires, or any two or more of them, thereby authorizing the said commissioners to enquire by the oaths of good and lawful men of the county of Tyrone whether the great proportion of Fentonagh in the barony of Clogher in the county aforesaid now in the possession of John Leigh, esquire, or of his assignes or undertenants, or any part thereof hath been aliened or let unto any person or persons ~~within the space of one year~~ being mere Irish, and to whom or to any other person or persons which within the space of one year before such demise or alienation have not taken the Oath of Supremacy or within six months after such alienation or demises; and further to enquire what lands or tenements lying within the said proportions or thereunto near adjoining and yet no parcel of the same have been occupied and enjoyed by the said Peter Peres(?)[44] John Leigh or by any other under whose right he claimeth without any lawful grant or title derived from his Majesty or any of his noble progenitors; and further giving authority to the said commissioners to distinguish and set forth one full fourth part of the said proportion to be let to mere Irish at the will and pleasure of the said John Leigh if he shall desire the same, and to enquire of what else shall be thought fitting to be enquired of in the discretion of the commissioners according [to] his Majesty's instructions in that behalf directed. And the same fairly engrossed to send us under your hand to be further passed as appertaineth. And for so doing this shall be a sufficient warrant. Given at his Majesty's Castle of Dublin 16th December 1628.

To our trusty and well beloved, his Majesty's attorney & solicitor general, or either of them.

H. d'Launc

42 Daniel Leigh, constable of Omagh Castle (see Hughes, *Patentee officers*).

43 Henry Tichbourne (Tichborne) (1581–1667), soldier and lord justice (see *DIB*).

44 The surname is crossed out and illegible.

25. [f. 90] 1629: LORD DEPUTY FALKLAND'S WARRANT FOR GRANTING A BARONETAGE TO JOHN MA[C]GRATH OF ALLE[S]OOLANE [*SIC*] IN COUNTY TIPPERARY [21 MAY 1629]

By the lord deputy

Falkland

Whereas his Majesty by his letters of the eighteenth of August hath been pleased to require and authorize us to give directions for passing several letters patents of the dignities of baronet of this kingdom unto two such persons as Sir Frederick Hamilton, knight,[45] should present and nominate unto us, and forasmuch as the said Sir Frederick hath by his instrument in writing under his hand and seal presented and nominated unto us John Macgrath of Allesollan in the county of Tipperary, esquire, to be one of those persons, these are to will and require you forthwith to draw up a fiant in due form of law containing a grant of the dignity of a baronet of this kingdom unto the said John Macgrath and the heirs males of his body begotten and to be begotten, to have and to hold the said dignity in as large and ample manner as by his Majesty's said letters (a copy whereof is herewith sent you) is warranted and required, inserting therein all such beneficial clauses as in grants of like nature are usual; and the same fair[ly] engrossed in parchment under your hand [to] send unto us to be further passed as appertaineth. For doing whereof this shall be your warrant. Given at his Majesty's Castle of Dublin the one and twentieth day of May 1629.

To our trusty and well beloved, his Majesty's attorney and solicitor general, or either of them.

John Veele

26. [f. 95] 1631: WARRANT FOR ENQUIRING INTO THE BREACH OF THE CONDITIONS FOR PLANTING ARDGART IN COUNTY FERMANAGH BY SIR JOHN HUME[46] [19 JULY 1631]

By the lords justices

Adam Loftus, chancellor, and Richard Cork.

These are to will and require you upon the receipt hereof to draw forth the form of a commission according [to][47] law to be directed to our well beloved Sir Andrew Stuart, baronet, Sir James Montgomery, knight,[48] Sir James Craig, knight, Walter Lackey, esquire, James Galbraith, esquire, and Edward Tarleton, gent, or any three, two or more of them, thereby authorizing the said commissioners to enquire by the oaths of good and lawful men of the county of Fermanagh whether the great proportion of Ardgart lying in the barony or precinct of Maghery Boy in the county of Fermanagh and formerly granted by letters patents to Sir John Hume, knight, the middle proportion of Moyglass in the said barony and county and formerly granted

45 Frederick Hamilton (*c.* 1590–1647), soldier (see *DIB*).

46 John Hume, a Scotsman and largest proprietor in Fermanagh. Also represented the county in 1634 parliament (see Hugh Kearney, *Strafford in Ireland, 1633–41: a study in absolutism* (2nd edn, Cambridge, 1989), p. 253).

47 Page torn.

48 James Montgomery (d. 1636), 1st Viscount Montgomery of the Ards.

by letters patents to William Fowler, esquire, and the small proportion of Dromcoose lying in the aforesaid barony or precinct and formerly granted by like letters patents from his late Majesty's to Alexander Hume, esquire, or any of the said proportions or any part or parcel of them or either of them hath been alienated or let to any person or persons being mere Irish, and to whom or to any person or persons whatsoever, which within one year before or six months after such demise or alienation have or hath not taken the Oath of Supremacy; and further to enquire what lands or tenements have been occupied and enjoyed by the said patentees or their assigns, or by any other without any lawful grant or title thereof derived from his Majesty or any of his noble progenitors; and likewise to enquire what bawns with stone houses are built upon the said proportions or every of them; and further giving authority to the said commissioners to distinguish and set forth by meres and bounds the full fourth part of each proportion to be let to the mere Irish at the will and pleasure of the said patentees or their assigns [**f. 95v**] if they shall desire the same; and also to enquire all such other matter and things according [to] his Majesty's late letters and instructions unto us in that behalf directed. And the same fair[ly] written under your hand to send unto us to be further passed as appertaineth. And for so doing this shall be your warrant. Given at his Majesty's Castle of Dublin this 19th of July 1631.

To our well beloved, his Majesty's attorney & solicitor general, or either of them.

27. [f. 96] 1631: WARRANT FOR A COMMISSION TO ENQUIRE ABOUT SIR STEPHEN BUTLER'S[49] LANDS IN COUNTY CAVAN [13 JULY 1631]

By the lords justices

Adam Loftus, chancellor, Richard Cork.

Whereas there hath been heretofore upon a former commission several enquiries concerning the great proportion of Clonose containing 2,000 acres of land and other the lands of Sir Stephen Butler, knight, lying within the county of Cavan and the middle proportion of Leitrim containing 1,500 acres, the middle proportion of Killspinan containing 1,500 acres and Dresternan containing one thousand acres, likewise the late possessions of the said Sir Stephen Butler, knight, lying within the county of Fermanagh, his Majesty is entitled unto the same lands and premises, together with certain other lands lying in or near adjoining unto the said proportions and premises which have been held and reputed as concealments, and that are not so fully found and expressed by the said late enquiries neither in their names nor quantities as the same ought to be, and also there are divers other parcels of lands lying in, or more adjoining unto, the said proportions that are ~~held as~~ concealments not found at all, the finding and making certain the particulars whereof will conduce to his Majesty's profit and increase of rent.

These are therefore to will and require you to draw forth the form of a commission according unto law to be directed unto Sir William Cole, knight, Edward Aldridge, esquire, Stephen Allen, his Majesty's attorney for Ulster, Charles Waterhouse, esquire,

49 Stephen Butler, undertaker from Bedfordshire. No relation to the Butler dynasty in Ireland.

Edward Hatton, clerk, Robert Allen, gent, the escheator and feodary or their deputies, and Martin ~~Baxter~~ Baxter, clerk, thereby authorizing of them the said commissioners or any two or more of them to enquire by the oaths of good and lawful men of the said several counties of Cavan & Fermanagh respectively what lands, tenements or other hereditaments are lying and being within the said several [**f. 96v**] proportions or were thereunto adjoining respectively that are no parcel thereof and yet are and have been possessed or occupied as concealments, or otherwise held without any lawful grant or title thereof unto him or them so possessing of the same derived from his Majesty that now is nor any other of his noble progenitors, and whereunto his Majesty is entitled by the grand office and are not as yet in charge with his Majesty's auditor, nor an[y?][50] rent answered unto his highness for the same and enquire further of the particular name or names there and the several and particular quantities, meres and bounds of the same, and of all other defects in these former offices and such other matters and things concerning the premises, as in the discretion of the sa[id] commissioners, shall be thought fitting to be enquired of and agreeable unto his Majesty's late instructions concerning the undertakers in Ulster unto us in that behalf directed. And the same fair[ly] written under your hand to send us to be further proceeded in as appertaineth. And for so doing this shall be your warrant. Given at his Majesty's Castle of Dublin the xiiith day of July 1631.

To our well beloved, his Majesty's attorney and solicitor general, or either of them.

< The particular of the concealments to be enquired of and not formerly certainly found are as followeth

Comitatu Cavan *vidzt*:
Vollolargen *alias* Vollacargagh 1 poll[51]
Corcreny *alias* Cornakilley *dimidium* poll
Reogh *dimidium* poll
Cornayrancreve 1 poll
Lisshanaderny 1 poll
Enysh *unum* pol[l]
and ~~dari~~ Darriada a parcel
Comitatu Fermanagh
Derrynishe *continet* vi *catenas*>

Memorandum that there be a clause inserted in the commission that fourteen days warning be given to the possessors of each parcels of these lands to be enquired of.

28. [f. 100] 1633: LORD DEPUTY WENTWORTH'S WARRANT FOR THE OFFICE OF COLLECTOR OF THE COMPOSITION RENTS IN MUNSTER TO RICHARD GETHING[52] [6 NOVEMBER 1633]

By the lord deputy

50 This is caught in the binding.

51 i.e. pole or perch.

52 Richard Gething (Gethings, Getking, Gitings) (1615?–1685), MP for Clonmel (see McGrath). See also warrant no. 113 in the Bodleian set; it is essentially the same warrant except it was issued on 2 December 1633.

Wentworth

Whereas the place or office of collector of his Majesty's composition rents in the province of Munster is now void & in his Majesty's gift, these are therefore to will & require you forthwith to draw up a fiant in due form of law containing a grant of the said place or office unto Richard Gething of Moyallo,[53] gent, to have, hold, possess & enjoy the said office, together with all the rights, duties, members, profits, privileges, pre-eminences, fees & appurtenances whatsoever ^thereunto belonging^ during good behaviour & in as large, ample & beneficial manner as Robert Morgan, gent, Sir Richard Morison, knight, & one Edward Merywether, or any other formerly held & enjoyed or of right ought to have held & enjoyed the same, the said office or place to be exercised by himself or his sufficient deputy during good behaviour as aforesaid, inserting therein ^a *non obstante* of the statute of 10 Henry Sept.[54] with^ all such clauses as in like cases are usual. And the same fairly engrossed in parchment under your hand to send unto us to be further passed as appertaineth. And for so doing this shall be your warrant. Given at his Majesty's Castle of Dublin the sixth day of November 1633.

To our right trusty & well beloved, his Majesty's attorney & solicitor general, or either of them.

Thomas Littell[55]

29. [f. 101] 1633: LORD DEPUTY WENTWORTH'S WARRANT FOR THE FAIR OF DONERAILE TO SIR WILLIAM ST LEGER[56] **[4 DECEMBER 1633]**

By the lord Deputy

Wentworth

Whereas our right trusty & well beloved Sir William St Leger, knight, lord president of the province of Munster, hath humbly petitioned unto us that we would be pleased to afford unto him the benefit of a weekly market & yearly fair to be kept at Doneraile in the barony of Fermoy in the county of Cork, we for that time did not think it fit to grant the same until such time as we certainly understood whether the granting thereof would be prejudicial to any other markets or fairs within the said county. Now inasmuch as it appeareth unto us by an inquisition taken the ~~17th~~ seventeenth day of September last that the same will be no annoyance, prejudice or hurt to any other fairs & markets as aforesaid, we therefore have thought fit and do accordingly hereby will & require you forthwith to draw up a fiant in due form of law containing a grant from his Majesty unto the said Sir William St Leger & his heirs of one weekly market to be kept upon the Thursday & one fair to be kept yearly the third day before the feast of St James the Apostle if it happen not to be a Sunday, & in that case to be held the day

53 Mallow.

54 Septimo, i.e. seventh.

55 Thomas Littell (d. 1641), secretary to lord deputy Wentworth, MP for Cashel (see McGrath).

53 See warrant no. 104, in the Bodleran set of warrants, which is essentially the same warrant, with minor differences, but the same date of issue.

following at Doneraile aforesaid, reserving thereout the sum of twenty shillings Irish rent to be paid unto his Majesty yearly, inserting therein all such clauses as in grants of like nature are usual; and the same fairly engrossed in parchment under your hand to send unto us to be further passed as appertaineth. And for so doing this shall be your warrant. Given at his Majesty's Castle of Dublin the fourth day of December 1633.

To our trusty & well beloved, his Majesty's attorney & solicitor general, or either of them.

<Warrant for fairs & market for the lord president of Munster>

30. [f. 102] 1634: A WARRANT FOR THE SECOND EXAMINATOR'S PLACE UNTO CHARLES AND GEORGE RYVES[57] [22 SEPTEMBER 1634]

By the lord deputy

Wentworth

These are to will and require you forthwith upon sight hereof to draw up a fiant in due form of law containing a grant from his Majesty unto Charles Ryves, late of All Souls College in the University of Oxford, Master of Arts, & George Ryves, late of the said university, Doctor in the Civil Laws of the office of second examinator of the Court of Chancery, with all fees, duties and perquisites thereunto belonging in as large and ample manner as the same was granted unto Sir Thomas Cary, knight,[58] by letters patents of our sovereign lord, the king, as likewise a grant unto the said Charles Ryves and George Ryves of the office of receiving, filing & transcribing copies of all depositions taken by commission on the part and behalf of any party or parties in any suit or cause depending or to be depending in the Court of Chancery in this kingdom in as large and ample manner as the same were heretofore granted unto the said Sir Thomas Cary & unto John Pitt & to Nathaniel Neave, or to any or either of them, to have and to hold the said several offices and either of them unto the said Charles Ryves during the term of his natural life and after his decease to the said George Ryves during the term of his natural life, inserting therein all such other clauses as in grants of like nature are usual; and the same fair[ly] engrossed in parchment under your hand to send us to be further passed as appertaineth. And for so doing this shall be your warrant. Given at his Majesty's Castle of Dublin the two & twentieth day of September 1634.

To our trusty and well beloved, his Majesty's attorney & solicitor general, or either of them.

Thomas Edmundes

[57] Charles and George Ryves (brothers), jointly held position of second examiners of the chancery from 1634. George also held the office of master in chancery (see Hughes, *Patentee officers*).

[58] Thomas Cary (Carry), master in chancery and prothonotary of court of common pleas 1627–34 (see Hughes, *Patentee officers*).

31. [f. 103] 1634: OFFICE OF MASTER OF CHANCERY TO GEORGE RYVES, LLD
[14 SEPTEMBER 1634]

By the lord deputy

Wentworth

These are to will and require you forthwith upon sight hereof to draw up a fiant in due form of law containing a grant from his Majesty unto George Ryves, Doctor in the Civil Laws, of the office of one of the masters of the Chancery in this Kingdom which is now void & in his Majesty's gift by the voluntary surrender & yielding up of the same by Sir Thomas Cary, knight, who formerly held & enjoyed the said office with a grant unto the said George Ryves of the annual fee or stipend of twenty pounds English for exercising of the said office, together with all other fees, wages, profits, salaries, advantages, commodities, pre-eminences and authorities to the said office belonging or appertaining to have, hold, use, exercise and enjoy the said office and other the premises unto the said George Ryves during his Majesty's will and pleasure in as large & ample manner & form as Sir Ambrose Forth, Sir William Temple, knight, the said Sir Thomas Cary, knight, or any of them, or any other formerly held & enjoyed the same, inserting therein all such other clauses as in grants of like nature are usual. And the same fairly engrossed in parchment under your hand to send unto us to be further passed as appertaineth. And for so doing this shall be your warrant. Given at his Majesty's Castle of Dublin the fourteenth day of September 1634.

To our trusty and well beloved, his Majesty's attorney & solicitor general, or either of them.

Thomas Edmundes

32. [f. 108] 1627: A WARRANT FOR A FIANT TO SIR WILLIAM ST LEGER OF THE OFFICE OF LORD PRESIDENT OF MUNSTER **[8 APRIL 1627]**

By the lord deputy

Falkland

These are to will & require you forthwith to draw up a fiant in due form containing a grant from his Majesty unto Sir William St Leger, knight, of the office of lord president of the province of Munster with all authorities, privileges, immunities, jurisdictions, pre-eminences & precedence thereunto in anywise appertaining in as large, ample & beneficial manner to all intents and purposes as Sir Henry Brunkard, the Lord Danvers, the earl of Thomond, Sir Edward Villiers, or any other president of that province, or of the province of Connacht in this kingdom, have held and enjoyed the place of presidents with all fees, commodities, entertainments and allowances whatsoever belonging and heretofore allowed to the presidents of that province or any of them according to the purport of his Majesty's letters unto us of the second of March last, a copy whereof for so much as concerns that particular we herewith send you. And for so doing this shall be your warrant. Given at his Majesty's Castle of Dublin, the viiith of April 1627.

To our well beloved, his Majesty's attorney & solicitor general, or either of them.

John Veele

<Sir William St Leger to be lord president of Munster>

33. [f. 109] 1637: THE PLACE OF ATTORNEY GENERAL OF THE PROVINCE OF CONNACHT TO EDWARD AYSCOUGH[59] [27 FEBRUARY 1638]

By the lord deputy

Wentworth

Whereas the office of his Majesty's attorney general for the province of Connacht is now void & in his Majesty's gift by the promotion of William Hilton, esquire, to be one of the barons of his Majesty's Court of Exchequer, and forasmuch as we have thought fit to confer that employment upon our trusty & well beloved Edward Ayscough, esquire, these are therefore to will and require you forthwith to draw up a fiant in due form of law containing a grant from his Majesty, his heirs & successors, unto the said Edward Ayscough of the said office of attorney general to his Majesty for the said province of Connacht to be held by him the said Edward Ayscough together with the yearly fee or stipend of twenty pounds sterling from his Majesty for the execution of the said office out of the revenues, fines, issues, forfeitures, & casualties happening, growing or from time to time arising within the said province of Connacht together with all other fees, profits, perquisites & emoluments whatsoever unto the said office belonging or anywise appertaining, & in as large, ample & beneficial manner as the said William Hilton or any other formerly held & enjoyed or of right ought to have held & enjoyed the same and to be exercised by him the said Edward Ayscough during good behaviour, inserting therein all such beneficial clauses as in grants of like nature are usual. And the same fairly engrossed in parchment under your hand to send unto us to be further passed as appertaineth. And for so doing this shall be a sufficient warrant. Given at his Majesty's Castle of Dublin the seven & twentieth of February 1637.

To our trusty and well beloved, his Majesty's attorney ~~general~~ & solicitor general, or either of them.

Edmundes

<Mr Ayscough to be attorney for Connacht>

59 Edward Ascough (Ayscough), attorney general of Ulster from 1634 and appears to have jointly held the position with the equivalent office in Connacht (see warrant no. 134).

34. [f. 111] 1637: LORD DEPUTY WENTWORTH'S WARRANT FOR THE PLACE OF BARON OF THE EXCHEQUER TO WILLIAM HILTON [29 JANUARY 1638]

By the lord deputy

Wentworth

Whereas the office or place of one of the barons of his Majesty's Court of Exchequer is now become void and in his Majesty's dispose by the death of Sir Lancelot Lowther, knight,[60] and forasmuch as (out of the even confidence we have in the integrity and abilities of our trusty & well beloved William Hilton, esquire) we have thought fit to confer that employment upon him, these are therefore to will & require you forthwith to draw up a fiant in due form of law containing a grant from his Majesty unto the said William Hilton of the said office of one of the barons of his Majesty's Court of Exchequer to be held by him, the said William Hilton (during his Majesty's pleasure), together with all such fees, stipends, vails, profits, perquisites, commodities, authorities, & privileges whatsoever unto the said office belonging or in anywise appertaining and in as large, ample, and beneficial manner as Sir John Elliott, knight,[61] or the said Sir Lancelot Lowther or any other formerly held and enjoyed or of right ought to have held and enjoyed the same, inserting therein all such clauses as in like cases are usual. And the same fairly engrossed in parchment under your hand to send unto us to be further passed as appertaineth. And for so doing this shall be a sufficient warrant. Given at his Majesty's Castle of Dublin the nine & twentieth day of January 1637[/8].

To our trusty & well beloved, his Majesty's attorney & solicitor general, or either of them.

Edmundes

<Mr Hilton to be one of the barons of the Exchequer>

60 Lancelot Lowther, third baron of the exchequer, 1617–25. Recommended by Sir Francis Bacon, lord keeper of the great seal of England, as 'a man learned in the profession of the law' (see *Lib. mun. pub. Hib.*).

61 John Elliot, third baron of the exchequer between 1589 and 1616 (*see Lib. mun. pub. Hib.*).

WARRANTS NO. 35–404

SEPTEMBER 1633–JANUARY 1634/5

BODLEIAN LIBRARY, MS ENG. HIST. C. 304

35. [f. 448r] <BISHOP OF KILFENORA[62] & STEPHEN ALLEN> [11 SEPTEMBER 1633]

By the lord deputy

Wentworth

Whereas upon humble suit made unto us by James, lord bishop of Kilfenora, & Stephen Allen, esquire, we have been pleased to give way that they shall be set at liberty. We therefore hereby require you forthwith to discharge & set at liberty the bodies of the said James, lord bishop of Kilfenora, & Stephen Allen, they paying their fees.[63] And for so doing this shall be your warrant. Given at his Majesty's Castle of Dublin this sixth day of September 1633.

To our well beloved Samuel Davis, esquire, constable of his Majesty's Castle of Dublin.

Thomas Littell

36. <SIR WILLIAM COLE> [11 SEPTEMBER 1633]

A like warrant made for the discharge of Sir William Cole, knight, directed to the constable of the Castle, Samuel Davis, esquire, dated the xith of September 1633.

Thomas Littell

37. [f. 448v] <A WARRANT FOR DRAWING UP A FIANT FOR THOMAS PRESTON, ULSTER KING AT ARMS> [14 SEPTEMBER 1633]

By the lord deputy

Wentworth

These are to will and require you forthwith upon sight hereof to draw up a fiant in due form of law concerning a grant from his Majesty unto Thomas Preston,[64] portcullis & of the office of Ulster king at arms in this kingdom, now void & in our hands & gift by the death of Daniel Molyneux & Adam Ussher[65] the last patentees thereof, together with the yearly fee or stipend of 40 marks sterling, good & lawful money of & in England for the exercise of the said office as also all such liveries, vestures, perquisites, stipends, wages, fees, salaries, customs, profits, commodities, pre-eminences, **[f. 449r]** privileges, advantages, rewards, jurisdictions & emoluments

62 James Heygate (d. 1638), bishop of Kilfenora.

63 Heygate and Allen, together with James, Lord Balfour, Sir William Cole, Sir John Dunbar and Captain Powell, were imprisoned in May 1633 for writing a letter on behalf of the Protestants of Fermanagh outlining their reasons for refusing to pay cess (see Mark Empey (ed.), 'The diary of Sir James Ware, 1623–66', *Analecta Hibernica*, no. 45 (2014), p. 94).

64 Thomas Preston (1585–1655), 1st Viscount Tara (see *DIB*).

65 Ussher jointly held the office with Molyneux from 1629 (see *Lib. mun. pub. Hib.*).

whatsoever unto the aforesaid office or officer by reason of the said office anyways belonging or appertaining, or at any time heretofore anciently or recently due or accustomed in as large & ample manner & form as the said Daniel Molyneux or Adam Ussher, or either of them, or one Nicholas Narbon[66] or Christopher Ussher,[67] or any other officer or officers in the said office within the kingdom of Ireland or in the kingdom of England, hath or ought to have received, taken or enjoyed, and as other kings at arms & principal heralds of the kingdom of England have or ought to have, to have & to hold the said office, fees, liveries, perquisites & premises unto the said Thomas Preston, portcullis, during good behaviour, inserting therein likewise all such other clauses as are mentioned in the former patent of the said office granted unto the said Daniel Molyneux & Adam Ussher as in like cases are usual. And the same fair[ly] engrossed in parchment to send unto us under your hand to be further passed as shall appertain. Given at his Majesty's Castle of Dublin this 14th day of September 1633.

To our well beloved, his Majesty's attorney general.

Thomas Littell

38. [f. 449v] <LORD BALFOUR HIS DISCHARGE>[68] [18 SEPTEMBER 1633]

By the lord deputy

Whereas upon humble suit made unto us by our very good lord, James, Lord Balfour, we have been pleased to give way that his lordship shall be freed from his present restrain & be set at liberty. We therefore hereby require you forthwith to discharge & set at liberty the body of him the said James, Lord Balfour, he paying his due fees; and for so doing this shall be your warrant. Given at his Majesty's Castle of Dublin this 18th day of September 1633.

To our well beloved Samuel Davis, esquire, constable of his Majesty's Castle of Dublin.

39. [f. 450r] <A WARRANT TO THE TOWN'S CLERK OF WATERFORD COMMANDING HIM TO DELIVER A BOOK TO RICHARD JONES, DEAN OF WATERFORD>

[18 SEPTEMBER 1633]

By the lord deputy

Wentworth

These shall be to will & require you forthwith upon sight hereof to deliver or cause to be delivered unto our well beloved Richard Jones, clerk, dean of the city of Waterford,[69] that book on which the mayor & other officers of that city do & have

[66] Nicholas Narbon, Ulster king at arms from 1566 to 1588 (see *Lib. mun. pub. Hib.*).

[67] Christopher Ussher, Ulster king at arms from 1588 to 1597 (see *Lib. mun. pub. Hib.*).

[68] See also warrant no. 35.

[69] Richard Jones, dean of Waterford between 1624 and 1634 (see Cotton, *Fasti*).

usually taken their oaths for the space of seven years last past [*sic*], at such time as they enter into their several offices and do take upon them the execution thereof. And hereof you are not to fail as you will answer the contrary at your uttermost peril. Given at his Majesty's Castle of Dublin this 18th of September 1633.

To Peirce Strange, town's clerk of the city of Waterford.

Thomas Littell

40. [f. 450v] <WILLIAM LONG> **[20 SEPTEMBER 1633]**

By the lord deputy

Wentworth

These are to will & require you forthwith to apprehend & attach the body of William Long, deputy sovereign of Baltimore, wheresoever he shall be found & immediately to bring him before ~~suc~~ us to answer such matters as at his coming shall be objected against him. And for so doing this shall be a sufficient warrant. In the due execution whereof we require all & every, his Majesty's officers, ministers & loving subjects whatsoever to be aiding & assisting unto you as there shall be cause, whereof you & they are not to fail at your & their perils. Given at his Majesty's Castle of Dublin the xxth day of September 1633. <*vide* page 59 for their discharge>

To any of his Majesty's pursuivants.

Thomas Littell

41. <THOMAS NEWMAN> **[20 SEPTEMBER 1633]**

The like attachment against Thomas Newman, deputy comptroller of the port of Baltimore, dated *ut supra*. <*vide* the affidavit whereupon these attach[ments] were grounded, petition book, page 140>

Thomas Littell

42. [f. 451r] <WILLIAM PEASLEY[70] TO ENJOY THE OFFICE OF SEARCHER IN THE PORT OF KINSALE> **[24 SEPTEMBER 1633]**

Wentworth

Whereas by the death of William Thornton, late searcher to his Majesty in the port of Kinsale, the said office is now become void & in our dispose, and forasmuch as we have been pleased to confer the same upon William Peasley, gent, these are therefore to will & require you forthwith to draw up a fiant in due form of law containing a grant from his Majesty unto the said William Peasley of the said office of searcher, packer & ga[u]ger in the said port of Kinsale & the creeks & members thereunto belonging, to have & to hold the said office with the yearly fee or stipend of six pounds, thirteen shillings, four pence sterling *per annum* together with all such other

[70] William Peasley (Peisley) (d. 1646), MP for Augher (see McGrath).

fees, stipends, profits, perquisites & emoluments whatsoever thereunto belonging or in anyway appertaining, & in as large, ample & beneficial manner as Sir William Hull, knight, sometime searcher of the said port, or the said William Thornton, formerly held & enjoyed or of right ought to have held & enjoyed the same during the said William Peasley, his good behaviour to be exercised by himself or his sufficient deputy or deputies, inserting therein all such clauses as in grants of like nature are usual. And the same fairly engrossed in parchment under your hand to send unto us to be further passed as appertaineth. And for so doing this shall be your sufficient warrant. Given at his Majesty's Castle of Dublin the 24th day of September 1633.

To our well beloved, his Majesty's attorney general.

Thomas Littell

43. [f. 451v] <WILLIAM HILTON> [24 SEPTEMBER 1633]

By the lord deputy

Wentworth

Whereas William Hilton of Awne[71] in the county of Limerick, esquire, hath been an humble suitor unto us that stay might be made to the enquiry of certain lands lately fallen unto him until your next sitting for that service after this in regard he is not possessed ~~which~~ ^of^ such writings, deeds & evidences as are necessary for him to produce, neither indeed can be part of them being in England, and the rest so dispersed in the hands of several persons as it is not possible for him to have them in readiness in this shortness of time as by his petition herewith sent you and affidavit made of the truth thereof may appear. These shall be therefore to will & require you to make stay of any such enquiry as aforesaid at this your present sitting at Kilmallock the last of this month & so to proceed therein as that the forbearance thereof may be no prejudice unto him; for which this shall your warrant. Given at his Majesty's Castle of Dublin this 24th day of September 1633. <*vide* the affidavit whereupon this was granted, petition book page 146>

To our well beloved Philip Perceval,[72] esquire.

Thomas Littell

44. [f. 452r] <ATTACHMENT VERSUS WAKEFIELD & SIMPSON> [26 SEPTEMBER 1633]

By the lord deputy

Wentworth

These are to will & require you forthwith to apprehend & attach the bodies of Thomas Simpson, customer of Cork, & William Wakefield, one of the waitors[73] for the farmers in that sort, wheresoever they shall be found & immediately to bring

[71] This may be Knockainy.

[72] Philip Perceval (Percival) (1605–47), landowner and government official (see *DIB*).

[73] i.e. weighers.

them before us to answer such matters as at their coming shall be objected against them; and for so doing this shall be your sufficient warrant. In the due execution whereof, we require all & every, his Majesty's officers, ministers & loving subjects whatsoever to be aiding & assisting unto you as there shall be cause; whereof you & they are not to fail at your & their perils. Given at his Majesty's Castle of Dublin this 26th day of September 1633.

To any of his Majesty's pursuivants.

Thomas Littell

45. [f. 453r] <ATTACHMENT *VERSUS* DR ~~ROBERG~~ ^ROBERT^ TRAVERS[74]> [28 SEPTEMBER 1633]

By the lord deputy

Wentworth

These are to will & require you forthwith to apprehend & attach the body of Sir Robert Travers, knight, wheresoever he shall be found & immediately to bring him before us to answer such matters as at his coming shall be objected against him as also to answer his contempt in not obeying our former warrant sent by the messenger; and for so doing this shall be your sufficient warrant. In the due execution whereof, we require all & every, his Majesty's officers, ministers & loving subjects whatsoever to be aiding & assisting unto you as there shall be cause whereof you & they are not to fail as you & they will answer the contrary at your perils. Given at his Majesty's Castle of Dublin the 28th day of September 1633.

To our well beloved, his Majesty's sergeant at arms.

46. [f. 453v] <THOMAS LAUGHER> [1 OCTOBER 1633]

By the lord deputy

Wentworth

Whereas Thomas Laugher by his humble petition hath informed us that having received in this kingdom a debt of two hundred & twenty pounds he hath endeavoured to return the same into England or Wales by bill of exchange but cannot at this present find conveniency for the same and the want thereof there (having great use for the said money) might prove very prejudicial ^unto^ him both in his estate & credit. He hath therefore been an humble suitor unto us to give licence unto him to transport the said sum of two hundred & twenty pounds *in specio*.

We, taking into consideration his necessity & the loss that may redound unto him for want thereof, have thought good to condescend to his request for this time and do hereby will & require you & every of you to permit & suffer the said Thomas Laugher to take, carry & transport with him the abovesaid sum of two hundred & twenty pounds sterling into England or Wales without any your trouble, seizure or

[74] Robert Travers (d. 1647), MP for Clonakilty (see McGrath).

molestation concerning the same whereof you may not fail; & for so doing this shall be your warrant. Given at his Majesty's Castle of Dublin the first day of October 1633.

To all & every, the officers of his Majesty's customs at this port, or at any other port, within the kingdom of Ireland whom the same may concern.

47. [f. 454r] <A WARRANT TO THOMAS LECHFORD[75] TO CONVEY THE BODY OF WILLIAM FREAKE TO LONDON> [4 OCTOBER 1633]

By the lord deputy

Wentworth

Whereas by the tenor of his Majesty's letters unto us directed bearing date at the court at Whitehall the eleventh day of March last 1632 & in the eight[h] year of his highness's reign concerning William Freake, esquire, we are required that the said Mr Freake shall forthwith make his personal appearance before the Master & Council of his Majesty's Court of Wards & Liveries in England. We do therefore herewith commit unto the custody of you Thomas Lechford, esquire, the body of him the said William Freake to be by you conveyed unto the city of London & from thence to the city of Westminster from this place by such ways as to ^you^ shall seem most convenient, there to be presented to the Master & Council of the Court of Wards & Liveries as aforesaid, hereby willing & requiring all mayors, justices of the peace, sheriffs, constables, bailiffs, officers and all other his Majesty's ministers & subjects to be aiding & assisting unto you as occasion shall be offered in the due performance & execution hereof, as they & every of them will answer the contrary at their perils. And for so doing this shall be unto you a sufficient warrant. Given under our hand & seal &c. this fourth day of October 1633.

To our well beloved Thomas Lechford, esquire, & to Henry Ashborne, or any others whom it may concern.

Thomas Littell

48. [f. 454v] <WILLIAM BRICKDALL> [4 OCTOBER 1633]

By the lord deputy

Wentworth

Whereas upon humble suit made unto us by William Brickdall we have been pleased to give way that he shall be set at liberty. We are contented to condescend to his request and therefore do hereby require you forthwith to discharge & set at liberty the body of him the said William Brigdall [*sic*], he paying his fees. And for so doing this shall be your warrant. Given at his Majesty's Castle of Dublin the 4th day of October 1633.

To any of his Majesty's pursuivants.

Thomas Littell

[75] Thomas Lechford (Lachford).

49. [f. 455r] <HIGH SHERIFF OF COUNTY CATERLOUGH[76] & LAURENCE KNOWLES> [4 OCTOBER 1633]

By the lord deputy

Wentworth

An attachment against the bodies of the high sheriff of the county of Caterlough & of Laurence Knowles of the town of Caterlough, merchant, dated the 4th of October 1633.

To any of his Majesty's pursuivants.

Thomas Littell

50. <A PROTECTION FOR 3 MONTHS TO GILES, LADY DOWAGER OF KERRY[77] & *AL.*> [10 OCTOBER 1633]

By the lord deputy

Wentworth

Whereas upon the humble petition of Giles, Lady Dowager of Kerry & Licksnawe[78], on the behalf of herself, Edmond Fitzmaurice and Garrett Fitzmaurice, esquires, her sons, and John Fitzgerald, esquire, her son in law, wherein it is set forth that by reason of the tedious suits & troubles between the petitioners & the Lord of Kerry[79] for divers years past [*sic*] they have been put to great extremity and to many & sundry inconveniences and are thereby also become much indebted unto divers persons both in the city & elsewhere in several sums of money, which hitherto their creditors have been contented to forbear in regard of their disabilities. <*vide* the petition thereupon, this was grounded ~~pet~~ in the common book of petitions, page 187> And whereas all the forementioned suits & differences between them are now ended & determined by virtue of an award, which is by us also lately confirmed, yet nevertheless they are humble suitors unto us to grant unto them a protection for some short time until they shall receive some benefit by the said award to enable them to satisfy their said creditors which they intend to do with all convenient expedition, [f. 455v] we, taking the premises into our consideration being fully persuaded that the reasons alleged are just & indifferent, are therefore pleased to condescend to this their request and do hereby make known that we receive the said Giles, Lady Dowager of Kerry and Licksnawe, the said Edmond Fitzmaurice & Garrett Fitzmaurice, her sons, & John Fitzgerald, her son in law abovementioned, their bodies, lands & goods into his Majesty's most gracious protection for the space of three months next ensuing the date hereof, hereby willing & requiring all his Majesty's officers, ministers & loving subjects whom it may concern not only to take due notice hereof but also to forbear to arrest, sue, trouble or molest them or any of them in their bodies, lands & goods as aforesaid during the time above limited; whereof they may not fail at their perils

[76] i.e. Carlow.

[77] Giles (Gilles or Julia) FitzMaurice, *neé* Power.

[78] Lixnaw.

[79] Thomas FitzMaurice (1574–1630), 18th Lord Kerry and Baron Lixnaw (see *DIB*).

provided that this extend not to protect them from any debt due unto his Majesty nor to free them from any former imprisonment. Given at his Majesty's Castle of Dublin under our hand & seal the xth day of October 1633.

To all mayors, sheriffs, justices of peace, portreeves, suffragans, bailiffs, constables, sergeants & all other his Majesty's officers, ministers & subjects & to every of them whom it may concern.

Thomas Littell

51. [f. 456r] <A WARRANT TO ROSS BOY McBRIAN McMAHON FOR THE APPREHENDING OF CERTAIN ILL PERSONS IN THE COUNTY OF MONAGHAN> [11 OCTOBER 1633]

By the lord deputy

Wentworth

Whereas we have received several informations & complaints of great wrongs, misdemeanours & enormities committed heretofore & still continued by a company of idle & ill disposed persons in the county of Monaghan, who have no manner of calling or trade of living but do frequently make stealths and that by night upon his Majesty's good subjects bordering upon them, & more especially from out of the lands of the next British undertakers inhabiting in the barony of Clanchy[80] in the county of Cavan, <*vide* the common book of petitions, page 187 for the certificate whereupon this warrant was grounded> and whereas sundry stealths have been of late time committed by such kind of people yet unknown upon the goods & chattels of Mathew Gambell, William Kernan & Richard Hill & divers others dwelling within the said barony to their damage of 40*li.* sterling as by their humble petition is set forth, all which stealths are credibly alleged & known to be dispersed in sundry parts of the said county of Monaghan amongst their relievers & abettors there residing, contrary to his Majesty's laws & justice in that behalf for the punishment of such offences and to the great discouragement of his ~~his~~ highness's good & loyal subjects who ought by all good ways & means to be by us relieved & protected (as much as in us lieth from rapine & spoil[)]. Now forasmuch as we are certainly informed that one Ross Boy MacBrian MacMahon is a person well able & no less well affected to do his Majesty's good service for the discovery & finding out of the said stolen goods, and for apprehending those malefactors their receivers, relievers & abettors, we have in consideration [f. 456v] thereof thought it fit & necessary upon the humble petition of the persons abovenamed and upon certificate of the truth thereof made unto us by our well beloved Sir Henry Peirs [sic], knight & baronet, & Sir William ~~Anterson~~ ^Anderson^, knight, to employ the said Ross Boy &c. in this service for the space of 3 months next ensuing the date hereof, taking into his company & for his assistants the said petitioners with such other persons as they and the said Ross Boy &c. shall think to be needful & shall make choice of, hereby willing & requiring all his Majesty's officers, ministers & loving subjects (as there shall be occasion) to be aiding

80 Clankee.

& assisting unto him the said Ross Boy and the rest of his assistants & conduitors in this employment during the time above limited as they will answer the contrary at their perils; and also affording them such necessary provision of meat & drink as the country will yield and as they shall stand in need of from time to time, they paining for the same the usual & accustomed rates and in all things behaving themselves honestly & orderly as they ought to do; for which their employment as aforesaid this shall be unto the said Ross Boy &c. and the rest a sufficient warrant. Given at his Majesty's Castle of Dublin under our hand & seal the eleventh day of October 1633.

To all mayors, sheriffs, justices of peace, provosts marshals, high & petty constables, bailiffs & all other his Majesty's officers, ministers & loving subjects whom it may concern.

Thomas Littell

52. [f. 457r] [DERMOD NESTOR] [11 OCTOBER 1633]

<Dermod Nestor: *vide* the affidavit whereon this was grounded, ~~petition book~~ page 16 in church affairs>

An attachment against the body of Dermod Nestor, clerk, dated the 11th day of October, directed to any of his Majesty's pursuivants, 1633.

Thomas Littell

53. <JOHN BRYCE> [11 OCTOBER 1633]

The like attachment against the body of John Bryce, dated *ut supra*, directed *ut supra*.

Thomas Littell

54. <CAPTAIN PUNCHER> [16 OCTOBER 1633]

By the lord deputy

Wentworth

Upon some informations lately exhibited unto us concerning one Captain Richard Puncher now being within your harbour at Waterford or within some creek near thereunto adjoining, these shall be to will & require you that presently upon the receipt hereof you make stay of him the said Captain Richard Puncher, his ship & company, until you shall receive our further directions in that behalf; whereof you may not fail. And for so doing this shall be unto you a sufficient warrant. Given at his Majesty's Castle of Dublin the 16th day of October 1633.

To our well beloved, the mayor of the city of Waterford ~~&~~ & to Lieutenant Stratford, commander of the fort of Duncannon in the harbour of Waterford, or to either of them.

Thomas Littell

55. [f. 457v] <JACOB JOHNSON[81]> [16 OCTOBER 1633]

By the lord deputy

Wentworth

Whereas a commission hath been heretofore granted by the Lords of the Admiralty in England unto Jacob Johnson, diver, bearing date the sixth day of June 1629 thereby requiring & authorizing him the said Jacob Johnson to employ his best art & industry in diving in all or any rodes, ports, harbours, creeks or havens, either on the coast of England or Ireland, where he shall know or understand that any bullion, ordnance, musters, either brass or iron anchors, cables or other goods or commodities whatsoever have been wrecked, sunk or lost, and there to use his best skill, cunning & industry for the getting up & regaining ~~of~~ such lost & wrecked goods of what kind soever rendering unto their lordships from time to time (for his Majesty's use) a true & perfect account ^for the same^ upon oath in the Court of Admiralty in England as by the said composition to him formerly granted, and a bond by him the said Jacob Johnson entered into for performance thereof doth further appear. And whereas the said Jacob Johnson, diver, hath humbly moved us for our furtherance and assistance for his better & more convenient accommodation in this his employment to the end he may without impediment or disturbance of any person or persons whatsoever ~~to~~ use and exercise his said art of diving for the getting up & regaining of all such lost & wrecked goods as aforesaid within any the rodes, ports, harbours, creeks or havens within this kingdom according to the tenor of the said commission, **[f. 458r]** we are therefore pleased to condescend to his request in that behalf hereby willing & requiring all vice-admirals, marshals & other officers of the Admiralty within this kingdom, mayors, sheriffs, justices of the peace, bailiffs, captains of castles & forts, captains & masters of ships, portreeves, constables, waterbailffs and all other his Majesty's officers, ministers & subjects whatsoever whom it may concern, not only to take notice of the said commission but also to permit & suffer him the said Jacob Johnson freely & quietly to work & use his said art of diving without any let, hindrance or interruption, and to aid & assist him as need shall require in the quiet & peaceable execution thereof, and not at any time to take out of his custody any such commodities or goods so by him taken up and recovered or to meddle therewith, otherwise then to certify unto us or unto the Lords of the Admiralty in England, the particulars thereof as they & every of them will answer the contrary at their perils. And for the performance of this his Majesty's service, this shall be unto the said Jacob Johnson a sufficient warrant. Given at his Majesty's Castle of Dublin under our hand & seal the sixteenth day of October 1633.

To our well beloved Jacob Johnson, diver.

Thomas Littell

81 Jacob Johnson of Aucusan, well known diver, hired by Venetian ambassador in 1622 (see John C. Appleby (ed.), *A calendar of material relating to Ireland from the high court of admiralty examinations, 1536–1641* (IMC, Dublin, 1992), p. 146).

56. [f. 458v] <ARCHIBALD CAMBELL> [17 OCTOBER 1633]

A warrant of attachment against the body of Archibald Cambell, dated the 17th day of October, directed to any of his Majesty's pursuivants, 1633.

Thomas Littell

57. <DAVID WALSH, ESQUIRE> [19 OCTOBER 1633]

An attachment *ut supra* against the body of David Walsh, esquire, dated 19th of October directed to any of his Majesty's pursuivants, 1633.

Thomas Littell

58. <ATTACHMENT *VERSUS* DANIEL DOYLE> [22 OCTOBER 1633]

By the lord deputy

Wentworth

<vide petition book page 200 for the petition whereupon this was grounded> These are to will & require you forthwith to make diligent search & enquiry for the body of one Daniel Doyle of Arklow in the county of Wicklow, merchant, & him there & wheresoever he can be found to attach immediately to bring him before us to answer the complaint of one Francis Portugal of Youghal & to be further dealt with as there shall be cause. <vide page 60> And for so doing this shall be your sufficient warrant. In the due execution whereof, we require all his Majesty's officers, ministers & loving subjects whatsoever to be aiding & assisting unto you as occasion shall require, whereof you & they are not to fail at your & their perils. Given &c. the 22nd of October 1633.

To any of his Majesty's pursuivants.

Thomas Littell

59. [f. 459r] <THOMAS MORGAN *VERSUS* EDWARD WADE> [23 OCTOBER 1633]

By the lord deputy

Wentworth

Whereas we are informed by Thomas Morgan, gent, victualler general of his Majesty's ships, appointed for the guarding of these coasts that you are indebted unto him in the sum of eighteen pounds sterling for wheat you bought of[f] him which was brought to Waterford in the ship, whereof one Anthony Tye was master, <*vide* the common book of entries, page 260> these are to will & require you immediately upon sight hereof to make present payment of the said sum of eighteen pounds unto the said Thomas Morgan or his assignee and thereof not to fail at your uttermost peril. <*vide* book of entries for the affidavit page 319> Given at his Majesty's Castle of Dublin the 23rd of October 1633.

Owen Brian.

To Edward Wade of Waterford, baker.
Thomas Littell
Owen ~~O Owen Brian~~

60. <A DISCHARGE *PRO* LONGE & NEWMAN> [2 NOVEMBER 1633]

By the lord deputy

Wentworth

~~A warrant to the constable in the Castle~~

A warrant to Mathew Bentley, one of his Majesty's pursuivants, commanding him to set at liberty the bodies of William Longe, late deputy sovereign of Baltimore, & Thomas Newman, deputy controller of the port of Baltimore. Dated 2nd of November 1633.

61. [f. 459v] <A WARRANT TO REMOVE DANIEL DOYLE FROM THE PURSUIVANT TO THE MARSHAL OF THE FOUR COURTS>[82] [2 NOVEMBER 1633]

By the lord deputy

Wentworth

Whereas upon the late complaint of one Francis Portugal of Youghal we have been pleased to grant our directions to his Majesty's pursuivant for the attaching of the body of one Daniel Doyle of Arklow in the county of Wicklow, who thereupon being brought before us & some other complaints being preferred against him of the nature, the said pursuivant hath made known unto us that by reason of the weakness of his house & that he hath no safe place to keep the said Doyle in custody he cannot keep him without danger of escape, wherefore the said pursuivant made humble suit unto us that we would be pleased to give order for the securing of the said Doyles person otherwise, whose request therein we have thought fit to grant. And therefore we do hereby will & require you forthwith to receive the body of the said Doyle into your custody & him to detain ~~in safe keeping~~ until you receive our further directions concerning him. Whereof &c. And for so &c. Dated 2 November 1633.

To John Dobb, marshal of the Four Courts.

62. <CAPTAIN PRONOVILLE[83]> [4 OCTOBER 1633]

By the lord deputy

Wentworth

Whereas we are advertised by Sir Richard Plumleigh, knight,[84] captain of all his Majesty's ships employed for guard of the coast of Ireland, of one Captain Richard Pronoville, who having commission from his Majesty the king of Spain & by exigency driven to betake himself into your port, hath there with all good discretion & civility demeaned & comported himself; now in regard it well suits the respective correspondency of both crowns that either subjects should mutually receive upon all just occasion civil & friendly usage the one ~~for~~ ^from^ the other, these are therefore

82 See also warrant no. 58.

83 Richard Pronoville (or Bromvile), naval officer (see *Cal. S. P., Ire, 1633–47*).

84 Richard Plumleigh (1595/6–in or after 1636), naval officer (see *ODNB*).

to will & require you & nevertheless straightly to charge & command you to [**f. 460r**] afford unto him the said Captain Pronoville ready supply & accommodation of victual & other whatsoever necessaries to himself, his ship or company appertaining, during his abode in these parts, he paying therefore the accustomed & usual rates; hereof fail you not ~~aswell~~ as you will answer the contrary at your uttermost perils. Given at his Majesty's Castle of Dublin the 4th day of October 1633.

To all mayors, sheriffs, justices of peace, sovereigns, governors, constables & customers in or about Crookhaven, and to all other his Majesty's officers, masters & subjects whom it may concern.

By the lord deputy general of Ireland.

63. <CAPTAIN PRONOVILLE>[85] [8 NOVEMBER 1633]

Wentworth

Whereas Sir Richard Plumleigh, knight, captain & commander of his Majesty's ships employed for the guarding of the coasts of Ireland, did lately (for certain reasons) grounded [*sic*] upon certain general instructions from the Lords & Commissioners of the Admiralty make stay of one Captain Richard Pronoville & his ship upon the western coasts of this kingdom, the said Captain Pronoville being commissioned by the king of Spain under whom he serves. Now inasmuch as we have received order from the said Lords & Commissioners of the Admiralty of England for the setting at liberty of the said Captain Pronoville & the restoring of the said ship into his full power & command, these are therefore to will & require as well the said Sir Richard Plumleigh as all others who are or may be entered with the keeping of the said ship in the said Sir Richard's absence either by [**f. 460v**] his directions or otherwise forthwith upon sight hereof, not only to restore and deliver back the said ship together with all the tackles, furniture, goods & provision whatsoever thereunto belonging unto the said Captain Pronoville without any the least diminution thereof, but also to use him & his company with all the fairest & most respective manner they can. And with all we do hereby declare & make it known unto all & every, his Majesty's officers, ministers & loving subjects whatsoever, that it is & may be free & lawful for them to see him the said Captain Pronoville & his said company (during the continuance of his said commission & whilst he doth not violate the same) provided either with victuals or any other necessaries which he or his said company shall want & desire to be furnished with, he & they paying therefore the usual & accustomed rates; whereof we require all whom it may concern not to fail at their perils. And for so doing this shall be a sufficient warrant. Given at his Majesty's Castle of Dublin the eighth day of November 1633.

[85] See *Cal. S. P., Ire., 1633–47*, p. 25.

64. <A WARRANT TO ALL OFFICERS TO MAKE STAY OF THE GOODS OF ROWLAND COLSTON> [9 NOVEMBER 1633]

By the lord deputy

Wentworth

Whereas Nicholas Astwood and William Wakefield, masters for the farmers of the customs in the port of Cork, having humbly petitioned unto us setting forth [**f. 461r**] that one Rowland Colston of Bristol, having put aboard 50 kilderkins of butter without any entry thereof, made with an intent to defraud his Majesty and the farmers of the customs do [*sic*] thereout, they the said masters seized thereon and have nigh put & given information into his Majesty's Exchequer, ~~fo~~ about the same they procured a writ of appraisement for the said butter with intention to proceed legally therein. But the said Colston understanding thereof, very cunningly and upon false suggestions, procured the custom of the said port to redeliver him the said butter (upon his own bare bond) which he forthwith put aboard and transported and as we are informed departed the kingdom and absents himself of purpose to decline the answering of the said information. We therefore (as well out of our care of his Majesty's just profits as that the farmers may not be prejudiced in their dues nor the petitioners either discouraged in their services for the future or be deprived of and lose the charges they have been put unto since the performing of the said information by their attendance here and solicitation thereof in the Exchequer) have thought fit and do accordingly hereby will and require all mayors, sheriffs, ^sovereigns,^ justices of the peace, bailiffs, constables, customers & searchers (who shall have notice of this our warrant) to make stay of all such goods and merchandize whatsoever which they shall find to belong unto the said Colston, wheresoever the same shall be found and safely to determine in your own custodies until upon advertisement or notice thereof sent from unto us we shall give forthwith directions therein; whereof they & every of them are not to fail at there perils. <*vide* the petition whereof this was grounded, petition book page 229> And for so doing this shall be ~~your~~ sufficient warrant. Given at his Majesty's Castle of Dublin the 9th day of November 1633.

65. [f. 462r] <ATTACHMENT *VERSUS* JOHN ARCHDEACON & *AL.*> [13 NOVEMBER 1633]

By the lord deputy

Wentworth

These are to will & require you to make diligent search & inquiry for the bodies of John Archdeacon & [blank] Gwins & them to attach wheresoever they may be found & being before us to answer such matters as on his Majesty's behalf shall be objected against them, for which this shall be your warrant. <This warrant granted upon affidavit of contempt in not appearing before commissioners for defective titles> In the due execution whereof we require all his Majesty's officers to be assisting &c. Given &c. 13th day of November 1633.

To any of his Majesty's pursuivants.

The affidavit whereupon the said attachment is grounded. 13 November 1633

<~~This warrant granted upon affidavit of contempt in not appearing before courts for the defective titles~~>

Brian Reilly made faith that on the 18th of September last past [*sic*] or thereabouts he showed a warrant signed by the right honourable, the lord deputy, & others the commissioners authorized, concerning defective titles, dated xth *Augusti* 1633, to John Archdeacon, gent, & one [blank] Gwins of Kinsale, clerk, whereby they as possessors of certain lands mentioned in a schedule annexed to the said warrant, or some others authorized & instructed for them, were to repair hither upon the 24th of September last to give satisfaction to the said commissioners concerning their interests in the said lands. <*vide* Reilly his petition ~~pe~~ book of entries page 237>

Paul Davis[86]

66. [f. 462v] <A COMMAND TO PRODUCE WITNESSES ON THE BEHALF OF MORRIS KIRTON & *AL.*> [13 NOVEMBER 1633]

By the lord deputy

Wentworth

Whereas we are informed by Maurice Kirton, gent, that you are meet & necessary witnesses to be examined in a difference depending before us between him & one David Walsh and inasmuch as the said difference is by us referred to be examined by Sir George Radcliffe, knight,[87] <*vide* page 68> these are to will & require you not to depart this town before you appear & be examined before & by the said Sir George Radcliffe in the said difference. Whereof &c. Given &c. 13 November 1633.

Marmaduke Shafby, Nicholas Herle & John Hawkins & to every of them.

67. <THE OFFICE OF SEARCHER OF CORK PAST [*SIC*] UNTO ROBERT PIERSY> [4 NOVEMBER 1633]

A warrant for the drawing up of a fiant of the searcher's place of Cork to be granted unto Robert Piersy upon the surrender of Richard & Joseph French, the patentees. The said Piersy to be searcher, weigher, packer & guager [*sic*] at the stipend of 5 *li. per annum* drawn according [to] the usual form, dated 4 November 1633.

68. <ATTACHMENT *VERSUS* SIR RICHARD OSBORNE & *AL.*> [15 NOVEMBER 1633]

By the lord deputy

Wentworth

These are to will & require you forthwith to make diligent search & enquiry for the bodies of Sir Richard Osborne, knight,[88] Richard Osborne,[89] his son, & one Donogh

[86] Paul Davies (or Davis) (d. 1672), clerk of the privy council and secretary of state (see *DIB*).

[87] George Radcliffe (1593–1657), lawyer and politician (see *DIB*).

[88] Richard Osborne (Osbourne) (d. 1667), MP for Waterford county (see *DIB*).

[89] Richard Osborne (Osbourne) (d. 1685), MP for Dungarvan (see *DIB*).

MacGillefoyle, & them to attach & bring before us to answer &c. <*vide* the petition and affidavit wherein this was grounded in church affairs page 31> Given &c. the 15th day of November 1633.

To any of his Majesty's pursuivants.

69. [f. 463r] <A WARRANT FOR A FIANT FOR JOHN SMYTH, CLERK> [15 NOVEMBER 1633]

By the lord deputy

Wentworth

These are to will & require you forthwith to draw up a fiant in due form of law containing a grant & presentation from his Majesty unto John Smyth,[90] clerk of the rectory of Eniskeen *alias* Enniskillen in the diocese of Clogher, *alias* the precentership of the cathedral church of St Macartin in the diocese of Clogher, being now void by lapse or otherwise, to have, hold, possess & enjoy the said rectory together with all the rights, duties, members, profits & appurtenances whatsoever thereunto belonging or in anywise appertaining, and in as large, ample & beneficial manner as any incumbent or incumbents formerly held & enjoyed or of right ought to have held & enjoyed the same, and directing his admission to the judge of the faculties, and inserting therein all such clauses as in like cases are usual. And the same fairly engrossed in parchment under your hand to send unto us to be further passed as appertaineth. And for so doing this shall be your warrant. Given at his Majesty's Castle of Dublin the 15th day of November 1633.

To our trusty & well beloved, the clerks of the Council, or either of them.

Thomas Littell

70. [f. 463v] <A WARRANT FOR EXAMINATION OF WITNESSES *INTER* KIRTON & WALSH>[91] [28 NOVEMBER 1633]

By the lord deputy

Wentworth

Whereas there is a difference depending before us between Maurice Kirton, plaintiff, & David Walsh, defendant, and forasmuch as the said parties do differ so much in the matter of fact as that the truth cannot well appear but by examination of witnesses, <*vide* the certificate whereupon this was grounded, petition book page 246> these are therefore to will & require you to examine all such witnesses & upon such interrogatories as either party shall produce concerning the matter in question. And having so done, to deliver copies of the depositions to either party under your hand provided that the defendant do in the meantime take a course that the sheep in question be delivered unto the complaint, and that you the clerk of the Council do

[90] John Smyth (or Smith), ordained decon in 1628, priest in 1629 and installed precenter on 26 November 1633 (Cotton, *Fasti*).

[91] See also warrant no. 66.

take good bonds with sufficient security that they stand to our order herein. And for so doing this shall be a sufficient warrant. Given at his Majesty's Castle of Dublin the xxviiith of November 1633.

To our right trusty & well beloved, the clerks of the Council, or either of them.

Thomas Littell

71. [f. 464r] <A PETITION FOR WILLIAM BOND FOR 6 MONTHS> [19 NOVEMBER 1633]

<*vide* the petition & certificate whereon this is grounded, petition book page 250 ~~150~~>

By the lord deputy

Wentworth

Whereas William Bond, merchant, hath petitioned unto us setting forth that for these many years together he hath furnished most of the western harbours & fishing places in the kingdom with salt for the saving of pilchards & other fish to the great benefit of the country & the advancement of his Majesty's customs, & still continueth the same, but by reason of some great losses he received lately by pirates at sea & the charge of about eighteen hundred pounds which he bestowed both in building & provision for two plantations begun by him in the west, he is become indebted unto several persons in certain sums of money amounting near unto six hundred pounds who expect present payment, which he being not able to give them & fearing to be arrested which he said would tend to his utter undoing & bring him in great danger to lose the employment he holdeth from divers merchants of England, Holland & Zealand, for the prevention of which inconvenience he humbly besought us to afford him his Majesty's protection for a time, whose request therein we have thought fit to grant and the rather in regard we have received very good certificate of the truth of what was contained in his petition as aforesaid and for that he said he is very ready & willing to give good security for the payment of his said engagements ~~as aforesaid~~ at any reasonable time. These are therefore to will & require you & every of you not only to take due notice thereof but also to afford him the full benefit of this protection in all respects by forbearing to sue, arrest, implead or any way molest him the said William Bond in his person or goods (he having [f. 464v] himself as becometh) for & during the space of six months next ensuing the date hereof, provided that by virtue hereof he do not endeavour to defeat any of his creditors but do in the interim to the uttermost of his powers use all care & industry to give them content & satisfaction that we may not be troubled with their complaints. And likewise our pleasure is that this extend not to protect him from any debt due to his Majesty nor to free him from any former imprisonment. And for so doing this shall be a sufficient warrant. Given at his Majesty's Castle of Dublin the nineteenth day of November 1633.

To all mayors, sheriffs, justices of peace, sovereigns, portreeves & bailiffs and to all others whom it may concern.

72. [f. 465r] <A WARRANT TO HIS MAJESTY'S ATTORNEY AND SOLICITOR GENERAL CONCERNING THE SEA [*SIC*] OF ARMAGH> [18 NOVEMBER 1633]

By the lord deputy

Wentworth

Whereas we gave order in August last for the issuing forth of a commission under the great seal (according to his Majesty's pleasure signified unto us by his letters of the 10th of May last) to enquire what lands, tenements or hereditaments do belong unto the sea [*sic*] of Armagh ~~Tyrone & Londonderry~~ and are quietly held & peaceably enjoyed by the now archbishop[92] thereof & his tenants in the three counties of Armagh, Tyrone & Londonderry, <*vide* the certificate of his Majesty's attorney and solicitor general, page 89 & 90> now inasmuch as the said commission hath been executed & three several inquisitions thereupon returned, these are therefore to will & require you two jointly to take into consideration, as well his Majesty's said letter of the 10th of May last as another letter from his highness of the 27th day of November in the sixth year of his reign, for passing of the said lands unto the see of Armagh & having so done upon perusal of the said inquisitions to consider whether they are pursuing & answerable to his Majesty's pleasure signified by his said letters, and whether the said letters be a sufficient warrant unto us for the passing of the premises and if we should give way thereunto whether any & what prejudice may arise thereby to the Crown all which, when you have duly digested & considered of, you are to certify us your opinions that thereupon we may give such order therein as there shall be cause. Given at his Majesty's Castle of Dublin the 18th day of November 1633.

To our trusty & well beloved, his Majesty's attorney & solicitor general.

73. [f. 465v] <ROBERT HOGSHEARD> [21 NOVEMBER 1633]

By the lord deputy

A warrant unto Robert Hogsheard, servant unto the Lord Eriskins [*sic*],[93] for transporting of a nag into Scotland for his own use, dated xxith November 1633, directed to all & every the officers of his Majesty's customs in the ports of Donaghadee & Bangor whom it may concern.

74. <WARRANT FOR A FIANT TO EDWARD SLACKE OF THE RECTORY OF CLEENISH> [21 NOVEMBER 1633]

By the lord deputy

Wentworth

Whereas the rectory of Cleenish in the diocese of Clogher is now void &c. and we have thought fit to confer the same upon Edward Slacke, Bachelor in the Arts, these require the drawing up of a fiant according to the usual form, <manicule> his

[92] James Ussher (1581–1656), archbishop of Armagh and distinguished scholar (see *DIB*).

[93] John Erskine (*c.* 1585–1653), 19th or 3rd earl of Mar (see *ODNB*).

admission directed to the bishop of the diocese & upon his refusal or absence to the judge of the faculties &c., dated xxith *Novembris* 1633.

To the clerks of the Council or either of them.

75. <ARCHIBALD ERISKIN> [23 NOVEMBER 1633]

By the lord deputy

Wentworth
An attachment against the body of Archibald Eriskin of Portoran in the county of Fermanagh, clerk, to answer the complaint of James Chadwick, esquire. Dated 23 *Novembris.*
<*vide* the common book of entries page 194 for the petition & affidavit whereon this is grounded>

To any of his Majesty's pursuivants.

Thomas Littell

76. [f. 466r] <A WARRANT TO RICHARD STRANGE & NICHOLAS POWER TO EXAMINE WITNESSES UPON THE DEATH OF WILLIAM WISE> [21 NOVEMBER 1633]

By the lord deputy

Wentworth
Whereas we are informed William Wise, esquire, of the body of King Henry the eighth, and after knight, (as it is said) died without any heirs males of his body the certainty whereof doth much concern his Majesty's service, these are therefore to will & require you to call before you & examine all such witnesses as shall be able to testify any thing material concerning the same asking them such questions of all such things & circumstances as may conduce to declare the truth herein and that of all your proceedings herein you forthwith certify us; whereof you may not fail. <Sir G. Radcliffe sent this to the entries>
Given at his Majesty's Castle of Dublin xxith November 1633.
~~Own Brien~~

To our trusty & well beloved ~~Nicholas~~ Richard Strange & Nicholas Power, esquires.

77. [WARRANT ORDERING THE PAYMENT OF 18*li.* TO THOMAS MORGAN] [N.D.]

Wentworth
~~Whereas we are informed by Thomas Morgan, victualler general of his Majesty's ships appointed for the guarding of these coasts, that you are indebted unto him in the sum of 18*li.* sterling for wheat you bought off him, which was brought to Waterford in the ship whereof one Anthony Tape was master, <*vide* the petition book, page 260 for Morgan's petition> <*vide* this book, page 59> these are to will & require you immediately upon sight hereof to make present payment of the said sum of 18*li.* unto the said Thomas~~

78. [f. 466v] <JOHN M[C]VICKON> [23 NOVEMBER 1633]

An attachment against the body of John McVickon now in town. Dated 23 November 1633. <the petition is unanswered & remains in our hands>

To any of his Majesty's pursuivants.

79. <THOMAS QUOAN> [23 NOVEMBER 1633]

Wentworth

An attachment against the body of Thomas Quoan of Waterford, dated *ut supra*, directed *ut supra.*

80. <WARRANT FOR RE-EDIFYING THE CHURCH OF DONEGAL> [25 NOVEMBER 1633]

By the lord deputy

Wentworth

Whereas it appeareth unto us, as well by certificate of the late commissioners nominated & appointed for the building & re-edifying of the churches in the county of Donegal unto the late lords justices as also to a petition presented unto us from the incumbent & the chiefest & greatest part of the conformable parishioners of the parish of Drumhome in the said county expressing the inconvenient situation of the parish church there and now altogether ruined, and that the abbey church of Donegal standeth more conveniently in the midst of the said parish and adjoining unto the corporation or borough of Donegal & town of Magherabeg where the most ^&^ chiefest of the British & conformable inhabitants are residing & dwell, <*vide* book of entries page 292 for the petition whereon this was grounded> we have thought it fit & so do order & appoint that the said abbey church shall be made the parochial church of the said parish of Drumhome & do hereby require the lord bishop of Raphoe[94] & the said commissioners formerly appointed by his Majesty for the re-edifying of churches within that county, or any three or more of them, to take care for the speedy & sufficient re-edifying **[f. 467r]** of the said abbey church of [ ] ^Donegal^ & to give from time to time their best furtherance thereunto. And we do likewise order that as well all such monies as have been lately by the said commissioners & parishioners applotted for the re-edifying of the parish church there, as also all such monies ^or^ ~~&~~ materials as remain in the hands of any person or persons whatsoever, & formerly designed for that good work shall be speedily ^& forthwith^ employed for & towards the re-edifying & building of the said ~~parish~~ ^abbey^ church, and in respect of the ease & commodity growing thereby to the inhabitants of the said borough of Donegal & town of Magherabeg, & the rest of the inhabitants in that part of the said parish, we do order that if the charge of re-edifying & building up the said abbey church shall amount to any greater sum then hath been already applotted upon the said parish & inhabitants then that they of the said borough of Donegal & town of Magherabeg, & such other of the inhabitants as receive ease & benefit, thereby

94 John Leslie (1571–1671), bishop of Raphoe (see *DIB*).

shall be at & undergo such further charges as shall be expended & laid out towards the finishing of the said abbey church & such of the inhabitants of the said parish as received no ease nor benefit thereby to ~~receive~~ be clearly freed from any further charge or contributing to the re-edifying thereof. Whereof all whom it may concern are required not to fail. <*vide* the petition whereon this was grounded, petition book page 292> And for so doing this shall be a sufficient warrant. Given at his Majesty's Castle of Dublin the ~~28~~ 25th day of November 1633.

81. [f. 467v] <A WARRANT FOR DRAWING UP A PARTICULAR OF THE MILLS AND LANDS FOUND FOR HIS MAJESTY IN THE COUNTY ANTRIM> [26 NOVEMBER 1633]

By the lord deputy

Wentworth

Whereas by virtue of his Majesty's directions unto us by his letters of the 14th of July last in the 9th year of his Majesty's reign ~~who~~ ^we^ gave our warrant for issuing forth of a commission under the great seal for an inquiry and office to be made and taken of what right, title and interest his Majesty then had to certain mills and lands in the county of Antrim that were in the possession (and properly did belong in his lifetime unto John Logan,[95] deceased), who upon return of this inquiry and by the confession of the parties in possession it appeareth plainly that his Majesty hath good right and title unto the said 4 mills, *vizt* the 2 mills of the bush, the mill of Donsenerick and Clanmanus and certain parcels of lands lying near the said mills, as by the said inquisition bearing date 24th of September last now at large doth and may appear, who hath commanded by his said letters in case the same should be so found that a grant thereof should be passed from him unto one William Logan, and the said William hath consented that Margaret Logan should have assured part of the said mills and lands during the continuance of the said leases. <vide page 84> These are therefore to will and require you **[f. 468r]** forthwith to make and draw up a particular of the said mills and lands by the said office so found for his Majesty reserving thereout ten pounds sterling *per annum* as a rent unto his Majesty that thereupon we may give further directions for passing the same as shall be fit; and for so doing this shall be your warrant. Given at his Majesty's Castle, 26th of November 1633.

To our right trusty & well beloved, his Majesty's surveyor & auditor general and to either of them.

82. <WARRANT TO THE LADY PHILLIPS FOR TRANSPORTATION OF HORSES INTO SCOTLAND> [30 NOVEMBER 1633]

By the lord deputy

Wentworth

Whereas upon humble suit made unto us in the behalf of Alice Lady Phillips who is (as we are informed) to make her present repair unto her husband Sir Thomas Phillips,[96]

95 Surname varies: Logan/Luggen/Loggen.

96 Thomas Phillips (*c.* 1560–1636), soldier and planter (see *DIB*).

who is employed in his Majesty's service in England, we have been pleased to give way & leave that her ladyship may carry over out of this kingdom into Scotland the number of six horses or saddle nags. These are therefore to will & require you to permit & suffer the said Phillips's servants to put aboard & transport the said number of horses or nags for herself & servants to ride on, any former general directions heretofore in this kind to the contrary notwithstanding. And for so doing this shall be your sufficient warrant. Given at his Majesty's Castle of Dublin xxxth of November 1633.

To all & every, the officers of his Majesty's customs in the ports of Donaghadee & Groomsport whom it may concern.

83. [f. 468v] <A WARRANT FOR A FIANT FOR ARTHUR GUINNE> [28 NOVEMBER 1633]

By the lord deputy

Wentworth

A warrant for drawing up of a fiant for Arthur Guinne, clerk, to enjoy the vicarages of Rathronan & Ardfinan & the rectory of Mortelstown <manicule> in the diocese of Lismore, to have &c. as in like cases are usual with a clause of union *pro hac vice tantum* together with all such other clauses as in like cases are usual, dated xxviiith day of November 1633.

To our trusty & well beloved, the clerks of the Council and either of them.

84. <LORD CAULFEILD & *AL.*> [23 NOVEMBER 1633]

By the lord deputy

Whereas there is a certain difference depending before us between William Lord Caulfeild[97] of the one side, and Anne Lady Dowager of Monaghan, Henry Lord Blaney,[98] Arthur Blaney, esquire,[99] Mary Martha & Lettice Blaney on the other side, as heirs, executors, administrators unto the late Lord Blaney,[100] about a certain debt of 1,200*li.* sterling with interest due unto the said Lord Caulfeild which he paid unto the Lord Balfour for him, the said Lord Blaney, <*vide* book of entries page 310 for an order whereupon this warrant is grounded> and forasmuch as the said parties are willing that the said Lord Caulfeild should be satisfied the said debts, after a rateable and proportionable share and rate out of each their **[f. 469r]** estates and interests respectively, we therefore (that it may be known and discerned how much ~~&~~ each and every of the said parties shall and ought to contribute for and towards the payment of the said debt until it be satisfied) have thought fit that a commission for that purpose shall issue under the great seal ~~of~~ to which end we do hereby pray and require your lordship to cause the same to issue accordingly and to be directed to our right trusty & well beloved

[97] William Caulfeild (1587–1640), 2nd Lord Caulfeild, baron of Charlemont.

[98] Henry Blaney (Blayney) (d. 1646), 2nd Baron Blayney, Welsh soldier, and governor of Monaghan (see Rhys Morgan, *The Welsh and the shaping of early modern Ireland, 1558–1641* (Woodbridge, 2014), p. 99).

[99] Arthur Blaney (Blayney), MP for Monaghan in 1634 (see Morgan, op. cit., p. 197).

[100] Edward Blaney (Blayney) (d. 1629), 1st Baron Blayney (see Morgan, op. cit., pp 97–9).

the Lord Viscount Moore,[101] the Lord Mountnorris,[102] the lord chief baron, <William Parsons, knight and baronet> ^Sir William Parsons, knight and baronet,^ & Sir Adam Loftus, knight, ~~& baronet~~ and to our trusty and well beloved Sir Robert King, knight, ^~~& baronet~~^ thereby giving them full power and authority to call before them the said parties and to inform themselves by all lawful ways and means whatsoever, as well by examination of witnesses as otherwise, what assets are yet remaining in the hands of the executors of the said late Lord Blaney <This warrant was renewed & dated 5 January and Sir William Parsons inserted instead of Sir Robert King, & returnable the last of Hill[ary] T[erm]> and whether the debts of the said late Lord Blaney satisfied since his death do exceed the parsonal estate which came to ^the^ executors' hands, and how much they do so and by whom they were paid, and also of what yearly value all & every the lands, tenements and hereditaments of and belonging unto them the said parties or any of them respectively as aforesaid are *ultra reprise*, and which descended and came unto them and every of them from and by the said late Lord Blaney. The said [**f. 469v**] commission to be returnable with as much expedience as conveniently they came and at the furthest by and before the feast of the body of our Lord God commonly called Christmas day next that thereupon we may set down such final order therein as shall be fit. And for so doing &c. Given &c. 23 November 1633.

To our very good lord, the lord chancellor.

85. [f. 470r] [APPOINTMENT OF WILLIAM FARRAR AS HIGH SHERIFF OF DONEGAL] [2 DECEMBER 1633]

By the lord deputy

Wentworth

We greet your lordship well. Whereas we have nominated and appointed our well beloved William Farrar, esquire, to be high sheriff of the county of Donegal for the year next coming, these are therefore to pray and require your lordship upon receipt hereof to make forth unto your letters patents under the great seal of this kingdom of the said office according [to] the usual and accustomed manner. And our pleasure is that before he do enter into the execution of the said office (besides the oath of sheriff) that he do take the Oath of Supremacy unto his Majesty according to the statute in that case made and provided, and do likewise enter into sufficient recognizance to his Majesty to be truly accountable in his highness's Exchequer for the said office as in such cases is usual. And for so doing this shall be your lordship's warrant. Given at his Majesty's Castle of Dublin, 2 December 1633.

To our very good lord, the lord chancellor.

101 Charles Moore (1603–43), 2nd Viscount Moore of Drogheda and royalist army commander (see *DIB*).

102 Francis Annesley (*c.* 1585–1660), Baron Mountnorris, 2nd Viscount Valentia, vice-treasurer and receiver-general of the king's revenue in Ireland (see *DIB*).

86. <KERRY> <SIR EDWARD DENNY[103]> **[2 DECEMBER 1633]**

Another warrant of the like nature for Sir Edward Denny to be high sheriff of the county of Kerry, dated 2 December 1633.

87. <ANTRIM> <ARTHUR HILL, ESQUIRE[104]> **[2 DECEMBER 1633]**

Another warrant of the like nature for Arthur Hill to be high sheriff of the county of Antrim, date *ut supra.*

88. <NICHOLAS WHYTE FOR TIPPERARY &C.> **[2 DECEMBER 1633]**

A warrant of the same date for Mr Nicholas Whyte to be sheriff of the county of Tipperary & Cross.

89. [f. 470v] <ROBERT WALSH FOR WATERFORD> **[2 DECEMBER 1633]**

A warrant for Mr Robert Walsh to be high sheriff of Waterford of the same date.

90. <JAMES FLEMING, COUNTY OF CAVAN> **[2 DECEMBER 1633]**

A warrant of the same date for him to be sheriff of the county of Cavan.

91. <JAMES BOURKE FOR LIMERICK> **[2 DECEMBER 1633]**

A warrant of the same date to make James Bourke sheriff of the county of Limerick.

92. <ARTHUR HILL FOR ANTRIM> **[2 DECEMBER 1633]**

A warrant of the same date for him to be sheriff of Tyrone.[105]

93. <DONNOGH O'BRIEN FOR CLARE> **[2 DECEMBER 1633]**

A warrant of the same date for him to be sheriff of Clare.

94. <HENRY SAVAGE, DOWN> **[2 DECEMBER 1633]**

A warrant for him of the same date to be sheriff of the county of Down.

95. <WILLIAM McHUGH, MONAGHAN> **[2 DECEMBER 1633]**

A warrant for him of the same date to be sheriff of Monaghan being of the same date.

103 Edward Denny (1605–46), MP for Kerry county (see McGrath).

104 Arthur Hill (1601–63), MP for Carysfort (see McGrath).

105 This must be a mistake. Hill was chosen sheriff of Antrim (see warrant no. 87) while Edward Tarleton was appointed sheriff of Tyrone (see warrant no. 100). See also entries for Hill and Tarleton in McGrath's thesis.

96. <EDMOND FITZGERALD, CORK> [N.D.]

A warrant for him to be high sheriff of the county of Cork.

97. <TYRONE, SIR WILLIAM HAMILTON> [N.D.]

A [warrant] for him to be high sheriff of the county of Tyrone.[106]

98. <ARMAGH, JOHN WALDRON> [N.D.]

A warrant for him to be high sheriff of the county of Armagh.

99. <FERMANAGH, ROGER ATKINSON[107]> [N.D.]

A warrant for him to be high sheriff of the county of Fermanagh being of the same date.

100. [f. 471r] <TYRONE, EDWARD TARLETON> [10 DECEMBER 1633]

By the lord deputy

signed: Wentworth

We greet your lordship well. Whereas we have nominated & appointed our well beloved Edward Tarleton, esquire, to be high sheriff of the county of Tyrone for~~thw~~ the year next ensuing, these are therefore to pray & require your lordship upon receipt hereof to make forth unto them letters patents under the great seal of this kingdom of the said office according [to] the usual & accustomed manner, inserting therein a clause of *non obstante* of the statute that none shall be sheriff twice for one county within 3 years space. And our pleasure is that before he do enter into the execution of the said office (besides the oath of sheriff) that he do take the Oath of Supremacy unto his Majesty according to the statute in that case made & provided, and do likewise enter into sufficient recognizance to his Majesty to be truly accountable in his highness's Exchequer for the said office or in such cases is usual. And for so doing this shall be your lordship's sufficient warrant. Given at his Majesty's Castle of Dublin the tenth day of December, 1633.

To our very good lord, the lord chancellor.

101. [f. 471v] <CAPTAIN NEALE O'NEALE> [2 DECEMBER 1633]

A warrant of attachment against Captain Neale O'Neale, dated 2 December 1633. <*vide* book of entries page 293 for the certificate whereupon this was grounded>

To any [of] his Majesty's pursuivants.

106 This must also be a mistake. A William Hamilton was made sheriff in 1638 although he was not knighted.

107 Roger Atkinson (1613–15), MP for Enniskillen in 1613 (see Brid McGrath, 'The membership of the Irish House of Commons (M.Litt. thesis, University of Dublin, 1985)).

102. <A WARRANT FOR THE FIANT TO WILLIAM LOGAN>[108] **[30 NOVEMBER 1633]**

<*vide* this book page 120>

By the lord deputy

Wentworth

Whereas by an inquisition taken the 24th day of September last the right, title & interest unto the mills, lands & patercourses in the above particular mentioned have been found to be in his Majesty [*sic*] who by his directions unto us of the 14th of July last hath been pleased to confer the same upon one William Logan, gent, in case the same should be so found. These are therefore to will & require you forthwith to draw up a fiant in due form of law containing a grant from his Majesty of all & singular the premises unto the said William Logan referring & saving only a third part thereof which, as well by our order (grounded upon very good reasons) as also by the assent & consent of the said William Logan, is by the said fiant to be passed unto one Margaret Logan sometimes wife unto John Logan, deceased, for & at the rent in the said particular mentioned unto his Majesty to be equally paid yearly by the said William & Margaret Logan according to their proportionable shares & divisions as aforesaid during the continuance of such leases as have been made of all & singular, the premises from our right trusty & right well beloved, the now earl of Antrim[109] and our well beloved James Óg McHenry, gent, unto whom the rents equally paid out of the premises are to be reserved, inserting [**f. 472r**] therein all such usual & beneficial clauses as in grants of like nature are usual. And the same fairly engrossed in parchment under your hand to send unto us to be further passed as appertaineth. And for so doing this shall be your sufficient warrant. Given at his Majesty's Castle of Dublin, 30th of November 1633.

To our trusty & well beloved, his Majesty's attorney & solicitor general, or either of them.

Thomas Littell

103. <RICHARD MARTIN> **[3 DECEMBER 1633]**

By the lord deputy

Wentworth

Whereas Richard Martin hath humbly petitioned unto us setting forth that he stands engaged to divers persons in England & Scotland towards whose satisfaction he had provided a certain quality of oats but by reason of the late proclamation against the transportation of corn & grain he is, as he affirmeth, like to be undone as having no way to vend & make away such a proportion of oats here, nor hath he any other means to keep touch with & satisfy his said creditors but by sale of the said oats. We therefore, as well upon the said Martin's humble suit as also for that we are informed that there is (God be thanked) such plenty & store of that kind of grain in & about the counties of Antrim & Carrickfergus as that the same may be spared in a reasonable

[108] See also warrant no. 81.

[109] Randall MacDonnell (1609–83), 2nd earl and 1st marquis of Antrim (see *DIB*).

measure towards the relief of other parts of his **[f. 472v]** Majesty's dominions, have thought fit and do accordingly hereby will & require you to permit & suffer the said Martin to put aboard & transport either by himself, his agents or servants, out of that port the quantity of 2,000*li.* barrels of ~~wheat~~ ^oats^ provided that you first make entry thereof in your custom books, and that you receive his Majesty's ^due^ customs thereout; whereof you are not [to] fail. And for so doing this shall be your sufficient warrant. Given ~~at his~~ &c. the 3 December 1633.

To all & every, his Majesty's officers of the customs in the port of Carrickfergus & the members & creeks thereof & to ~~such~~ ^such^ of the famers of the customs there whom it may concern.

Thomas Littell

104. <SIR WILLIAM ST LEGER>[110] **[4 DECEMBER 1633]**

By the lord deputy

Wentworth

Whereas our right trusty & well beloved Sir William St Leger, knight, lord president of ^the province^ of Munster, hath humbly petitioned unto us that we would be pleased to afford unto him the benefit of a weekly market & yearly fair to be kept at Doneraile in the barony of Fermoy in the county of Cork, <*vide* book of entries page 320> we for that time did not think fit to grant the same until such time as we certainly understood whether the granting thereof would be prejudicial to any other markets or fairs within the said county. Now inasmuch as it appeareth unto us by an inquisition **[f. 473r]** taken the 17th day of September last that the same will be no annoyance, prejudice or hurt to any other fairs or markets as aforesaid, we therefore have thought fit and do accordingly hereby will & require you forthwith to draw up a fiant in due form of law containing a grant from his Majesty unto the said Sir William St Leger and his heirs of one weekly market to be kept upon the Thursday, and one fair to be kept yearly upon St James the Apostle day, if it happen not to be a Sunday, and in that case to be held the day following at Doneraile aforesaid referring thereout the same of 20*s.* Irish rent to be paid to his Majesty yearly, inserting therein all such clauses as in grants of like nature are usual. And the same fairly engrossed in parchment under your hand to send unto us to be further past [*sic*] as appertaineth. And for so doing this shall be your warrant. Given at his Majesty's Castle of Dublin the 4th day of December 1633.

To our trusty & well beloved, his Majesty's attorney and solicitor general, or either of them.

~~Went~~

110 See also warrant no. 29. This is essentially the same warrant with minor differences but the same date of issue.

105. <ATTACHMENT *VERSUS* DANIEL O'BRIEN & CONNOR McGILLISHAGH>

[5 DECEMBER 1633]

A warrant of attachment against the bodies of Daniel O'Brien & Connor McGillishagh to answer the complaint of Mary Adrians *alias* Oring, widow, dated 5 December 1633. <*vide* book of entries, page 341>

To any of his Majesty's pursuivants.

Thomas Littell

106. [f. 473v] <A WARRANT FOR A FIANT FOR JOHN ANDREW> [10 DECEMBER 1633]

By the lord deputy

~~Wentworth~~ Wentworth

Whereas by the voluntary resignation of George Andrew[s], dean of Limerick and rector of Drumcliffe in the diocese of Killaloe,[111] and by the reason of the minority of Murrogh, lord baron of Inchiquin,[112] the said rectory is now become void and in his Majesty's gift. <manicule> These are therefore to will and require you forthwith to draw up a fiant in due form containing a grant and presentation from his Majesty unto the said rectory of Drumcliffe of John Andrew[s], clerk and Master of the Arts,[113] to have, hold, possess and enjoy the said rectory with all the rights, duties, members & appurtenances whatsoever thereunto belonging, and in as large, ample and beneficial manner as the said Dean Andrew[s], or any other incumbent or incumbents, formerly held and enjoyed or of right ought to have held and enjoyed the same, directing his admission to the judge of the faculties & inserting therein likewise all such clauses as in like cases are usual. And the same fairly engrossed in parchment under your hand to send unto us to be further passed as appertaineth. And for so doing this shall be your sufficient warrant. Given &c. the xth day of December 1633.

To our trusty & well beloved, the clerks of the Council, or either of them.

107. [f. 474r] <CERTIFICATE CONCERNING THE SEE OF ARMAGH>[114] [N.D.]

May it please your lordship.

Upon perusal & examination of the inquisitions taken for the lord primate in the several counties of Armagh, Tyrone & Londonderry, and of his Majesty's letters mentioned in your lordship's order of reference, and upon the credible relation of Mr Cragg (my lord primate's agent in following the said commissions) that convenient warning was given in each several county of the time & place appointed for the execution of the said commission and no complaint being made to the contrary, <*vide* page 71, the warrant underwritten concerns this> we do conceive that the said inquisitions are pursuant and answerable to his Majesty's pleasure signified by his letters of the 10th of May last;

111 George Andrews (*c.* 1575–1648), dean of Limerick and subsequently bishop of Ferns and Leighlin (see *DIB*).

112 Murrough O'Brien (*c.* 1616–73) 6th Baron and 1st earl of Inchiquin (see *DIB*).

113 John Andrews (d. 1674), rector of Drumcliffe and precentor of Killaloe (see Cotton, *Fasti*).

114 See also warrant no. 72.

neither do we perceive that the passing of the said lands can be anyways prejudicial to his Majesty and are likewise of opinion that by his Majesty's said letters of warrant there is sufficient authority given to your lordship for passing of the same. All which we humbly leave to your lordship's more grave consideration.

William Ryves[115]
Edward Bolton

108. <A WARRANT FOR DRAWING UP A FIANT ~~TO THE~~ FOR THE ARCHBISHOP OF ARMAGH FOR CERTAIN LANDS &C.>[116] [12 DECEMBER 1633]

Whereas we gave order in August last for the issuing forth of a commission (according to his Majesty's pleasure signified unto us by his letters of the 10th of May last) to enquire what lands, tenements or hereditaments do belong unto the see of Armagh and are quietly held & peaceably enjoyed by the now archbishop thereof & his tenants in the 3 counties of Armagh, Tyrone & Londonderry, now inasmuch as the said commission hath been executed & the inquisitions thereupon taken returned, one bearing **[f. 474v]** date the 9 of September last, the second dated the 16th, and the third inquisition bearing date the 23rd of September aforesaid, and for that the said archbishop hath humbly besought us to give further directions for the passing unto him of what hath been so found by the said inquisitions as his Majesty hath directed. These are therefore to will & require you forthwith to draw up a fiant in due form of law containing an effectual grant or grants, confirmation or confirmations, release or releases, from his Majesty unto the said now archbishop & his successors of the lands & premises (so found by the said 3 several late inquisitions which you are carefully to peruse & observe in your drawing of the said fiant) and by such names or howsoever otherwise they be called during such estate or estates & with such reservation or reservations, covenant or covenants, as are mentioned in & by his Majesty's letters of the 27th November in the sixth year of his reign, inserting therein all such clauses as in like cases are usual & warranted & required by his Majesty's said letters unto us of the 10th of May last, a copy whereof for your better instruction and information we have herewith sent you. And the same fairly engrossed in parchment under your hand to send unto us to be further passed as appertaineth. And for so doing this shall be your warrant. Given &c. 12 December 1633.

To our trusty & well beloved, his Majesty's attorney & solicitor general, or either of them.

109. [f. 475r] [WARRANT ORDERING LANDHOLDERS OF THE SEE OF KILLALOE TO APPEAR BEFORE THE COUNCIL CHAMBER] [9 DECEMBER 1633]

By the lord deputy

Wentworth

Whereas by virtue of his Majesty's commission to us directed we are authorized to call before us all such persons as do hold and possess any part of the ancient inheritance

[115] William Ryves (d. 1648), judge (see *DIB*).

[116] See also warrant no. 72.

of the bishopric of [the] see of Killaloe which have been by the now lord bishop's predecessors granted, leased or passed away by deeds of fee farms or leases without any valuable consideration or reservation given or preserved to the succeeding bishops of that see, and further to proceed as more at large in the said commission is expressed, these are therefore to will & command you the persons underwritten personally to appear before us in his Majesty's Council Chamber within the castle in Dublin on the 13th day of February next by 2 of the clock in the afternoon, bringing with you and every of you all such deeds of fee farms, leases, assignments and all other writings and miniments which you have or can be any way touching or concerning any the lands, tenements or other hereditaments of the said see now in your holding, or which your pretend to have any right, title or interest of whatsoever, to the end we may proceed further as by the said commission is prescribed. Whereof you and every of you may not fail at your perils, dated &c. the 9th of December, *anno domini* 1633.

The right honourable the earl of Thomond[117] or his agent sufficiently instructed.

Sir Daniel O'Brien, knight[118]
Sir Teig McMahon, knight
Sir John Morris, knight
Sir Rowland Delahide, knight

110. [f. 475v] [WARRANT FORBIDDING THE DEPARTURE OF A SHIP CALLED *ST JOHN OF LONDON*] [7 DECEMBER 1633]

By the lord deputy

Whereas the good ship called the *St John of London* (wherein one Don Francisco Nicolalde,[119] a Spanish gent, lately arrived there) is now riding in that harbour we, as well upon the said Don Francisco his request as for other reasons best known to our self, have thought fit and do accordingly hereby will and require you to take especial care that the said ship be not permitted to depart, nor that you give or deliver out cockets for any thing that may concern the same until Captain Richard Pronoville and his ship which now rides at or near Kinsale shall sail about to that harbour, <*vide* page 99 [&] 100> and that the said Don Francisco be returned from hence and his pleasure concerning the same be by him intimate~~ly~~ unto you, which when you receive you are punctually to observe and do hereby likewise will & require you to permit such as the said Don Francisco shall employ and appoint in that behalf to buy the worth of 20*li.* or thereabouts in flocks or lock wool for bedding & other uses, and the same together with such provision as shall be made there for the said shipping to put aboard and transport without paying any custom you giving bills of store for the same; whereof you and every of you are not to fail. And for so doing these shall be &c. Given &c. the 7th December 1633.

To our well beloved, the officers of his Majesty's customs in the port of Cork and to all others whom it may concern and to every of them.

[117] Henry O'Brien (d. 1639), 5th earl of Thomond (see *DIB*).

[118] Daniel O'Brien (*c.* 1577–1666), 1st Viscount Clare and politician (see *DIB*).

[119] Don Francisco Nicholalde, brother to the Spanish ambassador resident in London, Juan de Nicholalde.

111. [f. 476r] [WARRANT TO DELIVER GOODS BELONGING TO DON FRANCISCO NICHOLALDE] [7 DECEMBER 1633]

By the lord deputy

Whereas by our warrant of the 8th of November last we did require as well yourself as all others whom it might concern to deliver unto Captain Richard Pronoville the ship whereof he was captain and which had been stayed in those parts by Sir Richard Plumleigh, knight, commander of all his Majesty's ships appointed for guard of the coasts of Ireland, which directions we have thought fit to second by these, and therefore in case the said ship be not already delivered according unto our said former warrant our pleasure is, and we do accordingly require, that the same together with all the goods ^and^ tackles thereunto belonging be delivered forthwith unto Don Francisco Nicholalde, who is brother to the Spanish resident in England, if he shall so desire it. And in case any of the ging or company aboard the said ship have run into debt or score, any person unto whom such debts are due is left at his liberty to take a legal course for his relief against the person of everyone so indebted but not by any means to offer to make stay of the ship or any the goods or furniture thereunto belonging or appertaining. Whereof you and all ~~you~~ & every person or persons whom it may concern are required to take especial notice and thereof not to fail at your and their perils. And for so &c. Given &c. the 7th December 1633.

To our well beloved Henry Delany, esquire, & to all other his Majesty's ministers & subjects whatsoever whom it may concern and to every of them.

112. [f. 476v] <EARL OF NITHSDALE[120] HIS WARRANT FOR A FIANT> [16 DECEMBER 1633]

By the lord deputy

Wentworth

These are to will & require you forthwith to draw up a fiant of a commission in due form of law to be directed unto our right trusty & well beloved, the earl of Cork, the Lord Viscount Ranelagh,[121] lord president of Connacht, the Lord Viscount Baltinglass,[122] Sir William Parsons, knight & baronet, & Sir Gerald Lowther, knight, one of the barons of his Majesty's Court of Exchequer, thereby giving them, or any two or more of them, full power & authority whensoever our right trusty & right well beloved, the earl of Nithsdale, or his agents shall have any ground of charge against any person or his lands to consider whether or not it be fit to question or call in the debt so presented unto them, & do all other act & acts, thing & things, with such directions & limitations as by the letters of the late lords justices & the order of the lords' committee are prescribed, <*vide* the proceedings of the earl of Nithsdale in the first book of entries at the latter end of the book> these copies of all which we have herewith sent you which you are carefully to peruse & observe in the drawing up of the said commission, provided that according to the opinion of

120 Robert Maxwell (b. after 1586–1646), 1st earl of Nithsdale, politician and diplomat (see *ODNB*).

121 Roger Jones (d. 1644), 1st Viscount Ranelagh (see *DIB*).

122 Thomas Roper (*c.* 1587–1638), 1st Viscount Baltinglass.

the Lord Mountnorris, the lord chief baron & Sir George Radcliffe herewith likewise sent, you be very careful to omit in the said commission that clause (of the king's officers being to be restrained from sending of the process or levying of any of the debts) mentioned in the earl of Nithsdale his petition. And the same to send unto us under your hand to be further passed as appertaineth. And for so doing this shall be your warrant. Given &c. the xvith day of December 1633.

To our trusty & well beloved, his Majesty's attorney or solicitor general, or either of them.

113. [f. 477r] <A WARRANT TO RICHARD GETHING FOR THE OFFICE OF COLLECTOR IN THE PROVINCE OF MUNSTER>[123] [2 DECEMBER 1633]

By the lord deputy

Wentworth

Whereas the place or office of collector of his Majesty's composition rents in the province of Munster is now void & in his Majesty's gift, these are to will & require you forthwith to draw up a fiant in due form of law containing a grant of the said place of office unto Richard Gething of Moyall, gent, to have, hold, possess & enjoy the said office together with all the rights, duties, members, profits, privileges, pre-eminences, fees & appurtenances whatsoever thereunto belonging during good behaviour, & in as large, ample & beneficial manner as Robert Morgan, gent, Sir Richard Morrison, knight, & one Edward Meriwether, or any other formerly held & enjoyed or of right ought to have held & enjoyed the same, the said office or place to be exercised by himself or his sufficient deputy during good behaviour as aforesaid, inserting therein a *non obstante* of the statute of 10 Henry 7 with all such clauses as in like cases are usual. And the same fairly engrossed in parchment under your hand to send unto us to be further passed as appertaineth. And for so doing &c. Given &c. 2nd day of December 1633.

To our right trusty & well beloved, his Majesty's attorney & solicitor general, or either of them.

114. [f. 477v] <ATTACHMENT *VERSUS* STEPHEN ALLEN> [20 DECEMBER 1633]

By the lord deputy

Wentworth

These are to will and require you forthwith to repair to the dwelling house or place of abode of Stephen Allen and him, there or elsewhere, to attach and ~~bring~~ safely bring or cause to be brought before us to answer as well his contempt of an order of the board dated *quinto Decembris* 1633 as the complaints of Christopher Graham, Archibald Burn & William Slater; whereof you may not fail. And for so doing this shall be

[123] See also warrant no. 28. This is essentially the same warrant with minor differences including the date of issue.

sufficient warrant. Given at his Majesty's Castle of Dublin, xx December 1633.
Affidavit is made & entered.

Paul Davies

To any of his Majesty's pursuivants.

115. [f. 478r] <JOHN MOORE> **[18 DECEMBER 1633]**

By the lord deputy

Wentworth

Whereas John Moore of Bangor in this kingdom hath humbly petitioned unto us setting forth that not long since he was taken by Turkish pirates near the straits of Gibraltar after a long & cruel fight wherein many of his company were killed, most of them wounded, & himself and them & his ship taken & carried to Algier in Barbary where they were sold for slaves & his ship with goods to the value of five or six hundred pounds sold before his face, and he ~~being~~ himself kept & detained there as prisoner in miserable slavery and bondage until he paid for his ransom 1,000*li.* sterling, for payment whereof he was forced to sell & make away all that poor estate he had left, by reason whereof he hath ever since since [*sic*] lived in great want & misery. And being now grown aged and impotent he humbly besought us to licence him to ask the benevolence of well affected people towards his relief, whose request therein we have thought fit to grant & the rather in regard we have seen very good certificate of his losses & captivity, and inasmuch as we think it fit he should have our licence to that purpose for the province of Ulster only, these are therefore to pray and require all and every, his Majesty's officers, ministers and loving subjects within the said province, not only to permit and suffer the said John Moore to pass peaceably and quietly by them without any their lets, stays or molestations whatsoever, he demeaning himself as becometh, but also to be aiding & assisting unto him herein that he may repair as well to churches, fairs, markets & other public assemblies as to all cities, towns, corporate & not corporate, **[f. 478v]** villages & all other places within the said province to entreat and ask the benevolences of well disposed and charitable people to whose pity & commiseration, as well of his misfortunes as of his age & poverty, we recommend him; and do also hereby pray and require all preachers & ministers whatsoever in their several parish churches upon the Sabbath and holy days to signify & read publicly the contents hereof unto the congregation there gathered together, provided that this shall continue & be of force no longer then for the space of one whole year next ensuing the date hereof, and then to cease and ~~determine~~ determine. <*vide* common book of entries, page 383> Given at his Majesty's Castle &c. the 18th December 1633.

116. <RICHARD SHUKBOURGH[124] HIS WARRANT *PER* FIANT> [19 DECEMBER 1633]

By the lord deputy

Wentworth

Whereas the rectories of Squirea & Rathcanan in the diocese of Connorth[125] [*sic*] are now void and in his Majesty's gift by lapse <manicule> these are to require you forthwith to draw up a fiant ~~con &c.~~ containing a grant & presentation ~~to~~ ^from^ his Majesty unto the said rectories of Richard Shukbourgh, dean of Connorth, to have, hold &c. according [to] the usual form. Given &c. the nineteenth day of December 1633.

To our trusty & well beloved Sir William Ussher, knight,[126] & Paul Davies, esquire, clerks of the Council, or either of them.

117. [f. 479r] [LETTER TO FRANCISCO DE NICHOLALDE CONCERNING THE ARREST OF PRONOVILLE AND ROCH][127] [N. D.]

Sir

I have received yours together with Mr Gosnold's[128] letters touching the ship, the *St Jago*, under Captain Pronoville's command and by them an intimation of his harsh & unmannerly dealing (which though he thinks he may be bold & disrepute you) I hope shall be made to know himself & the duty his to bear & acknowledge towards me whilst he is within the reach of my command. To which purpose I have herewith sent directions to Mr Gosnold to cause as well Pronoville himself as Roch, the master of that ship, to be kept in safe custody & I shall advise with you not to adventure your own person with a fellow of so desperate a fortune & condition as Pronoville is by these his carriages manifested to be.

For the ship by you called the *St John* now residing at Cork harbour, although I were willing (for your better accommodation) she should be stayed for a time yet upon credible information given me of the great loss & prejudice the merchants & owners thereof are like to incur by detaining & staying of them (as by the enclosed being an abstract of a letter sent unto me in that behalf you will perceive), I cannot in justice refuse the setting her at liberty & for that purpose have given my directions.

As for the fardells of linen & other goods which did belong to the ship & are pawned for money or victual, you will conceive it just & reasonable the parties to whom they are so pawned *re vera* should be satisfied for the monies or victuals they are out for them & upon those terms have required Mr Gosnold to cause them to be restored & with all to take present order that the same with all the goods & furniture thereto belonging shall be forthwith delivered unto you. When I receive

124 Richard Shukbourgh or Shuckburgh (1628–40), dean of Connor (see Cotton, *Fasti*).

125 Connor.

126 William Ussher (*c.* 1610–71), clerk of the privy council, MP for Co. Wicklow (see McGrath).

127 See warrants no. 110 and 111 (and below).

128 Henry Gosnold, chief justice of Munster and judge of the vice admiralty court (see Appleby, *A calendar of material relating to …*, p. 252).

the examinations you mention to be taken against Pronoville & the master I shall thereupon give fitting directions. And so I rest.

To Seignior Francisco de Nicholalde.

<*verte fedum per* warrants>

118. [f. 479v] [WARRANT ORDERING THAT THE POSSESSIONS BELONGING TO DE NICHOLALDE BE DELIVERED TO HIM] [22 DECEMBER 1633]

By the lord deputy

Whereas by your letters of the 15th of this month & by us received this day, we find your care of the execution of our former directions in the behalf of Don Francisco de Nicholalde about the ship whereof Pronoville is captain & are glad to hear that himself & Roch, the master, are so well secured, & our pleasure is that they be continued [in] safe custody until you receive our further directions concerning them. And we do likewise require that the said ship & goods & furniture thereunto belonging be forthwith delivered wholly into the possession of the said Don Francisco according to our former directions to be disposed of as he shall think fit and in case any of the ~~said~~ goods be found to have been purloined or embezzled then to cause present restitution to be made thereof unto the said Don Francisco. But where any of them have been either sold or pawned *re vera* upon valuable consideration either of money, meat & drink, or other necessaries unto any of his Majesty's subjects, then it stands with reason and so we do expect that due satisfaction be made unto all such before any ~~such~~ restitution be made, which if it should be refused then every such person may lawfully keep what hath been so sold or pawned unto him until he be satisfied what shall appear justly due unto them. And for so doing &c. In the due execution whereof we require all & every, his Majesty's officers, ministers & loving subjects whatsoever to be aiding & assisting unto you, as there shall be occasion. Given &c. 22 December 1633.

To our trusty & well beloved Henry Gosnold, esquire.

119. [f. 480r] [WARRANT SETTING THE SHIP CALLED *ST JOHN OF LONDON* AT LIBERTY] [23 DECEMBER 1633]

By the lord deputy

Whereas upon the humble suit of Don Francisco de Nicholalde, brother to the Spanish resident in England, and for divers reasons us [*sic*] then & thereunto moving, we gave you directions by our warrant of the 7th of this month to make stay of & not to suffer the good ship called the ~~good~~ ^*St*^ *John of London* then & now residing in that harbour of Cork to depart until the said Don Francisco his return from hence, and that his pleasure herein were intimated unto you which you were required to observe. Now inasmuch as for good reasons enduring us thereunto we think it fit that the said ship should be forthwith cleared of the said restraint and embargos, these are therefore to will & require you forthwith to permit & suffer as well the said ship as the ging & company thereunto belonging to set to sea & depart from thence with their first & fittest opportunity & whensoever they please our said former warrant of the 7th of this month to the contrary notwithstanding, whereof you are not to fail. And for so doing &c. Given &c. xxiii December 1633.

To all & every, the officers of his Majesty's customs in the port of Cork & to all others whom it may concern.

120. [f. 480v] <THOMAS WHYTE, HIS PROTECTION FOR 6 MONTHS> [14 DECEMBER 1633]

By the lord deputy

Wentworth

Whereas Thomas Whyte of Clonmel, merchant, hath petitioned unto us setting forth that his losses at sea have been such and so great as that he is utterly disabled to give that content & satisfaction as he would willingly do unto certain persons unto whom he is engaged, who if they should arrest his person they should utterly undo him, <*vide* the certificate whereupon this is grounded. Book of entries page 309> wherefore he became an humble suitor unto us that we would to grant unto him his Majesty's protection for a certain time whose request therein we have thought fit to grant; and the rather in regard we received a certificate from the last lords justices confirming his said losses to have been great, and being protected by them in the time of their government he satisfied many of his creditors and their lordships, never received any complaint against him from any that was indebted unto during the time of his said protection. These are therefore to will & require you & every of you to take due notice thereof & to forbear suing, arresting or impleading the said Whyte in his person or goods for & during the space of 6 months next ensuing the date hereof he behaving himself as becometh, provided that this do not extend to protect him from any debt due to his Majesty or to free him from any former imprisonment, & that he do not by virtue hereof defeat his creditors but do his endeavours to the uttermost of his power to give them content & satisfaction. And the said Whyte is hereby likewise required to bring & leave with our secretary certificates what debts he shall discharge or take order for & during the [**f. 481r**] time at every 3 months end. Whereof you & every of you are not to fail. And for so doing this shall be your warrant &c. Given &c. 14 December 1633.

To all mayors, sheriffs, justices of the peace, bailiffs, constables & to all & every other his Majesty's officers, ministers & loving subjects whom it may concern.

121. <ART O'KEEFFE PROTECTION> [22 DECEMBER 1633]

By the lord deputy

Wentworth

Whereas Art O'Keeffe, gent, hath petitioned unto us setting forth that through the unjust prosecution of certain powerful adversaries of his he is not only thrust out & wrongfully dispossessed of a great estate by them, but is also vexed by their multiplicity of causeless suits as that he cannot for fear of their arrests solicit or go abroad to prosecute the recovery of his own. And forasmuch as he humbly besought us to recall our late directions for disannulling the protection granted unto him upon his Majesty's directions by the late lords justices & that he might have the same renewed by us for a time to the end he may be at liberty as well to follow his suits at the Council table as the recovery of a thousand pounds ordered him the last Hillary term in the High Court of Chancery, whose request therein we have thought fit to grant. And therefore we do hereby will & require you & every of you to **[f. 481v]** forbear suing or arresting his person for & until the beginning of the next term, at which time he is to appear before us & to answer & clear the objections that either ^already^ are, or shall be, made against his being protected, whereof if he fails his protection shall be dissolved & no more renewed provided that this protection do not free from any former arrests or imprisonments, or any debts due by him unto his Majesty. Whereof you & every of you are not to fail. And for so doing this shall be your sufficient warrant. Given at his Majesty's Castle of Dublin the 22nd day of December 1633.

To all mayors, sheriffs, justices of the peace, sovereigns, protections & bailiffs, and to all other his Majesty's officers, ministers & loving subjects whom it may concern & to every of them.

122. [f. 482r] <A WARRANT FOR ISSUING A COMMISSION TO EXAMINE *INTER* HEALAHY, HOLLIDAY & TRAVERS> [23 DECEMBER 1633]

By the lord deputy

Wentworth

Whereas divers complaints have been lately ~~made~~ preferred unto us by William Healahy & William Holliday, clerks, against Sir Robert Travers, knight,[129] Zachary Travers, Thomas Davis & William Wheeler for divers extortions, abuses, wrongs & misdemeanours by them done & committed unto & against the said Healahy & Holliday, <*vide* ~~book of~~ ^church^ entries page 48> now inasmuch as it is expedient that a speedy course should be taken for the bridling & restraining of such unlawful & unjust courses and to the end the ~~th~~ truth of what is objected & informed against the said Sir Robert & the rest may appear unto us, we have thought fit & do accordingly hereby pray & require your lordship forthwith to cause a commission to issue under the great seal of this kingdom to be directed unto ^Edmund^ Edward Barry, Edward Byam, chanter of Cloyne, James Nash & Oliver Healahy, gent, or any two of them or more, to enquire & examine by the oaths of good men & by all other lawful ways & means concerning the said pretended extortions, abuses, wrongs & misdemeanours; the said commission to be sat upon at Moyall[130] in the county of Cork and to be returnable with all convenient speed or at the furthest, by the last day of the next term, the said Sir Robert Travers, Zachary Travers, Thomas Davis & William Wheeler & every of them being to have ten days notice of the execution of the said commission before it be sat upon. And for so doing this shall be your lordship's warrant. Given at his Majesty's Castle of Dublin the xxiii of December 1633.

To our very good lord, the lord chancellor.

129 Robert Travers (d. 1647), MP for Clonakilty (see McGrath).

130 Mallow.

123. [f. 482v] <A WARRANT FOR DRAWING UP A COMMISSION BETWEEN THE ARCHBISHOP OF CASHEL[131] & REDMOND MAGRATH> [29 DECEMBER 1633]

Whereas there is a controversy concerning certain lands depending before us at the Council table between the now lord archbishop of Cashel, plaintiff, & Redmond Magrath, esquire, defendant, wherein the said defendant pretendeth he is likely to be greatly damnified if he hath not a commission granted him for the examination of ^his^ witnesses in the country whose age and imbecility of body (as he affirmeth) are such as that they are not able to travel hether to be examined before the clerk of the Council. We therefore, as well upon his humble suit as for divers reasons in his petition expressed, have thought fit & do accordingly hereby pray and require your lordship to cause a commission forthwith to issue under the seal to be directed unto Raph Leventhorp, esquire,[132] one of the examinators of the Chancery, authorizing him to examine for both parties, the said archbishop being to pay for the examination of his own witnesses, and for the rest of the fees & the charges of the said examinator's journey the same are to be born solely by the defendant upon whose request he is employed; the said commission to be returnable with all convenient speed & at the furthest by the middle of the next term of the execution, whereof (and in regard of the short return of the same) the defendant is required to give the plaintiff 4 days notice. And for &c. Given &c. Dublin, xxixth of December 1633.

To our very good lord, the lord chancellor.

124. [f. 483r] <HENRY PURESEY, HIS WARRANT FOR TRANSPORTATION OF OATS> [3 JANUARY 1634]

A warrant to Henry Puresey for transporting 2,000 barrels of oats into England or Scotland out of the port of Donaghadee & the members thereof, dated 3 *Januarii* 1633[/4]. This warrant is *verbatim* ~~w~~ by Richard Martin his warrant, page 85. <*vide* page 110 for a warrant of this nature at large, directed to the port of Strangford>

To all & every, his Majesty's officers of the customs in the ports of Donaghadee & the members & creeks thereof & to such of the farmers of the customs there whom it may concern.

125. <A WARRANT FOR ENLARGEMENT OF VALENTINE PAINE[133]> [8 JANUARY 1634]

By the lord deputy

Wentworth

Whereas Valentine Paine, being bound by recognizance to appear in his Majesty's Court of Exchequer the 6th day of the last term and render himself to the marshal of the said court, there to remain till he should be delivered by order of court, since which

131 Archibald Hamilton (1580?–1659?), archbishop of Cashel (see *DIB*).

132 Ralph Leventhorp (or Leventhorpe), MP for Ennis (see McGrath).

133 Valentine Paine, first comptroller of customs for the ports of Newcastle and other ports in Co. Down (see Hughes, *Patentee officers*).

time *vizt.* the 13th of November last upon motion of Mr Darcy of Council with the said Paine showing that he the said Paine had according to the condition ~~of~~ appeared & was in custody answerable as the condition of the recognizance reported, <*verte fedum per* certificate> it was then ordered that the said Paine should be dismissed & his recognizance cancelled if by the 16th of the said month cause were not shown to the contrary, after which day the said Paine again moved for his dismiss[al], which was then deferred him till such time as he should have compared his books with the farmers of the customs & cleared that account which, once **[f. 483v]** performed, he the said Paine to be dismissed without further motion. Now forasmuch as it appears unto us by the certificate of George Hull[134] & George Haughton that the said Paine hath compared his books & cleared the account according to the said rule of court (the barons being all this time out of town) we require you forthwith to discharge and set at liberty the body of the said Paine, paying his fees if his restraint with you be only grounded upon that cause so signified unto us. And for so doing this shall be your sufficient warrant. Given &c. 8 January 1633[/4].

To our well beloved, the marshal of his Majesty's Court of Exchequer.

[The account of Valentine Paine] [3 January 1634]

The account of Valentine Paine, collector of the customs in the port of Strangford from the 25th of March 1633[/4] till the 11th of June following.

The whole account in that port according to the book amounts unto 205*li.* 19*s.* 1*d.* Total: 205*li.* 19*s.* 1*d.*	205*li.* 19*s.* 1*d.* whereof paid into the Exchequer by retuned order of court 124*li.* 1*s.* 1*d.*, and so remaineth to balance this account 81*li.* 18*s.*

I acknowledge to have received the above sum of 81*li.* 18*s.* for the use of the farmers of his Majesty's custom. Witness my hand this third of January, 1633, George Hull.

<This account hath been examined by me & I find it true by the books, John Haughton>

126. [f. 484r] <A WARRANT TO THE CHIEF JUSTICE OF MUNSTER & AL. TO EXAMINE WITNESSES &C.>[135] [7 JANUARY 1634]

By the lord deputy

Wentworth

Whereas upon a former complaint made unto us by William Wakefield and Nicholas Astwood, weighers in the port of Cork, concerning a seizure made by them of 50 kinderkins of butter (belonging to one Rowland Colston of Bristol) aboard a ship called the *Messinger of London* by reason the customs was not paid nor entry made with any of his Majesty's officers of the customs before lading aboard the said ship,

[134] George Hull (d. *c.* 1632/3), customer and collector for the ports of Newcastle and other ports in Co. Down (see Hughes, *Patentee officers*).

[135] See also warrant no. 64.

which by misinformation ^of the said Colston^ he regained into his custody upon his own bond to answer a suit commenced against him in the Exchequer & so departed the kingdom, <*vide* the petition whereon this was grounded, book of entries, page 401> thereby to decline the answering of the said suit (as we alleged), he not being resident & having goods remaining here in the kingdom, we thought it meet to grant our warrant for the stay thereof whereby to cause him to be amenable to the law. And forasmuch as the said Colston being returned hither again & hath complained that he hath goods of great value now stayed by the sovereign of the town of Tallow by virtue of the said warrant and also hath been an humble suitor unto us that the truth of the business may be examined, & stands upon his justification, we, being no ways [*sic*] willing that merchants should be wronged in their occasions neither the officers discouraged in their just actions, have therefore thought fit to authorize & require you the chief justice of the province of Munster & Sir Randall Cleyton, knight,[136] to call before you the said Wakefield, Astwood, Colston & the rest of the officers of the port of Cork, and so to examine the truth of the matter, and in case it shall appear the said 50 kinderkins to be more then [*sic*] are mentioned in Colston's port cocket from Youghal, or have not paid custom before the seizure made, that then you take course to bind the said Colston over to answer the matter [at] the next assizes according to the statute in that case provided & also to bind over Wakefield & Astwood for prosecuting the cause in the behalf of his Majesty. And as for the goods now **[f. 484v]** stayed by the sovereign of Tallow (if he being found faulty) that then he putting in security to answer the value thereof, if he shall be hereafter convicted for the same and giving good caution for answering the information exhibited against him in the Exchequer, you give directions to the sovereign to deliver back to him his said goods. But if upon due examination it shall appear that the said Wakefield & Astwood have wronged the said Colston in seizing the said butter unduly then to certify us thereof whereby they may be punished for their error committed, and thereupon to give directions to the said sovereign for restoring unto Colston all his goods by him so stayed, without any further trouble. And for your so doing this shall be your warrant, dated at &c. of D.,[137] the 7th of January 1633[/4].

To our very loving friends, Henry Gosnold, esquire, chief justice of Munster, and Sir Randall Cleyton, knight.

127. <ROBERT ELLIOTT, HIS WARRANT FOR TRANSPORTATION OF OATS>

[8 JANUARY 1634]

By the lord deputy

Whereas Robert Elliott, gent, hath humbly petitioned unto us setting forth that he stands engaged to divers persons in England & Scotland towards whose satisfaction he had provided a certain quantity of oats but by reason of the late proclamation against the said transportation of corn & grain he is, as he affirms, like to be undone

136 Randall Cleyton, clerk of the council of Munster (see Hughes, *Patentee officers*).

137 Dublin, i.e. Castle of Dublin.

as having no way to vend & make away such a proportion of oats here, nor hath he any other means to keep forthwith & satisfy his said creditors but by sale of the said oats: we therefore, as well upon the said Elliott his humble suit as also that we are informed that [**f. 485r**] there is (God be thanked) such plenty & store of those kinds of grain in and about the county of Down as that the same may be spared in a reasonable measure towards the relief of other parts of his Majesty's dominions, have thought fit and do accordingly hereby will & require you to permit & suffer the said Elliott to put aboard & transport, either by himself, his agents or servants out of the nort[h], the quantity of 2,000 barrels of oats provided that you first make entry thereof in your custom books and that you receive his Majesty's due customs thereout; whereof you are not to fail. And for so doing this shall be our sufficient warrant. Given at his Majesty's Castle of Dublin the 8th day of *Januarii* 1633[/4].

To all & every, his Majesty's officers of the customs in the port of Strangford & the members & creeks thereof & to such of the farmers of the customs there whom it may concern.

128. <WARRANT FOR MR MEDCALFE TO TRANSPORT 25,000 PIPESTAVES>

[10 JANUARY 1634]

By the lord deputy

Wentworth

Whereas humble suit hath been made unto us by our trusty & well beloved Christopher Medcalfe of London, merchant, for our licence to transport out of this kingdom the number of two hundred & fifty thousand pipestaves to be embarked at the port of Waterford, which request we have thought fit to grant and do therefore hereby will & require you & every of you to permit & suffer the said Mr Medcalfe or his agents or servants to put aboard & transport the same accordingly, provided that you first make entry thereof in your custom books and receive as well his Majesty's due customs as also [**f. 485v**] over & above the said customs the sum of 30*s.* being the one moiety of 3*li.* sterling reserved to his Majesty upon every thousand so to be transported; the other moiety Mr Medcalfe hath undertaken and contracted shortly to come over hither & satisfy us himself. And you are likewise to be very vigilant that no other number of pipestaves under colour or pretence hereof be embarked contrary to your former directions in that behalf; whereof you may not fail. And for so doing this shall be your warrant. Given &c. the tenth day of January 1633[/4].

To all & every, the officers of his Majesty's customs of the port of Waterford.

129. ANOTHER WARRANT OF THE SAME EFFECT & DATE DIRECTED TO THE PORT OF KINSALE.

[10 JANUARY 1634]

Thomas Littell

130. <JOHN MAXFIELD, HIS WARRANT FOR TRANSPORTATION OF HORSES> **[9 JANUARY 1634]**

By the lord deputy

Wentworth

Whereas upon humble suit made unto us in the behalf of John Maxfield, captain & keeper of his Majesty's Castle & Fort of the Treive in Scotland, is to make his present repair thither, we have been pleased to give way & leave that he may carry over out of this kingdom into Scotland the number of 3 horses. These are therefore to require you to permit & suffer the said John Maxfield or his servants to put aboard & transport the said horses and former general directions heretofore in this kind to the contrary notwithstanding. And &c. Given &c. 9 *Januarii* 1633[/4].

~~To all and every, the officers of his Majesty's customs in the ports of Donaghadee &~~

<To all and every, the officers of his Majesty's customs in the port of Donaghadee & Groomsport>

131. [f. 486r] <THE EARL OF NITHESDALE HIS COMMISSION>[138] **[N.D.]**

Wentworth

Let a commission be made in due form of law according to the tenor of the words ensuing, (that is to say) Charles by the grace of God &c. To our right trusty & well beloved cousin & chancellor, Richard, earl of Cork, our high treasurer of our kingdom of Ireland, Roger, Lord Viscount Ranelagh, our president of our province of Connacht, Thomas, Lord Viscount Baltinglass, Sir William Parsons, knight & baronet, Master of our Court of Wards & Liveries, & Sir Gerard Lowther, knight, one of the barons of our ~~Excheq~~ Court of Exchequer, greeting. Whereas our right trusty & well beloved cousin Robert, earl of Nithesdale, hath undertaken by his petition unto us in that behalf addressed that he will by his industry, charge & endeavour discover & bring in sundry debts, duties, arrearages of rents & sums of money which grew due unto the Crown, as well in the Courts of Chancery, King's Bench, Common Pleas, Exchequer & Court of Wards of our kingdom of Ireland, as also before the justices of assize & gaol delivery, justices of the peace, clerk of the market, and before commissioners for ecclesiastical causes, or other judges of record within this kingdom from the 30th year of the reign of our late dear ~~coz~~ cousin of famous memory, Queen Elizabeth, until the first year of our reign, & which within the said time or ever since (through the neglect ~~or~~ and connivance of some inferior officers & clerks) have not been in any part answered unto us or our Crown, nor like to be hereafter, unless some extraordinary course be taken about the prosecuting and bringing in thereof.

Know ye therefore that we reposing especial trust & confidence ~~of~~ in your integrities & experience in the affairs of this kingdom by the advise [*sic*] & consent of our right trusty & well beloved cousin & chancellor Thomas, Lord Viscount Wentworth, our deputy general of our said realm of Ireland, and according to the tenor & effect of our letters under our privy signet bearing date at our manor of Greenwich the 24 day of

[138] See also warrant no. 112.

May, one thousand, six hundred, thirty & two, have nominated, constituted [**f. 486v**] & appointed, & by these presents do nominate, constitute & appoint you the said earl of Cork, Lord Viscount Ranelagh, Lord Viscount Baltinglass, Sir William Parsons & Sir Gerard Lowther, or any two or more of you to be our commissioners, and do hereby give full power & authority unto you or any two or more of you that when and as often as any ground of charge for and in our behalf shall be presented unto you or any two or more of you as aforesaid by the said earl of Nithesdale or his agents against any person or persons, his or their lands or goods, for or concerning any debts, duties or sums of money which have grown due to the Crown by any means whatsoever in the Courts of Chancery, King's Bench, Common Pleas, Exchequer & Court of Wards in this kingdom, or before the justices of assize & gaol delivery, justices of the peace, clerk of the market, & before commissioners for ecclesiastical causes & other judges of record, or by reason of the goods & chattels, real or personal, of any person or persons attainted of felony or treason, or for the mean profits of their lands, tenements, ~~& for~~ hereditaments, or for arrearages of rents incurred from the 30th year of ~~her~~ ^the^ reign of the said late Queen Elizab[eth] until the beginning of our reign; and whereof no part hath been paid or answered unto us, or our dear father of blessed memory, nor to the said late Queen Elizabeth since the 30th year of her reign nor any legal grant or discharge made thereof, that then you enter forthwith into consideration whether or not it be fit to call in the debts so presented unto you, either in respect of any general inconvenience which may thereby happen or in respect of any other consideration of state which may seem to depend thereupon; and thereupon either to proceed further or to forbear or suspend proceedings concerning any such debt as to you or any two or more of you with the advise of our said deputy general of this kingdom shall be thought fit. And as concerning such debts, duties, issues, arrearages of rents & sums of money ~~& to compound & sell~~ [**f. 487r**] which you or any two or more of you shall adjudge fit to question & be prosecuted, our will & pleasure is, and we do hereby ~~will~~ give full power and authority unto you or any two or more of you as aforesaid, to call before you all & every the persons interested or to be charged with the said debts, duties, arrearages of rents & sums of money, & to compound & sell all & singular the said debts of the natures aforesaid grown due or incurred mean between the thirtieth year of the reign of the said late Queen Elizab[eth] & the beginning of our reign & now owing unto us, & to acquit the parties thereof respectively that owe or are chargeable for the same, and what order or certificate of composition shall be made, that you cause the same to be entered with the several writing officers of our Court of Exchequer here, which shall be sufficient warrant for them to surcease writing for the said debt or duty and a good discharge unto the parties owing or chargeable for the same against us our heirs & successors. And if in your proceedings against those whom for any such debts or duties you shall think fit to question as aforesaid, the parties charged will stand upon their defence in law, then you are to cause the fines, recognisances, bonds & other assurances for the said debts to be estreated into our Court of Exchequer, and for any arrears of rents the same to be put in charge there as the several causes shall require, whereupon our officers of our Court of Exchequer are to write for the same whereby the matter may be brought to a legal trial, and upon eviction, if you shall not think fit to make any composition for the said debts, duties ^or^ fines of money of the natures & kinds aforesaid, then you are to take advice of our said deputy general or other chief governor or governors of this kingdom what part or portion of the said debts, duties or other sums so recovered shall be assigned unto the said earl for his pains and industry in discovering of the said debts, upon whose resolution therein you are to give notice thereof unto our Court of Exchequer that they may take order either by [**f. 487v**] sending forth the ordinary levying process of the Court or by recognizance or otherwise, that our part thereof be paid into our receipt and the said earl's part to be immediately paid unto him or otherwise respited upon ~~some~~ security as he and the party shall agree, and the acquittance of the said earl entered with the writing officers of the Court to be a good discharge unto the subject that shall pay the same. And in case any person or persons, charged with any debt or sum of money of the kinds and natures aforesaid, will submit & compound before any such fines, bonds & recognizances or other debts, duties or sums of money of the kinds and natures aforesaid shall be estreated or certified into our said Court of Exchequer, or any such rents put in charge as aforesaid, or after the same shall be so estreated or put in charge or written for, or after eviction as aforesaid, then you our said commissioners or any two or more of you as aforesaid shall have power nevertheless by this our commission to bargain and compound with all manner of persons for the said debts & sums of money, according to the discretions of you or any two or more of you as aforesaid as the cause shall require, and to certify the same unto our said Court of Exchequer there from time to time and with the advice of our said deputy general to assign a competent proportion thereof unto the said earl; for payment whereof, as well as for our own part thereof, you are to take such security and assurance as to you or any two or more of you as aforesaid in your discretion shall be thought fit, of which composition so to be made you are from time to time to make certificate under the hands of you or any two or more of you as aforesaid unto our said Court of Exchequer, commanding the same to be entered with the [**f. 488r**] several writing officers of the said Court which said certificate and entry with the several writing officers of the said Court, which said certificate & entry shall be sufficient warrant unto them to forbear any further writing for the same & a good discharge unto the parties that shall be so compounded with or pay the said debts against us, our heirs & successors, provided always that you do not admit of any composition for any fines, bonds or forfeited recognizances, debts, duties or other sums of money but of such only as were imposed or acknowledged & forfeited after the said 30th year of the reign of the said late Queen Elizabeth and before the first year of our reign; and whereof no part hath been answered unto us or any of our royal progenitors, nor of any arrearages of rents or mean profits of the lands of persons attainted as aforesaid but only such as grew due within the same time, and for the subsequent time since the beginning of our reign and the growing rents hereafter of the same, the same are to be put in charge in our Exchequer to our use. And for the better proceeding in this our service we do hereby straightly charge & command all our officers & ministers whom it shall or may concern that they & every of them upon the warrant or command of ~~your~~ you our said commissioners or any two or more of you as aforesaid ~~to~~ do show forth all manner of records and diminicles[139] of records & green-wax books whatsoever concerning the said debts & duties unto the said earl of Nithesdale and his agents, and they to take copies thereof as they shall have occasion to use the same for the better expedition of this our service; and because it may be requisite in some cases that our right & title to some part of the said debts growing out of the measure, rates & issues of the lands of persons attainted of treason or felony or outlawed persons shall be found by office~~rs~~ or inquisition, [**f. 488v**] these are therefore to will & require our chancellor or keeper of our great seal for the time being to issue forth such and so many commissions for the better effecting of this our service as by you, or any two or more of you shall be advised, and every signification or note in writing of you or any two or more of you to our chancellor or keeper of our great seal for the time being in that behalf shall be a sufficient warrant for the issuing of the same under the great seal of this kingdom, and for that also in some cases there may be occasion for you to inform yourselves by oath of some occurrences or circumstances concerning the premises. We do therefore hereby give full power and authority unto you or any two or more of you as aforesaid to administer any oath or oaths upon the Holy Evangelist to any person or persons upon any occasion concerning the premises and to receive & take affidavit or affidavits, oath or oaths, from any person or persons whatsoever as to you or any two or more of you in your discretions shall be thought fit. And we do hereby further give full power and authority unto you or any two or more of you as aforesaid upon information given you that any person or persons is indebted unto us in any sum and sums of money of the nature & kind aforesaid, to send for any such person or persons by your warrant to appear before you at such convenient time & place as by you shall be appointed, at which time and place if such person or persons so served or ~~commanded~~ ^summoned^ by your warrant shall refuse to appear or shall not appear before you then upon affidavit thereof made to issue attachments or to send any pursuivant or pursuivants for such person or persons for not appearing, or to use any other compulsory means [**f. 489r**] for the bringing of them in, and upon their appearance to punish them by fine or imprisonment as the quality of their offence shall deserve and as in other cases of like nature is usual; and as to you or any two or more of you as aforesaid in your directions shall be thought fit, willing & by these presents requiring all mayors, sheriffs, bailiffs, pursuivants, messengers and other our ministers & loving subjects whatsoever whom it shall or may concern, that they & every of them from time to time ~~ad~~ aiding, obedient & assisting unto you or any two or more of you as aforesaid in the execution of this our commission as becometh. And lastly, our will & pleasure is that at the end of every term, or whensoever else our said deputy general or other chief governor or governors of this kingdom shall require the same, you give an exact account unto our said deputy or other chief governor or governors of this kingdom for the time being of all your proceedings in the premises of such compositions as have been made, and of all such fines, bonds & recognisances as by your means shall be estreated into our Court of Exchequer, as also of all such rents as by your means shall be put in charge there from

139 i.e. breviate.

the time of your last account given to our said deputy general or other chief governor or governors of this kingdom concerning the same. This our commission to stand & be of full force during our will & pleasure, although it shall not be ~~convenient~~ continued from time to time by adjournment. In witness whereof &c. ~~Given &c.~~

William Ryves.

132. [f. 489v] <CAPTAIN NEALE O'NEALE'S WARRANT TO TRANSPORT SOLDIERS> [16 JANUARY 1634]

By the lord deputy

Wentworth

Although by letters of the 9th of March last you had directions from the late lords justices that by virtue of any commission or upon any other pretence you should give no passes or permission to any persons to go from this kingdom beyond the seas at that port, or any the creeks or members thereof, who should of purpose pass to serve any foreign prince or state whatsoever in the wars, yet forasmuch as his Majesty's pleasure hath been since signified unto us for giving leave unto such of his subjects in this kingdom as shall voluntarily desire to serve the king of Spain in his wars to be here levied & transported into Flanders for a supply of a regiment already serving there, we therefore in obedience to his Majesty's commandment do hereby require you (notwithstanding our former directions) that you permit and suffer such persons as shall be deputed ^for^ ~~for~~ that service in the behalf of the king of Spain (and by name this bearer Captain Neale O'Neale) to embark & transport out of that port such voluntary soldiers as to that purpose shall be presented in that port so as that they be not armed nor drawn together with any noise of drum or otherwise in any considerable number in one place, & that their passages be provided immediately from that port without landing in England. And we further require you that from time to time, and as frequently as you may, you advertise us diligently what numbers of men shall be so exported at that port and their names & qualities. And lastly, we require you to acquaint the magistrate there with these our letters whom we do hereby require to take special care from time ^to time^ for prevention of any disorder that may happen, that any men so coming thither to be transported as aforesaid be not admitted to enter any town under colour of waiting for a **[f. 490r]** passage or otherwise but that they remain in the suburbs & country & not be united in one body in any considerable number until the very instant of their taking shipping, and that they do commit no extortion or oppression on the subjects during their abode there and that they be not suffered to take any cess but that they pay for their meat, drink and lodging, ready money as other travellers do. And whereas one Patrick O'Daly & Hugh Mother have petitioned unto us setting forth that the said Captain Neale O'Neale hath entertained under his command and intended to transport with him one James McAnally, who had been impeached & stood indicted of felony, for whose appearance & forth coming they the said Patrick & Hugh were bound in recognizance which by reason of the said McAnally his flying away is become forfeited and now estreated into his Majesty's Court of Exchequer, we therefore upon the said petitioners humble suit [(]being seconded with the lord chief baron, his certificate &

opinion) did direct our warrant for the bringing in of the said Captain Neale O'Neale by pursuivant before us, who upon his coming affirmed that he hath not to his knowledge any such man under his command as the said McAnally although upon some earnest solicitation (as he remembers) he gave a note under his hand confessing the having of the said McAnally hoping that the forfeiture and estreating of the said recognizance might be thereby prevented whereupon, and for that we were very unwilling that the service should any way suffer by this his detention, we forthwith discharged him. But howsoever our pleasure is that when he, or any his officers shall intend to put aboard his men, that then you ~~to~~ call to him or such officers for a list of the names of those to be transported (which he & they are strictly required to give) & having so received the same you are as well then as at other times to make **[f. 490v]** diligent search & inquiry for the body of the said McAnally, and if you find him there or elsewhere you are to apprehend his body & him to commit to the next gaol there to remain until upon your certificate; thereof we shall give further directions concerning him wherein we require all mayors, justices of the peace, bailiffs, constables & all other his Majesty's officers, ministers, & loving subjects whosoever, to be aiding and assisting unto you as there shall be occasion. Whereof you & they are not to fail at your perils. And for so doing this shall be a sufficient warrant. Given &c. 16th of January 1633[/4].

To all & every, his Majesty's officers of the customs in the port of Carlingford, whom it may concern.

Thomas Littell

133. [f. 491r] <A WARRANT TO COMMIT SHELENICKE SWYNY[140] TO THE GAOL OF NEWGATE> [17 JANUARY 1634]

By the lord deputy

Wentworth

Whereas we are given to understand that Shelenicke Swyny hath in evasion of justice lately made an escape out of the common gaol of Lifford within the County of Donegal, these are therefore to require ~~you~~ & strictly command you forthwith to take her the said Shelenicke Swyny in your custody and safe keeping till you shall receive our further direction in that behalf. And for &c. Given &c. 17th *January* 1633[/4].

To the keeper of the gaol of Newgate or his deputy.

134. <WARRANT FOR EDWARD ASCOUGH TO BE ATTORNEY FOR ULSTER>[141] [20 JANUARY 1634]

By the lord deputy

Wentworth

Whereas the office of attorney for the province of Ulster (by the late surrender of Stephen Allen, esquire[)] is now become void and in our dispose, these are therefore

140 Shelenicke Swyny or MacSweeney.

141 See warrant no. 33.

to will and require you forthwith to draw up a fiant in due form of law containing a grant of the said office unto Edward Ascough, esquire, learned in the laws, to have, hold, exercise and enjoy the same with all such fees and profits, perquisites & emoluments whatsoever, unto the said office belonging or in anywise appertaining (during pleasure), and in as large, ample and beneficial manner **[f. 491v]** as the said Stephen Allen or any other formerly held and enjoyed or of right ought to have held and enjoyed the same, the fee of six pounds, four pence Irish *per annum* heretofore allowed for the execution of the place only excepted. And the same fairly engrossed in parchment under your hand to send unto us to be further passed as appertaineth. And for so doing this shall be your sufficient warrant. Given at his Majesty's Castle of Dublin the 20th day of January 1633[/4].

To our trusty & well beloved, his Majesty's attorney and solicitor general, or either of them.

135. [f. 492r] <WARRANT TO ROBERT WALSH TO BE MASTER OF THE GAME *PRO COMITATU* WATERFORD> [23 JANUARY 1634]

By the lord deputy

Whereas we perceiving the great abuses & enormities practised by sundry idle persons & men of loose life and mean quality in the unlawful destruction of all sorts & kind of game as dear, hares, conies, pheasants, partridges, quails & moore-game, with greyhounds, setting dogs, guns, buck-stalls, hay-nets, ferrets, hare-pipes, cords & other engines out of the limits of their own grounds, forests & parks, contrary to his Majesty's laws & sundry statutes made & provided in such cases, for presenting of which inconveniences and for divers good causes & considerations as thereunto moving we have thought fit hereby to give and grant unto our ~~right~~ trusty & ~~right~~ well beloved Robert Walsh, esquire, high sheriff of the county of Waterford, full power, licence and authority, either by his servants or such other person or persons as ~~he law~~ shall entrust and employ in that behalf from time to time henceforth (during our pleasure) to forbid and restrain all and every person or persons whatsoever (which by the laws are to be restrained) from the unlawful hunting, killing, destroying or taking of any manner of game, either of foul or beast, other then such foul or vermin as are noisome (which by the laws are ^to be^ destroyed out of their own lands and grounds) within & throughout the whole county of Down. <& the town> And if such as shall be so employed by ^him ~~him~~^ ~~his~~ Robert shall find any offending therein contrary to his Majesty's laws <not only> then to seize upon and take from them their dogs, nets, guns, ferrets & other engines, and the same to keep and detain until our further pleasure be therein known. And for so doing this shall be a sufficient **[f. 492v]** warrant. In the due execution whereof we require all & every, his Majesty's officers, ministers & loving subjects whatsoever to be aiding and assisting as there shall be occasion & as they will answer the contrary at their perils. Given &c. the 23rd of January 1633[/4].

136. <ROBERT WISE> **[18 JANUARY 1634]**

A warrant to the pursuivants to ~~all which~~ the bodies of Richard Butler & Robert Strange of Waterford, dated 18 January 1633[/4].

137. <WARRANT FOR THE CUSTOMERS PLACE OF LIMERICK TO WILLIAM WASHINGTON> **[23 JANUARY 1634]**

By the lord deputy

Wentworth

Whereas the office or place of customer & collector in the port of Limerick is become void by the late decease of William Perry, gent, who lately held the same, and forasmuch as we are pleased to confer the same upon William Washington, gent, these are therefore to will and require you forthwith to draw up a fiant in due form of law containing a grant from his Majesty, his heirs and successors, unto the said William Washington of the said office of customer & collector of the customs, subsidies, poundage & impositions within the said port of Limerick and the creeks & members thereunto belonging, to have, hold, exercise and enjoy the said office and to be exercised by himself or his sufficient deputy or deputies together with the yearly fee or stipend of thirteen pounds, six shillings, eight pence sterling to be paid yearly either by his Majesty's vice-treasurer or the farmers of the customs, together with all & singular other fees, profits, perquisites, commodities, privileges and pre-eminences [**f. 493r**] whatsoever unto the said office belonging or in anywise appertaining, and in as large and ample manner as the said Perry, or any other heretofore held and enjoyed or of right ought to have held and enjoyed the same, during the good behaviour of the said William Washington in the execution of the said office, inserting therein all such clauses as in grants of like nature are usual. And the same fairly engrossed in parchment under your hand to send unto us to be further passed as appertaineth. And for so doing &c. Given &c. xxiii of January 1633[/4].

To our trusty & well beloved, his Majesty's attorney & solicitor general, or either of them.

138. <A WARRANT FOR MR WILLIAM BUTLER TO TRANSPORT ONE HORSE> **[23 JANUARY 1634]**

By the lord deputy

Wentworth

Whereas upon humble suit made unto us by William Butler, gent, we have been pleased to licence him to transport for England one gelding or saddle horse for his own use to ride on, these are therefore to will and require you & every ~~of you~~ the officers of his Majesty's customs in what port so ever in the north of this kingdom where the said Butler shall embark himself to permit and suffer upon sight of this our warrant, to put aboard & transport the said gelding or saddle horse for the use aforesaid. And for so doing this shall be your warrant, any former general directions to the contrary notwithstanding. Given &c. xxiii *Januarii* 1633[/4].

Thomas Littell

139. [f. 493v] <ATTACHMENT *VERSUS* SIR RICHARD OSBORNE & *AL.*>[142] [24 JANUARY 1634]

By the lord deputy

Wentworth

These are to will and require you forthwith to make diligent search & inquiry ~~for~~ the bodies of Sir Richard Osborne, baronet, Richard Osborne, esquire, & Donagh McGillefoyle, yeoman, and them to attach wheresoever they can be found & immediately to bring before us to answer as well their contempt of our directions as the complaint of Thomas Ledsham, clerk. For doing whereof this shall be your warrant. Given of his Majesty's Castle of Dublin the 24th of January 1633[/4].

To any of his Majesty's pursuivants.

140. <TIRLAGH O'DANIEL> [26 JANUARY 1634]

Attachment *ut supra* against Tirlagh O'Daniel *adversus* William Blower, clerk, dated 26 *Januarii* 1633[/4].

141. <LAWRENCE MOORE> [27 JANUARY 1634]

Attachment *ut supra* against Lawrence Moore *adversus* inhabitants of Cavan &c., dated 27 *Januarii* 1633[/4].

142. <SIR GEORGE FLOWER[143]> [28 JANUARY 1634]

Attachment *ut supra* against Sir George Flower, dated 28 *Januarii* 1633[/4].

143. <ATTACHMENT AGAINST JOHN HAMILTON & *AL.*> [1 FEBRUARY 1634]

Attachment against John Hamilton, esquire, & Jane Hamilton, widow, to answer as well their contempt as the complaint of David Boyd &c., dated 1 February 1633[/4]. <*vide* the petition whereon this was grounded amongst the bundles>

To any of his pursuivants.

144. [f. 494r] <A WARRANT OF SUMMONS AGAINST SEVERAL PERSONS *ADVERSUS* JOHN POWER> [30 JANUARY 1634]

By the lord deputy

Wentworth

These are to will and require you & every of you the persons undernamed to make your personal appearance before us the 18th day of February next to answer this complaint of John Power, whereof you and every of you are not to fail as you will answer the contrary. Given under our hand & seal the 30th day of January 1633[/4].

[142] See warrant no. 68.

[143] George Flower, governor of Waterford Fort (see Hughes, *Patentee officers*).

<the petitioner whereon this is grounded resteth with us>
<*vide* book of entries page 474>
Nicholas Power of Kilballikilty – *comparit xvi die Februarii*
Richard Power of Carruleigh
John Power of Clondonell – *comparit xvi die Februarii*
Edmond Power of Gland-Patrick – *comparit ut supra*
Charles Everard of Lower Park – *comparit xvi Februarii*
Alexander Power of Kilgaynieghter – *comparit* 17 *die Februarii*
Thomas Prendergast of Kilganioughtuigh
<*comparit xvi Februarii*> Richard Power, fitz-Geffey of Ballyclohowghtengh
Rowne O'Neale of the same – *comparit 19th Februarii* 1633[/4]

145. <WILLIAM WASHINGTON HIS LICENCE OF ABSENCE FOR 6 MONTHS>

[31 JANUARY 1634]

By the lord deputy

Wentworth W. Wen
A licence of absence to William Washington, customer of Limerick, to go into England for 6 months, according [to] the usual form, dated *ultimo Januarii* 1633[/4].

146. <CAPTAIN [O']DONOGHOE> [3 FEBRUARY 1634]

A warrant of attachment against ~~one~~ Captain Roger O'Donoghoe *adversus* John Carpenter, dated 3 February 1633[/4].

To any of his Majesty's pursuivants.

147. [f. 494v] <A WARRANT FOR SEIZING THE GOODS OF JOHN HASSARD> [5 FEBRUARY 1634]

By the lord deputy

Wentworth
Whereas Christian Borr of Dublin, merchant, hath humbly petitioned unto us setting forth that he, upon the earnest request and entreaty of one John Hassard of Youghal, merchant, hath been drawn of late to undertake & engage himself to his correspondents at London for the said Hassard in the sum of 1,000*li.* or more upon the said Hassard's engagement that the bills of exchange by him signed here should be currently paid in England, of which the said Borr as he affirmeth hath received no advice as yet but, to the contrary, understandeth that some of the bills have been refused and so thinketh he hath good cause to fear the acceptance & discharge of the rest. <*vide* book of entries page 442 for the petition whereon this is grounded> In regard whereof he became an humble suitor unto us that (for the prevention of his the said Borr's present & utter ruin) we would be pleased to afford him some relief (in a case so equitable and especially in a matter of this nature wherein the said

Borr cannot secure himself in a legal way, the said ~~Hassalls~~ ^Hassard's^ goods being paid for with the said Borr's money and immediately to be transported out of the kingdom, and so Borr left remediless), we have thought fit to grant. And therefore we do hereby require and authorize you and every of you within the precincts of your several offices forthwith upon sight hereof, not only to make diligent search for but also to seize upon and take into your custodies by inventory all such goods and merchandizes of the said Hassard's, as either now **[f. 495r]** are or henceforward shall or may be tendered & offered to be shipped within any of the ~~cr~~ ports, creeks or members thereunto belonging, where you are officers to the value of 1,000*li.* & the same to detain safely in your hands until either the said Borr shall be served that the said bills of exchange be truly satisfied or that our further pleasure be signified unto you herein. And for so doing this shall be your sufficient warrant, in the due execution whereof we require as well the mayors of Cork & Youghal as the sovereign of Kinsale, and all other his Majesty's officers & ministers whom it may concern to be aiding and assisting unto you as there shall be occasion, whereof you and they are not to fail. Given at his Majesty's Castle of Dublin under our hand & seal the 5th day of February 1633[/4].

To all and every, his Majesty's officers of the customs in the ports of Cork, Youghal & Kinsale.

148. <CAPTAIN OLIVER SHORTALL> **[6 FEBRUARY 1634]**

A warrant of attachment against Captain Oliver Shortall, *adversus* Edward Butler, dated ~~18 January~~ 6 *Februarii* 1633[/4].

To any of his Majesty's pursuivants.

149. [f. 495v] <SIR THOMAS ESMOND[144]> **[11 FEBRUARY 1634]**

An attachment against the body of Sir Thomas Esmond to answer as well his contempt as the complaint [of] John Fanning, chirurgeon, dated 11 February 1633[/4]. <*vide* amongst the bundles for the petition and affidavit &c.>

To any of his pursuivants.

150. <A WARRANT FOR SIR JOHN CLOTWORTHY,[145] HIS FAIR & MARKET> **[10 FEBRUARY 1634]**

By the lord deputy

Wentworth

These are to will and require you forthwith do draw up a fiant in due form of law containing a grant from his Majesty unto our trusty & well beloved Sir John

144 Thomas Esmond (d. 1674), soldier and confederate (see *DIB*).

145 John Clotworthy, 1st Viscount Massereene and politician (see *DIB*).

Clotworthy, knight, of one market to be kept on Tuesday weekly and one yearly fair to be kept ^on^ the 10th day of May if it happen not to be on a Sunday, and in that case to be held the day following at the town of Moneymore *alias* Draperstown in the county of Londonderry, reserving thereout the sum of 20*s.* sterling rent to be paid yearly unto his Majesty, inserting therein all such clauses & provisions as in grants of like nature are usual. <*vide* common book of entries page 450 for the petition whereon this was grounded> And the same fairly engrossed in parchment under your hand to send unto us to be further passed as appertaineth, for doing whereof this shall be your warrant. Given at his Majesty's Castle of Dublin the 10th day of February 1633[/4].

To our trusty & well beloved, his Majesty's attorney & solicitor general, or either of them.

151. [f. 496r] <A WARRANT FOR APPREHENDING ONE JOHN McVICKON>[146] [12 FEBRUARY 1634]

By the lord deputy

Wentworth

These are to will & require you forthwith to make diligent search and inquiry for the body of one John McVickon of Clounty in the county of Clare, and him wheresoever he can be found to apprehend and in sure and safe manner to bring before us by the 20th day of the next month to answer such matters as at his coming shall be objected against him whereof, or to certify us by that time, your reasons to the contrary you are not to fail at your peril. And for so doing this shall be your warrant. In the due execution whereof we require all & every, his Majesty's officers, ministers & loving subjects whom it may any way concern to be aiding and assisting unto you & such bailiffs or others as you shall employ, either in the apprehension or conveyance of him the said [Mc]Vickon unto us. <*vide* amongst the bundles for the petition whereon this is grounded> Given at his Majesty's Castle of Dublin the 12th day of February 1633[/4].

To our well beloved, the high sheriff of the county of Clare.

152. [CAPTAIN NEAL O'NEALE'S WARRANT TO TRANSPORT SOLDIERS] [N.D.]

By the lord deputy

Wentworth

~~Although by letters of the ninth of March last <*vide* book of marshal affidavits> you had directions from the late lords justices that by virtue of any commission, or upon any other pretence, you should give no passes or permission to any persons to go from this kingdom beyond the seas at that port, or any the creeks or members thereof, who should of purpose~~ [f. 496v] ~~pass to serve any foreign prince or state whatsoever in the wars, yet forasmuch as his Majesty's pleasure hath been since signified unto us for~~

146 See warrant no. 78.

~~giving leave unto such of his subjects in this kingdom as shall voluntarily desire to serve the kingdom of Spain in his wars, to be here levied and transported~~.

153. <CAPTAIN FORTESCUE, HIS WARRANT TO TRANSPORT A NAG> [18 FEBRUARY 1634]

By the lord deputy

Wentworth

Whereas upon humble suit made unto us by Captain Edmond Fortescue we have been pleased to licence him to carry over into England one gelding or saddle nag for his own use to ride on, these are therefore to will and require you to permit and suffer the said gelding or saddle nag to be put aboard & transported out of this port into England, any former general directions to the contrary notwithstanding. And for so doing &c. Given &c. xviiith *Februarii* 1633[/4].

To William Scott, esquire, searcher in the port of Dublin.

154. <JOHN DANIEL, SEARCHER, PACKER & GUAGER [*SIC*] IN THE PORT OF LIMERICK> [22 FEBRUARY 1634]

A warrant for a ~~fyar~~ fiant unto John Daniel for the offices of searcher, guager [*sic*] & packer in the port and harbour to the city of Limerick with the creeks &c. with a stipend of 5*li.* English for executing the same &c., dated 22 February 1633[/4]. <This I entered by the fiant because Sir G.R.[147] had sent away the warrant itself which came not again to the office>

To our well beloved, his Majesty's attorney & solicitor general, or either of them.

155. [f. 497r] <ATTACHMENT *VERSUS* SIR STEPHEN BUTLER> [19 FEBRUARY 1634]

By the lord deputy

A warrant of attachment against Sir Stephen Butler to answer as well his contempt as the complaint of Mary Montgomery &c., dated 19th February 1633[/4].

To any of his Majesty's pursuivants.

156. <MR GUINN'S WARRANT FOR A VICARAGE> [19 FEBRUARY 1634]

By the lord deputy

Wentworth

These are to will and require you forthwith to draw up a fiant in due form containing a gift & presentation from his Majesty <manicule> of <u>the vicarage of Moycleare *alias* Mockler & Temple Michael</u> a member of the same in the diocese of Lismore (being now void and in his Majesty's gift by lapse[)] unto Roger Guinn, clerk, to have & to hold the said vicarage with all the members, rights, duties, profits & perquisites

[147] Sir George Radcliffe (1593–1657), lawyer and politician (see *DIB*).

whatsoever thereunto belonging, and in as large, ample & beneficial manner as any other incumbent or incumbents formerly held & enjoyed or of right ought to have held & enjoyed the same, <*vide* the bundle of petitions for that, whereon this was grounded> inserting therein a clause of union *pro hac vice tantum* of the said vicarage & member thereof unto the vicarages of Caslane & Tibraghny already in the said Guinn's possession directing his admission to the judge of the faculties. And the same fairly engrossed &c. Given &c. 19th February 1633[/4].

To our trusty & well beloved, the clerk of the Council or either of them.

157. [f. 497v] <A WARRANT TO THE LORD MARQUIS HAMILTON[148] TO PERMIT TRANSPORTATION OF HORSES> [19 FEBRUARY 1634]

By the lord deputy

Wentworth

Whereas towards the better accommodation of his Majesty's horse troops in this his realm of Ireland, as well with serviceable horses presently trained to such employment as also to raise a good race & breed of horses (lately much impaired) here, his Majesty by his letter of the 16th of January hath been graciously pleased to licence our transportation hither of such horses as to those ends & purposes we shall hold conducing, (wherein notwithstanding we shall ever carry on advised & moderate hand) provided that first under our hand & seal we certify your lordship thereof. These are therefore, in obedience and pursuance of such his Majesty's good pleasure to us in that behalf signified, to certify your lordship that we have accordingly desired this gent, the bearer hereof Mr Richard Scott, to provide for use & bring over with him twenty horses or geldings towards the purposes and employments abovesaid. In testimony whereof we have hereunto set our hand & seal at his Majesty's Castle of Dublin the nineteenth day of February 1633[/4].

To the right honourable our very good lord, the Lord Marquis Hamilton.

158. [f. 498r] <JOHN RAGGETT> [21 FEBRUARY 1634]

An attachment against John Raggett to answer such matters as at his coming shall be objected against him, dated 21 ~~April~~ ^*Februarii*^ 1633[/4].

159. <TIRLAGH O'DANIEL>[149] [21 FEBRUARY 1634]

An attachment *versus* Tirlagh O'Daniel to answer as well his contempt as the complaint of William Blower, dated 21 *Februarii* 1633[/4].

To any of his Majesty's pursuivants.

148 James Hamilton (1606–49), 1st duke of Hamilton (see *ODNB*).

149 See warrant no. 140.

160. [A WARRANT ORDERING THE REMOVAL OF CORN POWDER FROM CARRICKFERGUS] [22 FEBRUARY 1634]

By the lord deputy

Wentworth

Master of the Ordnance. These are to pray & require your lordship to cause to be removed from Carrickfergus hither by sea, with all the convenient expedition that may be, 10 barrel[s] of corn powder[150] for answering the occasions of his Majesty's service here. And for your so doing these shall be unto your lordship a sufficient ~~power~~ warrant. Given at his Majesty's Castle of Dublin the 22nd day of February 1633[/4].

To our very good lord, the Lord Caulfeild, Master of the Ordnance in Ireland.

<These my lord sent by Mr Care>

161. [WARRANT TO TAKE UP A BOAT AT CARRICKFERGUS FOR THE SAFE TRANSPORTATION OF POWDER] [22 FEBRUARY 1634]

By the lord deputy

Wentworth

Whereas we have given directions that 10 barrels of powder shall with all expedition be brought hither from Carrickfergus to sea upon some special occasion of his Majesty's service, these are therefore to will & require you to press & take up within that harbour one sufficient boat, close decks or small barques, [**f. 498v**] for the safe transporting of the same powder hither for the fraught of which boat or barque ready money shall be paid as the clerk of the stores at Carrickfergus shall agree according to his Majesty's usual & accustomed rates; hereof you may not fail as you will answer the contrary at your uttermost peril. Given at his Majesty's Castle of Dublin this 22nd of February 1633[/4].

To our well beloved, the mayors of the town of Carrickfergus.

162. [ATTACHMENT AGAINST CAPTAIN JOHN PERKINS] [25 FEBRUARY 1634]

By the lord deputy

Wentworth

A warrant of attachment against Captain ^John^ Perkins (Captain Chichester's[151] lieutenant) *adversus* William, Lord Caulfeild, baron of Charlemont, dated 25 February 1633[/4].

To any of his Majesty's pursuivants.

[150] Corn powder is gun powder that has been 'corned' or granulated to facilitate drying (*Oxford English Dictionary).*

[151] Arthur Chichester (1606–75), 1st earl of Donegal, soldier and administrator (see *DIB*).

163. <WILLIAM ALDRICH> **[4 FEBRUARY 1634]**

By the lord deputy

Wentworth

<manicule> A warrant for drawing up a fiant in due form containing a presentation of William Aldrich, clerk, unto the rectory of Drumgoon in the county of Cavan & diocese of Kilmore being now void by lapse, to have &c. according [to] the usual form, dated 4 February 1633[/4].

To our trusty & well beloved, the clerks of the Council, or either of them.

164. [f. 499r] <A WARRANT TO THE DUKE OF LENNOX,[152] HIS AGENT, TO TRANSPORT 250*li.*> **[26 FEBRUARY 1634]**

By the lord deputy

Wentworth

Whereas our very good lord, the Duke of Lennox, his agent here hath been an humble suitor unto us that we would be pleased to licence him to send over into England the sum of 250*li.* in specie[153] for his the said Duke of Lennox his use, being part of his rents due out of his lands in this kingdom, whose request therein we have thought fit to grant and the rather in regard the said agent affirmeth that he cannot have the same returned by exchange, though he did endeavour it with large proffer of advantage to the undertaker. These are therefore to will and require you & every of you to permit & suffer the bearer hereof to put aboard & transport for England the said sum of 250*li.* without any your hindrances, or any seizure thereof to be made, whereof you & every of you are not to fail. And for so doing this shall be &c. Given &c. 26th February 1633[/4].

To all & every, his Majesty's officers of the customs in the port of Dublin and to all other his Majesty's officers & ministers whom it may concern & to every of them.

Thomas Littell

165. [f. 499v] <A WARRANT FOR A COMMISSION *INTER* SIR THOMAS STAPLES, MILES & JAUNCY> **[26 FEBRUARY 1634]**

By the lord deputy

Wentworth

Whereas upon the hearing of the cause between Anthony Jauncy, ~~&~~ plaintiff, & Sir Thomas Staples, knight & baronet, defendant, which was referred formerly unto us by the lords of his Majesty's most honourable privy council in March last concerning a debt of threescore pounds, fifty pounds principal, 20*li.* costs & damages ~~forfor~~ formerly paid by the said Jauncy unto one Humphrey Lee <*vide* book of Common

[152] James Stuart (1612–55), 4th duke of Lennox and 1st duke of Richmond (see *ODNB*).

[153] i.e. minted pieces of metal.

entries [pages] 400 & 449> upon a bond of 100*li.* for the payment of 50*li.* entered into by the said Jauncy to the said Lee for the proper debt of the said defendant, Sir Thomas Staples, as is alleged by the petitioner. <& now book of entries page 33> And inasmuch as the defendant allegeth that the said plaintiff entered into the said bond in acquittal of a like debt of the petitioner's own owing to one Henry Miles who was thereupon to have so much defaulted out of some debts the said Miles owed the defendant, we (for the better manifestation of the tenth & our further satisfaction in the matter) have thought fit that 2 several commissions shall be granted & directed unto the persons undernamed being commissioners of the parties own choosing & election, the one of the said commissions to be sat upon & executed at Londonderry in the county of Londonderry in this kingdom, and the other to be executed in London in the realm of England. And to that end we do hereby pray & require your lordship to cause the said commissions to issue accordingly, thereby giving full power & authority unto the said commissioners respectively as they are commissioned to enquire & examine upon oath whether as well at the time of the bond entered into by the said plaintiff, Jauncy unto Lee, he the said plaintiff was indebted in any such sum unto the said Miles, and how much & [**f. 500r**] upon what accounts, bills, bonds or otherwise as also whether at the same time the said Miles was indebted unto the said defendant in the said 50*li.*, or how much & upon what account, bills, bonds or otherwise; the said commission to be returnable with all convenient speed and at the furthest by the first day of the next Trinity term. And for so doing this shall be a sufficient warrant. Given &c. the 25th day of February 1633[/4].

The names of the commissioners in England: Hugh Saunders, esquire; Henry Payton, esquire, *pro defendente*; Charles Jones, esquire; William Firth gent, *pro querente.*

The names of the commissioners for this kingdom: Sir John Vaughan, knight, Henry Hart, esquire, *pro defendente*; John Perkins, esquire, John Richardson, clerk, *pro querente.*

To our very good lord, the lord chancellor.

166. <A WARRANT FOR A COMMISSION BETWEEN THE DEAN & CORPORATION OF WATERFORD>[154] [25 FEBRUARY 1634]

By the lord deputy

Wentworth

Whereas there is a difference depending before us between Richard Jones, dean of the city of Waterford, plaintiff, and the mayor & corporation of the said city, defendants, concerning certain revenues, plate, jewels & ornaments pretended to have been belonging to the said cathedral church ~~of~~ there and are now come into the hands of the mayors & corporation aforesaid, <*vide* church affairs page 88> but for our further satisfaction in the premises & to the end the truth may the better [**f. 500v**] appear, our pleasure is, and so we pray & require your lordship, to issue forth a commission under the great seal & to be directed unto our well beloved Richard Strange, Andrew

[154] See warrant no. 39.

Lynn, Thomas Wadding & Geoffrey Baron, gent, thereby giving them or any 3 or 2 of them full power and authority to examine all such witnesses as either party shall produce concerning the matter in question, the said commission to be returnable with all convenient speed and at the furthest by the second return of the next term. And for so doing this shall be a sufficient warrant. Given at his Majesty's Castle of Dublin the 25th of February 1633[/4].

To our very good lord, the lord chancellor.

167. [ATTACHMENT *VERSUS* FRANCIS HILL] [5 MARCH 1634]

By the lord deputy

Wentworth

An attachment *versus* Francis Hill, esquire, to answer as well his contempt of our directions as the complaint of Richard Shukburgh, dean of Connorth [*sic*],[155] dated 5 *Martii* 1633[/4].

To any of his Majesty's pursuivants.

Thomas Littell

168. [f. 501r] <DERMOD NESTOR>[156] [5 MARCH 1634]

By the lord deputy

Attachment against Dermod Nestor, clerk, to answer such matters as shall be objected against him, dated 5 *Martii* 1633[/4]. <*vide* church affairs page 90>

To any of his Majesty's pursuivants.

169. [ATTACHMENT *VERSUS* THOMAS PRENDERGAST][157] [3 MARCH 1634]

By the lord deputy

Wentworth

Attachment *versus* Thomas Prendergast to answer as well his contempt as the complaint of John Power, dated 3 March 1633[/4].

To any of his Majesty's pursuivants.

170. <THOMAS BURGESS, HIS *MITTIMUS* TO THE MARSHALLSEA> [25 FEBRUARY 1634]

By the lord deputy

Wentworth

These are to will and require you forthwith to receive & take into your custody the body of Thomas Burgess, one of the weighers of the customs in the port of Kinsale,

155 Connor.

156 See warrant no. 52.

157 See warrant no. 144.

& ^him^ having so received safely to detain & keep until our further pleasure be known, whereof you may not fail. And for so doing this shall be your warrant. Given &c. 25 of February 1633[/4]. <*verte fedum per liberate*>

To John Dobb, gent, marshal of the Four Courts.

171. [f. 501v] [WARRANT TO SET THOMAS BURGESS FREE] [10 MARCH 1634]

By the lord deputy

Wentworth

Upon receipt hereof you are to enlarge & set at liberty the body of Thomas Burgess, one of the weighers of the customs of the port of Kinsale, whom you have in your custody upon our former warrant to you directed, he paying his due & accustomed fees. And for so doing this shall be your warrant. Given &c. the 10th of March 1633[/4].

To John Dobb gent, marshal of the Four Courts.

Thomas Littell

172. <WARRANT FOR THOMAS WATSON TO TRANSPORT A HORSE> [12 MARCH 1634]

By the lord deputy

Wentworth

Whereas the bearer hereof William Watson, merchant, is to make his present repair into England & to take his journey through Scotland, these are to will and require you the officers of that port, wheresoever he shall present this our warrant, to permit & suffer him to put aboard & transport for England one gelding or saddle nag for his own use to ride on. And for so doing this shall be your warrant, any former general directions to the contrary notwithstanding. Given &c. 12 *Martii* 1633[/4].

173. [f. 502r] <A WARRANT FOR LIEUTENANT WEST TO TRANSPORT HORSES> [15 MARCH 1634]

By the lord deputy

Wentworth

Whereas upon humble suit made unto us by William West, esquire, we have been pleased to licence him to carry for England four horses for himself, his son-in-law & their men to ride on, these are therefore to will and require you to permit and suffer the said four horses, gelding or saddle nags (so they be not horses of service) to be put aboard & transported out of this port, any former general directions to the contrary notwithstanding. And for so doing this shall be a sufficient warrant. Given &c. 15 *Martii* 1633[/4].

To our well beloved William Scott, esquire, searcher to his Majesty in the port of Dublin.

174. <WILLIAM SYMS, GENT> **[18 MARCH 1634]**

By the lord deputy

Wentworth
A warrant for transporting of 2 horses or saddle nags ~~at~~ for England out of the port of Youghal, dated eighteenth of March 1633[/4].

To all & every, his Majesty's officers of the customs in the port of Youghal.

175. [f. 502v] [A WARRANT OF ATTACHMENT AGAINST THE MAYOR & RECORDER OF CORK, & *AL.*] **[18 MARCH 1634]**

By the lord deputy

Wentworth
A warrant of attachment against the several persons undernamed, dated 18 *Martii* 1633[/4], to answer as well their contempt as the complaints of Thomas Bate &c.

The mayor & recorder of Cork

William Lumberd
William Coppinger
John Skiddy
John Flynn &
James Galway now in this town

} all of Cork

<*vide* least [*sic*] book of entries page 129>

This attachment issued upon the certificate & affidavit following.

At the request of Thomas Bate, merchant, we the persons undernamed on the 10th day of this ~~instant~~ present month went with the said Bate unto the mayor & recorder of Cork & showed them an order from the right honourable the lord deputy, upon a petition preferred unto his lordship by the said Bate, requiring the mayor, recorder & 4 young men named in the petition to redeliver back again unto the said Bate the 346*li.* of tobacco formerly unjustly seized and detained by the said young men, or else to appear before his lordship. The mayor & recorder desired time until the next day in the afternoon whether they would redeliver the tobacco or appear before his lordship. The next day the mayor & recorder were willing to redeliver the one half of the tobacco conditionally that if the young men evicted the said Bate that then he should pay so much money to the mayor & aldermen as the tobacco should be worth, and the [**f. 503r**] said young men protesting in open court that they would not deliver the tobacco but would spend rather their whole estates in law, ad[d]ing? that if Mr Bate spent a thousand pounds it should not cost them a shilling a piece. And on the same day, showing the lord deputy's warrant in open court, one James Galway FitzEdward went & seized of 3 rolls of tobacco of one Robert Fennell's, sold unto one John Court going through the town of Cork, the said Robert Fennell dwelling in St Francis Abbey where divers English merchants have inhabited & freely traded for many years. Notwithstanding his said warrant he the said Galway detaineth the tobacco and hath received a sum of money of[f] them to be their agent to answer his lordship's warrant & to justify the seizures. And for the manifestation of the truth thereof we have hereunto set our hands this 12th day of March 1633[/4].

Thomas Simpson
Richard French
Daniel Cuffe.

176. <AFFIDAVIT AGAINST THE MAYOR OF CORK & *AL.*> **[N.D.]**

Morris McEdmond Hay, yeoman, made faith that on the 10th of this instant or thereabouts he was present when one Richard French of Cork, merchant, showed the right honourable the lord deputy's direction, dated 24 February 1633, to the mayor & recorder of the city of Cork, and to William Lumberd, William Coppinger, John Skiddy & John Flynn of Cork, merchants, by which direction aforesaid the said mayor & recorder of Cork [**f. 503v**] as all & every the persons aforesaid were required forthwith to restore unto Thomas Bate, merchant, the tobacco in the said Bate's petition mentioned or failing so to do to appear forthwith to show cause to the contrary; and in the meantime to forbear molesting or troubling the said Bate for the said tobacco or any other matter of that nature until upon the hearing thereof the lord deputy should give such order therein as there should be cause. And the deponent ~~al~~ deposeth that he was also present when the aforesaid Richard French desired the said mayor & recorder & the persons aforesaid to restore to the said Thomas Bate the tobacco aforesaid whereupon the mayor & recorder offered the said French half the said tobacco but the parties aforesaid, namely William Lumberd, William Coppinger, John Skiddy & John Flynn, merchants, said openly that they would not suffer the said tobacco to be restored but would spend 1,000*li.* to the said Thomas Bate his shilling rather then they would restore it, whereupon the said mayor & recorder & the rest stayed all the said tobacco & still do detain the same.

Copia Vera

William Ussher.

177. [f. 504r] <A WARRANT OF ASSISTANCE FOR LIMERICK> **[17 MARCH 1634]**

By the lord deputy

Wentworth

Whereas there is complaint made unto us by the farmers & officers of his Majesty's customs that there are divers goods & merchandizes landed ~~la~~ in several ports & creeks ~~of~~ ^in^ this kingdom without due entry made thereof which his Majesty's officers in that behalf appointed, and the merchants having so indirectly gained the said goods & merchandizes they afterwards carry the same by land to the cities, towns and other places of their dwelling and there do allege that the customs & other duties due to his Majesty were formerly paid at their first landing thereof and yet do not bring any certificate or warrant to manifest the same. And forasmuch as we are given to understand that upon the like complaint made to the barons of the Exchequer *anno* 1619 by agents of the then farmers of his Majesty's customs, who weighing the great damage, might thereby ensur[e] it was then by them ordered that all merchants trading into this kingdom of what kind so ever they should be & carrying any [of] their goods, wares & merchandizes from any port or creek of their said landing to any city, town and place over land should there take out & bring with them a true certificate under the hands & seals of the customer & farmers' deputies of the said port where the said goods & merchandizes were so landed, expressing the true quantities & qualities of the said goods & signifying the true payment of the said customs & other duties due as aforesaid; and in failing thereof that it should be lawful for the said officers, as well of his Majesty as the farmers, to [**f. 504v**] seize any the said goods to his Majesty's use as they might do if the same were carried from one port to another by sea, which order we conceive to be right & just; and now we are informed that the said officers have often endeavoured to put the said order in execution in the port of Limerick but have received many affronts in executing the same by such merchants in refusing either to show any certificate or suffering them to view their said goods, forthwith they deserve to be severely punished. These are therefore to will & require you the mayor, sheriff, constables & all other officers whatsoever in the said city of Limerick & ^or^ elsewhere that you be hereafter aiding & assisting as well to his Majesty's officers as the farmers in the due execution as well of the premises as also in all other matters that may concern his Majesty or the farmers of his customs. And if any merchant or others shall contemptuously refuse to obey the same or give disturbance unto them in executing their employments that then you take a course to bind him or them over to appear before us to answer their contempts, of which fail you not as you will answer the contrary at your perils. Given &c. 17th March 1633[/4].

To all mayors, sheriffs, justices of the peace, constables and all other his Majesty's officers & loving subjects whom it may concern.

Thomas Littell

178. [f. 505r] <A WARRANT FOR GEORGE HULL TO BE CUSTOMER & COLLECTOR IN THE PORTS OF NEWCASTLE & *AL.*>[158] [20 MARCH 1634]

By the lord deputy

Wentworth

Whereas by the death of ^George Hull, gent,^ William Pitt, gent, late customer & collector in the ports of Newcastle, Dundrum &c., the said office is now become void & in our dispose and forasmuch as we have thought fit to confer the same upon George Hull, gent, these are therefore to will & require you forthwith to draw up a fiant in due form of law containing a grant from his Majesty unto the said George Hull of the said office of customer & receiver of his Majesty's customs, imposts & subsidies in the ports of Newcastle, Dundrum, Killough, Ardglass, Strangford, Killcliffe,

[158] See warrant no. 125.

Loughcoyne, Portaferry, Bangor, Donaghadee & Hollywood, with all the creeks and members to them & every of them belonging in the county of Down, <*vide* page 169> to have, hold, execute, exercise & enjoy the said office & offices of customer & receiver in the said ports & creeks together with the fee or stipend of ten pounds harps *per annum* from his Majesty, <~~by he death of George Hull who lately held the same~~> together with all other fees, profits, perquisites, privileges & emoluments whatsoever unto the said office or offices belonging or in anywise appertaining from & immediately after the day of the death of the said William Pitt, <Thomas Belfield, gent> and in as large, ample and beneficial manner as the said William Pitt formerly held & enjoyed or of right ought to have held and enjoyed the same, or as any other his Majesty's customers & receivers in any his highness's ports in this kingdom usually receive & enjoy, the said office to be exercised by the said George Hull or his sufficient deputy or deputies during good behaviour, inserting therein all such clauses as in like grants are usual and the same fairly engrossed in parchment under your hand to send unto us to be furthe[r] passed as appertaineth. And for so doing &c. Given &c. the twentieth day of March 1633[/4].

To our trusty & well beloved, his Majesty's attorney & solicitor general, or either of them.

Thomas Littell

179. [f. 505v] <WARRANT FOR THE ERECTING OF PARSONS, VICARS CHORAL &C. IN ARMAGH>[159] **[DATE]**

These are to will and require you forthwith upon sight hereof to draw up a fiant in due form of law containing first a clause of disappropriation of the several rectories of Mullaghbrack, the rectory & vicarage of Creggan, the rectory & vicarage of Teagly *alias* *~~als~~* Derrynoose, the rectory of Tynan, the rectory of Mountechenry *alias* Townaghlry in the vicarage of the church of Levalliglees in the county of Armagh, & the rectory of Donaghmore & the rectory of Clonfeacle, and the tithes of Tomackbryn, parcel of the rectory of Kilsleeve in the county of Armagh heretofore impropriated to the priory of Culdees of Armagh, <*vide* church affairs, page 82, 93> and by inquisition lately taken found to belong unto his Majesty by reason of the dissolution of the said priory and then making & creating the said rectories to be presentative & collative as the case shall require with cure of souls, <manicule> and that there shall be incumbents upon them forever for the discharge of the cure of souls in the several parishes whereof the said rectories are; and where there are any vicarages endowed out of the said rectories there to unite & consolidate the vicarages to the said rectories again & to make them entire rectories, and after such disappropiation made then to contain a new plantation of the now incumbents hereunto again and, if you shall think it necessary, to make a new incorporation of every of the said incumbents to be a body politic by the name of parson of every of the said parishes & his successors respectively, and by that name to have perpetual succession and to be capable of

[159] The end of the warrant is badly torn.

any grant to be made unto them of the several tithes & glebes of the said rectories respectively, and of new a [**f. 506r**] grant of the said glebes and tithes to be made unto them & their successors respectively. The said fiant likewise to contain a grant of the advowsons & rights of patronage, presentation & collation to the said several rectories with the several vicarages respectively to be united unto them, unto James, lord archbishop of Armagh, and his successors forever in pure & frank-almoign, with a covenant on the part of the said lord archbishop of Armagh that neither he nor any of his officers shall demand any fees from the several persons to be presented to the said rectories, or any of them, for or in respect of any such new union, jurisdiction or induction to the said see, to be made presentative or collative parsonages respectively with a clause of exoneration of all first fruits, mesne rates & profits of the said lands, tithes; and several rectories with a grant also in the said fiant to be contained of foundation of a new college in the church of St Patrick's, Armagh, consisting of eight vicars chorals, four choristers & one organist to celebrate divine service in the said church, ^the said college^ to be called by the name of the college of King Charles in the church of St Patrick's Armagh, the lord archbishop of Armagh & his successors to name the said vicars choral, choristers & organist, as well for the time present ~~p~~ as to come; and to give them a perpetual succession & a common seal with power to purchase lands not exceeding ~~100*li*.~~ two hundred pounds English *per annum*, and to acquire any goods or chattels with a grant of all lands, parcels of lands, tenements & hereditaments, with their appurtenances at any time heretofore found by inquisition to be granted and to have been belonging to the late priory or Culdees of Armagh & [**f. 506v**] formerly granted by letters patents unto George Kirk, one of the grooms of his Majesty's bed chamber, and his heirs, reserving all such rents as were at any time heretofore paid unto Christopher, late archbishop of Armagh,[160] or unto the present archbishop wherein is to be contained a covenant on the part & behalf of the new to be erected incumbents of the said rectories; that in case the said ^town^lands & other temporal lands, tenements and parcels anciently belonging to the said priory or Culdees, shall upon inquisition be found not to be worth 115*li*. English *per annum* that then the several incumbents of the said rectories shall make effectual grants to such persons for such estates & in such manner as to us the lord deputy, with the advice of the lord chancellor, shall seem most convenient to the use of the said vicars choral, choristers & organists of such several & competent pensions & yearly sums to issue out of their said rectories, having regard to their several values as together with the uttermost rent of the said lands, ~~yearly~~ ^parcels^ & tenements, being freed from all former incumbencies & reprises shall amount to the sum of 115*li*. English *per annum* with a signification of his Majesty's pleasure that the maintenance of the said vicars choral, choristers & organist shall be suspended for the space of one year from the date of the letters patents to be past [*sic*] upon these presents, or until such time as the rents & profits which shall accrue & issue out of the said lands from the first day of November last past [*sic*] shall amount to a competent sum sufficient to defray the charge of the letters patents to pass hereupon & other things concerning [**f. 507r**] the establishment of the premises; and to buy a pair of organs for the quire as by the

160 Christopher Hampton (1552–1625), archbishop of Armagh (see *DIB*).

advice of the now archbishop of Armagh and his successors & the lord chancellor of this kingdom for the time being shall be thought fit, inserting therein likewise a grant from his Majesty unto the said lord archbishop of Armagh & his successors forever of one fair to be held within the town of Armagh upon St Peter's day, yearly to continue for that day and the day next following provided always that if the said St Peter's day shall happen upon Saturday or Monday then the said fair to be held upon the Tuesday & Wednesday following, and likewise of one weekly market to be kept upon Saturday in the said town of Armagh with such courts, tolls, liberties and customs to any other fairs or markets within this kingdom belonging, and the benefits of the fines and amerciaments of such courts, tolls, liberties & customs; The said courts… by the seneschal or seneschals…archbishop and his successors…lawful deputy or dep…purport ^& intent^ of his M…of the 24 of…for your better instruc… And the same…under your hand…passed as app… Given &c.

<This warrant was renewed…this condition that the fairs…markets should pass with…rent reserved to his Ma…dated according [to] the first …>

180. [f. 507v] <WARRANT FOR A FERRY, MARKET & FAIR FOR MR CANNING>[161] **[22 MARCH 1634]**

By the lord deputy

Wentworth

Whereas George Canning, gentleman, hath petitioned unto us setting forth that about some 15 years last past [*sic*] he passed letters patents under the great seal of this kingdom for a ferry over the river of the Bann in the county of Londonderry and also one weekly market & a yearly fair at a town called Aghagene in the said county, <*vide* the last book of common entries page 176 & 234 for the petition & certificate whereon this was grounded> but in regard the town of Coleraine in the said county have a clause in their charter that no fair or market should be kept within seven miles of that town he the said Canning affirmeth he could receive no benefit by his, although he duly paid his Majesty's rent thereout being 40*li.* Irish; he therefore…besought us to give directions for the…of the said letters patents for the…where it formerly was & now is…weekly market & yearly fair…town of Gravahy in the…ver, being distant from…ten miles at least…[whe]rein we have thought fit…redoubling of the rent… therefore we do hereby…you to draw up & make…the said ferry & of a…to be kept on Friday and…of July forever at the…Gravahy, reserving [**f. 508r**] thereout unto his Majesty the yearly rent of three pounds sterling. And the same fairly engrossed in parchment under your hand to send unto us to be further passed as appertaineth. And for so doing this shall be a sufficient warrant. Given at his Majesty's Castle of Dublin the xxii of March 1633[/4]. <*vide* page 164: a warrant for a fiant>

To our trusty & well beloved, his Majesty's surveyor & auditor general.

Thomas Littell

161 The end of the warrant is badly torn.

181. <RICHARD WATERS> **[22 MARCH 1634]**

By the lord deputy

Wentworth
A warrant of attachment against Richard Waters of Moyrion in the county of Cork to answer such matters as at his coming shall be objected against. Given &c. 22nd of March 1633[/4]. <*vide* new book of entries page [blank] for petition & articles against him & amongst the bundles for the affidavits>

To any of his Majesty's pursuivants.

182. [f. 508v] <*MITTIMUS* FOR RICHARD ROCH>[162] **[26 MARCH 1634]**

By the lord deputy

Wentworth
These are to will and require you forthwith to receive & take into your custody the body of Richard Roch, late master of a ship called the *St Jago of Dunkirk*, and him safely to detain & keep close prisoner until our further pleasure be known; whereof you may not fail. And for so doing this shall be your sufficient warrant. Given at his Majesty's Castle of Dublin, 26th *Martii* 1634.

To our well beloved Samuel Davis, esquire, constable of his Majesty's Castle of Dublin.

Thomas Littell

183. <ATTACHMENT AGAINST JOHN HARRIS> **[26 MARCH 1634]**

By the lord deputy

Wentworth
These are to will and require you to make diligent search & inquiry for the body of John Harris, & him having found to attach & forthwith being before us, to answer as well his contempt of our directions as the complaints of Bartholomew Lincoln &c. Given &c. the 26th March 1634. <*vide* the affidavit amongst the bundles>

To any of his Majesty's pursuivants.

Thomas Littell

184. [f. 509r] <A WARRANT TO THE LORD BLANEY TO SEND ROSS BOY &C. TO THE CASTLE OF DUBLIN>[163] **[27 MARCH 1634]**

By the lord deputy

Wentworth
Whereas we are given to understand that Ross Boy McBrien Sanagh McMahon, a notorious rebel & malefactor, is lately by our warrant & directions apprehended

[162] See also warrant no. 117.

[163] See warrant no. 51.

& taken and is now by the sheriff of the county of Monaghan committed to safe custody, <*vide* book of letters page 49, 50, 51> these shall be therefore to will and require you immediately upon the receipt hereof to receive unto your custody the body of the said Ross Boy McBrien Sanagh McMahon from the sheriff of the said county of Monaghan to whom we have directed our warrant for delivering him unto you accordingly; and him safely manacled & fettered under the conduct & safeguard of thirty soldiers of their company with their lieutenant or other officer-in-chief to convey to Mellifont to our very good lord the Lord Viscount Moore[164] to be delivered to him or to his immediate officer, together with this our warrant, who is likewise hereby required to convey the said prisoner Ross Boy &c. under the guard of ten horsemen of his troop with their officers and such others as his lordship shall think fit to the constable of this his Majesty's Castle of Dublin. And we do likewise hereby will and require all and every his Majesty's subjects, whom the same may concern, to afford unto the said officers, soldiers & prisoner, competent meat, drink and lodging in their passage hither, they paying ready money or leaving ticket for the same according to his Majesty's usual and accustomed rates. The said officers & soldiers being also hereby commanded not to commit any extortion, exaction or outrage upon peril of their [**f. 509v**] lives but to march the direct way towards this city of Dublin after the rate of fifteen miles a day at least. And for so doing this shall be unto you & every of you a sufficient warrant; in the due execution whereof &c. Given &c. 27th March 1634.

To our very good lords, the Lord Blaney & the Lord Viscount Moore, & to the officers commanding their several companies in chief, and to all others whom it may concern.

185. <WARRANT TO MR BLANEY TO PROSECUTE REBELS IN THE COUNTIES OF MONAGHAN, CAVAN, TYRONE, FERMANAGH, ARMAGH & LOUTH> [26 MARCH 1634]

By the lord deputy

Wentworth

Whereas divers robberies, felonies and other insolences are daily committed as we are informed within the several counties of Monaghan, Cavan, Fermanagh, Tyrone, Armagh and Louth by sundry persons whose names cannot yet be known to the terror & grief of his Majesty's good subjects, the contempt of his laws & the bad example of others ill disposed, <*vide* book of letters page 51, this warrant renewed page 186> and whereas we have reposed special trust in our well beloved Richard Blaney, esquire, for the prosecution & apprehension of the said malefactors, we have therefore thought fit and do hereby give full [**f. 510r**] commission & authority to the said Richard Blaney to pursue, attach, apprehend and by all good ways & means to prosecute the said malefactors, their relievers or abettors, and them or any of them so apprehended forthwith to examine & commit, or convey or cause to be conveyed, before his Majesty's next justice or justices of peace, who are to examine & commit

164 Charles Moore (1603–43), 2nd Viscount Moore of Drogheda (see *DIB*).

them to the next gaol within that county where they shall be so taken to be kept in safe custody till they may be proceeded against by due course of law, and such good as being suspected to be stolen & shall be found in the custody of the said malefactors, or any their receivers or abettors, to seize upon & safely keep till it shall appe[ar] to whom the same shall legally appertain. And for the better effecting hereof we do hereby require all & every, or any of the captains or officers of companies within the counties aforementioned, to furnish & accommodate the said Richard Blaney with such soldiers as he shall from time think necessary & useful to be employed by him in the service aforesaid, which said soldiers are in all lawful things to obey his directions, hereby further charging and requiring the inhabitants of the several towns & places, whereunto the said Richard Blaney & the soldiers aforesaid shall have occasion to resort, to afford them competent meat, drink & lodging at his Majesty's usual rates during the time of such prosecution provided that they commit no extortion nor oppression in the [**f. 510v**] county upon peril of their lives; and provided also that this commission continue in force for the space of 3 whole months from and after the date hereof and no longer, in the due execution whereof &c. Given &c. ~~And &c.~~ 26 *Martii* 1634.

186. <PROTECTION FOR CORMAC RAWER O'DUFFEY FOR 3 MONTHS> [26 MARCH 1634]

By the lord deputy

Wentworth

Whereas for reason best known to ourself we are pleased to take into his Majesty's protection the body of Cormac ^Rawer^ O'Duffey for the space of 3 months from & after the date hereof. We do therefore hereby will and require you to take due notice thereof & to forbear suing, arresting, apprehending or otherwise molesting the said Cormac Rawer O'Duffey in his person ~~&~~ ^or^ goods for & during the said time & term of 3 months. And for so doing this shall be a sufficient warrant. Given at his Majesty's Castle of Dublin the 26th of March 1634. <*vide* page 185>

To all mayors, sheriffs, justices of peace, sovereigns, portreeves, bailiffs & all other his Majesty's officers, ministers and loving subjects whom it may concern.

187. [f. 511r] <ATTACHMENT *VERSUS* WILLIAM FURLONG & *AL.*> [1 APRIL 1634]

By the lord deputy

Wentworth

~~These~~ An attachment ^*versus*^ William Furlong, Nicholas Devorix & Anthony Coleclough to answer as well their contempts as the complaint of John Fagan, dated 1 April 1634. <*vide* least [*sic*] book of common entries, page 74>

To any of his Majesty's pursuivants.

188. <GEORGE SILL> **[1 APRIL 1634]**

An attachment against George Sill to answer such matters as at his coming shall be objected against him. Sir George Radcliffe gave directions for this. Given 1 April 1634.

To any of his Majesty's pursuivants.

189. <THOMAS BENNETT> **[1 APRIL 1634]**

An attachment against Thomas Bennett, deputy customer of Baltimore, to answer such matters as at his coming shall be objected against him, dated 1 April 1634.

To any of his Majesty's pursuivants.

190. [f. 511v] <GEORGE CANNING, WARRANT *PRO* FIANT>[165] **[2 APRIL 1634]**

By the lord deputy

Wentworth

These are to will and require you forthwith to draw up a fiant in due form of law containing a grant from his Majesty unto George Canning, esquire, ^his heirs & assigns forever^, of the ferry over the river of the Bann in the county of Londonderry and of a yearly fair & a weekly market to be kept at the town of Garvahy in the said county as the same are contained in this particular, <this was granted upon Sir William Parsons's return of the ~~certificate~~ particulars> the fair to be kept on the 15th day of July and the market on Friday weekly, forever reserving thereout unto his Majesty the rent of 3*li.* sterling *per annum* provided that if the said 15th day of July shall fall to be upon a Sunday that then the said fair to be kept upon the day following. Inserting therein all such clauses as in like cases are usual, the said George Canning, being to surrender the former patent past [*sic*] unto him for the said ferry and a fair & market to have been kept at Aghivee in the said county before this now grant, be permitted to pass the great seal. And the same fairly engrossed in parchment under your hand to send unto us to be further passed as appertaineth; for doing whereof this shall be your warrant. Given &c. 2 *Aprilis* 1634.

To our trusty & well beloved, his Majesty's attorney & solicitor general, or either of them.

191. [f. 512r] <WARRANT FOR A FIANT FOR ELIZABETH ASLABY TO HAVE A GENERAL COLLECTION THROUGH ALL IRELAND, EXCEPT IN THE PROVINCE OF MUNSTER> **[3 APRIL 1634]**

By the lord deputy

Wentworth

Whereas his Majesty hath been graciously pleased by his highness's letters, bearing date the 13th day of August in the third year of his highness's reign of England &c., to give

[165] See warrant no. 180.

order to the late lords justices of this kingdom to grant letters patents under the great seal thereof unto Elizabeth Aslaby for the collection of the benevolence of all his Majesty's well disposed subjects of this said kingdom of Ireland, in consideration that many & great losses which the said Elizabeth her husband had sustained by thieves, fire and otherwise, <*vide* the least [*sic*] book of entries page 254 for his Majesty's letter whereupon this was grounded> and forasmuch as she was then limited by the said lords justices to the province of Munster only for the said collection which was conceived to be far short for any competent satisfaction of the said losses, these are therefore to will and require you to draw up a fiant in due form of law containing a grant of licence unto the said Elizabeth Aslaby to take, gather & collect the charitable & Christian benevolence of all his Majesty's well disposed subjects within Ɨ ^this^ kingdom of Ireland (the said province of Munster only excepted), inserting therein a direction to the minister of the several churches thereof respectively for the stirring up of the devotion of their parishioners for performance of the intent of his Majesty's charitable work herein, together with the **[f. 512v]** usual clauses of grants of this or the like nature according to the effect of his Majesty's letters bearing date the eleventh day of February 1633 to us in that behalf directed, a copy whereof for your better instruction we have herewith sent you to peruse; the said grant or licence to continue for the space of 18 months next ensuing the date hereof. And the same fairly engrossed in parchment to send unto us under your hand to the end the same may be further passed as shall appertain. And for so doing this shall be your warrant. Given &c. 3 *Aprilis* 1634.

To our right trusty & well beloved, his Majesty's attorney & solicitor general, or either of them.

Thomas Littell

192. [f. 513r] <A PROTECTION FOR 6 MONTH[S] FOR KATHERINE MAISTERSON *ALIAS* BUTLER[166]> **[2 APRIL 1634]**

By the lord deputy

Wentworth

Whereas Katherine Maisterson *alias* Butler, widow, hath humbly petitioned to us setting forth that in regard of divers losses and unnatural suits commenced against her by a son-in-law she is become engaged in certain debts which she is not possibly able for the present to discharge, <I copied this from Mr Edmund's office[167]> and for her better liberty to follow her several occasions without danger of arrests which might in some sort enable her to the payment thereof did humbly pray us to afford her his Majesty's protection for a time, which we did for the present decline and deny to grant unto her. Yet being since informed by our very good lord, the Lord Esmond, to whose mediation we referred the said petition, that she hath made very reasonable offers of payment at a years' day to some of the creditors of the sums due unto them with damages for the

166 Katherine Butler (d. 1646). She left most of her estate to her grandson, Peter Butler (1606–after 1670), MP for Gowran (see McGrath).

167 Thomas Edmundes.

forbearance as namely to one Cleere, to whom she offered 50*li.* for a debt of 37*li.*, who doth nevertheless violently press for present payment which she is not able to make and that though she hath made offer unto him of her bond for payment accordingly, which the said Lord Esmond conceives sufficient and which he himself would accept for so much debt yet is the same also refused, we have thought fit upon her second humble petition to grant her request and do therefore hereby will and require you & every of you not only to take due notice thereof but also to forbear suing, arresting, impleading or otherwise molesting the said Katherine either [**f. 513v**] in her person or goods for and during the space of six months next ensuing the date hereof she behaving herself as becometh, provided that by virtue hereof she defeat not her creditors but do her endeavour to the uttermost of her power to give them content and satisfaction that we may not be troubled with their complaints; and provided that she doth forthwith make offer of her bond to the said Cleere to make good payment of the said 50*li.* in such sort as aforesaid, neither is this protection granted either to free her from any debt due to his Majesty or from any former imprisonments; whereof she & you are not to fail. Given at his Majesty's Castle of Dublin the second day of April 1634.

To all mayors, sheriffs, justice of the peace, sovereigns, portreeves & bailiffs, and to all and every, his Majesty's other officers, minsters and loving subjects whom it may concern.

193. [f. 514r] <WARRANT TO WATERHOUSE, CRIMBLE & *AL.* IN BEHALF OF GEORGE HULL> **[10 APRIL 1634]**

Wentworth

Whereas the office of customer & collector of the customs, subsidies, imposition & poundage in the ports of Strangford, Donaghadee & Bangor with the ports, havens & creeks thereunto belonging being lately void & in our gift by the death of # <#George Hull> William Pitt, gent, late customer there, is now granted to George Hull, gent, by letters patents under the great seal, together with all fees, profits & perquisites of right belonging to the said office, have since the death of the said William Pitt been collected & received by Charles Crimble as sequestrator of the said office & by other officers of the customs <*vide* page 151 this went from Sir George Radcliffe> and many are yet due & detained by the merchants & masters of ships or barques who are ready to pay the same if they know to whom the said perquisites belong, <*vide* page 174> we therefore, at the humble request of the said George Hull, have thought meet to declare unto you that those fees & perquisites received since the decease of the said William Pitt do of right belong & are due to the said George Hull, the now patentee & his assigns, who is to receive the same and besought us further for our warrant to assist him in the receiving thereof. We do therefore require the said Charles Crimble as sequestrator, and all & every officer & officers of the customs in the said ports and all merchants, owners & others who have received any of the said fees & perquisites & detain them and all merchants & others, that since the death of the said William Pitt have entered any ships, wares or merchandizes, inwards or outwards, or alongst the coast by cocket let pass or otherwise, that upon sight hereof & notice of this our direction they pay [**f. 514v**] unto the said George Hull all the said fees & perquisites to the use of him the said Hull, which upon account or otherwise shall be found due, and that from henceforth they permit the said George Hull or his deputy to receive the same in all & every the said ports. Whereof they nor any of them may not fail as they will answer the contrary at their perils. Given &c. xth *Aprilis* 1634.

To our well beloved Charles Crimble, sequestrator of the office of customer in the ports of Strangford, Donaghadee & Bangor, & to the controllers, surveyors, & collectors of the customs for the farmers, & to all merchants & masters of ships & others whom it may concern & every of them.

194. <A WARRANT FOR JOHN PERRY TO TRANSPORT INTO ENGLAND OR SCOTLAND 500 CATTLE &C.> [11 APRIL 1634]

By the lord deputy

Wentworth

Whereas upon humble suit made unto us by John Perry of Skenergitt in the county of Tyrone, gent, we have been pleased to licence him to transport into England or Scotland the number of 500 cattle, oxen & cows, there to be sold for the discharge of some debts due by him to be paid. These are therefore to will & require you & every of you to permit and suffer the said John Perry by himself, his servants, or assignees by him authorized upon sight of this our licence, or a true copy thereof to put aboard & transport the said number of [**f. 515r**] cattle from any [of] the ports in the province of Ulster, provided you first make entry of them in your custom book & receive his Majesty's due customs thereout; and that likewise you take him or his assignees bound in good bonds not to transport them into any other foreign parts but only into England or Scotland as aforesaid, and thereof to return you[r] certificate by a certain limited time he being to transport the aforesaid number by or before the feast of All Saints next ensuing the date hereof. Whereof &c. And &c. Given &c. the eleventh day of April 1634.

To all & every, his Majesty's officers of the customs in any the ports within the province of Ulster.

Thomas Littell

195. <A WARRANT FOR WILLIAM HALL TO APPEAR AS A WITNESS &C.> [11 APRIL 1634]

By the lord deputy

Wentworth

Whereas there is a cause in controversy depending between James Slack, plaintiff, & Art O'Neill & others, defendants, which cause is to receive a hearing the next Easter term, and whereas we are informed that your testimony will be very necessary for the clearing of some difficulties & doubts concerning the same, these shall be therefore to will and require you that you be, & personally appear before us, at his Majesty's Castle of Dublin upon Monday the 5th of May next then & there to certify your knowledge [**f. 515v**] concerning the said cause as you shall be thereunto required.

Whereof you are not to fail as you will answer the contrary at your peril. Given &c. the eleventh day of April 1634.

To our trusty & well beloved William Hall, sub-sheriff of the county of Fermanagh.

196. <WARRANT FOR REDMOND ÓG MAGUIRE *AD TESTIFICANDID* [*sic*]> [11 APRIL 1634]

The like warrant directed to Redmond Óg Maguire of Balliculway to appear as a witness the 5th of May next, twixt James Slack, plaintiff, & the Lord Balfour, Eleazer Middleton & others, defendants, dated *ut supra.*

<These warrants issued by Doctor Bramhall's[168] directions & no former proceedings ~~h~~ with us>

To our trusty & well beloved Redmond Óg Maguire of Balliculway, gent.

197. <ATTACHMENT JOHN CRAYFORD[169] & *AL.*> [11 APRIL 1634]

Attachment *versus* John Crayford, dean of Emly, John Magrath, esquire, & Robert Hamilton, clerk, to answer such matters as at their coming shall be objected against them ~~with a clause of assistance~~, dated xith April 1634. *Vide* church affairs page 125.

To any of his Majesty's pursuivants.

<~~*defendente*: Crayford *comparit 16 die Aprilis* 1634~~>

<~~*defendente*: Hamilton & Jo[hn] wherupon~~>

198. [f. 516r] <A WARRANT TO MR BURNETT'S TENANTS TO PAY THEIR RENTS TO MR BLANEY> [11 APRIL 1634]

By the lord deputy

Wentworth

Whereas we are given to understand that the rents payable unto Thomas Burnett, gent, by you the farmers & tenants of his lands in the county of Monaghan are due by you to be paid at May day next & so henceforth ~~all y~~ half yearly, these are therefore to will & require you the said tenants & occupiers of the said lands not to make payment of the said rents ^& duties^ to the said Thomas Burnett, or to any other, by his appointment authorized to receive the same, but that (for reasons best known unto us) you pay the same over half yearly as they shall grow due unto the hands of Richard Blaney, esquire, who is by us authorized to receive the same for the use of the said Thomas Burnett during our pleasure and for which he is to be accountable; and his acquittance or acquittances under his hand testifying the receipt thereof shall be unto you a sufficient discharge; hereof fail you not as you will answer the contrary at your peril. Given &c. 11th April 1634.

To the tenants & farmers of the lands of Thomas Burnett, gent, in the county of Monaghan.

Thomas Littell

168 John Bramhall (1594–1663), bishop of Derry (see *DIB*).

169 John Crayford (Croford), prebendary of Cashel and subsequently dean of Emly (see Cotton, *Fasti*).

199. [f. 516v] <ROBERT BRANDON> [14 APRIL 1634]

By the lord deputy

Wentworth
An attachment against Robert Brandon to answer the complaint of ~~Rob~~ Ferderagh Hanlan, with a clause of assistance, dated 14th April 1634.

200. <PHILIP MACSHAN O'REILLY, ESQUIRE> [14 APRIL 1634]

The like attachment against Philip MacShan O'Reilly, ^esquire^, to answer unto such matters as at his coming shall be objected against him with a clause of assistance, dated 14th April 1634.

201. <A WARRANT OF ATTACHMENT AGAINST CHARLES CRIMBLE>[170] [1 MAY 1634]

By the lord deputy

Wentworth
Attachment against Charles Crimble to answer as well his contempt ~~of~~ as the complaint of George Hull with a clause of assistance, dated 1 May 1634. *Vide* this book page 169 for the original hereof. The affidavit is in the bundles.

202. <MURROGH MCBRIEN> [30 APRIL 1634]

Attachment against Murrogh McBrien & Brian McTirlagh to answer as well their contempt as the complaint of ~~Donnogh~~ Mahon McDonnogh, with a clause of assistance dated *ultimo Aprilis* 1634.

203. [ROBERT COGAN] [1 MAY 1634]

An attachment ~~from Thomas Newsam~~ against the body of Robert Cogan ~~dated the first day of May 1634~~ ^to answer as well his contempt as the complaint of Thomas Newsam^ with a clause of assistance, dated *primo Maii* 1634.

204. [f. 517r] <EUSEBIUS BROOK> [3 MAY 1634]

Wentworth
Attachment against Eusebius Brooke, esquire, to answer as well his contempt as the complaint of Nicholas Leach, dated 3 May 1634. <*vide* first book of entries page ~~586~~ 526 for the petition>
Affidavit in bundles. <delivered to Mr Bentley,[171] 3 May 1634>

To any of his Majesty's pursuivants.

[170] See warrant no. 193.

[171] Mathew Bentley (Bently), first pursuivant at arms (see *Lib. mun. pub. Hib.*).

205. [f. 517v] <WARRANT TO PASS THE RECTORY OF VENTRY UNTO MR BARHAM> **[1 MAY 1634]**

By the lord deputy

Wentworth

A warrant for a fiant to pass the rectory of Ventry in the diocese of Ardfert unto Henry Barham, clerk, according [to] the usual form, inserting therein a clause of union <manicule> *pro hac vice tantum* of the said rectory of Ventry unto the 2 vicarages of Killarney & Killcomin in the diocese of Aghado[e] ^which he now holds^, directing his admission to the judge of the faculties &c. Given &c. 1 *Maii* 1634.

To our trusty & well beloved Sir William Ussher, knight, & Paul Davies, esquire, clerks of the Council, or either of them.

206. [f. 518r] <A PASS FOR THE SPANIARDS &C.> **[6 MAY 1634]**

By the lord deputy

Wentworth

Whereas the persons undernamed being Spaniards & Portugalls [*sic*] by their country have made known unto us that upon their late coming from Brazil their ship was surprised & taken at sea by a certain Holland free-boater who was ϵ shortly after (as they say) sank himself by certain Biscayners, but they the said persons undernamed were with much ado preserved from perishing by a Flemish ship who took them aboard herself & set them in shore in this kingdom. Now inasmuch as they are resolved to make their speedy repair unto their own native countries, we upon their humble suit have thought fit to grant them these our letters of passport & accordingly we do hereby will & require all & every, his Majesty's officers, ministers & loving subjects whatsoever to permit & suffer them to travel pass by them, either towards the city of Waterford or any other town, place or port in this kingdom (where they shall intend to take shipping) without any their lets or stays whatsoever they demeaning themselves as becometh. And &c. Given &c. 6 *Maii* 1634.

Gaspar Alures, Pascoall Miz, Michaell Lopez, Jeronimo Andre, Michaell Chamber, Visente Dyaz, Antonio Matias, Nigell Royt.

<*vide* our lease for a letter to the officers of the customs of Waterford about the Spaniards' transportation>

Thomas Littell

207. [f. 518v] <A LETTER TO THE OFFICERS OF THE CUSTOMS OF WATERFORD ABOUT THE SPANIARDS' TRANSPORTATION> **[6 MAY 1634]**

After our hearty commendations there lately came hither certain Spaniards & Portugals [*sic*] who (as they inform us) were lately taken at sea by a Holland free-boater in their return from Brazil, who himself was shortly after sunk at sea by certain Biscayners. But these being preserved with much ado by a Flemish ship who took them aboard they were put ~~aboard they were~~ ashore in this kingdom and being resolved to ~~and~~ repair with speed to their countries we, in consideration of their distress & upon their humble suit, have thought fit that order should be taken for their transportation hence, and understanding that there are some shipping in that port which are bound for Spain & Portugal our pleasure is, and so we require you, to take a course with the merchants & owners of those ships that they take with them & transport the said persons being in number eight whose names are hereunder written, whereof you and the said merchants, masters & owners are not to fail. So we bid you farewell from &c. 6 *Maii* 1634.

Your loving friend, Wentworth

Gaspar Allures [*sic*], Pascoall Miz, Michaell Lopez, Jeronimo Andre, Michaell Chamber, Visente Dyaz, Antonio Matias, Nigell Royt.

208. [f. 519r] <CHRISTIAN CARPENTER'S PROTECTION> **[7 MAY 1634]**

By the lord deputy

Wentworth

Whereas Christian Carpenter, widow, late wife & administratrix unto John Carpenter, gent, deceased, hath humbly petitioned unto us setting forth that her said husband at the time of his death stood indebted in certain sums of money unto divers persons who now prosecute her with all eagerness unto whom (if she might be born with & dispensed for a time) she is very confident that she will be able in short time to give all fitting and reasonable content. But divers of them being not to be persuaded with, or drawn by fair means, to accept of any other satisfaction but present payment, which not lying within the compass of her ability ~~or~~ ^&^ power ^to give^, she humbly besought us (in tender commiseration of her distressed estate & to preserve her & her 5 children from utter ruin) to be pleased to receive her for a time into his Majesty's protection that so she may be at liberty to sue for & endeavour to recover such debts as were due unto her said husband which are many & due from divers persons that live far remote from her habitation, whose request therein we have thought fit to grant. And therefore we do hereby will and require you & every of you to take due notice thereof and to forbear suing, arresting, impleading or troubling the said Christian in her person, lands or goods, for and during the space of six months next ensuing the date **[f. 519v]** hereof, provided that by virtue & under colour hereof she do not defeat her creditors but do her endeavour to the uttermost of her power to give them content ~~their content~~ & satisfaction. And we likewise require her the said Christian, by her self and some other sufficient person or persons jointly bound with her, to enter into bonds of two hundred pounds before the clerk of the Council within six days next ensuing the date hereof that she shall not during the continuance of this protection depart this kingdom unless she doth first satisfy her creditors, otherwise this protection to be void. Neither is it our intention that the said Christian shall be protected by virtue hereof from any debt due to his Majesty, nor freed from any former restraint & imprisonment, whereof you & every of you are not to fail. And for so doing &c. Given &c. the seventh day of May 1634.

<*vide* amongst the bundles for the petition whereon this was grounded>

To all mayors, sheriffs, justices of the peace, bailiffs, constables & to all & every other his Majesty's officers, ministers & loving subjects, whom it doth or may concern.

Thomas Littell

209. <CHRISTIAN CARPENTER> [22 OCTOBER 1634]

Christian Carpenter's protection renewed for 6 months from the day of the expiration of the above written, dated 22 *Octobris* 1634.

210. [f. 520r] <WARRANT FOR DAVID THOMAS[172] FOR 2 VICARAGES>[173] [6 MAY 1634]

By the lord deputy

Wentworth

A warrant for a fiant unto David Thomas, clerk, of the vicarages of Tallow in the diocese of Lismore and also of Lisronagh in the said diocese became void by reason of simony, according [to] the usual form, dated 6 *Maii* 1634, <manicule> inserting a clause of union of these 2 & the vicarages of Mogelly in the diocese aforesaid *pro hac vice tantum* directing his admission to the judge of the faculties.

To our trusty & well beloved Sir William Ussher, knight, & Paul Davies, esquire, clerks of the Council, or either of them.

211. <LANDELL'S WARRANT FOR 3 VICARAGES> [6 MAY 1634]

By the lord deputy

Wentworth

<Manicule> A warrant for a fiant unto David Landell, clerk, of the vicarages of Moylary, Dunleer & Kildimock in the diocese of Armagh, to have & hold the same according [to] the usual form, dated 6 *Maii* 1634, inserting a clause of union therein *pro hac vice tantum* directing his admission to the judge of the faculties. Directed *ut supra.*

212. <A WARRANT TO ISSUE A COMMISSION BETWEEN MELVILL & PURDAM> [7 MAY 1634]

By the lord deputy

Wentworth

Whereas there is a controversy depending before us between one William Melvill, gent, & 2 of his brethren, plaintiffs, against Adam Purdam, gent, defendant, about the estate of Sir John Melvill, deceased, which is pretended by the said plaintiffs to have been sinisterly gotten & gained by their elder brother Robert Melvill, deceased,

172 David Thomas (d. *c.* 1641), appointed chancellor of Lismore in 1636 (see Cotton, *Fasti*).

173 See warrant no. 232. This is the same warrant with only slight differnces.

whose [**f. 520v**] relict the said Purdam hath married. Now inasmuch as we think it fit that a commission should issue to examine witnesses upon oath for the better finding out of the truth in the matter, these are to pray and require your lordship forthwith to cause a commission ^should^ [*sic*] to issue to examine witnesses upon oath for the better finding out of the truth in the matter. These are to pray & require your lordship forthwith to cause a commission to issue to that purpose, & the same to be directed unto our right trusty & well beloved the Lord Viscount Conway[174] & the lord bishop of Dromore[175] authorizing them to require & also to examine upon oath all & every such witnesses as shall be produced by either party to be examined concerning this matter, & upon such interrogatories as either party shall present & exhibit the said commission to be returnable with all convenient speed & at the furthest by the ~~middle~~ ^end^ of the next term, <*vide* first book of common entries page 361 & 469> provided the plaintiffs do give 15 days notice of the execution of the said commission unto the defendant that he likewise may be prepared & ready against the time of the execution ~~of the said commission unto the defendant that he likewise may be compounded & ready against the licence of execution~~. And &c. Given &c. 7th *Maii* 1634.

~~<*vide* the petition amongst the bundles>~~

To our very good lord, the lord chancellor.

213. [f. 521r] <WARRANT FOR THE LORD INCHIQUIN TO TRANSPORT HORSE & MARE> **[8 MAY 1634]**

By the lord deputy

Wentworth

A warrant for Murrogh, lord baron of Inchiquin, to transport for England a horse & mare directed to any the ports in the province of Munster, dated eight[h] day of May 1634.

214. <JOHN & JAMES SMYTH> **[8 MAY 1634]**

Wentworth

Attachment against John Smyth & James Smyth to answer as well their contempt as the complaint of Arnold Cosby, dated 8 *Maii* 1634.

215. <WARRANT *PER* FIANT TO JOHN GARDNER[176]> **[8 MAY 1634]**

By the lord deputy

Wentworth

These are to will and require you forthwith to draw up a fiant in due form of law containing a grant & presentation from his Majesty unto John Gardiner, clerk,

174 Edward Conway (1594–1655), 2nd Viscount Conway and Killultagh, nobleman and army officer (see *DIB*).

175 Theophilus Buckworth (1580–1652), bishop of Dromore (see *DIB*).

176 John Gardner or Gardiner.

<manicule> of the parsonage of Kilurie & the vicarage of Ballyheigue in the diocese of Ardfert being void & in his Majesty's gift ~~by law~~ ^*pleno jure*^, to have, hold & enjoy the said parsonage & vicarage unto him the said John Gardiner together with all the rights, duties, members, profits and appurtenances whatsoever thereunto belonging or anywise appertaining, and in as large, ample & beneficial manner as any other incumbent or incumbents formerly held & enjoyed or of right ought to have held & enjoyed the same, inserting therein a clause of union *pro hac vice tantum* [**f. 521v**] and directing his admission to the judge of the faculties. And the same fairly engrossed &c. And &c. Given &c. 8 May 1634.

To our trusty & well beloved Sir William Ussher, knight, & Paul Davies, esquire, clerks of the Council, or either of them.

216. <WARRANT FOR A RECTORY & VICARAGES TO CARR> **[9 MAY 1634]**

By the lord deputy

Wentworth

<Manicule> A warrant for a fiant containing a grant unto Patrick Carr, clerk, of the rectory & vicarage of Dunach *alias* Dunbought & of the vicarage of Glynn in the diocese of Connor void by lapse, to have &c. according [to] the usual form with a clause of union *pro hac vice tantum* & directing his admission to the judge of the faculties. Given &c. 9th *Maii* 1634.

To our trusty & well beloved Sir William Ussher, knight, & Paul Davies, esquire, &c.

Thomas Littell

217. [f. 522r] <PHILIP MCSHAN O'REILLY> **[10 MAY 1634]**

By the lord deputy

Wentworth

Warrant to the constable of the castle to detain in his custody the body of Philip McShan O'Reilly, esquire, ~~and him to det~~ until our further pleasure be known, dated 8 *Maii* 1634.

To our well beloved Samuel Davis, esquire, & constable of his Majesty's Castle of Dublin.

218. <RICHARD COLLIER> **[10 MAY 1634]**

A warrant for Richard Collier to transport a horse or nag at the port of Youghal, dated xth *Maii* 1634.

219. <CORMAC ~~REARY~~ ^RAWER^ O'DUFFEY'S PROTECTION>[177] **[10 MAY 1634]**

By the lord deputy

Wentworth

Whereas upon information given us that Cormac ~~Reary~~ ^Rawer^ O'Duffey (who was then out upon his keeping) was a person that could do acceptable service both in the prosecution and also by his discovery of divers malefactors who have lately committed divers stealths & robberies in the counties of Cavan, Monaghan, Tyrone, Fermanagh & Armagh, we were pleased to receive him for a time into his Majesty's protection. Since which time we are given to understand that some good service have been already effected by his means & more may be done & such as may merit favour if his [**f. 522v**] protection, which is now near expiration, might be renewed for a longer time which we for the reasons aforesaid have thought fit to do. And therefore we do hereby will and require you & every of you to forbear either apprehending, troubling or molesting the person of the said Cormac for & during the space of 3 months next ensuing, the day of the expiration of the former protection which was dated the 26th day of March last & was to continue for 3 months after. Whereof &c. dated x *Maii* 1634.

<This protection was again renewed for 6 months from the 26th of September, dated 19 September 1634>

To all mayors, sheriffs, justices of the peace, bailiffs, constables & to all other his Majesty's officers, ministers & loving subjects, whom it doth or may concern.

220. <WARRANT TO MR BLANEY TO PRESENT REBELS>[178] **[10 MAY 1634]**

Wentworth

Whereas divers robberies, felonies and other insolences and outrages are daily committed as we are informed within the several counties of Monaghan, Cavan, Fermanagh, Tyrone, Armagh & Louth by certain idle & negligent persons whose names are not yet certainly known to the great terror and grief of his Majesty's good and well affected subjects, the contempt of his laws and ^to^ the bad example of others that are ill disposed, and inasmuch as we have reposed special trust and confidence in our trusty & well beloved Richard Blaney, esquire, as a person fit to be entrusted & enabled both for the prosecution, apprehension & bringing to justice of the same malefactors, [**f. 523r**] we therefore have thought fit & do accordingly do [*sic*] hereby give full power & authority unto him the said Richard Blaney to pursue, attach & by all good means to apprehend & prosecute the said malefactors, relievers & abettors, and them or any of them so apprehended forthwith to examine & commit or cause, convey or cause to be contained, before his Majesty's next justice or justice of the peace who are to examine & commit them to the next gaol within that county where they shall be so taken there to be safely kept until they be delivered thence by a due course of law, and all such goods as being suspected to him stolen & shall be found

[177] See warrant no. 186.

[178] See warrant no. 185.

in the custody of the said malefactors, or any their receivors or abettors, to seize upon & safely keep until it shall appear unto whom the same shall legally appertaining. And for the better effecting hereof we do hereby require all and every of the captains & chief officers of companies within the foresaid counties to send an officer together with such & so many soldiers to attend the said Richard Blaney from time to time as he shall think fit & necessary to be employed by him in the service aforesaid, he being likewise authorized to employ & make use of in this business such and so many other person or persons for the better advancement of the service as he shall likewise think fit which said officer & soldier are in all lawful things to obey his directions during their being abroad upon this occasion, hereby further charging and requiring ^all^ and every the ^inhabitants of the^ several towns & place whereunto the said Richard Blaney & the said officer & soldiers shall have occasion to resort, to afford them competent meat, drink and lodging at his Majesty's usual & accustomed rates during the time of ^their^ being so employed, provided that upon the peril of their lives they commit no extortion nor oppression in the [f. 523v] country and that this our warrant is to continue in force but during pleasure. In the due execution all and every, his Majesty's offices, ministers & loving subjects whatsoever to be aiding and assisting unto the said Richard Blaney as there shall be occasion, and thereof not to fail at their perils; for doing whereof this shall be a sufficient warrant. Given at his Majesty's Castle of Dublin, 10 May 1634.

221. <WARRANT FOR MR HARBERT TO APPEAR & ANSWER PALMER> [12 MAY 1634]

By the lord deputy

Wentworth

These are to will & require you to make your personal appearance before us & to bring with you all such letters and directions as you received, either from the late lord of Falkland alone during his government or from him & the Council jointly issued unto you in the year of your sheriffwick for the King's County *anno* 1627, for the levying of any monies there towards the maintenance of the army in that time and with all you are to bring & produce all such acquittances & discharges as have been taken by you from the officers & soldiers for such monies as were by you paid unto them & especially unto Anthony Palmer, sergeant, unto Sir John Ogle's[179] foot company. Whereof you are not to fail. Given &c. 12th May 1634.

To our well beloved Nicholas Harbert, esquire.

222. [f. 524r] [WARRANT TO SEARCH AND APPREHEND O'REILLY & *AL.*] [12 MAY 1634]

By the lord deputy

Wentworth

These are to require & command you in his Majesty's name to make diligent search ~~& inquiry~~ for the persons undernamed & then to apprehend wheresoever they can be

179 John Ogle (bap. 1569–1640), army officer (see *ODNB*).

found within the precincts of your liberty & immediately in sure and safe manner to convey & deliver over unto the sheriff of the next county in the way directly hither, who is likewise required to receive them & to deliver over to the next sheriffs, that so they may be conveyed from sheriff to sheriffs until they be brought hither where being come we shall give such further directions concerning them as there shall be cause. Whereof you and the said several sheriffs are not to fail as you & they will answer the contrary at your uttermost perils. And for so doing this shall be your sufficient warrant. Given &c. 12th *Maii* 1634.

Mulmore McPhillip O'Reilly, gent
Hugh McMulmore O'Reilly
Phillip McDonnell O'Reilly
David McConyn
<by directions from Sir G. R.[180]>

To our trusty & well beloved, the high sheriff of the county of Cavan.

223. [f. 524v] <A WARRANT TO RICHARD BLANEY, ESQUIRE, TOUCHING MR BURNETT>[181] [13 MAY 1634]

By the lord deputy

Wentworth

Whereas upon information given [to] us that John Burnett of ^the county of^ Monaghan, esquire, lately deceased, left a good and competent estate in lands unto his eldest son, Thomas Burnett, who is joint administrator with his mother, who being as yet but young & not of years of ability & judgment to manage what hath been so left him by his father, it is greatly feared by those who are tender & careful of his good[s] that no care will be taken for the preservation & improvement of his estate in this time of his minority by those who are entrusted to look unto & manage the same, by which means great loss & disadvantage may ensue unto the young gent which we, taking into consideration & being desirous that the same may be prevented, have thought fit & do accordingly (out of the confidence & ~~honesty~~ trust we repose in your honesty and integrity[)] hereby authorize you from time to time henceforward for these three years next ensuing the date hereof, not only to set the lands of the said Thomas Burnett to the best improvement & to turn the duties & customs into rent but also to call all those to account that have had the receiving of his rents & duties since the said John Burnett's death & likewise for the half year when he died, & to require due payment of what shall be found to be due unto the said Thomas Burnett from those who have had the receiving and collecting thereof. And we do also hereby authorize you to call for, demand & receive all such sum or sums of money as are to be repaid by any person or persons during the time of 3 years aforesaid for all such lands as are held in mortgage and also the moiety of the rents payable out of such lands as are left in lease & are due unto the said Thomas **[f. 525r]** Burnett as joint

180 Sir George Radcliffe (1593–1657), lawyer and politician (see *DIB*).

181 See warrant no. 198.

administrator, willing & hereby requiring all & every person & persons whom it may concern not only to come to a speedy account with you concerning the premises but also to pay over unto you all such monies, either for rent or otherwise, as either already are or hereafter shall become due during the time aforesaid, which being so received by you, ^you^ are safely to keep and detain in your hands until you shall be required to give an account & make restitution thereof provided that competent allowance be given & made yearly thereout unto the said Thomas Burnett towards his education & maintenance. And for so doing this shall be a sufficient warrant. Given at his Majesty's Castle of Dublin the 13th of May 1634.

To our well beloved Richard Blaney, esquire.

224. [WARRANT TO APPREHEND SEVERAL PERSONS] [13 MAY 1634]

By the lord deputy

Wentworth
These are to will and require you to receive & take into your custody the bodies of the several persons undernamed and them safely to detain until our further pleasure be known; whereof you may not fail. And for so doing this shall be your warrant. Given &c. the 13th of May 1634.
John Johnson
Peter Lyon
Adrian Chandremire
Jaques Le Ferre
Cornelius Martin
John Nodin
John Simion
John Erme &
John Smyth

To our well beloved Samuel Davis, esquire, constable of his Majesty's Castle of Dublin.

225. [f. 525v] <ROBERT LEFTWICH> [13 MAY 1634]

An attachment against Robert Leftwich to answer as well his contempt as the complaint of George Hull with a clause of assistance, dated 13th *Maii* 1634. *Vide* page ~~159~~ ^169^ for the original warrant.

226. <SIR ALEXANDER MCDONNELL[182]> [13 MAY 1634]

An attachment against Sir Alexander McDonnell, knight, to answer as well his contempt as the complaint of William Hamilton. Given &c. 13th *Maii* 1634. *Vide* 2 book of entries page 71 for the petition whereon this is grounded.

[182] Alexander MacDonnell (d. 1647), clan leader (see *ODNB*).

227. <RICHARD ISACKE, HIS *LIBERATE*> **[15 MAY 1634]**

By the lord deputy

Wentworth
Whereas you have in your custody the body of Richard Isacke committed unto you by our former warrant, these are to require you upon sight hereof to set him at liberty paying his fees. And &c. Given &c. 15 May 1634.

To our well beloved Samuel Davis, esquire, constable of his Majesty's Castle of Dublin.

228. [f. 526r] <FLAN MCBRUODINE & *AL.*> **[17 MAY 1634]**

By the lord deputy

Wentworth
An attachment with a clause of assistance against the several persons undernamed to answer such matters as at their coming shall be objected against them.
This is grounded upon the petition of Teige Entaramon which is in the bundles dated 17th *Maii* 1634.

Flan McBruodine high constable of the barony of Tullagh.
John O'Dwena
Thomas MacShanduff
Edmond O'Brollanc &
Therelagh O'Dwine
} Petty constables of the several parishes of Moyneo & Thomgreny
Rory O'Tiffy
Teige O'Tiffy
Sulluduffe O'Mollony
Um: Ni Cormocan
Any Ni Tiffy &
John McVickon

To any of his Majesty's pursuivants.

229. [SIR RICHARD OSBORNE] **[20 MAY 1634]**

Wentworth
An attachment against Sir Richard Osborne, baronet, to answer such matters as at his coming shall be objected against him. Given 20th *Maii* 1634.

230. [f. 526v] <JOHN NORFOLK> **[20 MAY 1634]**

Wentworth
Attachment against John Norfolk to answer as well his contempt of our directions as the complaint of John Flineaghan Fitzdonagh with a clause of assistance, dated 20th *Maii* 1634. *Vide* the second book of entries page 205 for the original.

231. <JOHN NAYLOR> **[20 MAY 1634]**

A warrant for John Naylor to transport 2 horses or saddle nags at the port of Youghal, dated 20th *Maii* 1634.

To all & every, his Majesty's officers of the customs, the port of Youghal.

232. <DAVID THOMAS>[183] **[6 MAY 1634]**

A warrant for a fiant unto David Thomas of the vicarages of Tullagh[184] *alias* Tullageagh & Lisronagh *alias* Kilsronagh in the diocese of Lismore void by lapse &c., to have &c. according [to] the usual form, inserting therein a clause of union *pro hac vice tantum* of the said 2 vicarages & the rectory of Moyelly in the diocese of Cloyne and directing his admission to the judge of the faculties, dated the sixth day of May 1634.

To our trusty & well beloved Sir William Ussher, knight, & Paul Davies, esquire, clerks of the Council, or either of them.

233. [f. 527r] <THOMAS NEWSAM> **[19 MAY 1634]**

Attachment *versus* Thomas Newsam to answer such matters as at his coming shall be objected against him, dated 19th *Maii* 1634.

234. <ROBERT ELLIOT TO BE CUSTOMER OF LONDONDERRY> **[21 MAY 1634]**

Wentworth

~~The~~ A warrant for a fiant to make Robert Elliot customer & collector of Londonderry & Coleraine with the creeks of Portrush, the Bann, Lough Foyle & Lough Swilly & Ballyshannon & the creeks & ports thereunto belonging, being void upon the surrender of Arthur Tirry who held the same by patent. No fee from his Majesty allowed but the ordinary perquisites, dated 21 May 1634.

235. <THOMAS WATSON'S PROTECTION> **[20 MAY 1634]**

By the lord deputy

Wentworth

Whereas one Thomas Watson hath petitioned unto us setting forth that by reason of sundry losses he hath had of late, as well by mortality that came amongst his cattle as also by the ill payment & abuse of bad debtors, his estate is brought to so low an ebb as that he cannot possibly satisfy some debts that are due by him, neither will some of those unto whom he standeth so engaged be contented with any satisfaction but present payments which he being no way able to give, & fearing if he should be once arrested & imprisoned he should be utterly undone & be deprived from all hopes [*sic*] either by gaining & recovering of his own debts or by any other means to be able to

183 See warrant no. 210. This is the same warrant with only slight differnces.

184 Tallow, Co Waterford.

give his said creditors content, wherefore he humbly besought us to receive him for a time into his Majesty's protection whose requests therein we have thought fit to grant & the rather in regard that James Watson of Dublin, alderman,[185] hath promised & undertaken by a note under his hand shortly either to satisfy or at least to compound with his the said Thomas Watson's creditors for the debts due by him the said Thomas (being his brother) unto him. And therefore we do hereby will and require you and every of you not only to take due notice thereof but also to forbear, suing, **[f. 527v]** arresting, troubling or any way molesting the said Thomas Watson in his person or goods for & during the space of six months next ensuing the date hereof, he behaving himself as becometh, provided that by virtue & under colour hereof he do not defeat his creditors but do his endeavour to the uttermost of his power to give them content and satisfaction so as we [will] not be troubled with their complaints. Neither is it our intention that the said Thomas should be protected by virtue hereof from any debt due from him to his Majesty nor freed from any former restrain or imprisonment, whereof you and every of you are not to fail. And for so doing this shall be a sufficient warrant. Given at his Majesty's Castle of Dublin the twentieth of May 1634.

To all mayors, sheriffs, justices of the peace, bailiffs, constables & to all and every other his Majesty's officers, ministers and loving subjects whom it doth or may concern.

236. [f. 528r] <RANDALL INCE, CLERK> [21 MAY 1634]

<manicule> A warrant for a fiant for him for the vicarage of Kinally *alias* Kinawley in the diocese of Kilmore, dated 21 May 1634, the same being void by lapse.

237. <CHRISTOPHER LEE, CLERK> [22 MAY 1634]

<manicule> A warrant for a fiant for the parsonage & vicarage of Dungorne in the diocese of Cloyne being void by lapse, dated 22 May 1634.

238. <WARRANT FOR DOCTOR BRAMHALL TO BE BISHOP OF DERRY> [22 MAY 1634]

By the lord deputy

Wentworth

Whereas the bishopric of Derry in this kingdom is become void by the death of the late bishop thereof and inasmuch as his Majesty hath been graciously pleased to confer the same upon our trusty & well beloved John Bramhall, doctor in divinity, these are therefore to will and require you forthwith to draw up a fiant in due form of law containing a donation from his Majesty as well of the said bishopric unto the said John Bramhall <manicule> as also for his investiture, consecration & ~~in~~^re^stitution of the temporalities of the said bishopric, and all jurisdictions, powers, authorities, privileges,

185 James Watson, alderman and later mayor of Dublin in 1637 (see J. T. Gilbert, *Calendar of ancient records of Dublin* (18 vols, Dublin, 1892), iii, 334).

pre-eminences, advowsons, tithes, profits, rents, benefits, immunities, emoluments, members & appurtenances whatsoever to the same belonging or in anyway appertaining, to have and to hold unto him the said ~~Doctor~~ ^John^ Bramhall during his natural life in as large, ample and beneficial manner and form to all intents & purposes whatsoever as any of his predecessors have heretofore had or enjoyed, or ought to have had & enjoyed the same, according to the purport of his Majesty's letters unto us of the ninth of this month, a copy whereof for your better information we have herewith sent you. And the same fairly engrossed in parchment under your hand to send unto us to be further passed appertaineth; for doing whereof this shall be your ~~warrant~~ sufficient warrant. Given at his Majesty's Castle of Dublin, 22nd day of May 1634.

To our trusty & well beloved Sir William Ussher, knight, & Paul Davies, esquire, clerks of the Council, or either of them.

239. [f. 528v] <SIR ARTHUR LEIGH> **[22 MAY 1634]**

Attachment against Sir Arthur Leigh, baronet, to answer as well his contempt as the complaint of Dame Mary Leigh, widow, dated 22nd May 1634. <Delivered to Mr Gilbert[186] 24th *Maii* 1634> *Vide* the affidavit in the bundles enclosed in the petition of the Lady Lee.

240. <GARRET FITZGERALD, CLERK,[187] & JOHN CROFORD> **[22 MAY 1634]**

An attachment issued against Garret Fitzgerald, clerk, & John Croford, clerk, dean of Emly, to answer such matters as at their coming shall be objected against them, dated 22nd *Maii* 1634. <Mr ~~Gilbert~~ Bently[188] delivered it 23 May> *Vide* the fourth book of entries page 89 & so forward & the second book of entries page 193.

241. <THOMAS BENNETT, RICHARD BARRON> **[23 MAY 1634]**

An attachment against Bennett, Whyte & Richard Barron to answer such matters as at their coming shall be objected against them, dated 23rd May 1634. <Delivered to Mr Bently[189] 24 *Maii* 1634> *Vide* second book of entries page 193 & 4th book of entries [pages] 86, 87.

242. <THOMAS BUTLER, THOMAS STAPLETON, REDMOND MOCKLER> **[23 MAY 1634]**

Attachment against Thomas Butler, Thomas Stapleton & Redmond Mockler to answer as well their contempt as the complaint of Redmond Magrath, dated 23 *Maii* 1634. <Delivered to Mr Bently 23 May 1634> *Vide* second book of entries page 103 for the former petition & in the bundles for the affidavit.

186 Robert Gilbert, second pursuivant at arms (see *Lib. mun. pub. Hib.*).

187 Garret (or Gerald) Fitzgerald, archdeacon of Emly (see Cotton, *Fasti*).

188 Mathew Bentley (Bently), first pursuivant at arms (see *Lib. mun. pub. Hib.*).

189 Mathew Bentley, as above.

243. [f. 529r] <MR WOOD'S WARRANT FOR A PREBEND> [24 MAY 1634]

By the lord deputy

Wentworth

These are to will and require you forthwith to draw up a fiant in due form of law containing a presentation from his Majesty of Edward Wood, Master in the Arts & one of our chaplains, to the prebend of Ballihag~~h~~ in the cathedral church of Cloyne, to have, hold, possess & enjoy the said prebend unto him the said Wood, the said prebend (being now void & in his Majesty's gift by lapse) together with all <manicule> rights, duties, members, profits and appetencies whatsoever thereunto belonging, and in as large, ample & beneficial manner as any other incumbent or incumbents formerly held & enjoyed or of right ought to have held & enjoyed the same, directing his admission to the judge of the faculties. And the same fairly engrossed &c. And &c. Given &c. 24th *Maii* 1634.

To our trusty & well beloved Sir William Ussher, knight, & Paul Davies, esquire, clerks of the Council, or either of them.

244. [f. 529v] <WARRANT FOR A VICARAGE FOR KITSON> [23 MAY 1634]

By the lord deputy

Wentworth

~~These are~~ A warrant for a fiant containing a presentation from his Majesty of William Kitson, clerk, to the vicarage of Killeneffe in the diocese of Killaloe in his Majesty's gift by reason of the wardship of Gerald Grace, gent, <manicule> to have &c., inserting a clause of union *pro hac vice tantum* unto the said vicarage of two other vicarages called Goughallary & Burgesbeg within the diocese aforesaid, dated 23 *Maii* 1634.

To Sir William Ussher & Paul Davies &c.

245. <PETER BAKER & HIS 2 SONS, PROTECTION> [24 MAY 1634]

By the lord deputy

Wentworth

Whereas Peter Baker of Tallow in the province of Munster, grazier, hath petitioned unto us setting forth that he for many years together hath used to transport into England fat cattle, oxen, cows & sheep, & yearly paid great sums of money for customs, & for the maintenance of the trade used his 2 sons, Francis & William Baker, & together with his own & their credit employed great sums of money of several persons with whom he & his sons have dealt fairly & honestly, and that of late by reason of sundry great losses by shipwrecks, pirates & other calamities he & his sons have been disabled to continue that trade as also to make payment of his & their just debts, they having lost thereby a thousand pounds sterling. And being now all three reduced to great extremity & his & their fortunes & estate come to a low ebb there are divers of **[f. 530r]** his creditors who prosecute him & his said sons with all the extremity of law that may be & will be contented with no other manner of satisfaction but present payment, which he being not able to give them he and his said sons are in great danger to be imprisoned which if it come to pass they are all three undone forever. For prevention therefore of their utter & apparent ruin, he humbly besought us to receive him & his said sons for a time into his Majesty's protection to the end that being freed from arrests & imprisonments he may as well by seeking to recover his own debts from others, as by other his good endeavours, procure some means to give his said creditors satisfaction, whose request therein we have thought fit to grant & the rather in regard our very good lords, the late lords justices, have certified unto us that the said Peter & his said 2 sons are very honest, painful & laborious men, and that their lordships to preserve them from utter ruin had in the time of their government granted them his Majesty's protection during which time they paid & compounded for the greatest part of their debts & that in their lordship's opinion it would be a work of charity & justice to renew their protection. These are therefore to will & require you & every of you to forbear saving troubling, arresting or molesting the persons or goods of the said Peter, Francis & William Baker for & during the space of six months next ensuing the date hereof, they behaving themselves as becometh, provided that by [**f. 530v**] virtue & under colour hereof they do not endeavour to defeat their creditors but to the uttermost of their power shall give them all reasonable content & satisfaction. And we do hereby declare that it is not our intention that they, nor any one of them, shall be protected by reason or virtue hereof from any debt due to his Majesty nor freed from any former arrests or imprisonment, whereof you & every of you are not to fail. And for so doing this shall be a sufficient warrant. Given &c. 24th *Maii* 1634. <*vide* the third book of entries page 125 & 184 for petition & certificate whereon this protection is grounded>

To all mayors, sheriffs, justices justices [*sic*] of the peace, bailiffs, constables & all other his Majesty's officers, ministers & loving subjects whom it may concern.

Thomas Littell

246. <WARRANT TO THE EARL OF ORMOND[190] FOR PRIZE WINES> [24 MAY 1634]

By the lord deputy

Wentworth

Whereas our very good lord, the earl of Ormond & Ossory, hath petitioned unto us setting forth that where the merchants, as well natives as strangers, arriving in the harbours & ports of Carrickfergus, Bangor and Donaghadee with their ships laden with wines do commonly, after entry made in his Majesty's Custom House of such wines as they have aboard, refuse to permit the said earl's agents and factors to open their decks or suffer them to mark or taste their wines, by means whereof the said earl many times is defeated of his prize wines [**f. 531r**] and his Majesty of such rents as should accrue to him thereout. We therefore upon his lordship's humble suit have thought fit and accordingly do will & require as well all merchants, strangers as natives, and all others whom it may concern from time to time, not only to permit the said earl's agent and factors of his lordship's lease of the said prize wines before

190 James Butler (1610–88), 12th earl and 1st duke of Ormond, lord lieutenant of Ireland (see *DIB*).

bulk be broke to take up taste & mark such wines as shall respectively grow due to him, according to the ancient custom of prize wines as they & every of them will answer the contrary at their perils. And we likewise require all his Majesty's officers of the customs in the said ports & every of them and also all mayors, sheriffs, bailiffs, portreeves, provosts and other his Majesty's officers in the said ports, or any of the creeks and members thereof or to any of them belonging, to be aiding and assisting to the said earl's agent in the execution of this our warrant as they and every of them will answer the contrary at their perils. Given &c. 24th *Maii* 1634.

Thomas Littell

247. <WARRANT TO MAKE STAY OF BOYES'S TO ANSWER SIR JOHN THROUGHGOOD[191] &C.> **[27 MAY 1634]**

By the lord deputy

Whereas complaint hath been made to us in the behalf of Sir John Thoroughgood, knight, that he having employed over hither and entrusted one Thomas Boyes as well with the receipt as the disposing of divers and sundry sums of money to his the said Sir John's use, he the said Boyes (as we are credibly informed) hath converted the same wholly to his own ~~use~~ proper use both in buying of cattle and otherwise, which cattle as it is thought he intends to transport out of that port, which if he should be permitted to do before the said Sir John Throughgood be secured of his said monies he is in great danger wholly to loose the same. We therefore upon humble suit made unto us in his behalf have thought fit and do accordingly hereby will and ~~join~~ require you [**f. 531v**] and every of you not only to make stay of all such cattle and other goods as he shall offer to transport out of the port, but also of his person & him so stayed to commit to safe custody until he shall put in very good & sufficient security (of persons well known unto you or some of you[)] to answer the said Sir John Throughgood's demands, or that you received our further directions to the contrary. Whereof you & every of you are not to fail. And for so doing this shall be your warrant. Given &c. 27th *Maii* 1634.

To our well beloved, the mayors & bailiffs of the town of Youghal & to all & every, his Majesty's officers of the customs in the port of Youghal aforesaid.

248. <WARRANT FOR THE FREE SCHOOL OF CASHEL> **[27 MAY 1634]**

By the lord deputy

Wentworth

Whereas by the resignation of Thomas Gilbert, late schoolmaster of his Majesty's free school within the united diocese of Cashel & Emly, the said free school is now become void of a schoolmaster to teach & instruct the children & youth in those parts, and forasmuch as we have received good testimony as well of the learning &

[191] John Throughgood or Thoroughgood. The family had strong links with Ennis. His kinsman, Simon Thoroughgood, was MP for Ennis (see McGrath).

sufficiency as also the good life & conversation of Raphe Carr, Master of the Arts, these are therefore to will and require you upon the receipt hereof to draw up a licence in the usual form containing a grant of the said place of schoolmaster unto the said Raphe Carr, together with all rights, duties, fees, wages, [**f. 532r**] perquisites & profits to the same belonging or in anywise appertaining in as large, ample & beneficial manner as the said Gilbert or any other heretofore enjoyed the same during his good behaviour, inserting therein such clauses as in like grants are usual. And the same fairly engrossed in parchment under your hand to send unto us to be further passed as appertaineth. And for so doing &c. Given &c. 27th *Maii* 1634.

To our trusty & well beloved Sir William Ussher, knight, &Paul Davies, esquire, clerks of the Council, or either of them.

249. <RICHARD GRAY, HIS WARRANT *PER* FIANT> [29 MAY 1634]

By the lord deputy

Wentworth

These are to will and require you forthwith to draw up a fiant in due form of law containing a grant & donation from his Majesty unto <manicule> Thomas Gray, clerk,[192] of the deanery of Waterford being now void and in his Majesty's gift by the cession and removal from thence of Richard Jones, clerk, who lately held the same to be dean of Elphin, to have, hold, possess & enjoy the said deanery unto him the said Thomas Gray, together with all the rights, duties, unions, annexations, jurisdictions & appurtenances whatsoever thereunto belonging in as large, ample & beneficial [**f. 532v**] manner as the said Richard Jones, ~~clerk, who lately held the same~~ or any other dean of the said church, formerly held, possessed & enjoyed the same, requiring also the chapter of the said cathedral church, or any one or more of them, to install the said Thomas Gray as in like case is usual. And the same fairly engrossed in parchment under your hand to send unto us to be further passed as appertaineth, for doing &c. Given &c. 29th *Maii* 1634.

To the clerks of the Council, or either of them.

250. <A WARRANT TO THE MARSHAL OF THE 4 COURTS TO KEEP SAFE THE BODY OF JOHN MCNEMARA *ALIAS* MCVICKON>[193] [27 MAY 1634]

By the lord deputy

Wentworth

Whereas there was one John McNemara *alias* McVickon lately delivered to your custody by Mathew Bentley, one of his Majesty's pursuivants, and inasmuch as the said McNemara is a notorious turbulent person and one that hath for this long time not only disobeyed all loyal courses & ways ~~but~~ being now under proclamation of rebellion, but also hath often contemned and slighted our commands & directions,

192 Thomas Gray, installed dean of Waterford 17 May 1635 (see Cotton, *Fasti*).

193 See warrant nos 78 and 151.

for which his misdemeanours and contemptuous carriage we are resolved to have him exemplarily punished. And therefore we do hereby will & require you to be very careful to see that he be kept in sure & safe manner till you receive our directions for his enlargement. Whereof &c. And &c. Given &c. 27 *Maii* 1634.

To the Marshal of the Four Courts.

251. [f. 533r] <A WARRANT TO THE LORD CHANCELLOR TO ISSUE A COMMISSION TO SEVERAL PARTS FOR EXAMINATION OF MERCHANTS OF SHIPS> [22 MAY 1634]

By the lord deputy

Whereas we have directed our former warrant to your lordship bearing date the 9th day of December last past [*sic*] for issuing out a ~~pet~~ commission under the great seal ~~of~~ to his Majesty's customer, controller, surveyor & collector for his Majesty's farmers of the customs of the port of Carrickfergus for examining of masters of ships, merchants or any other person or persons whatsoever for and concerning custom affairs, these are therefore to pray and require your lordship to issue out the like commission under the great seal directions to the several customers, controllers, surveyors & collectors as aforesaid of the several ports following (*vizt.*) Wexford, Waterford, Youghal, Cork, Kinsale, Dingle-Inch,[194] Limerick, Galway, Sligo, Londonderry and Drogheda according to the instructions annexed to our said former warrant, for which doing this shall be your lordship's warrant; from his Majesty's Castle of Dublin the 22nd day of May 1634.

To ~~every~~ our very good lord, the lord chancellor.

252. <SIR ARTHUR LOFTUS[195]> [31 MAY 1634]

By the lord deputy

Wentworth

Whereas upon humble suit made unto us by Sir Arthur Loftus, knight, we have been pleased to licence him to send into England 12 cast of marlins to be bestowed upon some friends of his therein. These are therefore to will & require you to permit & suffer the said Sir Arthur Loftus, his servant, to put aboard & transport the said hawks for England as aforesaid, any former general directions to the contrary notwithstanding. Given &c. 31st May 1634.

To all & every, his Majesty's officers of the customs in that port from whence the said Sir Arthur Loftus shall desire to transport the said hawks.

194 Anglicised version of the Irish town Daingean Uí Chúis (now Dingle).

195 Arthur Loftus (1616–59), MP for Wexford county (see McGrath).

253. [f. 533v] <CAPTAIN DALLENSON'S SHIP TO BE RESTORED & THE MEN TO BE ENLARGED> **[2 JUNE 1634]**

By the lord deputy

Wentworth

Whereas upon your information given us by your letters of the tenth of the last month & the examinations therewith sent concerning a stay you had made of one Captain Charles Dallenson & his ship called the *Hope of Newhaven*, we were pleased by our letters of the ~~10th of the last month~~ 15th of the same to approve of your act & to require you as well to secure the ship as to restrain the men thereunto belonging & with all to send unto us two or three of the chiefest of them; whereupon there came hither the said captain & one Daniel Frecquett, who being both examined & their commission perused, were found to be such as against whom no suspicion of piracy or any other just exceptions can be taken that do require their longer detention. We therefore have thought fit & do accordingly hereby will & require you & all other whom it may concern forthwith upon sight hereof not only to restore & deliver back the said ship, together with the goods, merchandize, sails & ~~forfeiture~~ furniture whatsoever to the same belonging without any manner of diminution, but also to enlarge & set at liberty the men so restrained & to permit & suffer him & them to depart without any further stay or hindrances at his & their wills & pleasure. And you are also required to permit him & them to furnish themselves for their money with any kind of provision they **[f. 534r]** want, whereof you & all others whom it doth or may concern are not to fail. And for so doing this shall be your warrant. Given &c. 2 *Junii* 1634.

To our well beloved, the mayor of Youghal & to all others whom it doth or may concern.

254. <~~CHARLES~~ CAPTAIN CHARLES DALLANSON'S *LIBERATE* &C.> **[2 JUNE 1634]**

A warrant to the constable of the Castle to enlarge Captain Charles Dallanson & Daniel Frecquett, paying their fees &c., dated 2 *Junii* 1634.

To Samuel Davis.

255. <ATTACHMENT *VERSUS* TIRLAGH OGE MCHUGH &C. ~~MR~~ TO MR GILBERT[196] 5 JUNE 1634 WITHOUT FEE> **2 JUNE 1634]**

Attachment against Tirlagh Oge McHugh & Patrick McHugh to answer such matters as at their coming shall be objected against them with a clause of assistance, dated 2 *Junii* 1634. *Vide* church affairs page 71 ~~for~~ & so forward for the petition & certificate whereon this was grounded.

196 Robert Gilbert, second pursuivants at arms (see *Lib. mun. pub. Hib.*).

256. <WILLIAM SOMERVILL> [2 JUNE 1634]

Attachment against William Somervill to answer such matters as at his coming shall be objected against him with a clause of assistance, dated 2 *Junii* 1634 <delivered to Mr Gilbert[197] 5 *Junii* 1634 *nullis feodis*>. *Vide* the third book of entries page 186 for the petition of Peter Dickenson, whereon this is grounded.

257. [f. 534v] <FRANCIS BLENERHASSETT> [4 JUNE 1634]

An attachment against Francis Blenerhassett to answer such matters as at his coming shall be objected against him with a clause of assistance dated 4th *Junii* 1634. <Delivered to Gilbert[198] 5th *Junii* 1634> *Vide* the third book of entries page 195 & 165, and first book of entries ~~&c.~~ page 499.

258. <A WARRANT FOR A COMMISSION BETWEEN BOYD & JANE HAMILTON>[199] [6 JUNE 1634]

By the lord deputy

~~After~~ Whereas there is a difference depending before us between David Boyd, plaintiff, and Jane Hamilton, widow (as executrix to her late husband William Hamilton, deceased), defendant, and inasmuch as the truth therein cannot appear without the examining of witnesses upon oath, we therefore have thought fit and do accordingly hereby pray and require your lordship forthwith to cause a commission to issue to that purpose under the great seal and the same to be directed to our well beloved Patrick Savage, Nicholas Ward and Valentine Paine, esquires, <*vide* third book of entries page 214 for the petition whereon this is grounded> authorizing them or any two of them to examine upon oath all and every such witnesses as shall be produced by either party to be examined concerning this matter & upon such interr[ogations] as either party shall present & exhibit. The said commission to be returnable with all convenient speed and at the furthest by the tenth day of the next month provided the plaintiff do give 15 days notice of the execution of the said commission unto the defendant that she likewise may be prepared and ready against the time of the execution thereof. And for so doing this shall be your lordship's warrant. Given at his Majesty's Castle of Dublin the 6th of June 1634.

To our very good lord, the lord chancellor.

259. [f. 535r] <WARRANT OF POSSESSION FOR MR COSBY> [5 JUNE 1634]

By the lord deputy

Wentworth

Whereas for our better satisfaction of the truth in a difference depending before us between Arnold Cosby, esquire, plaintiff, and James and John Smith, defendants,

197 Robert Gilbert, as above.

198 Robert Gilbert, as above.

199 See warrant no. 143.

about the towns & lands of Ballimanus, Ballyreder, Kilrory and Knockanbrae in the Queen's County, we referred the examination of the whole matter unto our right trusty and well beloved Sir George Radcliffe, knight, and one of his Majesty's privy council in this kingdom, who having fully heard both sides and examined the difference at large in the presence of them and their counsel learned hath certified us that the petitioner Cosby hath good right and title in law unto the said town and lands, <*vide* fourth book of entries page 117 for the certificate whereupon this was grounded> and that although the said defendant's estate was fully ended by the death of Richard Cosby, the petitioner's brother, yet such is their obstinacy as that they refuse (although it was offered them) to accept of a new lease from the petition at a reasonable rent & fine. We therefore have thought fit and do accordingly hereby require and authorize you the sheriff of the Queen's County forthwith to enter into the towns and lands of Ballimanus, Ballyreder, Kilrory and Knockanbrae aforesaid and to remove from thence the said defendants and the quiet & peaceable possession thereof to deliver unto the said Peter Cosby, or his assigns, and him and them therein to maintain from time to time until the same be evicted from him either by a due course of law or that we shall be pleased to revoke or countermand this our warrant. Whereof you the said sheriff are not to fail. And for so doing this shall be a sufficient warrant. Given at &c. 5 *Junii* 1634.

To our well beloved, the sheriff of the Queen's County as well for the time being as which hereafter for the time shall be.

260. [f. 535v] <WARRANT TO THE CONSTABLE OF THE CASTLE TO BURY JOHN NODIN> **[5 JUNE 1634]**

By the lord deputy

Wentworth

Whereas one John Nodin, who was lately committed to your custody for suspicion of piracy, is yesterday deceased in this Castle, these are therefore to will & require you upon receipt hereof to take present order that the body of the said Nodin be carried forth of the said Castle & buried in St Werbugh's churchyard in this city; whereof you may not fail. And for so doing this shall be your warrant. Given &c. 5 *Junii* 1634.

To our well beloved Samuel Davis, esquire, constable of his Majesty's Castle of Dublin.

261. <JOHN GROVES> **[5 JUNE 1634]**

By the lord deputy

Wentworth

Whereas upon humble suit made unto us by John Groves we have been pleased to licence him to carry for England 2 horses or saddle nags &c. according [to] the usual form, dated 5 *Junii* 1634.

Port of Youghal.

262. [f. 536r] <A WARRANT FOR CAPTAIN DALLENSON TO SELL PART OF HIS GOODS & NOT BREAK BULK>[200] [7 JUNE 1634]

Whereas one Charles Dallenson, captain of the ship called the *Hope of Newhaven*, hath made known unto us that ^himself & the company^, by reason of their tedious voyage from the Indies & their long stay at Youghal, ~~they~~ are become destitute of ready money to supply themselves with such necessaries as they want and are not able to pay and discharge such debts and engagement as they have already come into, unless they may have licence to make sale of some part of their goods & merchandize for that use which he humbly besought us to afford, whose request therein we have thought fit to grant and that by the ~~consent~~ general consent of the farmers. And therefore we do hereby will and require you and every of you to permit and suffer the said Dallenson and his company to bring on shore and sell some part of their goods & merchandize to furnish themselves with such provision as they want and not to impute the same unto him or them as a breaking of bulk, and to receive custom for no more then they so sell which through our favour extended unto them they are permitted to do, although in strictness they ought not to break bulk before they had entered their goods and so paid custom for all. Whereof you and every of you are not to fail. And for so doing this shall be your sufficient warrant. ~~Dated~~ Given &c. 7 *Junii* 1634.

To our well beloved, the mayor & bailiffs of Youghal & to all & every, his Majesty's officers of the customs there.

263. [f. 536v] <JOHN CROFORD>[201] [7 JUNE 1634]

By the lord deputy

Wentworth

A warrant to the pursuivant to enlarge the body of John Croford, dean of Emly, committed at [the] suit of Piers Sheakin, paying his fees provided he were detained for no other matter, dated 7 *Junii* 1634.

To the pursuivant in whose custody the said John Craford remaineth.

264. <ATTACHMENT *VERSUS* STOUTE & SCOTT, THE MATTER & THE CAUSE RESTING WITH SIR GEORGE RADCLIFFE> [7 JUNE 1634]

An attachment against Edward Stoute, customer in the port of Youghal, & Edward Scott, dated 7 *Junii* 1634. <Delivered to Mr Thomas Littell, 7 *Junii* 1634>

265. [f. 537r] <WARRANT FOR 3 HORSES FOR THE MASTER [OF THE] ROLLS[202]> [10 JUNE 1634]

Wentworth

Whereas by warrant from the right honourable & our very good lord, the Lord Marquis Hamilton, there are directions given that it should be free for us to have

200 See warrants no. 253 and 254.

201 See warrants no. 197 and 240.

202 Christopher Wandesford (1592–1640), master of the rolls and lord deputy of Ireland (see *DIB*).

the number of twenty horses of service to be brought hither out of England for the better raising of the troop of horse which his Majesty for our better support in the government here alloweth unto us. And forasmuch as our right trusty & well beloved Christopher Wandesford, esquire, Master of the Rolls & one of his Majesty's privy council in ~~England~~ this kingdom, hath three horses to be brought over hither as upon the said warrant for twenty & for that the said three horses are to be of our troop, we therefore have thought fit & do accordingly hereby will & require you & every of you, as well the officers of his Majesty's customs in that port where the same shall be shipped as also all other his Majesty's officers, ministers & loving subjects whom it may concern to permit & suffer; the bearer hereof to put aboard & transport hither the said number of 3 horses for the said Master of the Rolls his use & to be employed in our troop as aforesaid. Given &c. 10th *Junii* 1634.

Thomas Littell

266. [f. 537v] <A WARRANT FOR MR BANASTER[203] TO BE MASTER OF THE GAME IN THE COUNTY OF CORK> [30 MAY 1634]

By the lord deputy

Wentworth

Whereas we are credibly informed that it is a common practise & custom with divers idle and loose persons in most parts of this kingdom to kill & destroy deer, lares, conies, pheasants & partridges which they sell up and down in that abundance to gain themselves a living & subsistence by, as that it is justly to be feared that unless a timely course be taken for prevention thereof the game of all sorts will be in a short time utterly destroyed, which we having taken into consideration and being ready and willing to abolish and extirpate such obnoxious and insufferable ~~wrongs~~ abuses, we have of late directed our warrants to divers of the nobility ~~and~~ and other persons of quality in divers parts of this kingdom whom we have thereby authorized & enabled to bridle & curb such disorderly & idle persons as shall henceforth apply themselves to such courses. And calling to mind ~~that~~ ^how^ we have not as yet nominated any to be masters of the game in that county of Cork we, out of the confidence in repose in your integrity and judgment, have thought fit & do accordingly hereby give you full power & authority either by yourself, your servants or such other person or persons as you shall entrust & employ in that behalf, not only to forbid from time to time and with all to restrain all and every person or persons whosoever within that county of Cork (which by the laws are to be restrained from unlawful hunting, killing, destroying ^or taking^ of any manner of game, either beast or fowl other then such foul or vermin as are noisome[)], but also to seize upon and take away their guns, dogs, buck-stalls, hay-nets, ferrets, hare-pipes & other engines. And with all you are to cause the persons of such offenders to be attached & carried before the ~~judg~~ next justice of the peace who is to commit them to the gaol, there to remain till they & every of them do put in good security to answer their transgressions before the next coming **[f. 538r]** judges of assize for that county who are to inflict such

203 Peregrine Bannister (d. 1647–59), master of the game and MP for Clonakilty (see McGrath).

punishment upon them as the quality of their several offences shall demerit; and for so doing this shall be ~~your appear interest~~ a sufficient warrant (which is to continue during our pleasure). In the due execution whereof, we require all & every, his Majesty's officers, ministers & loving subjects whom it doth or may concern to be aiding & assisting unto you as there shall be occasion & as they & every of them will answer the contrary at ~~y~~ their perils. Given &c. 30 May 1634.

To our trusty & well beloved Peregrine Banaster.

267. <WARRANT FOR MR BODKIN TO TRANSPORT 30,000 PIPESTAVES> [14 JUNE 1634]

By the lord deputy

Wentworth

Whereas upon humble suit made unto us and for divers good reasons as thereunto moving, we have been pleased to licence Alexander Bodkin of Galway, merchant, to transport out of this kingdom the number of thirty thousand pipestaves. These are therefore to will & require you to permit and suffer the said Alexander Bodkin by himself or his servants to put aboard & transport the said number of pipestaves out of that port provided that you first make entry thereof in your custom books & receive his Majesty's due customs thereout; besides which custom you are also to take 3*li.* sterling for every 1,000 of the said pipestaves and having so received the same you are to account for it unto us as a part from the said custom monies & to return it unto us with the first conveniency that shall be offered. And inasmuch as the said ship wherein the said pipestaves ~~is~~ ^are^ to be transported is a Spanish vessel, we have thought thought [*sic*] it fit to intimate thus much unto you that it is our pleasure that the Spaniards in her should be used in a fair ^&^ respective ~~way~~ manner the more to encourage them and others of that nation to fall into a commerce and trading with this kingdom which doubtless [**f. 538v**] would lend much to the benefit of both the Crowns; hereof you are not to fail. And for so doing &c. Given &c. *Junii* 14, 1634.

To all & every, the officers of his Majesty's customs in the port of Limerick or any other port in the province of Munster where the said Bodkin shall make entry of this our warrant.

268. <A WARRANT FOR A COMMISSION BETWEEN MRS MONTGOMERY & SIR STEPHEN BUTLER> [14 JUNE 1634][204]

By the lord deputy

Wentworth

Whereas there is a difference depending before us between Mary Montgomery, plaintiff, & Sir Stephen Butler, knight, defendant, and inasmuch as it is denied by the defendant that Robert Montgomery, the younger son unto Robert Montgomery the older, had ever an estate of freehold in a tate of land called Killmackbrack being part of the 150 acres in Leitrim past [*sic*] unto him and perfected by Sir John Wishert,

[204] See warrant no. 155.

knight, and for that we expect to be resolved and satisfied whether the said defendant had the said estate from the said Robert the younger by virtue of an order of the late Lord Caulfeild[205] and the Lord Angier,[206] both deceased, to the end therefore the truth may appear in both those points. We pray and require your lordship forthwith to cause a commission to issue to that purpose under the great seal and the same to be directed unto our well beloved Henry Manning and Captain Roger Atkinson, esquires, Richard Morse, clerk, & Nicholas Simpson, gent, authorizing them or any 2 or 3 of them to examine upon oath all and every such witnesses as shall be produced to be examined concerning those 2 points and such interrogatories as shall be presented & exhibited in that behalf. The said commission to be returnable with all [**f. 539r**] convenient speed & at the furthest within these 3 weeks next following provided the plaintiff do give the defendant 8 days notice of the prevention of the said commission that both parties may be ~~proved~~ provided at the time that the same shall be sat upon. And for so doing this shall be a sufficient warrant. Given &c. 14 *Junii* 1634.

To ~~the~~ our very good lord, the lord chancellor.

269. <WARRANT FOR PETER HILL TO BE SERGEANT AT ARMS> **[12 JUNE 1634]**

By the lord deputy

Wentworth

These are to will & require you forthwith to draw up a fiant in due form of law containing a grant from his Majesty, his heirs & successors, unto Peter Hill, esquire, of the office or place of one of the sergeant at arms to attend at all times when he should be required, but more especially to attend the speaker of the House of Commons for the time being at every parliament & parliaments to be holden hereafter within this realm of Ireland. And further, to perform such other services in the said House of Commons (as is or hath been heretofore done & performed by his Majesty's sergeant at arms for their or the like since in England[)] the same being now void by the voluntary surrender of William Peisley, esquire, and George Peisley, gent, to have and to hold the said place or office of one of the sergeant at arms as aforesaid unto him the said Peter Hill, together with all and singular fees, perquisites, profits, rewards, pre-eminencies and emoluments whatsoever thereunto belonging & in anywise appertaining, and in as large, ample & beneficial manner as Edward Davies, gent, or the said William & George Peisley, or any of them, formerly held & enjoyed or of right ought to have held & enjoyed the same, & to be exercised by himself or his sufficient deputy during good behaviour the fee of twenty pounds sterling allowed for the execution of the place only excepted, inserting therein all such clauses as in ~~such~~ like grants are usual; and the same fairly engrossed in parchment under your hand to send unto [**f. 539v**] us to be further passed as appertaineth. For doing whereof this shall be your warrant. Given &c. 12 *Junii* 1634.

To our trusty & well beloved, his Majesty's attorney & solicitor general, or either of them.

[205] Toby Caulfeild (1565–1627), 1st Baron Charlemont, soldier and administrator (see *DIB*).

[206] Francis Aungier (1558–1632), lawyer and adminstrator (see *DIB*).

270. <LOWE & TUCKER'S LICENCE TO TRANSPORT 200,000 BARRELSTAVES> [13 JUNE 1634]

By the lord deputy

Wentworth

Whereas John Lowe & Mansfield Tucker, merchants, have made known unto us that they (amongst others being adventurers in the royal fishing of great Britain & Ireland) have made a journey hither out of England of purpose to provide a certain number of barrelstaves to be transported to the Ile of Lewis in Scotland for the barrelling up of theirs and others, the adventurers' fish to be taken there this approaching season. For the transportation whereof they humbly besought us to afford them our licence which we have thought fit to grant & the rather in regard the right honourable and our very good lord, the lord ^high^ treasurer of England, hath written unto us to that purpose in their behalf. And therefore we do hereby will & require you & every of you the officers of that port, where they shall make entry of this our warrant, to permit & suffer them the said Lowe and Tucker by themselves & their servants to put aboard & transport the number of two hundred thousand barrelstaves provided you first make entry thereof in your custom books & receive his Majesty's due customs thereout, and that you take good security of them not to transport the said barrelstaves to any other foreign parts but only to the said Isle of Lewis, & to be there employed as aforesaid; and that they return us a good & well attested certificate thereof & the like unto you by a certain convenient time to be by you appointed, whereof you are not to fail. And for so doing this shall be your sufficient warrant. Given &c. 13 *Junii* 1634.

To all every, the officers of his Majesty's customs in the ports of Londonderry & Carrickfergus & the creeks & members thereunto belonging.

271. [f. 540r] <EDWARD STANHOPE HIS WARRANT FOR 2 VICARAGES> [10 JUNE 1634]

<Manicule> A warrant for a fiant containing a presentation from his Majesty of Edward Stanhope, clerk, unto the vicarages of Kiltaughorke in the diocese of Ardagh & Drumreilly in the diocese of Kilmore according [to] the usual form with a clause of union, dated 10th *Junii* 1634.

272. <A WARRANT FOR THE FREE SCHOOL OF ARDFERT> [18 JUNE 1634]

By the lord deputy

Wentworth

Whereas the place of schoolmaster of his Majesty's free school within the united diocese of Ardfert & Aghado[e] in the province of Munster is now become void & in his Majesty's gift, and forasmuch as we have received good testimony as well of the learning & sufficiency as also of the good life & conversation of William Fell, Master of the Arts, <*vide* petition in the bundles> these are therefore to will and require you upon the receipt hereof to draw up a licence in the usual form <manicule> containing a grant of the said place of school master unto the said William Fell ^with the yearly fee or stipend of 30*li.* yearly^, together with all rights, duties, fees, wages, perquisites & profits to the same belonging or anyway appertaining in as large, ample & beneficial manner as the same hath been heretofore enjoyed by any other during his good behaviour, inserting therein such clauses as in like grants are usual. And the same fairly engrossed in parchment under your hand to send unto us to be further passed as appertains. And for so doing &c. ~~And~~ Given &c. 18 of June 1634.

To our trusty & well beloved Sir William Ussher, knight, & Paul Davies, esquire, clerks of the Council, or either of them.

273. [f. 540v] <SIR JOHN HUME> **[17 JUNE 1634]**

By the lord deputy

A warrant for Sir John Hume to be Master of the Game for the county of Fermanagh, dated 17th June 1634. This agreeth *verbatim* with Bannister's warrant, page 216.

To our trusty & well beloved Sir John Humes [*sic*], knight.

274. <GREGORY DICKENSON> **[20 JUNE 1634]**

Wentworth

A warrant for a fiant containing as well his Majesty's free gift & donation of the treasureship of the cathedral church of Kilfenora unto Gregory Dickenson, clerk, as also a presentation from his highness of the said ~~dic~~ Dickenson to the rectory & vicarage of Rathburne & the rectory & vicarage of Dromcree in the said diocese of Kilfenora, now all void & in his Majesty's gift by lapse, <manicule> to have & to hold the said treasurership together with all & every the said rectories & vicarages & all the duties, members, rights, profits, perquisites & appurtenances whatsoever thereunto belonging or in anyway appertaining, & in as large, ample & beneficial manner as any other incumbent or incumbents formerly held & enjoyed or of right ought to have held & enjoyed the same, directing his installation & admission thereunto to the dean & chapter of the said diocese, & the judge of the faculties as **[f. 541r]** is usual, inserting therein a clause of union *pro hac vice tantum* together with all other accustomed clauses. And the same fairly engrossed &c.; for doing whereof &c. Given &c. 20th *Junii* 1634. <*vide* the bundles for the petition>

To our trusty & well beloved Sir William Ussher, knight, & Paul Davies, esquire, clerks of the Council, or either of them.

275. [WARRANT TO TRANSPORT HORSES FOR SCOTLAND] **[21 JUNE 1634]**

Warrant for Peter Floswick & Volcardus Voss to transport 2 horses out of any port in the north for Scotland, dated xx *Junii* 1634.

276. <EARL OF ANTRIM> **[21 JUNE 1634]**

Warrant for the earl of Antrim to be Master of the Game in *comitatu* Antrim according [to] the usual form, dated 21 *Junii* 1634.

277. <WARRANT FOR A VICARAGE FOR MR LEADBITTER> **[26 JUNE 1634]**

By the lord deputy

Wentworth

These are to will & require you forthwith to draw up a fiant in due form of law containing a presentation from his Majesty ~~unto~~ of George Leadbitter, clerk, unto the vicarage of Castletown in the diocese of Cloyne being now void & in his Majesty's gift by lapse, <manicule> to have, hold, possess & enjoy the said vicarage together with all the rights, duties, members, profits & appurtenances whatsoever thereunto belonging or in anyway appertaining, & in as large, ample & beneficial manner as any other incumbent or incumbents formerly held & enjoyed or [**f. 541v**] of right ought to have held & enjoyed the same, directing his admission to the judge of the faculties. And the same fairly engrossed in parchment under your hand &c. Given &c. 26 *Junii* 1634.

To Sir William Ussher & Paul Davies.

278. <WARRANT FOR FIANT FOR THOMAS WAY[207]> **[25 JUNE 1634]**

Wentworth

These are to will & require you forthwith to draw up a fiant in due form of law containing a grant & presentation from his Majesty unto Thomas Way, clerk, of the vicarages of Skull & Caragh *alias* Cateragh in the diocese of Cork void by lapse, <manicule> to have, hold &c. according [to] the usual form, inserting a clause of union & directing his admission to the judge of the faculties, dated 25th *Junii* 1634.

To Sir William Ussher & Paul Davies.

279. <WARRANT FOR WILKINSON FOR 2 VICARAGES> **[25 JUNE 1634]**

Warrant for a fiant containing a presentation for his Majesty of John Wilkinson unto the <manicule> vicarages of Cloone & Anaghduffe in the diocese of ~~Kilmore~~ ^Ardagh^ in his Majesty's gift by lapse, inserting therein a clause of union & directing his admission to the judge of the faculties, dated 25 *Junii* 1634.

To Sir William Ussher & Paul Davies.

280. [f. 542r] <WARRANT FOR A PARTICULAR FOR MR WARTER'S FAIRS &C.>[208] **[25 JUNE 1634]**

By the lord deputy

Wentworth

Whereas upon humble suit made unto us by William Warter, esquire, we have been pleased to grant unto him the benefit of one weekly market & two yearly fairs to

[207] Thomas Way, native of Kinsale, plundered by the rebels in 1641 of property amounting to £1,000 (see Cotton, *Fasti*).

[208] See warrant no. 287. This is the same warrant with only slight differences.

be kept in the town of Cullen in the county of Cross Tipperary, we thereupon did require the then next going judges of assize to cause it to be enquired whether the granting thereof would not be prejudicial to any of the neighbouring fairs or markets, <*vide* first book of entries page 283 & third book of entries 247 for the former proceedings> which being enquired of by the grand jury it was by them returned that if the said market were kept upon a Saturday & the fairs upon Corpus Christi & St Luke's day that then the same would not prove prejudicial to the public. We therefore have thought fit & do accordingly hereby will & require you forthwith to draw up a particular of the said market & fairs, reserving thereout the sum of 40*s.* sterling rent yearly unto his Majesty. And the same fairly engrossed in parchment under your hand to send unto us to be further passed as appertaineth; for doing whereof this shall be your warrant. Given &c. 25 *Junii* 1634.

To our trusty & well beloved, his Majesty's surveyor & auditor general, or either of them.

281. [f. 542v] <LORD CONWAY, HIS LICENCE TO TRANSPORT HORSES & HAWKS> [27 JUNE 1634]

By the lord deputy

Wentworth

Whereas our very good lord, the Lord Viscount Conway & Killultagh, hath made known unto us that his lady, the Lady Viiscountess Conway,[209] being to make her present repair into England, his lordship humbly besought us to be pleased to give our directions that he might be permitted to send into England six coach mares & fourteen geldings ~~or~~ ^and^ saddle nags, as well for the coach as for the servants' use to attend her ladyship in her journey to ride on & for the carriage of trunks & other necessaries, whose request as well therein as for the sending over of two cast of goshawks we have thought fit to grant. And therefore we do hereby will & require you the officers of that port to permit & suffer his lordship's servants to put aboard & transport the said mares, geldings & hawks into England as aforesaid, any former general directions to the contrary notwithstanding. And for so doing &c. Given &c. 27th *Junii* 1634.

To all & every, his the officers of his Majesty's customs in the port of Strangford.

282. [f. 543r] <JAMES BRUSE> [28 JUNE 1634]

Warrant for a fiant containing a presentation from his Majesty of James Bruse, clerk, of the <manicule> vicarage of Bridgetown being now void & in gift by lapse, to have &c. according [to] the usual form, directing his admission to the judge of the faculties. Given &c. 28th *Junii* 1634.

To Sir William Ussher & Paul Davies.

[209] Frances Conway (née Popham), Lady Viscountess Conway.

283. <ROBERT MILNER'S WARRANT FOR A RECTORY & VICARAGE> [27 JUNE 1634]

~~Warrant for a fiant containing a prosecution from his Majesty of Robert Milner, clerk, unto the rectory & vicarage of Rincorran in the diocese of Cork void by lapse, to have &c. according [to] the usual form, directing his admission to the judge of the faculties. Given &c. 27 *Junii* 1634.~~

~~To Sir William Ussher & Paul Davies, clerks of the Council, or either of them.~~

284. [f. 543v] <~~A WARRANT TO BRING UP SUCH AS HOLD LANDS FROM THE SEE OF KILLALOE~~> [N.D.]

285. <A BEGGING PASS FOR LILLY> [3 JULY 1634]

By the lord deputy

Wentworth

Whereas William Lilly, a poor decayed merchant, hath petitioned unto us setting forth that he being a man of late ~~of good~~ brought to extreme indigency & poverty, as well by the loss of 3 barques & all his goods at sea in one year to the value of 300*li.* sterling & after falling into the hands of thieves was robbed of all he had, & besides other miseries he had of late by misfortune one of his legs broken whereby he is now become so lame & impotent as that he is not able any longer to subsist or support himself & family without the charitable benevolence of good & well disposed Christians. Wherefore he humbly besought us to be pleased to grant him our licence to ask & crave relief of such as in pity & consideration of his distressed estate will be pleased to afford the same, whose request therein for this city of Dublin & the whole province of Ulster we have thought fit to grant & the rather in regard we have received very good testimony of his leases & misfortunes. These are therefore to pray & require all & every, his Majesty's officers, ministers & loving subjects whatsoever within the said city of Dublin & province of Ulster, not only to permit & suffer him the said Lilly to pass peaceably & quietly by them without any their lets, stays **[f. 544r]** or molestations whatsoever he demeaning himself as becometh, but also to be aiding & assisting unto him herein that he may repair as well to churches, fairs, markets & other public assemblies as to all cities, towns, corporate & not corporate, villages & all other places within the said province to entreat the benevolence of all well disposed & charitable people to whose pity & good consideration we do hereby recommend him. And we do hereby pray & require all archbishops, bishops, preachers & ministers within their several dioceses & parishes upon the Sabbath & holidays[210] to signify & read publicly the contents hereof unto their several congregations there gathered together, provided that this shall continue & be in force no longer then for the space of one whole year next ensuing the date hereof. And for so doing this shall be ~~yo~~ a sufficient warrant. Given &c. 3 *Julii* 1634.

<*vide* amongst the bundles for the petition of William Lilly whereupon this was grounded>

Thomas Littell

210 i.e. holy days.

286. [f. 544v] <VALENTINE BLACKER & GEORGE BLACKER, THEIR *LIBERATE*> [3 JULY 1634]

Wentworth

Whereas you have in your custody the bodies of Valentine Blacker & George Blacker, his son, committed unto your custody upon our former warrant, these are to require you to set them at liberty paying their fees provided they give sufficient security for their appearance of the next assizes before the judges of assize for the county of Armagh to answer such matters as at their being there shall be objected against them. And for so doing this shall be your warrant. Given &c. 3 *Julii* 1634.

To any of this Majesty's pursuivants.

287. <WARRANT FOR A FIANT FOR MR WARTER'S MARKET & FAIRS>[211] [3 JULY 1634]

Whereas upon humble suit made unto us by William Warter, esquire, we have been pleased to grant unto him the benefit of one weekly market & two yearly fairs to be kept in the town of Cullen in the county of Cross Tipperary, we thereupon did require the last going judges of assizes to cause it to be enquired whether the granting thereof would not be prejudicial to any of the neighbouring fairs & ^or^ markets, which being enquired of by the said grand jury, <*vide* first book of entries page 283 & third book of entries page 247 & 248 &c. for certificate whereon this is grounded> it was by them returned that if the said [**f. 545r**] market were kept upon a Saturday & the fairs upon Corpus Christi & St Luke's day that then the same would not prove prejudicial to the public. These are therefore to will and require you forthwith to draw up a fiant in due form of law containing a grant from his Majesty unto the said William Warter, his heirs & assigns, of the said market & fairs within mentioned reserving thereout unto his Majesty the yearly rent of 40*s.* sterling, inserting therein all such clauses as in grants of like nature are usual. And the same fairly engrossed &c. Given &c. 3 *Julii* 1634.

To our trusty & well beloved, his Majesty's attorney & solicitor general, or either of them.

288. [f. 545v] <WARRANT FOR SIR RICHARD OSBORNE TO TRANSPORT 3 NAGS> [3 JULY 1634]

A warrant for Sir Richard Osborne, baronet, to transport for England 3 geldings or saddle nags for his own use at the port of Youghal, dated 3 *Julii* 1634.

289. <WARRANT FOR TRANSPORTATION OF SHORN SHEEP> [2 JULY 1634]

Wentworth

Whereas there lately issued a warrant unto you from us prohibiting the transportation of any sheep out of those ports into the realm of England without our licence first obtained, we do therefore make known unto you that by our said inhibition we did

[211] See warrant no. 280. This is the same warrant with only slight differences.

not intend that sheep which were already shorn this season might not be exported as formerly but that our restraint should extend only to the prohibiting of the transportation of sheep that were unshorne. These are therefore to require & authorize you for the future (notwithstanding our said restraint[)] to permit & suffer Henry Stanes, esquire, or his servants or any other whatsoever, to transport such sheep only as already are shorn into the realm of England paying only his Majesty's customs as the[y] usually did before our said restraint. And &c. Given &c. 2 *Julii* 1634.

To the officers of the customs in the ports of Waterford and Ross.

290. [f. 546r] <SIR RICHARD OSBORNE, HIS LICENCE OF ABSENCE> [JULY 1634]

Wentworth

Whereas upon humble suit made unto us by our trusty & well beloved Sir Richard Osborne, baronet, clerk of the Crown ~~and~~ & peace in the city & county of Limerick & the county of Tipperary & Cross, we have been pleased to licence him to make his repair into England & there to remain about the dispatch of some special affairs of his own for & during the space of six months next ensuing the date hereof. These are therefore to require all & every, his Majesty's officers, ministers & loving subjects whom it may concern not only to take due notice thereof but also to afford him the full benefit of this our licence without any prejudice to be suffered or any forfeiture to be made of his said offices by reason of his absence during the time aforesaid; whereof they & every of them are not to fail. And for so doing this shall be a sufficient warrant. Given &c. *Julii* 1634.

Thomas Littell

291. [f. 546v] <A PASS FOR SMITH> [4 JULY 1634]

Whereas the bearer hereof Thomas Smith, calling himself yeoman of the powder room in the king's ship called the *Bonaventure* & commanded by Sir Richard Plumleigh, hath made known unto us that he having fallen sick of late when the said ship was (of late) upon this coast & being now recovered, he is to make his repair towards the western parts of this kingdom where he hopeth to find the said ship. These are therefore to will & require you & every of you to permit & suffer him the said Smith to travel & pass without ~~any~~ any your lets or stays whatsoever he demeasning [*sic*] himself as becometh. Whereof you & every of you are not to fail. Given &c. 4 *Julii* 1634.

To all mayors, sheriffs, justices of peace, bailiffs, constables and all other his Majesty's officers, ministers & loving subjects whom it may concern & to every of them.

292. <WARRANT FOR MR HARTBURNE TO CARRY OVER HORSES & HAWKS> [5 JULY 1634]

~~A warrant for~~ Whereas upon humble suit made unto us by Richard Hartburne & Francis Moore, gent, we have been pleased to licence them to transport into England for their own use 4 horses, 6 cast of marlins, one falcon & one tarsell gent [*sic*].[212] These are therefore to will & require you ~~the~~ to permit & suffer them the said Hartburne & Francis Moore to put aboard & transport the said number of horses & hawks as aforesaid, any former general directions to the contrary notwithstanding. And for the doing &c. Given &c. 5 *Julii* 1634.

To all & every, his Majesty's officers of the customs ~~of~~ in the port of Carrickfergus.

293. [f. 547r] <WILLIAM FELL> [5 JULY 1634]

A warrant for a fiant for William Fell, Master in the Arts, to the rectory of Killeen in the diocese of Ardfert, ^void by lapse^, to have, hold &c. according [to] the usual form, inserting therein a clause to enable him the said Fell to hold the said rectory <manicule> notwithstanding the clause inserted in his warrant for the place of schoolmaster in the diocese of Ardfert, that if he did accept of any church living then the said place of schoolmaster conferred upon him to be void together with all such other clauses as in like nature are usual, ^directing his admission &c.^ Given &c. 5th *Julii* 1634.

To our trusty & well beloved Sir William Ussher, knight, & Paul Davies, esquire, clerks of the Council, or either of them.

294. <HENRY STANES> [7 JULY 1634]

Warrant for Henry Stanes to transport for England 4 geldings or saddle horses at the port of Youghal, dated 7th *Julii* 1634.

295. <HENRY RUFFIN> [8 JULY 1634]

Warrant for Henry Ruffin to carry for England 3 horses or saddle nags at the port of Youghal, dated 8th *Julii* 1634.

296. [WARRANT TO DETAIN O'REILLY & *AL.*][213] [3 JULY 1634]

A warrant to the constable of the castle to receive into his custody the body of Philip McDonnell O'Reilly, David McConyn & Hugh McMulmore O'Reilly & them to detain until our further pleasure known. Given &c. 3 *Julii* 1634.

To Samuel Davis &c.

212 i.e. tercel gentle, the male of any kind of hawk, particularly in falconry.

213 See warrant no. 222.

297. [f. 547v] **<A WARRANT FOR SEQUESTRATION OF THE LADY DOWAGER BLANEY &C., LANDS FOR THE LORD CAULFEILD>[214]** **[3 JULY 1634]**

Whereas his Majesty, having taken into special consideration the humble requests of our very good lord, the Lord Caulfeild, about an engagement he had undertaken to the Lord Balfour for the late Lord Blaney, his highness was graciously pleased by his letters of the 7th of July 1633 to require us to take an effectual order for the just satisfaction & saving harmless of the said Lord Caulfeild. Whereupon we falling into a serious examination of the whole state of the difference & finding that the said Lord Caulfeild had paid twelve hundred pounds principal & three hundred & forty pounds damages & interest amounting in all to the sum of fifteen hundred & forty pounds sterling for the mere & proper debt of the said Lord Blaney's, we did order by the consent of the then defendants being the now Lord Blaney, the Lady Dowager Blaney, Mr Arthur Blaney, Mary, Martha & Lettice Blaney, that they & every of them should contribute & pay their proportionable shares out of the estates to them severally come & descended from the late Lord Blaney towards the satisfaction of the said Lord Caulfeild, amongst whom the said Lady Dowager [**f. 548r**] Blaney, Arthur Blaney, Mary, Martha & Lettice Blaney were ordered to pay (*vizt.*) the said lady Dowager the sum of 200*li.* sterling, Mr Arthur Blaney the sum of six hundred pounds sterling & the three daughters Mary, Martha & Lettice each of them fifty pounds sterling a piece unto the said Lord Caulfeild, who now complains unto us & made it likewise appear by affidavit that the said Lady Dowager, Arthur Blaney & the said three sisters have contemptuously neglected & delayed the payment of their said shares to the great prejudice of him the said Lord Caulfeild, who had already much suffered by his good offices employed & done for the said late Lord Blaney & who in conscience & equity ought to have relief which we upon his humble & earnest request have thought fit to afford him. And therefore we do hereby require & authorize as well the sheriff of the county of Monaghan as the sheriffs of such other counties (as well now being as to come) where the said Lady Dowager, Arthur Blaney & the said three sisters' lands & estates do remain either in their possession or whereof they or any of them do receive the rents & profits to enter unto & upon the same, & having so done to take security of the several tenants to pay the growing rents & profits of the said lands from time to time as the same shall grow due; & having so received the same to deliver over & make payment thereof unto the said Lord Caulfeild or his assigns until his lordship be fully satisfied & paid what they the said Lady Dowager, [**f. 548v**] Arthur Blaney & the said 3 sisters, Mary, Martha & Lettice Blaney ought to pay severally, together with the forbearance thereof for the times limited it should have been paid after 10*li. per centum*, according to the true intent & meaning of our said order. A copy whereof is hereunto annexed whereof they the said sheriffs & every of them are not to fail upon pain of 1,000*li.* And for so doing this shall be a sufficient warrant. Given &c. 3 *Julii* 1634.

[214] See warrant no. 84.

298. <WARRANT FOR A COMMISSION TO EXAMINE WITNESSES NICHOLAS JOY & THE EARL OF ANTRIM>[215] [7 JULY 1634]

~~By the lord deputy~~

~~Wentworth~~

~~Whereas there is a difference depending before us between Nicholas Joy, plaintiff, & our very good lord, the earl of Antrim, defendant, concerning certain parcels of land called by the names of Blackote & Sanogenagh containing 400 acres of upon both parties' humble suit in that behalf, <*vide* first book of entries, page 326> now inasmuch as we think it fit that a commission should issue to examine witnesses upon oath for the better finding out of the truth in that matter &c. accordingly the usual form [*sic*] & directed to Sir Andrew Moneypenny & William Hewson, esquire, William Reading, gent, & Thomas Piers, the elder clerk &c., returnable with all convenient speed & at the furthest by the first day of the next Michaelmas term provided the plaintiff do give 15 days notice of the execution hereof to the defendant, dated 7 *Julii* 1634.~~

~~To our very good, lord the lord chancellor.~~

299. [f. 549r] <MR MILNER'S WARRANT FOR A RECTORY AND A VICARAGE> [16 JULY 1634]

By the lord deputy

Wentworth

These are to will & require you forthwith to draw up a fiant in due form of law containing a presentation of Robert Milner, clerk, unto the rectory & vicarage of Rincorran in the diocese of Cork being now void in his Majesty's gift & presentation by reason of the minority of Peter *alias* Pierce Gold, his higness's ward, to have, hold, possess and enjoy the said rectory and vicarage unto him <manicule> the said Milner together with all rights, duties, members, profits and appurtenances whatsoever thereunto belonging & in anywise appertaining, and in as large, ample & beneficial manner as any other incumbent or incumbents formerly held and enjoyed or of right ought to have held & enjoyed the same, directing his admission to the ~~judge of the faculties~~ ^bishop of Cork, Cloyne & Ross[216] or, in his absence, to his vicar general or any other whom it may concern^. And the same fairly engrossed in parchment under your hand to send unto us to be further passed as appertaineth. For doing whereof this shall be your warrant. Given &c. 16 *Julii* 1634.

To our trusty & well beloved Sir William Ussher, knight, & Paul Davies, esquire, clerks of the Council, or either of them.

215 See warrant no. 305 for amended version.

216 Richard Boyle (d. 1645), bishop of Cork, Cloyne and Ross (until 1638) and later archbishop of Tuam (see *DIB*).

300. <MR BAPTHORPE'S WARRANT FOR A FIANT> [10 JULY 1634]

Wentworth

<manicule> Warrant for a fiant containing a prosecution of Richard Babthorpe [*sic*], clerk, unto the several vicarages of Kilmacabea & Dremnagh in the diocese of ~~Cloyne~~ Ross void by lapse or otherwise, to have &c. according [to] the usual form, directing his admission to the judge of the faculties with a clause of union &c. Given &c. 10th *Julii* 1634.

To Sir William Ussher & Paul Davies.

301. [f. 549v] <WARRANT FOR MR VAUGHAN[217] FOR A PARSONAGE> [10 JULY 1634]

By the lord deputy

Whereas Charles Vaughan, clerk, hath petitioned unto us setting forth that the right reverend father in God, the late lord bishop of Derry,[218] having presented him to the parsonage of Banagher cum Dungiven together with the prebendary of Comyer in the diocese of Derry, <*vide* church affairs, page 177 for the petition wherein this is grounded> he the said Charles (being doubtful that his title is weak thereunto) hath humbly besought us for the better corroboration of his said title to confirm the premises unto him by a grant thereof from his Majesty ^as being in lapse^, whose request therein we have thought fit to grant. <manicule> And therefore we do hereby will & require you forthwith to draw up a fiant in due form of law containing his Majesty's gift & presentation of him the said Vaughan unto the said parsonage of Banagher cum Dungiven together with the prebendary of Comyer, to have, hold, possess & enjoy the same together with all the rights, duties, tithes, profits, members and appurtenances whatsoever to them belonging, & in as large, ample & beneficial manner as any other incumbent or incumbents formerly held & enjoyed the same, directing his admission to the bishop of the diocese, ~~or the judge of the faculties~~ inserting therein likewise a clause of union *pro hac vice tantum.* <by directions from bishop of Derry> And the same likewise fairly engrossed in parchment under your hand to send unto us to be further passed as appertaineth for &c. Given &c. 10 *Julii* 1634.

To our trusty & well beloved William Ussher, ^knight^, & ~~Mr~~ Paul Davies, esquire, clerks of the Council, or either of them.

302. [f. 550r] <MAURICE ROCH> [12 JULY 1634]

Warrant to the constable ~~to~~ of the Castle of detain in his custody the body of Maurice Roch & him to detain until further pleasure known, dated 12th *Julii* 1634.

To the constable of the Castle.

217 Charles Vaughan (d. in or after 1664), prebend of Derry (see Cotton, *Fasti*).

218 George Downham (d. 1634), bishop of Derry prior to Bramhall (see *DIB*).

303. <WARRANT FOR THE CREATING OF CLAUDE HAMILTON, LORD HAMILTON>[219] **[17 JULY 1634]**

By the lord deputy

Whereas upon the voluntary surrender made unto his Majesty's hands by our very good lord, James, now earl of Abercorn, in the realm of Scotland of the style, title, degree, dignity & honour of Lord Hamilton, baron of Strabane, which he the said earl held in this kingdom of Ireland (& which was passed unto him by letters patents from our late sovereign King James of happy memory), <this was altered as in page 253> his highness hath been pleased to require that a commission should issue from hence unto our trusty & well beloved Sir William Jones & Sir Robert Barkley, knights, 2 of the justices of his Majesty's Court of Chief Place in England, authorizing them or either of them to make the acknowledgment of a fine (according to a statute of the 4th year of Henry the 7th in that case provided) from the said James, earl of Abercorn, of the said state, degree, dignity, style, title, name & honour of Lord Hamilton, baron of Strabane, to his Majesty, his heirs & successors. And forasmuch as it appeareth by an order of his Majesty's High Court of Chancery here of the third of February 1633[/4] that the said commission hath issued & is ^executed^ accordingly and that the fine (as is usual) hath been recorded in the Court of Common Pleas here, the said former letters patents cancelled & [f. 550v] a *vacat* entered upon the enrolment thereof. These are therefore to will and require you forthwith to draw up a grant in due form of law containing a fiant from his Majesty, his heirs & successors, unto Claude Hamilton, esquire, brother unto the said earl of Abercorn of the name, style, title, degree, dignity & honour of Lord Hamilton, baron of Strabane, unto him the said Claude Hamilton in the county of Tyrone in the province of Ulster, to have, hold, possess & enjoy the said name, title, dignity, style & honour of Lord Hamilton, baron of Strabane, unto him the said Claude Hamilton & to the heirs males of his body lawfully begotten & to be begotten, & for want of such issue to the heirs males of the body of James, late earl of Abercorn (father unto the now earl of Abercorn & the said Claude Hamilton) lawfully begotten, and that the said Claude Hamilton & the heirs males of his body lawfully begotten. And for want of such issue, the heirs males of the body of the said James, late earl of Abercorn, lawfully begotten may have & enjoy the same place, voice in parliament & elsewhere & all other right privileges, pre-eminences & benefits in as ample & beneficial manner as the said James, now earl of Abercorn, had or ought to have by virtue of the said recited letters patent & any other baron of this realm hath or ought to have & enjoy the same. And the same fairly engrossed in parchment under your hand to have send unto us that the same may be further passed as appertaineth according to the purport of his Majesty's letters unto us of the 7th of May in the 9th year of his reign, a copy whereof for your better information we have herewith sent you; for doing whereof &c. Given &c. 17 *Julii* 1634.

To our trusty and well beloved, his Majesty's attorney and solicitor general.

[219] See warrant no. 324 for 'altered' or corrected version.

304. [f. 551r] <MR BINGHAM'S WARRANT FOR TRANSPORTATION OF 6 CAST OF MERLINS> **[19 JULY 1634]**

By the lord deputy

Whereas upon humble suit made unto us by Thomas Bingham, esquire, we have been pleased to give way that he shall send over ~~for~~ ^into^ England 6 cast of merlins, these are therefore to will & require you & every of you not only to take notice of this our pleasure but also to permit his servant or such other as he shall entrust in that behalf to put aboard and transport the said hawks as aforesaid any directions heretofore to the contrary notwithstanding. And for so doing &c. Given &c. 19 July 1634.

To all & every, his Majesty's officers of the customs in the port of Waterford.

305. <WARRANT FOR A COMMISSION *INTER* JOY & THE EARL OF ANTRIM>[220] **[23 JULY 1634]**

By the lord deputy

Whereas there is a difference depending before us between Nicholas Joy, plaintiff, and our very good lord, the earl of Antrim, defendant, concerning certain parcels of land called by the names of Blackote & Sanogenagh containing 400 acres, now inasmuch we think fit upon both parties' humble suit in that behalf that a commission should issue to examine witnesses upon oath for the better finding out of the truth in that matter. These are therefore to pray and require your lordship forthwith to cause a commission to issue to that purpose and the same and the same [*sic*] to be directed to our well beloved Sir Hercules Langford, knight, William Reading, gent, Dr Andrew Moneypenny and Edward Cousins, esquire, or to any 2 or 3 of them, to enquire and examine upon oath all and every such witnesses as shall be produced by either party to be examined concerning this matter, and upon such interrogatories as either party shall present and exhibit the said commission to be returnable with all convenient speed and at the furthest by the first day of the next Michaelmas term, provided the plaintiff do give 15 days notice of the execution of the said commission unto the defendant that he may likewise be prepared and ready against the time of the execution thereof. And for so doing this shall be your lordship's warrant. Given at his Majesty's Castle of Dublin, this 23rd day of July 1634.

To our very good lord, the lord chancellor.

306. [f. 551v] [WARRANT TO PAY PHILLIPS AND PHILLIPS 500*li.*] **[21 JULY 1634]**

By the lord deputy

Whereas Sir Thomas Phillips, knight, and Dudley Phillips, his son, have surrendered unto his Majesty's hands in cause of the sum of 500*li.* sterling a pension of six shillings, eight pence sterling *per diem* which they were to hold during their lives by a grant from our late sovereign King James of happy memory, these are therefore to

[220] See warrant no. 298.

pray and require your lordship to make present payment unto the said Sir Thomas Phillips and Dudley Phillips, or the assigns of either of them, of the sum of 500*li.* sterling out of the rent of his Majesty's customs in this kingdom due at Our Lady Day last past [*sic*] in full satisfaction of their surrender of the said pension, provided that the payment thereof from his highness be made unto them only till the feast of the Annunciation of the Blessed Virgin Mary last past [*sic*] and from that time to cease and be determined according to the purport of his Majesty's letters unto us of the fifth of April last, a copy whereof for your better information we have herewith sent. And for so doing this shall be your lordship's sufficient warrant. Given at his Majesty's Castle of D.,[221] 21 *Julii* 1634.

To our very good lord, the Lord Mountnorris, his Majesty's vice-treasurer & receiver general of his revenues in Ireland.

307. <CAPTAIN DENNY, HIS *LIBERATE*> [23 JULY 1634]

Forasmuch as we think it fit that Captain Benjamin Denny who hath remained long in your custody upon our former directions should be now enlarged, these are therefore to require you to set him at liberty paying his fees. <This is grounded upon the certificate of the lord chancellor on the other side> And for so doing &c. Given &c. 23rd *Julii* 1634.

To Samuel Davis, esquire, constable of his Majesty's Castle of Dublin.

308. [f. 552r] <CERTIFICATE OF THE LORD CHANCELLOR ~~UPON~~ CONCERNING CAPTAIN DENNY> [22 JULY 1634]

According to your lordship's directions of this instant I have taken a recognizance of 200*li.* sterling off Captain Denny for his Majesty's use with condition that he shall from henceforth behave himself as a loyal & dutiful subject to his Majesty & that he shall not serve any foreign prince or state without special licence from his Majesty, dated this 22nd of July 1634.

Adam Loftus, chancellor.

309. <WARRANT FOR MR FITZGERALD'S APPEARANCE> [24 JULY 1634]

Wentworth

These are to will and require you forthwith to make your personal & undelayed appearance before us and at your coming we shall give you to understand the cause of this your being sent for; whereof you may not fail. Given &c. 24th July 1634.

To our well beloved ~~Gerald~~ Garrett FitzGerald of Dromany in the county of Waterford.

[221] Dublin.

310. [f. 552v] <WARRANT FOR A COMMISSION BETWIXT BENSON & BENSON>[222] **[26 JULY 1634]**

<this warrant was altered as in page 256>

~~By the lord deputy~~

~~Wentworth~~

~~Whereas there is a certain difference depending before us between Elizabeth Benson, widow, plaintiff, & Peter Benson, esquire, concerning a certain assurance in land & the laying out of 400*li.* sterling in money towards the buying of a lease, & the same to be directed unto the said lord keeper of Drogheda, estated wholly upon the plaintiff upon her intermarriage with William Benson, deceased, son unto the said defendant, <*vide* third book of entries page 191> now inasmuch as the truth cannot well appear therein, unless witnesses be examined upon oath and that both parties have desired & agreed unto it that a commission should issue to that purpose unto the right reverend father in God, John, lord bishop of Derry, these are therefore to pray & require your lordship forthwith to cause a commission to issue to that purpose & the same to be directed unto the said lord bishop of Derry (as a commissioner indifferently chosen by both parties[)], thereby authorizing his lordship to examine upon oath all and every such witnesses as shall be produced by either party concerning this matter and upon such interrogatories as either party shall present & exhibit. The said commission to be returnable with all convenient speed & at the furthest by the beginning of the next Michaelmas term, provided the plaintiff do give the defendant 15 days notice of the time & place of the execution of the said commission. And for so doing this shall be your lordship's sufficient warrant. Given &c. 26 *Julii* 1634.~~

~~To our very good lord, the lord chancellor.~~

311. [f. 553r] <WARRANT FOR HUNT & FRANCIS TO SEARCH A SPANISH SHIP WHICH WAS BOUND FROM GALWAY TO THE RIVER OF KILMARR> **[N.D.]**

By the lord deputy

Whereas we are credibly informed that there lately arrived in the port of Galway a Spanish ship freighted thither with wine and other merchandizes by some merchants belonging to the said port who have dealt very fraudulently with his Majesty and the farmers of his customs upon landing their said goods, and that upon the reloading of the said ship back again the said merchants and others have also fraudulently conveyed & laden ~~divers~~ aboard divers prohibited goods and other merchandizes of great value before entry made thereof with his Majesty's officers of the customs, or any custom paid for the same as they ought to have done, which by the laws of this his Majesty's realm are become [ ] ^forfeited^ as also the ship wherein the said goods are laden & the laders thereof, together with their abettors, are to be accounted as felons which abuses & wrongs we conceive to be unsufferable and do not only tend to the disabling [of] his Majesty's farmers of his customs in paying their great rent (as is alleged), but also very prejudicial to the commonwealth by carrying away such prohibited ~~goods~~

222 See warrant no. 326 for amended version.

^commodities^ into foreign parts that are most useful here in his Majesty's kingdom. And whereas we are further given to understand that after the said prohibited goods & other merchandizes were laden aboard as aforesaid that the said ship departed the said harbour of Galway whereby the[y] could not be made stay of there, and is from thence bound for the river or harbour of Kilmarr there to be taken in others lading, these are therefore to will & require you & every of you to take notice that Edmond Hunt & Richard Francis, gent, are specially employed to search & examine the said Spanish ship whereby to find out the truth & that you from time to time, as often as need shall require, be aiding and assisting unto them or any of them or to any other when they shall ^have cause to^ employ; and also to be aiding & assisting to them in providing of men & boats for the better furthering of that service they paying them reasonable wages for their pains as also ^for the^ taking ashore of the sails, seizing of the said ship & goods if occasion shall so require; and likewise [f. 553v] for the apprehending & making stay of all such persons as the said Hunt or Francis shall inform you fitting to be made stay ~~of all such persons~~ and them to cause to be kept in safe custody until you shall receive our further order therein. All which we require you & every of you to observe & perform carefully as you will answer the contrary at your uttermost perils.

To all mayors, ~~sovereigns~~ sufferances, justices of the peace, vice admirals, captains of his Majesty's ships, the sheriffs of the counties of Cork & Kerry, & to all constables & other his Majesty's officers & loving subjects whatsoever.

312. WARRANT TO THE SHERIFF OF CORK TO KEEP MILNER IN POSSESSION> [N.D.]

~~By the lord deputy~~

~~Whereas the rectory & vicarage of Rincorren in the diocese of Cork were lately void & in his Majesty's gift by the minority of Peter *alias* Pierce Gould, the same being unjustly & illegally held.~~

313. <EARL OF THOMOND, MASTER OF THE GAME, *PRO COMITATU* CLARE> [30 JULY 1634]

A warrant for the earl of Thomond to be Master of Game in the county of Clare, dated 30th *Julii* 1634. This warrant agreeeth *verbatim* with Bannister's, page 216.

To our very good lord, the earl of Thomond.

314. [f. 554r] <PATRICK DUNCAN> [30 JULY 1634]

A warrant for a fiant containing a prosecution unto Patrick Duncan, clerk, of the <manicule> vicarage of Donamore in the diocese of Dromore void by lapse, directing his admission to the judge of the faculties, dated 30th *Julii* 1634.

To Sir William Ussher & Paul Davies.

315. <NATHANIEL BUCKLEY> [29 JULY 1634]

A warrant for a fiant containing a presentation of Nathaniel Buckley, clerk, unto the <manicule> vicarage of Temple Drummen ^*alias* Templedrome^ & Kilmore in the diocese of Aghado[e] void by lapse, directing his admission to the judge of the faculties & inserting therein a clause of union of the said vicarages unto the vicarage of Killadysert in the diocese of Killaloe (& already held by the said Buckley) *pro hac vice tantum*, dated 29th *Julii* 1634.

To Sir William Ussher & Paul Davies

316. <EARL OF THOMOND> [29 JULY 1634]

Warrant for the earl of Thomond to transport at Youghal one cast of falcons & a tassel-gentle, dated 29th *Julii* 1634.

317. [f. 554v] <WARRANT FOR FLORENCE McCARTY UNTO THE RECTORY & VICARAGE OF KILMOREMARON> [29 JULY 1634]

A warrant for a fiant containing a presentation from his Majesty of Florence McCarty, clerk, unto the rectory & vicarage of Kilmoremaron in the diocese of Down void by lapse, <manicule> directing his admission to the judge of the faculties & inserting therein a clause of union *pro hac vice tantum*, dated 29th *Julii* 1634.

To Sir William Ussher & Paul Davies.

318. <WARRANT TO THE SHERIFFS OF THE COUNTY OF CORK TO GIVE MR MILNER POSSESSION>[223] [29 JULY 1634]

Whereas the rectory & vicarage of Rincorran in the diocese of Cork were lately void & in his Majesty's gift by the minority of Peter, *alias* Pierce Gould, the same being unjustly & illegally held by the present pretended incumbent, one Richard Owen, we in the maintenance & preservation of his Majesty's right have thought fit to confer the same upon Robert Milner, clerk. Now inasmuch as the said Milner having past [*sic*] the said livings under the great seal complaineth that the said Owen doth disturb him in the quiet possession thereof, we therefore upon his humble suit have thought fit & do accordingly hereby require & authorize you to enter into the said rectory & vicarage & the quiet & peaceable [f. 555r] possession thereof to deliver unto the said Milner & him to keep & maintain therein from time to time hereafter until he be thereout evicted by due course of law. Whereof you are not to fail. And for so doing &c. Given &c. 29th *Julii* 1634.

To our well beloved, the high sheriff of the county of Cork now being & to the sheriff of the said county that from time to time shall be.

[223] See warrant no. 299.

319. <JOHN McMACKON McNEMARA, HIS *LIBERATE*>[224] [29 JULY 1634]

Whereas upon the complaint of one Teige Entaramon we commited unto your custody the body of John McMackon McNemara, these are to require you to set the said McNemara at liberty, paying his fees provided there be no other cause for his restraint. And for so doing this shall be your warrant. Given &c. 29th *Julii* 1634. <*vide* the bundles for McNemara's petition & proceedings>

To our trusty & well beloved John Dobb, esquire, Marshal of the Four Courts.

320. [f. 555v] <WARRANT FOR A PARTICULAR FOR FRANCIS[225] &C. FOR THE LORD IKERIN[226]> [29 JULY 1634]

By the lord deputy

Wentworth

Whereas our very good lord, the Lord Viscount Ikerin, became an humble suitor unto us that we would be pleased to grant unto him the benefit of certain fairs & markets to be kept yearly within the manor of Lismalin and Tullogh, we thereupon did require the next going judges of assize for the county of Tipperary to cause it to be enquired whether the granting thereof would not be prejudicial to any the neighbouring fairs or markets, which being enquired of by the grand jury it was by them returned that if 2 fairs were yearly kept within the said manor of Lismalin, *vizt.* one upon the 23rd day of June & the next day following, & the other upon the 24th day of July & the next day following with a market overt to be kept there likewise on every Monday weekly, and that if 2 other yearly fairs were kept in the manor of Tullogh, the one upon the sixteenth of September & the next day following, & the other upon the 4th day of August & the next day following with a market overt there on Thursday weekly, there would ensue thereof neither inconvenience, damage or prejudice to any other person or persons having either late or ancient of fairs or markets. We therefore have thought fit and do accordingly hereby will & require you forthwith to draw up a particular of the said fairs & markets reserving thereout the sum of 4*li.* sterling rent yearly unto his Majesty. And the same fairly engrossed in parchment under your hands to send unto us to be further passed as appertainieth. Given &c. 29th *Julii* 1634.

To our trusty & well beloved, his Majesty's surveyor & auditor general & to either of them.

Thomas Littell.

321. [f. 556r] <EDWARD TRENCHER> [3 JULY 1634]

A warrant for Edward Trencher to transport 2 horses or saddle nags at the port of Youghal, dated 3 *Julii* 1634.

224 See warrant no. 228.

225 No surname is provided.

226 Piers Butler (d. 1660?), 1st Viscount Ikerrin, confederate commander (see *DIB*).

322. [WILLIAM LEWELLIN] 1 AUGUST 1634]

A warrant for William Lewellin to transport for England 4 horses or saddle nags at the port of Youghal, dated 1 *Augusti* 1634.

323. <WARRANT FOR A FIANT FOR JOHN BINNS, CLERK[227]> [1 AUGUST 1634]

<manicule> Containing a presentation from his Majesty of John Binns to the vicarages of Cahirdown and Bothan *alias* Buttivant in the diocese of Cloyne void by lapse, directing his admission to the judge of the faculties & inserting a clause of union of the said vicarages unto other 2 vicarages now held by the said Binns called Wallestown & Corkbeg in the same diocese & so to remain united *pro hac vice tantum*, dated 1 August 1634.

To the clerks of the Council.

324. <WARRANT FOR MR CLAUDE HAMILTON[228] TO BE LORD HAMILTON &C.> [2 AUGUST 1634]

Wentworth

Whereas upon the voluntary surrender made into his Majesty's hands by our very good lord, James now earl of Abercorn,[229] in the realm of Scotland of the style, title, degree, dignity & honour of Lord Hamilton, baron of Strabane, which he the said earl held in this kingdom (& which was passed unto him by letters patents from ~~his Majesty~~ our late sovereign King James of happy memory), his highness hath been pleased to require that a commission should issue forth from hence unto our trusty & well beloved Sir William Jones & Sir Robert Barkley, knights, two of the justices of his Majesty's Court of Chief Place in England, authorizing them ~~authorizing him~~ or either of them to take the acknowledgment of **[f. 556v]** a fine (according to a statute of the 4th year of King Henry the seventh in that case provided) from the said James, earl of Abercorn, of the said state, degree, dignity, style, title, name & honour of Lord Hamilton, baron of Strabane, to his Majesty, his heirs & successors. And forasmuch as it appeareth by an order of his Majesty's High Court of Chancery here of the third of February 1633[/4] that the said commission hath issued & is executed accordingly and that the same (as is usual) hath been recorded in the Court of Common Pleas here, the said former letters patents cancelled and a *vacat* entered upon the enrolment thereof, these are therefore to will & require you forthwith to draw up a fiant in due form of law containing a grant from his Majesty, his heirs & successors, unto Claude Hamilton, ~~his heirs & successors~~ esquire, brother unto the said earl of Abercorn of the name, style, title, degree, dignity and honour of Lord Hamilton, baron of Strabane, in the county of Tyrone in the province of Ulster, to have, hold, possess & enjoy the said name, title, dignity, style & honour of Lord Hamilton, baron of Strabane, unto

[227] John Binns, prebandary of Cloyne and treasurer of Cloyne in 1641 (see Cotton, *Fasti*).

[228] Claud Hamilton (*c.* 1606–1638), 2nd Lord Hamilton.

[229] James Hamilton (*c.* 1604–*c.* 1670), 2nd earl of Abercorn.

him the said Claude Hamilton & to the heirs males of his body lawfully begotten & to be begotten. And for want of such issue to the heirs males of the body of James, late earl of Abercorn (father unto the now earl of Abercorn and the said Claude Hamilton) lawfully begotten and that the said Claude Hamilton & the heirs males of his body lawfully begotten may have & enjoy place & voice in parliament & elsewhere according to his now creation, and for want of such issue then the heirs males of the body of the said James, late earl of Abercorn, lawfully begotten are to have & enjoy the said honour & title of Lord Hamilton, baron of Strabane, together with the same place [&] voice in parliament & elsewhere & all other rights, privileges, pre-eminences & benefits in as ample & beneficial manner as the said James, now earl of Abercorn, had or ought to have by virtue of the said recited letters patents & any other baron of this realm hath or ought to have & enjoy. And the same fairly engrossed in parchment under your hand to send unto us [**f. 557r**] to be further passed as appertaineth according to the intent & meaning of his Majesty's letters unto us of the 7th of May in the 9th year of his reign, a copy whereof we have herewith sent you; for doing whereof this shall be your warrant. Given &c. 2 August 1634.

To our well beloved, his Majesty's attorney & solicitor general, or either of them.

325. <WARRANT FOR A COMMISSION *INTER* FOX & WATERS> **[2 AUGUST 1634]**

Wentworth

Whereas there is a difference depending before us between Nicholas Fox, gent, ~~and~~ agent unto Sir Richard Fleetwood, baronet, plaintiff, and one Richard Waters, gent, defendant, wherein amongst other misdemeanours it is alleged by the plaintiff that the defendant by himself & his tenants hath ploughed up, digged [*sic*] & sown the churchyard of Mocrony with corn & potatoes, which by the said defendant is denied; we therefore, for the better finding out of the truth & by the consent of both parties, have thought fit that a commission should issue forth for the examination of witnesses in that behalf. <*vide* 3 book of entries page 184 & 331> And accordingly we pray and require your lordship to cause a commission to issue forthwith under the great seal and to be directed unto our trusty & well beloved Sir William Fenton, knight, & John Tobin Fitz Edmond, gent, Sir Arthur,[230] knight, & Edward Byam, clerk, authorizing them or any 2 of them to examine upon oath all and every such witnesses as shall be pardoned to be examined concerning the bounds of the said church or chapel yard, how far the consecrated ground did extend, & how the parishioners used to be buried, and whether the defendant, Waters, or any of his servants or tenants or any other by his command, consent or approbation have digged [*sic*] or ploughed up any part thereof or converted the ~~same~~ corn fruits or roots growing there to his or their use, and also if he or they & if any who they were that have invaded the said glebe-land belonging to the said church, and also upon ^such^ other interr[ogations] as either party [**f. 557v**] shall present & exhi[b]it. The said commissioners to be returnable with all convenient speed and at the furthest by the middle of the next

[230] No surname is provided.

Michaelmas term, provided that the plaintiff do give the defendant 15 days notice of the execution thereof. And for so doing &c. Given &c. 2 August 1634.

To our very good lord, the lord chancellor.

326. <WARRANT FOR A COMMISSION *INTER* BENSON & BENSON> [2 AUGUST 1634]

Wentworth
Whereas there are certain differences depending before us between Elizabeth Benson, widow, plaintiff, & Peter Benson, esquire, defendant, concerning a certain assurance in land & the laying out of 400*li.* sterling in money towards the buying of a lease, and the same to be estated wholly upon the plaintiff upon her intermarriage with William Benson, deceased, son to the said defendant, & other matters contained in the said Elizabeth Benson's petition, <*vide* 3 book of entries page 291> now inasmuch as the truth cannot well appear therein unless witnesses be examined upon oath, & for that both parties have desired that a commission should issue to that purpose unto the right reverend father in God, John, lord bishop of Derry. These are therefore to pray and require your lordship forthwith to cause a commission to issue to that purpose and the same to be directed unto the said lord bishop of Derry (who is indifferently chosen by both parties to hear, end & fully to determine the said differences before us depending), thereby authorizing his lordship to examine upon oath all & every such witnesses as shall be produced by either party concerning the said differences for the better informing his lordship of the true state of the cause, provided that the said cause be examined, heard & determined by his lordship before Michaelmas term next. And that the plaintiff do give the defendant ten days warning of the time and place of execution of the said commission. And for so doing this shall be your lordships warrant. Given &c. the 2 of August 1634.

To our very good lord, the lord chancellor.

327. [f. 558r] <MR GRAINE,[231] HIS WARRANT FOR 3 VICARAGES> [2 AUGUST 1634]

A warrant for a fiant containing a presentation from his Majesty of Edward Graine, clerk, to the <manicule> vicarages of Kilcroghan, Kilcreddan & Templenoe in the diocese of Ardfert & Aghado[e] void by lapse, directing his admission to the judge of the faculties & inserting therein a clause of union *pro hac vice tantum*, dated 2 *Augusti* 1634..

328. <THOMAS CHUTE> [2 AUGUST 1634]

<mannicule>A warrant containing a presentation from his Majesty unto Thomas Chute to the vicarage of Ballinaheglish in the diocese of Ardfert void by lapse, directing his admission to the judge of the faculties and inserting therein a clause of union *pro hac vice tantum* of the said vicarages of Ballinaheglish unto the chancellorship of the cathedral church of St Brendan's & the vicarage of Kilnaughtin in the said diocese which the said Chute already houldeth, dated 2 *Augusti* 1634.

231 Edward Graine (or Grayne).

329. [f. 558v] <WARRANT FOR A COMMISSION TO ENQUIRE CONCERNING THE LORD TREASURER'S TOMB> [4 AUGUST 1634]

By the lord deputy

Wentworth

These are to pray and require your lordship forthwith to issue a commission under the great seal and to be directed unto us, his Majesty's deputy general of Ireland, the most reverend father in God, the lord primate of Armagh, the archbishop of Dublin,[232] & to the right reverend father in God, the lord bishop of Limerick,[233] the lord bishop of Raphoe,[234] the lord bishop of Kilmore, the lord bishop of Derry, & also to our well beloved the dean[235] & chapter of St Patrick's near Dublin & to the dean[236] & chapter of Christ Church in Dublin, thereby giving unto us & them or unto any six of us, whereof we his ^said^ Majesty's deputy general to be always one full power & authority, to enquire of the fitness of the placing of a monument or tomb lately built & erected by our very good lord, the earl of Cork, in the quire of St Patrick's Church aforesaid & whether it standeth not in the place where the high altar did ~~stand~~ anciently stand, together with such other circumstances as we or any six of the ^said^ commissioners, whereof ourself to be one, shall think fit to inform ourselves of concerning the same according to the purport of his Majesty's letters unto us, his Majesty's said deputy general of the 16th of April last, a copy whereof for your better information we have herewith sent you. The said commissioners to be returnable with all convenient speed and at the furthest by the middle of the next Michaelmas term. And for so doing this shall be your warrant. Given &c. 4 August 1634.

To our very good lord, the lord chancellor

330. <WARRANT FOR THE EARL OF ORMOND TO BE MASTER OF THE GAME IN *COMITATU* TIPPERARY> [12 JULY 1634]

This warrant was made by Mr Bannister's page 216 [*sic*] & dat[ed] 12 July 1634.

331. [f. 559r] <~~WARRANT~~ LICENCE OF ABSENCE FOR THE LORD BISHOP OF DROMORE> [4 AUGUST 1634]

By the lord deputy general of Ireland

Wentworth

Whereas upon humble suit made unto us by the right reverend father in God, Theophilus, lord bishop of Dromore, we have been pleased to licence his lordship to make his repair into England and there to remain during the space of six months next ensuing the date hereof. These are therefore to will & require you & every, his

[232] Lancelot Bulkeley (1568/9–50), archbishop of Dublin (see *DIB*).

[233] Francis Gough (d. 1634), bishop of Limerick.

[234] William Bedell (1571–1642), bishop of Kilmore and scholar (see *DIB*).

[235] Benjamin Culme (Cullen), dean of St. Patick's cathedral (see Cotton, *Fasti*).

[236] Henry Tilson (d. 1655), chaplain of lord deputy Wentworth, dean of Christ Church cathedral, later bishop of Elphin.

Majesty's officers, ministers & loving subjects whatsoever, not only to take due notice thereof but also to afford him the full benefit of this our licence without any loss or prejudice to be incurred by him by reason of his absence during the time aforesaid, provided that his lordship before his departure do leave his proxy for the next session of parliament with some such person as his lordship shall think fit and is capable thereof. Given at his Majesty's Castle of Dublin the 4th of August 1634.

Thomas Littell.

332. <McVICKON'S *LIBERATE*>[237] [4 AUGUST 1634]

Wentworth
Whereas upon the complaint of one John Bourke we formerly committed unto your custody the body of John McVickon McNemara whereby you were required to keep him in restraint until he had answered an information exhi[b]ited against him by the said Bourke in the Court of Castle Chamber & with all entered good security to be present at the hearing & then not to depart without special licence. Now forasmuch as the said John McVickon McNemara hath performed the contents of our said directions as appear by the annexed certificate from the clerks of the said Court of Castle Chamber, we think it fit and so do require that upon sight hereof you enlarge & set him the said McNemara at liberty, paying his fees (if ~~in case~~ there be no other ~~place~~ ^cause^ for his detention); whereof you may not fail. And for so doing &c. Given &c. 4 *Augusti* 1634.

To our Marshall of the 4 Courts.

<This was grounded in the certificates overleaf>

333. [f. 559v] <JOHN BOURK, PLAINTIFF, JOHN McNEMARA & *AL.*, DEFENDANTS>[238] 25 JUNE 1634

The said John McNemara having stood out the process of this court unto a commission of rebellion & being now in the custody of the marshal of this court upon the humble motion of Mr Alexander,[239] it is ordered that the said John, having appeared & answered the plaintiff's bill being examined on personal interrogatories entered into bonds with good sureties to appear in this court at the hearing of this cause & paid the costs of attachments, shall be discharged of his contempt.

William Stoughton, *deputatus clericus Curia Camerae Castelli.*[240]

2 August 1634
According [to] the order above written the said John [Mc]Mackon McNemara hath put in 2 several answers to both the plaintiff's bills in this court: the one of the said answers was exhibited on the 30th of July last, the other was exhibited this present

[237] See warrants no. 78, 151 and 250.
[238] See warrant no. 319.
[239] Jerome Alexander (1590–1670), judge and administrator (see *DIB*).
[240] William Stougton (or Stoughton), deputy clerk of Dublin Castle.

day, & no interrogatories are as yet exhibited against him in either of the said causes which interrogatories the plaintiff hath 4 days exclusive to enter after the coming in of the said answers respectively. I have also taken bonds of the said John [Mc]Mackon with sureties *vizt.* Tirlagh Brien of Tullamore in the county of Clare, esquire, & Brian O'Brien of Pallisbeg in the county of Limerick, gent, to appear at the hearing of the said causes. I have likewise received the costs of attachments issued against the said John [Mc]Mackon & the rest.

William Stoughton, *deputatus clericus Curia Camerae Castelli.*

334. [f. 560r] <PETER HILL'S *LIBERATE*> [5 AUGUST 1634]

Wentworth

Whereas you have in your custody the body of Peter Hill committed unto you upon our former ~~pet~~ directions, these are to require you to enlarge & set him at liberty, paying his fees (if there be no other cause for his detention[)]. And for so doing &c. dat[ed] 5 August 1634.

<grounded upon a certificate of Conn Maguire's in the bundles>

To any of his Majesty's pursuivants.

Thomas Littell

335. <WARRANT FOR A COMMISSION BETWEEN THE BISHOP OF WATERFORD & BAYNTON> [7 AUGUST 1634]

Wentworth

Whereas the right reverend father in God, Michael, lord bishop of Lismore and Waterford,[241] together with one Edward Baynton, gent, have jointly petitioned unto us setting forth that he the said Baynton, holding as from the see of Lismore by a long lease the towns and lands of Donoghmore and Graignebrenagh in the county of Tipperary being part of the temporalities of the said diocese of Lismore, is now willing to surrender up the same unto the said lord bishop's hands upon condition to have a new lease confirmed by the said lord bishop; <*vide* in the bundles for petition with the affidavits> and therefore they jointly besought us to give way thereunto and to give directions for a commission to issue to enquire of the yearly value of the premises, whose request therein we have thought fit to grant. And therefore we do hereby pray and require your lordship to issue forth a commission under the great seal to that purpose and to be directed unto our well beloved John Gwyn, clerk, Richard Busher, clerk, and George Butler, gent, authorizing ^them^ or any two of them to examine upon oath all such witnesses as shall be produced by ~~all~~ either party before them concerning the premises, and with all to view the same themselves and ^to^ return unto us what they find. [f. 560v] The said commission to be returnable with all convenient speed and at the furthest by the middle of the next Michaelmas term, provided that each party have fifteen days notice of the time & place of the execution

[241] Michael Boyle (d. 1635), bishop of Waterford and Lismore.

of the said commission. And for so doing this shall be your warrant. Given at his Majesty's Castle of Dublin the seventh of August 1634.

To our very good lord, the lord chancellor.

Thomas Littell

336. <MR LEADBITTER'S WARRANT OF POSSESSION>[242] [7 AUGUST 1634]

Whereas the vicarage of Castletown in the diocese of Cloyne was lately void & in his Majesty's gift by lapse, the same being unjustly held by our very good lord, the Lord Viscount Roch,[243] under pretence of a lease made by the former incumbent, one John Binns, who, as appeareth by his affidavit, did farm the same to his lordship which by the said Binns's resignation is now become void. <*vide* ~~the former book~~ church affairs for the petition of George Leadbitter with the affidavit ~~enclosed~~> We, in maintenance and preservation of his Majesty's right, have thought fit to confer the same upon George Leadbitter, clerk, now inasmuch as the said Ledbitter, having passed the said vicarage by patent under the great seal, complaineth (and so made it to appe[ar] by affidavit[)] that the said Lord Roch doth disturb him in the quiet possession thereof. We therefore upon his humble suit have thought fit and do accordingly hereby require & authorize you to enter into the said vicarage and the quiet & peaceable possession thereof to deliver unto the said Ledbitter and him to keep and maintain therein from time to time hereafter until he be thereout evicted by due course of law; whereof you may not fail. And for so doing this shall be your warrant. Given at &c. the seventh of August 1634.

To our well beloved, the high sheriff of the county of Cork now being & to the sheriff of the said county that from time to time shall be.

Thomas Littell

337. [f. 561r] <SIR THOMAS STANDISH'S WARRANT TO TRANSPORT HORSES> [8 AUGUST 1634]

Whereas Sir Thomas Standish, knight, hath employed his servant into England upon the dispatch of some special affairs and for such as he made suit unto us ~~and for such~~ that we would please to licence him to transport one horse or gelding for his said servant's use &c., according [to] the usual form &c. from the port of Youghal.

338. <A BEGGING PASS FOR COOK> [8 AUGUST 1634]

According to Lilly's warrant, page 228,[244] for the ~~city of Dublin &~~ counties of Cavan & Armagh (for the causes in the petition mentioned which is in the bundles), dat[ed] 8 of August 1634 ~~for~~ to continue for 6 months from the date.

[242] See warrant no. 277.

[243] David Roch (Roche) (*c.* 1573–1635), 2nd Viscount Fermoy (see *DIB*).

[244] See warrant no. 285.

339. <WARRANT FOR A CARTULER FOR BOYD> [12 AUGUST 1634]

By the lord deputy

Wentworth

Whereas his Majesty by his gracious letters of the 20th of July in the 2nd year of his reign hath been pleased to require that a grant should be made in due form of law unto Robert Boyd, gent, of all such lands, tenements & hereditaments as should be found by inquisition to have been purchased by his father David Boyd, deceased, from Sir Hugh Montgomery, knight, now Lord Montgomery, viscount of the Ards,[245] and inasmuch as an inquisition hath been taken accordingly at Down in the county of Down on the 4th day of September 1633 by our very good lord, the lord chief baron, and Sir Samuel Mayart, knight, one of the justices of his Majesty's Court of Common Pleas, by virtue of his Majesty's commission to them & others under the great seal ~~to them~~ directed, these are therefore to will and require you (having perused and advisedly considered) as well of his **[f. 561v]** Majesty's letters [(]a copy whereof we have herewith sent you as also the said inquisition) to draw up a particular of the said lands by the said office or inquisition found for the said Robert Boyd to be ~~him~~ by him held of his Majesty as formerly, and by such tenures & ancient since proportionably as his lordship held the same & according to the purport of his Majesty's said letters unto us. And also thereby pressing the said Lord Montgomery's interest to the premises according to his Majesty's pleasure signified also from Sir Henry Holcroft, knight,[246] then secretary to his Majesty for Irish affairs, bearing date the 17th of October 1626 and directed to the late Lord Falkland being the then lord deputy here, a copy whereof we herewith likewise send you; and also yielding unto his Majesty, his heirs & successors, 40*s.* sterling of English money of increase of rent yearly. And the same fairly engrossed ~~under~~ in parchment under your hand to send unto us to be further passed as appertaineth; for doing whereof &c. Given &c. 12 August 1634. <*vide* first book of entries, page 528 ~~for~~ &c.>

To our trusty & well beloved, his Majesty's surveyor & auditor general & to either of them.

The letter following from Sir Henry Holcroft mentioned in the warrant above.

My noble lord, whereas an information was made here on the behalf of one Mr Robert Boyd that Colonel David Boyd, his father, did in his lifetime purchase for a valuable consideration ~~of~~ ^in^ money of the Lord Viscount Montgomery certain lands in Ulster which upp [*sic*] office found of the said Colonel Boyd not denization ought to escheat unto his Majesty [*sic*]. It pleased his Majesty being thereunto moved by order of the lord of the Council to direct his letters to your ~~letter~~ lordship of the 20th of July last for the issuing of a commission to find what lands were so purchased by Colonel Boyd of the Lord Montgomery, **[f. 562r]** the said Boyd being no denizon and upon finding his Majesty's title for his not denization to grant the same in Mr Robert Boyd & his heirs to be holden of his Majesty by the same tenures, rents & servic[e]s proportionably as the same were formerly held by the Lord Montgomery with an increase of 40*s.* rent to the king, but now his Majesty hath been informed on the part of the said lord viscount

245 Hugh Montgomery, 3rd Viscount Montgomery of the Ards and 1st earl of Mount-Alexander (see *DIB*).

246 Henry Holcroft (*fl.* 1600–50), king's secretary for Irish affairs (see *DIB*).

that the said lands are held of him & were by him granted to Colonel Boyd in fee farm and lest they should now pass as is warranted by the letter abovementioned it would be very prejudicial to his lordship & extinguish his seigniory in the said lands & his ~~ancient~~ ^rents &^ duties payable to him for the same. ~~his~~ His Majesty, being herein moved, ~~he~~ hath commanded me to let your lordship know that his intention in the granting of the said letter to Mr Boyd was but to put him in as good case as if Colonel Boyd & his father had died a free denizon of that kingdom, not purposing to extinguish or prejudice the interest of the Lord Montgomery in his seigniory of the said lands held of him nor in his rents & all other duties. And therefore it is his pleasure that in the passing of any grant to Mr Boyd by virtue of the said letter due care be taken therein for preventing any prejudice that may come to the said viscount thereby. And even so I kiss your lordship's hands, resting your most humble servant.

Subscribed Henry Holcroft.

<Westminster, 17 Octob[e]r 1626>

To the right honourable his very noble lord, the Lord Viscount Falkland, lord deputy of Ireland.

340. [f. 562v] <WARRANT FOR A RECTORY FOR MR FERCKER> [13 AUGUST 1634]

<manicule> Warrant containing a prosecution of George Fercker, clerk, to the rectory of Cleenish in the diocese of Clogher void by lapse or otherwise, directing his admission to the judge of the faculties, dated 13th *Augusti* 1634.

To Sir William Ussher, &c.

341. <A WARRANT FOR A COMMISSION ABOUT THE CONCEALED LANDS OF ST MARY'S IN LIMERICK> [13 AUGUST 1634]

By the lord deputy

Wentworth

Whereas Robert Gough, chanter, Hugh Gough, chancellor, and Thomas Lodge, treasurer of the cathedral church of St Mary the Virgin in Limerick, have petitioned unto us setting forth that there are ~~certain~~ sundry parcels of glebe lands concealed & kept away wrongfully for these many years from their several dignities by divers persons <*vide* petition in the bundles> who have no manner of right or interest therein for the better finding out and recovery, whereof they humbly besought us to give our directions for issuing forth of a commission under the great seal to examine & ~~com~~ enquire of the same, whose request therein we have thought fit to grant and accordingly we do hereby pray and require your lordship to cause a commission to issue by that purpose and to be directed unto our well beloved George Courtney, Captain Charles Price & Thomas Searle, esquire, giving them or any two of them full power and authority to examine upon oath all such witnesses as the said petitioners shall produce and upon such inter[rogatorie]s as they shall present & exhibit concerning the said glebe lands so wrongfully withheld from the church. The said commission to be returnable with all convenient speed & at the furthest by the first return of the next Michaelmas term, provided the petitioners do give ~~the~~ 15 days notice of the execution of the said commission unto all & every such person or persons who are interested [**f. 563r**] in the matter and who hold any part of the premises so to be enquired after; for doing whereof this shall be your lordship's sufficient warrant. Given &c. 13 August 1634.

To our very good lord, the lord chancellor.

342. <WARRANT FOR THE LORD ARCHBISHOP OF CASHEL[247] TO HOLD 2 RECT[ORIES] *IN COMMENDAM*> [13 AUGUST 1634]

By the lord deputy

Wentworth

~~Whereas~~ These are to will & require you forthwith to draw up a fiant in due form of law containing his Majesty's presentation of the most reverend father in God, the lord archbishop of Cashel &c., to the rectories of Slewlen *alias* Gostila & Bowcola *alias* Gallen in the diocese of Achonry being void & in his Majesty's gift *pleno jure seu alio quocunque modo*, to have, hold, possess & enjoy the said rectories unto his lordship by way of *commendam* (whereunto he is sufficiently enabled & qualified by virtue of <manicule> his Majesty's letters patents under the great seal of this kingdom and bearing date the first day of April in the 6th year of his Majesty's reign), together with all rights, duties, members, ^profits^ and appurtenances whatsoever thereunto belonging & in anywise appertaining, & in as large, ample & beneficial manner as any other incumbent or incumbents formerly held & enjoyed or of right ought to have held & enjoyed the same, directing his admission to the judge of the faculties. And the same ~~fir~~ fairly engrossed in parchment under your hand to send unto us to be further passed as appertaineth; for doing &c. Given &c. 13th of August 1634.

To Sir William Ussher &c.

343. [f. 563v] <WARRANT TO PERMIT THE EARL OF ARUNDEL'S[248] HORSES TO BE TRANSPORTED> [15 AUGUST 1634]

By the lord deputy

Wentworth

Whereas the right honourable our very good lord the earl of Arundel is to make his repair into England and to have horses carried over for his lordship's use & his ~~lordship's~~ followers and servants, these are therefore to will and require you the officers of the ~~of~~ customs in that port where this our licence shall be presented & his lordship shall take shipping to permit & suffer his lordship's said horses, nags & geldings to be put aboard & transported for England as aforesaid. And &c., dated 15 *Augusti* 1634.

247 Archibald Hamilton (1580?–1659?), archbishop of Cashel (see *DIB*).

248 Thomas Howard (1585–1646), 14th earl of Arundel, 4th earl of Surrey, and 1st earl of Norfolk (see *ODNB*).

344. <GERRARD'S WARRANT TO TRANSPORT HORSES> [16 AUGUST 1634]

Warrant for Thomas Gerrald [sic] to transport for England 3 horses or saddle nags, dated 16th August 1634.

345. <THOMAS ASHTON> [16 AUGUST 1634]

A warrant *ut supra* for Thomas Ashton to transport 4 nags, dated *ut supra.*

346. <EDWARD BUTLER> [16 AUGUST 1634]

The like to Edward Butler for 3 geldings or saddle nags, dated *ut supra.*

To the Port of Waterford.

347. [WARRANT PROHIBITING THE TRANSPORTATION OF WOOL, FLAX, LINEN, ETC.] [12 AUGUST 1634]

These are to will & require you & every of you that you from henceforth take especial notice & care <from Sir G.R.[249]> that no wool, flax, linen, yarn, woollen yarn, sheep-fell, red dear-fell, tallow dear-fell, unwrought beef, butter & tallow, tallow wrought in candles or otherwise, wax & wax wrought in candles or otherwise, be henceforth shipped or put on board any barque or boat to be transported out of your port of Strangford, or out of any port creek, haven, or member to the same belonging or appertaining, upon pain of incurring the penalties & [**f. 564r**] punishments mentioned in the several statutes prohibiting the transportation thereof. And likewise that you cause to be levied all prisages & all impositions, payments & duties expressed in the new book of rates established by grant to the now farmers of the customs for wines, oil & salt inwards, and for as many native commodities outwards as are not prohibited by this our present warrant & direction (*vizt.*) hides into foreign parts, cows, rugs, herring, pillchards &c. And lastly that you receive & levy wholly to the use of the said farmers of the customs all such payments, duties & impositions as shall be due & payable for all goods & merchandizes whatsoever imported or exported by any freeman of the cities of Dublin & Waterford & of the towns of Drogheda & Galway & dwelling in any [of] the said cities & towns, together with all petty customs due by merchants, strangers, or aliens; whereof &c. Given &c. 12th *Augusti* 1634.

To our well beloved, the customer, surveyor, comptroller & searcher in the ports of Strangford & the creeks & members thereof, and to the collectors for the farmers there & every of them.

[249] Sir George Radcliffe (1593–1657), lawyer and politician (see *DIB*).

348. [f. 564v] <WARRANT FOR A COMMISSION ^INTO ENGLAND^ BETWEEN JUNS & BEVANS> **[18 AUGUST 1634]**

By the lord deputy

Wentworth

Whereas there is a difference ~~defference~~ depending before us between Alexander Juns, gent, & his wife, plaintiff, & Maude Bevans, ~~deceased~~ defendant, concerning the rectory of Donaghmore in the county of Meath & certain other goods & estate of Sir Robert Jacobs, knight,[250] deceased, pretended by the plaintiff to have come to the hands of Edward Bevans, deceased, husband to the defendant, and for which (as he ought) he hath not accounted, all which is denied by the said defendant for the better finding out ~~of the better finding out~~ of the truth. Wherein we think fit & do accordingly hereby pray & require your lordship forthwith to issue a commission under the great seal directed to our well beloved Sir William Slingsby, knight, & Sir Edward Leich, knight,[251] Robert Bisse of Lincoln's Inn[252] & Peter Trevor of Gray's Inn, esquires, or any two of them, whereof one of the defendant's commissioners to be always one, to examine upon oath all such witnesses as shall be produced & upon such interr[ogatories] as shall be exhibited by either party concerning this matter. The said commissioners to be returnable with all convenient speed and at the farthest by the last return of the next ~~Michaelmas~~ Hillary term and in regard the plaintiff hath the carriage of the commissioners into England, where the same is to be executed the plaintiff is to give the defendants's commissioners 14 days ~~notice~~ warning & notice of the execution hereof. And for so doing &c., dated 18th August 1634.

To our very good lord, the lord chancellor.

349. [f. 565r] <WARRANT FOR A COMMISSION BETWEEN WISE AND BUTLER> **[18 AUGUST 1634]**

By the lord deputy

Wentworth

Whereas there is a difference depending before us between Robert Wise, esquire, plaintiff, & Richard Butler, esquire, defendant, concerning certain injuries, wrongs & abuses pretended to have been done and used by the said Butler against the said Wise upon the late election of knights of the shire for the county of Waterford, and inasmuch as the truth therein cannot well appear without the examination of witnesses upon oath, we therefore have thought fit and do accordingly hereby pray and require your lordship forthwith to issue a commission under the great seal to be directed unto John Sherlock & Thomas Wadding, esquires, Sir Peter Aylward, knight, and James Walsh, esquire, authorizing them or any 2 or more of them to examine upon oath all such witnesses as either party shall produce, & upon such interr[ogatories] as

250 Robert Jacobs (or Jacob), solictor general and commissioner of the Court of Wards (see Hughes, *Patentee officers*).

251 Edward Leich (or Leech), clerk of the Pells (see Hughes, *Patentee officers*).

252 Robert Bysse (d. 1643), lawyer and MP of Roscommon (see McGrath).

they shall exhibit concerning this matter; <*vide* third book of entries page 393 for the petition> the said commission to be returnable with all convenient speed and at the furthest by the middle of the next Michaelmas term, provided the plaintiff do give the defendant 15 days notice of the time & place of the execution thereof. And for so doing &c. Given &c. 18 August 1634.

To our very good lord, the lord chancellor.

350. <WARRANT FOR ALIENATION IN MORTMAIN OF THE CHURCH OF DERRY> [18 AUGUST 1634]

By the lord deputy

Wentworth

~~Whereas~~ These are to will and require you forthwith to draw up a fiant in due form of law containing a grant of a licence <*vide* the petition in the bundles> from his Majesty unto the society, the governor and assistant of London of the new plantation ~~of~~ in Ulster, to alien in Mortmain <manicule> unto the right reverend father in God, John, lord bishop of Derry, and his successors, in pure & [**f. 565v**] perpetual almoigne, all that fabric of a church together with a chancel, a library, vestry house & tower with the appurtenances, & also a churchyard & place of burial lying about it within the city of Londonderry to the end the same may be consecrated & dedicated to the service of God according to the rites & ceremonies in such cases accustomed. The said church to serve as well for a cathedral church as also a parochial for the use of the inhabitants of the said city & of the parish of Derry *alias* Templemore. And the same fairly engrossed &c.; for doing &c. Given &c. 18 August 1634.

To our trusty & well beloved, his Majesty's attorney & solicitor general & either of them.

351. <WARRANT FOR A FIANT FOR MR BOYD>[253] [18 AUGUST 1634]

By the lord deputy

~~Wentworth~~ Wentworth

These are to will and require you forthwith upon sight hereof to draw up a fiant in due form of law containing a grant from his Majesty unto Robert Boyd, gent, his heirs and assigns, of all such lands, tenements and hereditaments as were found by office lately taken to have been granted or enfeoffed by Sir Hugh Montgomery, knight, now lord viscount of the Ards, unto Colonel David Boyd and his heirs or which came unto his Majesty by reason ~~of~~ the said Colonel David Boyd was an alien ~~to~~ beholden of his ~~hand~~ Majesty, his heirs and successors, by such tenure and services as the same were formerly held before the said enquiry taken, reserving to his Majesty, his heirs and successors, the yearly rent of 3*li.* sterling *vizt* 20*s.* thereof as part of the old rent payable by the said Lord Montgomery before he enfeoffed the said Colonel David Boyd (and of so much the said Lord Viscount Montgomery

253 See warrant no. 339.

to be exonerated) and the other 40s residue as a **[f. 566r]** new increase of rent unto his Majesty, concerning likewise unto the said Lord Montgomery the yearly rent of 16*li.* sterling being the rent reserved to the said Lord Montgomery ~~the yearly rent of~~ upon the estate granted to the said Colonel David Boyd and all other rents, duties and services due, payable or performable unto the said Lord Montgomery by the true intent & meaning of the said indenture of feoffment made by the said Lord Montgomery unto the said Colonel David Boyd so as the said Robert Boyd may be in as good state and condition for his rents and tenures as he was before the said lands were found for his Majesty and no otherways according to the tenor of his Majesty's letters of the 20th of July in the second year of his reign & a letter of explanation written by Sir Henry Holcroft, knight, by his Majesty's command bearing date the 17th day of October 1626, which you are carefully to peruse and observe, inserting therein ~~all~~ further all such other clauses as in grants of like nature are usual. And the same fairly engrossed &c. And for so doing &c. Given &c. 18 August 1634.

To our trusty & well beloved, his Majesty's attorney & solicitor general & to either of them.

352. <WARRANT FOR ATTACH[MENT] ONE JAMES GYRE FOR NOT PAYING HIS CUSTOMS> [21 AUGUST 1634]

By the lord deputy

Wentworth

Whereas we are credibly informed that one James Gyre of Weymouth in England, merchant, and who is now residing in some of the western ports hath not long since deceived his Majesty & the farmers' officers in the payment of his Majesty's customs to a great value, we therefore have thought fit and do accordingly hereby require and authorize you to attach the body of the said Gyre wheresoever he shall be found and him to carry before the 2 next justices of the peace **[f. 566v]** who are to take him bound in good bonds with sufficient ^& know[n]^ sureties for his present appearance before us to answer the premises. And for so doing this shall be your warrant, in the due execution &c. whereof they are not to fail at their utmost perils. Given &c. 21 August 1634.

To our well beloved William Lewis, gent, collector of the customs in the port of Youghal.

353. <MR TRAFFORD'S WARRANT FOR A FIANT> [20 AUGUST 1634]

By the lord deputy

A warrant for a fiant containing a presentation of Thomas Trafford, clerk, unto the vicarages of Teysynod & Mohill in the diocese of Ardagh void by lapse with a clause of union, directing his admission to the judge of the faculties, dat[ed] 20 August 1634.

To Sir William Ussher & Paul Davies &c.

354. <MR CHRISTIAN'S LICENCE OF ABSENCE, COMPTROLLER OF THE CUSTOMS &C.> **[22 AUGUST 1634]**

By the lord deputy general of Ireland

Wentworth

Whereas upon humble suit made unto us by Mynard Christian, comptroller of the customs in the port of Waterford, we have been pleased to licence him to make his repair into England and there to remain during the space of three months next ensuing the date hereof about the dispatch of certain special affairs of his own. <*vide* petition in the bundles with a certificate of Sir George Radcliffe> These are therefore to will and require all and every, his Majesty's officers, ministers & loving subjects whom it may concern not only to take due notice thereof but also to assure him the full benefit of this our licence without any forfeiture to be made of his ~~place~~ said office or other prejudice to be incurred by reason of his absence during the time aforesaid, he leaving an able & sufficient deputy to discharge the employment in ~~his~~ his absence, whereby they & every of them are not to fail. Given &c. 22 of August 1634.

355. [f. 567r] <RICHARD RICKSON> **[20 AUGUST 1634]**

A warrant for Richard Rickson to transport 5 horses or saddle nags ~~at the~~ for England at the port of Donaghadee, dated 20 *Augusti* 1634.

356. <WILLIAM HAMOND> **[20 AUGUST 1634]**

<Manicule>A warrant for a fiant containing a presentation of William Hamond, clerk, unto the 2 vicarages of Oughtera in the diocese of Kilmore & Shrower in the diocese of Ardagh void by lapse, directing his admission to the judge of the faculties & instering therein a clause of union, *pro hac vice tantum*, dated 20th *Augusti* 1634.

To Sir William Ussher & Paul Davies &c.

357. <MR CRESSY'S WARRANT FOR A RECTORY> **[21 AUGUST 1634]**

These are to will and require you forthwith to draw up a fiant in due form of law containing a presentation from his Majesty of Hugh Cressy, clerk, <manicule> to the rectory of Taghboyne *alias* Taboyne in the diocese of Raphoe being void by lapse or otherwise, to have, hold, possess and enjoy the said rectory together with all the rights, duties, members, profits & appurtenances whatsoever thereunto belonging or in anywise appertaining, and in as large, ample and beneficial manner unto him the said Cressy as any other incumbent or incumbents formerly held & enjoyed or of right ought to have held & enjoyed the same, directing his admission to the judge of the faculties. And the same fairly engrossed in parchment under your hand to send unto us to be further passed as appertaineth; for doing whereof this shall be your warrant. Given at &c. xxith August 1634.

To our trusty & well beloved Sir William Ussher, knight, & Paul Davies, esquire, clerks of the Council, or either of them.

358. [f. 567v] <SIR JAMES OLLIPHANT[254]> [21 AUGUST 1634]

A warrant for Sir James Olliphant to transport for England three horses or saddle nags at the ports of Donaghadee or Groomsport, dated 21st *Augusti* 1634.

359. <MR BRADISH, HIS WARRANT FOR POSSESSION> [26 AUGUST 1634]

Whereas John Bradish, clerk, hath complained unto us that he being collated to the two vicarages of Castrachore & Moyally in the diocese of Cloyne by the most reverend father in God, the lord archbishop of Cashel, & being likewise thereunto canonically inducted & in possession of the fruits thereof by the free consent of the propriety of the rectories of the said vicarages, being Sir John Fitzgearld, knight, <*vide* ~~book of warrants~~ ^church affairs^ page 224 & in the bundles for petition of Sir John FitzGerald with certificate from bishop of Derry> yet he the said Sir John by himself & his servants (as appears by the said Bradish, his affidavit) doth hinder him the said Bradish in the preception & taking up of the fruits & harvests thereof in causing his men to be beaten & abused. We therefore upon the said Bradish his humble suit have thought fit & do accordingly hereby require & authorize you to enter into the said vicarages & the quiet & peaceable possession thereof to deliver unto the said Bradish, & him to keep & maintain therein from time to time hereafter until the same be evicted by an order of the Council table here, where a trial for the eight thereof may be had by the said Sir John, if any he hath thereunto; whereof **[f. 568r]** you may not fail. And for so doing &c. Given &c. 26 *Augusti* 1634.

To our well beloved, the high sheriff of the county of Cork now being & to the sheriff of that county that from time shall be.

360. <ROCH'S PROTECTION FOR 4 M[ONTHS]> [25 AUGUST 1634]

By the lord deputy

Wentworth

Whereas James Roch hath petitioned unto us setting forth that by reason of a long & tedious suit which hath ~~been~~ depended for many years concerning certain lands whereunto he pretends to have good right, he hath been brought to that poverty and his estate reduced to that low ebb as that he is not able to pay for his meat & drink. And inasmuch as he is afraid that some creditors of his who threaten to arrest him will be contended with no other satisfaction but ready money, which he being no way able to give, he humbly besought us to receive him into his Majesty's protection whose request therein we have thought fit to grant; & the rather in regard his suit being depending before us at the Council table as to come to a hearing this next Michaelmas term, these are therefore to will and require you and every of you not only to take due notice thereof but also to forbear suing, troubling or arresting the person of the said Roch for & during the space of four months next ensuing the date hereof he behaving

[254] James Olliphant of Newton (d. 1648), Lord of Seffion, expelled from the bench in 1632 for shooting his gardner (see John P. Wood, *The antient and modern state of the parish of Cramond* (Edinburgh, 1744), p. 25).

himself as becometh, provided that by virtue hereof he deceive not his creditors but do his endeavour to the uttermost of his power to give them content and satisfaction; neither is it our intention that this protection shall free him from any former arrests or any debt due to [**f. 568v**] his Majesty from him if any be. Whereof you & every of you are not to fail. And for so doing &c. Given &c. 25 August 1634.

To all mayors, sheriffs ~~&c.~~ justices of the peace, porteeves, sovereigns, bailiffs & sergeants & to all & every others his Majesty's officers, ministers & loving subjects whom it may concern.

361. <WARRANT TO JOHN BUTCHER, KEEPER OF THE MARSHALSEA, TO DETAIN GIDION PIERCE & JOHN KING> [26 AUGUST 1634]

These are to will & require you to receive into your custody the body of Gidion Pierce & John King, two of the foot company under the command of Sir Barnaby [O']Brien, knight,[255] and them having so received to keep in sure and safe manner until you receive our directions for their enlargement; for doing whereof &c. Given &c. 26th *Augusti* 1634.

To John Butcher, keeper of the city Marshalsea.

362. [WARRANT TO DETAIN BIGNELL[256] AND WREN][257] 26 AUGUST 1634]

A warrant *ut supra* directed to the constable to take into his custody John Bignell & John Wren, two of the foot company under Sir Barnaby [O']Brien's command, dated 26th *Augusti* 1634.

363. [f. 569r] <SPARKE'S *LIBERATE*> [29 AUGUST 1634]

Whereas it appeareth unto [us] that George Sparke, gent, (who now by our directions & upon the complaint of Sir Faithful Fortescue, knight[)][258] remaineth in your custody, hath engaged himself either to satisfy the said Sir Faithful Fortescue what he claimeth from him this next Michaelmas term, or failing to submit and render himself then to your custody again, we therefore upon humble suit have thought fit and do accordingly hereby require you to set the body of the said Sparke at liberty, paying his fees. And for &c. Given &c. xxixth of August 1634.

To Robert Gilbert, one of his Majesty's pursuivants.

255 Barnaby O'Brien (*c.* 1590–1657), 6th earl of Thomond (see *DIB*).

256 John Bagnall (Bignell).

257 See warrant no. 369.

258 Faithful Fortescue (*c.* 1581–1666), MP for Armagh county (see McGrath).

364. <ARTHUR SHURLRY[259]> **[1 SEPTEMBER 1634]**

A warrant for Arthur Shurlry to transport four horses or saddle nags at the port of Youghal, ~~or~~ Cork ^or Waterford^, dated 1 Septembe[r] 1634.

365. <WARRANT FOR THE CONVEYANCE OF 2 PRISONERS FROM WATERFORD> **[2 SEPTEMBER 1634]**

Whereas we think it fit that John Preston & John Murth, now prisoners in the gaol of Waterford upon suspicion of piracy, shall be forthwith brought & conveyed hither, these are therefore to will & require you to deliver their bodies forthwith unto the sheriff of that county that lieth directly on the highway hither, **[f. 569v]** who is to take & deliver them over to the next sheriff that so they may be conveyed from sheriff to sheriff until they be delivered over to the constable of this his Majesty's Castle of Dublin who is required not only to receive but also safely to detain them until our further pleasure be known. Whereof he & the said several sheriffs are not to fail at their perils. And for so doing &c. Given &c. 2 *Septembris* 1634.

To our well beloved, the sheriffs of the city of Waterford & to all other sheriffs of the several counties from thence hither whom it may concern & to every of them.

366. <A WARRANT TO SIR CHARLES COOTE[260] ABOUT THE CONCEALED COMPOSITION> **[2 SEPTEMBER 1634]**

By the lord deputy

Whereas our trusty & well beloved Sir Charles Coote, knight & baronet, hath petitioned unto us setting forth that there are several quarters of lands within the several baronies of the province of Connacht & the county of Clare *alias* Thomond which pay not their composition rent to his Majesty, <*vide* 4th book of entries page 331 for the petition whereupon this is grounded> whereof the said Sir Charles Coote being the collector humbly besought us to give our warrant for the issuing forth of a commission to enquire of such concealed lands & who **[f. 570r]** they are that hold the same many quarters, whereof he is in good hope (as he saith) to bring into charge. And therefore his request (being so reasonable & conducing to his Majesty's benefit in his revenue) we have thought fit to grant and accordingly we do hereby will & require you forthwith to draw up a fiant of a commission in due form to be directed unto the said Sir Charles Coote & Edward Ormesby, esquire, his deputy, thereby giving them & either of them full power & authority from time to time & so often as it may stand with the conveniency of his Majesty's service to empanel a jury of freeholders or other sufficient men within every of the baronies of the said province & county of Clare, to enquire what lands remain & lie waste & void of manurance, & what & how many quarters of land are so concealed, & who held the same that are liable to pay 10*s.* yearly rent to his Majesty for each such concealed quarter, and what shall be found upon such inquisition to certify us thereof from time to time with all convenient

259 Arthur Shirley (Shurlry).

260 Sir Charles Coote (d. 1642), army officer (see *DIB*).

speed. And the same fairly engrossed to send unto us under your hand to be further passed as appertaineth. For doing whereof &c. Given &c. 2 Septembe[r] 1634.

To our trusty & well beloved, his Majesty's attorney & solicitor general.

367. [f. 570v] <WILLIAM GRAHAM'S PETITION FOR 3 MONTHS> [10 SEPTEMBER 1634]

By the lord deputy

Wentworth

Whereas humble suit hath made unto us, Lieutenant William Graham, setting forth that he being muster master of the plantators, servitors & natives within the province of Ulster, hath been at great charge & pains by himself & his deputies in taking view of mustering & training the forces for those northern parts and hath thereupon several arrears as yet unpaid him due in that province for his said charge & pains till the receipt whereof he rests thereby disenabled to give present satisfaction to his own creditors. And besides, whereas by order of the late lords justices & Council dated the 24th of December 1630, he is required yearly to give certificate to the chief governor or governors for the time being of the names & several weapons of the persons by him yearly so mustered with a particular account of his own ~~daily~~ diligence in that employment now, to the end that he might as well undisturbed accordingly attend us with such certificate & account as also that thereupon making it appear to us what arrears are already unjustly due unto him, he might (as formerly) receive our order for due payment thereof to the better enabling him to satisfy his creditors, he made his humble request to us for his Majesty's protection for a time which out of the aforesaid considerations we think fit to grant him. [**f. 571r**] These are therefore to will & require you ~~to~~ & every of you not only to take due notice thereof but also to afford him the full benefit of this our protection in all respects by forbearing to sue, arrest, implead, or any ways molest him the said William Graham in his person or goods (he behaving himself as becometh) for & during the space of three months next ensuing the date hereof, provided that in the interim he endeavour to his ability to content & satisfy his creditors that we be not troubled with their complaints. And likewise our pleasure is that this extend not to protect him from any debt due to his Majesty nor to free him from any former imprisonment. And for so doing this shall be a sufficient warrant. Given &c. 10th *Septembris* 1634.

To all mayors, sheriffs, justices of peace, portreeves & bailiffs & to all others whom it may concern.

368. [f. 571v] <CAPTAIN PINNER'S[261] WARRANT TO BE OVERSEER OF HIS MAJESTY'S FORTIFICATION &C. FOR A FIANT> [22 AUGUST 1634]

By the lord deputy

Wentworth

Whereas his late Majesty, King James of famous memory, by his letters patents under the great seal of this kingdom bearing date the 27th day of February in the 15th year

[261] Nicholas Pinner, naval officer.

of his reign of England &c., did give & grant unto Sir Thomas Rotheram, knight,[262] & Captain Nicholas Pinner the office & place of overseer & director general of all his highness's fortifications & plantations in this kingdom, to have & to hold the same during our lives & the longest liv[er] of them together with the fee & entertainment of 10*s.* *per diem*, <*vide* the entry of the king's letter in book of letters page 107> and forasmuch as the said Sir Thomas Rotheram & Captain Nicholas Pinner are willing & ready to surrender into his Majesty's hands, as well the said letters patents as the fee hereby reserved unto them, upon condition that the said place or office be part unto the said Captain Pinner alone & at half the fee or entertainment reserved unto them jointly by the said letters patents as aforesaid, and to that end they humbly besought us to give directions to renew the said grant whose request therein we have thought fit to condescend unto and the rather in regard his Majesty by the renovation thereof saves the sum of 5*s.* sterling *per diem*. And therefore we do hereby will & require you to draw up a fiant in due form of law containing a grant from his Majesty unto the said ^Captain^ Nicholas Pinner alone of the said place or office of overseer & director general of his Majesty's satisfactions & plantations in & throughout this kingdom as aforesaid, to have, hold, possess & enjoy the said place or office unto him the said Captain Nicholas Pinner for & during his natural life together with the fee & entertainment of 5*s.* ~~*per diem*~~ sterling English money *per diem* as aforesaid, & in as large, ample & beneficial manner as Sir Josias Bodley, knight,[263] or they the said Sir Thomas Rotheram & Captain Nicholas Pinner held & enjoyed or of right ought to have held & enjoyed the same, inserting therein all such clauses as in ~~like cases are usual~~ grants of like nature are usual. And the same fairly engrossed in [**f. 572r**] parchment under your hand to send unto us to be further passed as appertaineth; for doing whereof this shall be your warrant. Given &c. 22 August 1634.

To our trusty & well beloved, his Majesty's attorney & solicitor general, ~~&~~ or either of them.

369. <JOHN BAGNALL AND JOHN WREN, TWO OF THE SOLDIERS UNDER BARNABY [O']BRIEN'S COMMAND>[264] [10 SEPTEMBER 1634]

Their *liberate*, dated the tenth of September 1634.

To the constable of the Castle &c.

370. <FRANCIS BLENERHASSETT>[265] [10 SEPTEMBER 1634]

Francis Blenerhassett, his *liberate*, at suit of Sir William Cole, dated 10th September 1634, directed to Gilbert, the pursuivant,[266] provided there be no other cause for his detention but that at Sir William's suit.

[262] Thomas Rotherham (d. *c.* 1648), MP for Tuam (see McGrath).

[263] Josias Bodley (*c.* 1550–1617), soldier and military engineer (see *ODNB*).

[264] See warrant no. 362.

[265] See warrant no. 257.

[266] Robert Gilbert, second pursuivant at arms (see *Lib. mun. pub. Hib*).

371. <WARRANT FOR IMPRESTING 50*li.* TO THE LORD CAULFEILD> [SEPTEMBER 1634]

Whereas by direction from his Majesty there is to be impressed unto the Master of the Ordnance of this kingdom out of the 50*li.* *per annum* for extraordinaries the sum of 200*li.* sterling by the year for answering all occasions incident to his office, the same to be paid unto him by equal portions at the beginning of every half year, these are therefore to pray & require your lordship to satisfy & pay [**f. 572v**] unto our very good lord, the Lord Caulfeild, the sum of 100*li.* sterling for the half year beginning the first of March last passed. And for so doing these, with his acquittance acknowledging the receipt thereof to be accountable for the same unto his Majesty, shall be unto your lordship & the commissioners of your account sufficient warrant & discharged. Given at ~~his &c.~~ the Phoenix [blank][267] of September 1634.

To our very good lord, the Lord Mountnorris, his Majesty's vice-treasurer & general receiver for Ireland.

372. <*LIBERATE* FOR JOHN BERMINGHAM & *AL.*> [11 SEPTEMBER 1634]

By the lord deputy

~~These are to will~~
Wentworth
Whereas you have in your custody the bodies of the several persons underwritten committed unto you upon our former warrant, these are to require you to set them at liberty, paying their fees. And for so doing &c. Given &c. 11 September 1634.
John Bermingham
Lucas Athy &
Stephen Lynch.

To our well beloved Samuel Davis, the constable of the Castle.

373. [f. 573r] <WARRANT FOR CONVEYING MARGARET DUCKETT [TO] MOYALLOE[268]> [23 SEPTEMBER 1634]

By the lord deputy

Wentworth
Whereas you have in your custody the body of Margaret Duckett who being for some misdemeanours and abuses committed by our very good lord, the lord president of Munster, to the custody of Rawly Nudigate, his lordship's gentleman porter, as his prisoner, and upon pretence of want of health obtained liberty to walk abroad to take the air and so by that means made an escape in mans apparel and is come hither to this city with a purpose immediately to go for England as by the humble petition of the said Rawley Nudigate & affidavit thereof made may more at large appear. <*vide* 3 book of entries page 479 for the petition whereon this issued> And being now apprehended by our directions & questioned concerning the same hath confessed in effect as much

[267] Likely Phoenix Park.

[268] Mallow.

as is therein set forth & alleged, these shall be therefore to will & command you to take charge of the said Margaret Duckett & to see her safely conveyed to the town of Moyalloe in the province of Munster & delivered to the said gentleman porter from when she made her escape as aforesaid, there to be proceeded with all according to the nature & quality of her offence; and for so doing this shall be unto you a sufficient warrant in the due execution whereof we require all mayors, sheriffs, bailiffs, portreeves, constables and all other his Majesty's officers, ministers & loving subjects whatsoever to be aiding & assisting unto you; whereof you & they are ^not^ to fail as you and they will answer the contrary at your peril. Given &c. 23 September 1634.

To Mathew Bentley, one of his Majesty's pursuivants.

374. [f. 573v] <WARRANT FOR REDELIVERY [OF] SALT &C. TO CAPTAIN PRONOVILLE> **[24 SEPTEMBER 1634]**

By the lord deputy

Wentworth

Whereas we are advertised that Richard Pronoville, captain of the *St Jago*, lately separated from his company by distress of weather & having commission from his Majesty, the king of Spain, was by that exigency driven to betake himself to that port and there landed some barrels of salt whereby to provide himself & company with fresh victual with salt, we understand is by the customers there detained till our further pleasure therein known. Now in regard of the mutual correspondency of both Crowns that either subjects should upon all just occasions respectively receive friendly & civil usage the one from the other, and also that we are informed he hath as well at that port as in his passage thither civilly demeaned & comported himself without disturbance to the peace or commerce of any of his Majesty's subjects, & in like fair manner intends forthwith after his accommodation to depart thence ~~from~~ for Spain, these are therefore to will and require you & all others who have, or may have, the said salt in custody to restore & deliver back the same (without impair or diminution[)] to him the said Captain Pronoville, and also to afford him accommodation of necessaries to his ship or company, he paying therefore the usual & accustomed rates. Hereof fail you not as you will answer the contrary at your perils. Given &c. 24th Septemb[er] 1634.

<To all mayors, sheriffs, justices of peace, sovereigns, governors, constables & customers in or about the port of Wexford, & to all other his Majesty's officers, ministers & subjects whom it may concern.>

375. [f. 574r] <HAWKER'S LICENCE TO TRANSPORT 100,000 HOGSHEAD STAVES> **[20 SEPTEMBER 1634]**

By the lord deputy

Wentworth

Whereas the lords of his Majesty's most honourable privy council by their letters of the tenth of December 1632 requiring the then lords justices to give strict & effectual order that no ship, timber nor pipestaves should be transported out of this kingdom without special directions from his Majesty or their lordships, and forasmuch as Humphrey Hawker of Cork, merchant, hath been an humble suitor unto us to licence him, ~~to~~ his agents or assigns, to transport out of that port a certain quantity of hogshead staves which we conceive are not prohibited nor within their lordship's intention of prohibition, the rather having been long since cut & brought to the waterside & therefore will not be any breach if their lordship's commands being done by our warrant; we are therefore pleased to grant his request & do hereby will & require you & every of you notwithstanding any former restraint to permit & suffer him the said Humphrey Hawker by himself, his agents or assigns, to load & transport out of that port the quantity of 100,000 of hogshead staves, he paying his Majesty's custom for the same, whereof you & every of you are not to fail at your perils. Given &c. 20 September 1634.

To our well beloved, the officers of ^his Majesty's^ ~~the~~ customs in the port of Cork.

376. <GABRIEL DE LA PORT'S WARRANT TO TRANSPORT 16,000 HOGSHEAD STAVES> **[1 OCTOBER 1634]**

The like warrant for Gabriel de la Port, a merchant stranger, to transport sixteen thousand hogshead staves at the port of Limerick, dated 1 *Octobris* 1634.

377. [f. 574v] <HENRY KETTLE> **[27 SEPTMEBER 1634]**

A warrant for Henry Kettle to transport 2 saddle nags for England at the port of Youghal, dated 27 September 1634.

378. <GEORGE BUTLER'S POST WARRANT> **[27 SEPTEMBER 1634]**

By the lord deputy

Wentworth

Whereas our right trusty & well beloved George Butler, esquire, one of the gent[lemen] of his Majesty's privy chamber, is to make his present repair to the city of York in the realm of England about his Majesty's special affairs, these are therefore to will & require you & every of you wheresoever the said George Butler shall land to be very careful to see him provided from thence from stay to stay of six good & able post-horses with a guide, he paying therefore according to his Majesty's usual & accustomed rates, whereof you are not to fail. Given &c. 27 September 1634.

To all mayors, sheriffs, justices of the peace, bailiffs, constables, postmasters and to all other his Majesty's officers, ministers & loving subjects whatsoever whom it may concern.

379. <BRIAN PALMES> **[27 SEPTEMBER 1634]**

The like warrant for ~~Bryan~~ our trusty & well beloved Brian Palmes, esquire, for 4 post-horses & a guide to Nottingham, dated *ut supra.*

Directed *ut supra.*

380. <HENRY MUSGRAVE, BARONET> **[27 SEPTEMBER 1634]**

The like warrant for Sir Henry Musgrave, baronet, for 3 post-horses & a guide to Skipton in Yorkshire, dat[ed] *ut supra.*

Directed *ut supra.*

381. [f. 575r] <KIREN'S *LIBERATE*> **[7 OCTOBER 1634]**

By the lord deputy general

A warrant to the pursuivant in whose custody the said Kiren remained to enlarge & set him at liberty, paying his fees (if there were no other cause for his detention), dated 7th *Octobris* 1634.

382. <WARRANT FOR WITNESSES TO APP[EAR] BEFORE REFEREES> **[7 OCTOBER 1634]**

By the lord deputy

Wentworth

Whereas we have been pleased by our orders of the 6th day of this month to refer the examination of a complaint preferred unto us by Richard Grace, gent, in behalf of himself & others against Daniel O'Brien & others, defendants, unto certain referees in the country, we now upon the said Grace, his humble suit, have thought fit and do accordingly hereby require you & every of you the persons undernamed (whom he pretends to be very material witnesses for him) not only to appear before the said referees but also to deliver the truth of your several knowledges concerning the said difference whensoever you shall be thereunto required. Whereof you & every of you are not to fail at your perils. Given &c. 7 *Octobris* 1634.

Owen O'Kennedy & *al.*[269]

383. <SERGEANT MAJOR [O']DONELLY, HIS POST WARRANT> **[8 OCTOBER 1634]**

Whereas the bearer hereof, Sergeant Major Patrick O'Donelly, is to make his present repair from hence unto the city of London about certain special affairs, ~~of his own~~ these are therefore to will & require you & every of you to be very careful to see that he be provided from place to place of two good & able horses with a guide, he paying therefore according to the usual & accustomed rates, whereof &c. And &c. Given &c. 8th October 1634.

269 This is as it appears. No further names are mentioned in the manuscript.

<To all mayors, sheriffs, justices of peace, port masters, bailiffs, constables & to all & every other his Majesty's officers &c.>

384. [f. 575v] <SIR JOHN LEAKE, HIS WARRANT TO TRANSPORT HIS HORSES> [10 OCTOBER 1634]

Whereas our trusty & well beloved John Leake, knight, being to make his present repair into England, we upon his humble suit have thought fit to licence him to have eight geldings or saddle nags transported for himself and his men to ride on. These are therefore to will & require you & every of you to permit & the said Sir John Leake's servants to put aboard & transport the said horses for England as aforesaid without any your lets or hindrances whatsoever. And for so doing this shall be your warrant. Given &c. 10th *Octobris* 1634.

To the officers of the customs in the port of Youghal.

385. <WARRANT ABOUT A COMMISSION FOR THE [O']MOLLONYS> [16 OCTOBER 1634]

Whereas the persons undernamed have petitioned unto us setting forth that they being accused for the unfortunate killing of one James Morish, <*vide* book of pardons page 40 & so forward> their estates thereupon as well in lands as goods have been seized by divers persons who had neither of themselves any right thereunto nor any legal authority to [**f. 576r**] enter upon the same. And forasmuch as the said persons undernamed have made humble suit unto us that for the better discovery of what state & goods they have been so p dispossessed of, we would be pleased to cause a commission to issue to certain indifferent persons to enquire thereof. We have thought fit to grant their request and therefore we pray and require your lordship to cause a commission to issue forthwith under the great seal and to be directed unto our well beloved Thomas Lodge, archdeacon of Killaloe,[270] Robert Sibthorpe, clerk,[271] Thomas Arthur, esquire, and Nicholas Fanning of Limerick, alderman, <these commissioners Mr Justice Cressy[272] did certify were fit men for this service which is in the bundles> giving them, or any three or two of them, full power & authority to examine & enquire as well by the oaths of good men as by all other good ways & means what estate <*vide* the return of the commission 5 book p[age] 531> either in lands or goods the said persons undernamed were really possessed of at the time of the killing of the said Morish, by whom the same were so taken away in whose hands they did, and do still remain, what loss & damage they the said persons undernamed have sustained thereby, how long it is since their lands were taken from them, and of what yearly value the said lands are, and what spoil or waste have been committed upon the said [**f. 576v**] estate. The said commission to be returnable with all convenient speed and at the furthest by the beginning of the next Hillary term. And for so doing this shall be your lordship's sufficient warrant. Given &c. 16th *Octobris* 1634.

270 Thomas Lodge, archdeacon of Killaloe and treasurer of Limerick (see Cotton, *Fasti*).

271 Robert Sibthorpe (d. 1649), bishop of Kilfenora and subsequently of Limerick (see Cotton, *Fasti*).

272 Hugh Cressy, justice of the king's court of chief place (see *Lib. mun. pub. Hib.*).

Owen O'Mollony
Eleanor Fanning *alias* Mollony
Honora Ni Connor
James O'Mollony
Teig McDonnell Kierigh
John O'Mollony
Danniel O'Cahassa
Teig O'Mollony
Melaghlin O'Mollony
Finola Ni Killin
John O'Doragh

To our very good lord, the lord chancellor.

386. <WARRANT TO KEEP TOTTIE CLOSE PRISONER> [17 OCTOBER 1634]

Whereas you have remaining in your custody the body of one Thomas Tottie, these are to will and require you (for reasons best known to ourself) to keep the said Tottie close prisoner henceforward <by directions from Sir George Radcliffe> and not to permit him to talk or converse with any person until our further pleasure be known. Whereof &c. dated 17th *Octobris* 1634.

To our well beloved, the Marshal of the 4 Courts.

387. [f. 577r] <WARRANT TO THE SHERIFF OF DOWN TO RESTORE MR PAINE'S CATTLE>[273] [20 OCTOBER 1634]

Whereas Valentine Paine, esquire, hath humbly petitioned unto us setting forth that he holding some three townlands from Mrs Bagnoll of the Newry upon which his cattle did graze and he (about some three weeks past [*sic*]) being removing of them from thence unto some other lands which he had seven miles of[f], there came and followed after him by the special command & directions of the said Mrs Bagnall in a most riotous & rebellious manner to the number of one hundred and fifty armed men with swords, pikes, darts and fowling-pieces, & did not only several times violently assault the said Paine <*vide* third book of entries page 496 for the petition of Valentine Paine & 506 for an affid[avit] with certific[ate]> and such as drove the said cattle by his directions, but also drove & carried away (as he allegeth) the number of one hundred cows, thirty garrons & one hundred & ninety sheep, all which the said Mrs Bagnall hath taken into her own possession & will (as the said Paine affirmeth), suffer neither sheriff nor any other his Majesty's officers to reploy the same as standing upon certain pretended liberties & privileges belonging to her manor, and not therewith contented she the said Mrs Bagnall about the time aforesaid commanded her men to man out a boat to surprise a barque of the said Valentine Paine's which was laden with fish and lay at anchor in the Newry harbour which she likewise detaineth. Now inasmuch as these courses are so exorbitant & of so dangerous a consequence as that they are not to be suffered in a civil commonwealth, we therefore upon the said Valentine Paine, his humble suit, have thought fit & do accordingly hereby require & authorize you forthwith to make diligent pursuit & enquiry after the said cattle & wheresoever they shall be found, either within liberty or without, within that county to ~~sees~~ seize upon

[273] The page is torn at the end of the warrant.

and taken the same, together with the said barque & the fish therein contained into your own custody, and the same having so taken up to restore & deliver unto the said Valentine Paine, he giving you good & sufficient security to stand, to abide & [f. 577v] perform such order as (upon examination... whole matter & the hearing of what...alleged of either side) we shall think fit to give. Whereof you are not to fail as you will answer the contrary at your peril. And for so doing this shall be your warrant. Given at his Majesty's Castle of Dublin the twentieth of October 1634.

To our well beloved, the sheriff of the county of Down.

388. <ARLENTER USSHER> **[21 OCTOBER 1634]**

A warrant to the pursuivant to detain in his custody the body of Arlenter Ussher until our further pleasure be known, dated 21st *Octobris* 1634.

To any of his Majesty's pursuivants.

389. [f. 578r] <WARRANT FOR THE LADY ROE> **[20 OCTOBER 1634]**

Whereas his Majesty having taken into his princely consideration the great charge & expense that the right reverend father in God, George, late lord bishop of Derry, deceased, had been put unto in the building of a convenient house for himself & his successors upon part of the mensals of the said ~~bp~~ bishopric, ~~that became due at May last in the vacancy whereof the said see~~ his highness hath been thereupon graciously pleased to require us to give order that Dame Margery Roe, the relict of the said bishop, should receive to her own use one quarters rent & revenue of the said bishopric that became due at May last in the vacancy of the said see. We therefore, in pursuance of his Majesty's said directions, have thought fit & do accordingly hereby authorize & give full power & authority unto William Clemens, servant, unto the said Dame Margery Roe (whom she hath thereunto likewise appointed) not only to demand, levy, ~~&~~ receive & take up, but also to pay over unto the said Dame Margery Roe the said quarters rent & revenue due as aforesaid provided the same (as his Majesty hath required) do not exceed the sum of 200*li.* And in case the said rent or any part thereof be already levied either by his Majesty's officers or any other, then we do hereby will and require as well such [f. 578v] officer & officers, person or persons, who have levied the same to make presen[t] payment & restitution thereof unto the said Dame Margery Roe that so she may reap the full benefit of what his Majesty hath been pleased by his said letters to confer upon her. Whereof all whom it may concern are required to take notice & to observe what they are hereby enjoined and thereof not to fail. And for so doing this shall be a sufficient warrant. Given &c. 20th *Octobris* 1634.

To William Clemens, servant, unto the said Dame Margery Roe.

<The letter from his Majesty whereupon this is grounded followeth>

390. CHARLES REX **[22 SEPTEMBER 1634]**

Right trusty & right well beloved cousin & councillor, we greet you well. Whereas Dame Margery Roe, the relict of the right reverend father in God, George, late bishop of Derry, deceased, hath by her humble petition showed unto us that her late husband being desirous to build & plant upon some part of the mensals of the said bishopric a convenient house for himself and his successors, did in his life effect the same to the expense of two thousand marks sterling, or thereabouts, of his own and her means [**f. 579r**] the revenues of his bishopric being (as she pretends[)] most expended in hospitality & marrying of her children, whereupon she is now an humble suitor unto us for the quarters rent & revenue of the said bishopric grown due at May last, her husband dying about one week before the quarters day. We being graciously inclined to cherish the memory of so commendable a work of the said bishop in his life time and understanding likewise that the present bishop doth renounce any pretence or claim unto the same rents, we hereby require and authorize you to give warrant to our officers there whom it may concern to suffer the said Dame Margery Roe to take & enjoy the benefit of the said quarters rent grown due at May last as aforesaid so as the same be under the same of two hundred pounds, or in case the same or any part thereof be already paid to any [of] our officers for our use, that you give present order for delivering thereof unto her according to our pleasure herein signified. And for so doing these our letters shall be your sufficient warrant and discharge. Given under our signet at our honour of Hampton Court the two & twentieth day of September in the tenth year of our reign.

To our right trusty & well beloved cousin & councillor Thomas, Viscount Wentworth, our deputy of Ireland & president of our Council established in the north parts of our kingdom of England.

Francis Windebank[274]

391. [f. 579v] <OWEN PRICHARD'S WARRANT FOR THE SCHOOL OF KILFENORA>[275] **[22 OCTOBER 1634]**

Wentworth

Whereas the place of school[master] of the free-school of Kilfen[ora] is now void and in our dispose & inasmu[ch] as upon the good testimony we received of the sufficiency of the good life & consideration of Owen Prichard, clerk, we have thought fit to confer the same upon him, the said Prichard. These are therefore to will and require you upon the receipt hereof to draw up a licence in the usual form containing a grant of the said place of schoolmaster unto the said Owen Prichard together with all rights, duties, fees, wages, perquisites & profits to the same belonging or anywise appertaining in as large, ample & beneficial manner as any other heretofore enjoyed or of right ought to have enjoyed the same during the said Prichard's good behaviour, inserting therein all such clauses as in like grants are usual. And the same fairly engrossed in parchment

274 Francis Windebank (bap. 1582–1646), secretary of state (see *ODNB*).

275 The page is torn at the edges.

under your hand to send unto us to be further passed as appertaineth. And for so doing this shall be a sufficient warrant. Given &c. 22nd *Octobris* 1634.

To our trusty & well beloved Sir William Ussher, knight, & Paul Davies, esquire, clerks of the Council, or either of them.

<Dr Alec Colrill, Dr in Divinity>

392. [f. 580r] <[WARRANT] FOR PRESTON & [JO]HN [MOO]RTH>[276] [3 NOVEMBER 1634]

A warrant to the constable of his Majesty's Castle of Dublin to set at liberty the bodies of John Preston & John Moorth, paying their reasonable fees, dated 3 *Novembris* 1634.

To Samuel Davis, esquire, &c.

393. <A CUSTODIAN OF THE TEMPORALITIES OF THE SEE OF LIMERICK>[277] [6 NOVEMBER 1634]

Whereas by the death of the late lord bishop of Limerick[278] the temporalities of the said bishopric ought to be seized unto his Majesty's hands & the profits thereof duly answered unto his highness during the vacancy of the said see, <the petition of Elizabeth Gough whereupon this is grounded is in the bundles> and inasmuch as upon the suit of Elizabeth Gough, late wife unto the said late lord bishop, we have been pleased to grant unto her a custodian of all & singular the temporalities belonging unto the said see and which ought to be forged upon unto his Majesty's hands. These are therefore to will and require you & every of you to pass & grant unto the said Elizabeth under his Majesty's seal of that court, a grant of all and singular the premises with th[e] appurtenances thereunto belonging at the usual & accustomed ~~rates~~ rents & services with full power & authority to the said Elizabeth by herself or her agents to receive the rents, issues & profits thereof during the vacancy of that see, and the same to deliver unto her with all convenient expedition provided that she do first enter into bonds of five hundred **[f. 580v]** pounds with good sureties to be truly a… for the same unto his Majesty whensoever…shall be called upon or thereunto required. And for so doing this [is] a sufficient warrant. Given at his Majesty's Castle of Dublin, 6 *Novembris* 1634.

To our very good lord, the lord chief baron & the rest of the barons of his Majesty's Court of Exchequer & to all & every other his Majesty's officers & ministers of that court, or otherwise, whom it may concern.

394. <MR SLINGSBY TO BE COMMITTED TO THE CASTLE> [8 NOVEMBER 1634]

Wentworth

Whereas Francis Slingsby, esquire,[279] hath been attached by the pursuivant by virtue of our warrant and inasmuch as we think it fit he should be committed to your custody,

276 The page is torn at the edges.

277 The page is torn at the end of the warrant.

278 Francis Gough (d. 1634), bishop of Limerick.

279 Francis Slingsby, later clerk of the pipe and chief engrosser of the Exchequer (see *Lib. mun. pub. Hib.*).

these are therefore to will and require you upon sight hereof to take & receive into your custody the body of the said Francis Slingsby & him to detain in sure and safe manner until you received our further directions concerning him. Whereof you may not fail. And &c., dated 8th *Novembris* 1634.

To Samuel Davis, esquire.

395. [f. 581r] <[MERED]ITH [GUYLIN], HIS [WARRANT F]OR 2 [VICARA]GES>[280] [12 NOVEMBER 1634]

These are to will and require you forthwith to draw up a fiant in due form of law containing his Majesty's prosecution of Meredith ~~Guyllem~~ Guylin, clerk, to the vicarages of Ballenderry & Linavy <manicule> in the diocese of Down being void and in his Majesty's gift *pleno jure seu alio quocunque modo*, to have, hold &c. according [to] the usual form &c., inserting a clause of union *pro hac vice tantum* & directing his admission to the bishop of the diocese, dated 12th *Novembris* 1634.

To Sir William Ussher & Paul Davies.

396. <HENRY CAPLRY> [12 NOVEMBER 1634]

A warrant for a fiant containing a presentation from his Majesty of Henry Caplry, clerk, unto the <manicule> vicarages of Cahir, Killanane & Glanbegh in the diocese of Ardfert void by lapse, to have, hold &c. according [to] the usual form, inserting a clause of union & directing his admission to the judge of the faculties, dated 12th *Novembris* 1634.

To Sir William Ussher & Paul Davies.

397. <JOHN BURROWS> [N.D.]

A warrant ~~to~~ for John Burrows to transport six horses or saddle nags out of the port of Kinsale or the creeks or members thereof.

398. [f. 581v] <JAMES BRUCE, HIS WARRANT FOR 2 VICARAGES> [14 NOVEMBER 1634]

<This warrant next underwritten> ~~A warrant containing a presentation from his M[ajesty] of James Bruce, clerk, [of] the vicarages of Knocktemple [and] Liscarroll in the diocese of Cloyne void by lapse or otherwise, to have, &c. according [to] the usual form, inserting a clause of union *pro hac vice tantum* and directing his admission to the judges of the faculties, dated 14th November 1634.~~

To Sir William Ussher & Paul Davies.

<James Bruce[281]>

280 The page is torn in the marginalia.

281 James Bruce, prebend of Iniskenny in 1637, and subsequently prebendary of Cloyne in 1640 (see Cotton, *Fasti*).

These are to will and require you forthwith to draw up a fiant in due form of law containing a presentation from his Majesty of James Bruce, clerk, unto the <manicule> vicarages of Knocktemple and Liscarroll in the diocese of Cloyne being now void & in his Majesty's gift by lapse or otherwise, to have, hold, possess & enjoy the said vicarages with all the rights, duties, members, profits and appurtenances thereunto belonging or in anywise appertaining, and in as large, ample and beneficial manner as any other incumbent or incumbents formerly held & enjoyed or of right ought to have held & enjoyed the same, inserting therein a clause of [**f. 582r**] union of the said two vicarages unto the vicarage of Ahern, which the said James Bruce now holdeth *pro hac vice tantum*. And directing his admission to the judge of the faculties and the same fairly engrossed &c. And for so doing &c. Given &c. 14th *Novembris* 1634.

To Sir William Ussher & Paul Davies.

399. <HUGH NEEVING> **[28 NOVEMBER 1634]**

A warrant for a fiant containing a presentation from his Majesty of Hugh Neeving, clerk, unto <manicule> the vicarages of Donekedy and Ballyrolly in the diocese of Down void ~~by lapse~~ ^*pleno jure sive devoluto seu alio quocunque modo,*^ to have &c. according [to] the usual form with a clause of union *pro hac vice tantum*, directing his admission to the ~~judge of the faculties~~ ^bishop of the said diocese,^ dated ~~15~~ ^28th^ *Novembris* 1634.

To Sir William Ussher & Paul Davies.

400. <JOHN WATSON[282]> **[18 NOVEMBER 1634]**

A warrant for a fiant containing a presentation of John Watson, clerk, unto the <manicule> rectory of Ballymore in the diocese of Armagh void by lapse or otherwise, to hold the same according [to] the usual form, inserting therein a clause of union of the said rectory unto the vicarage of Clonkearney which the said Watson now holdeth *pro hac vice tantum*, directing his admission to the judge of the faculties, dated 18th *Novembris* 1634.

401. [f. 582v] <MR MARKANT'S WARRANT ABOUT THE MINES>[283] **[18 NOVEMBER 1634]**

By the lord deputy

Whereas his Majesty hath been please by his [letters] patents under the great seal of this k[ingdom] to pass a grant of all the royal m… mineral works of gold, silver, copper, quit…, holding silver, or mixed with silver, opened or unopened, in the province of Munster unto Captain Th[omas] Whitmore & William Webb, gent. And foras[much] as the said Whitmore & Webb having for certain good considerations

[282] John Watson, prebend of Mullaghbrack (or Mullabrack) from 1628. Charles made the four livings of Mullabrack, Tynan, Loughgall, and Ballymore presentative by a grant in 1627 (see Cotton, *Fasti*).

[283] The page is torn at the edges.

~~sharged~~ ^shared^ the new works of Ardmore in the said province with Dr Bovill & Captain Christopher Burgh, <*vide* the petition of Markant in the 3 book of entries page 610> they the said Bovill & Burgh (as appeareth under the said Burgh's hand) made away, conveyed & assigned ^over^ the right title & interest in the said works unto John Hayes, esquire, and William Penington of London, merchant, which [the] said John Hayes hath employed over hither one Edmund Markant, gent, (as appeareth under his hand) as his deputy & agent in that behalf. But he, the said Markant, fearing least some opposition might be made by the workmen, or their overseers, or that he should find a backwardness in the county people to furnish him with such necessaries as he should want & to be assistant unto him otherwise with that readiness as they would be had he [*sic*] the original patent in his custody, we therefore, upon his humble suit, have thought fit to grant him a warrant for his better countenance in the service. And accordingly we do hereby will & require all & every, as well the overseers of the said works as the workmen themselves, not only to take due notice of the said Markant's present employment as being derived from the said John Hayes but also to permit & suffer him to perform & do for & in the behalf of the said Hayes what of right **[f. 583r]** he may & ought to do concerning the premises, hereby likewise giving & granting unto him the said Markant absolute & free power to do, execute & perform all & all manner of act or acts, thing or things in & about the premises for so much as concerns the said Hayes, his interest therein, and in as large & ample manner as the said Whitmore and Webb being the prime patentees may, or ought to do, if they were personally present according to the said letters patents. And finally we do hereby require all & every, his Majesty's subjects who live in these parts & whom it may concern not only to take due notice thereof but also to permit & suffer him ~~finally~~ fully to discharge, perform & put in execution the trust reposed in him as aforesaid without any their least lets, oppositions or hindrance whatsoever. Whereof they & every of them are not to fail at their peril. And for so doing this shall be a sufficient warrant. Given &c. 18 November 1634.

Sir, Mr Little[284] desires that you would recite unto his honour what part of the mine yourself & Dr Bovell did sell unto Mr Hayes & Mr Penington & this shall give his honour satisfaction; ~~therein~~ three or four lines is enough which I pray send me by man & I shall rest, your loving friend.

At your service, Edmund Markant.

<This was acknowledged before William Cadogan[285] & Abraham Wright>

Mr Little, I sold to Mr Penington & Mr Hayes of London, merchants, three eights of the mine of Ardmore being all that belonged to me, the rest being Dr Bovill's & Walter Bateman's. Dr Bovill sold Mr Penington one eight[h]. This is all I can certify you & so I rest.

Your assured friend, Christopher Burgh, November 15, 1634.

[284] Thomas Littell, secretary to lord deputy Wentworth, MP for Cashel (see McGrath).

[285] William Cadogan (1601–61), MP for Monaghan (see McGrath).

402. [f. 583v] <RICHARD COUTILLON>[286] [15 NOVEMBER 1634]

Warrant for a fiant containing [a] presentation from his Majesty [of] Richard Coutillon, clerk, unto [the] vicarage of Finogh & Balti[more] in the diocese of Ardfert voi[d] by lapse, to have &c. according [to] the usual form, inserting therein a clause of union ~~to~~ of the said <manicule> two vicarages unto the vicarage of Kilwily, which the said Richard Coutillon now holdeth *pro hac vice tantum*, directing his admission to the judge of the faculties, dated 15th *Novembris* 1634.

To Sir William Ussher & Paul Davies.

403. <THOMAS BARHAM[287]> [N.D.]

A warrant for a fiant containing a presentation of Thomas Barham, clerk, unto the <manicule> rectory & vicarage of Durrus in the diocese of Cork & the prebend of Donoghmore in the cathedral church of Lismore being all void and in his Majesty's presentation by lapse, to have, hold &c. according [to] the usual form, inserting therein a clause of union *pro hac vice tantum* together with all such[288]

404. [f. 584r] <BARNARD[289] TO BE DEAN OF [KILM]ORE & VICAR OF DROGHEDA>[290] [14 JANUARY 1635]

These are to will and require you forthwith to draw up a fiant in due form containing ~~a~~ ^his Majesty's^ grant & donation unto Nicholas Barnard, clerk, and Master of Arts of the deanery of the cathedral church of St Phelim of Kilmore & also a presentation from his highness of the said Nicholas Barnard to the <manicule> vicarage of ^St Peter's in ~~Drogheda~~^ Drogheda in the diocese of Armagh, the said deanery being void *pleno jure* and the said vicarage likewise void *pleno jure, jure devoluto seu alio quocunque modo*, to have, hold and possess the said deanery & vicarage unto him the said Nicholas Barnard, together with all the rights, duties, tithes, unions, ^annexations^, jurisdictions & appurtenances whatsoever thereunto belonging or in any way appertaining, & in as large, ample & beneficial manner as any other incumbents formerly held & enjoyed or of right ought to have held & enjoyed the same, directing his installation to the deanery unto the chapter of the said cathedral church, or any one or more of them, & his admission to the said vicarage to the judge of the faculties, inserting therein a clause of union of the said vicarage to the said deanery *pro hac vice tantum*. And the same fairly engrossed &c., dated 14th January 1634[/5].

To Sir William Ussher & Paul Davies.

286 This page is torn at the edges.

287 Thomas Barham, he was also prebendary of Cloyne since 1631 but was allowed to hold this preferment in addition to the prebendary of Donoghmore and Kiltegan (see Cotton, *Fasti*).

288 Eight folios have been torn out after this point; the current foliation does not take account of this (see note on the manuscript p. xxxi).

289 Nicholas Barnard (or Bernard) (d. 1661), Church of Ireland cleric and writer (see *DIB*).

290 The page is slightly torn in the marginalia.

WARRANTS NO. 405–628

JUNE 1634–*c.* 1637

EAST RIDING ARCHIVES AND

LOCAL STUDIES SERVICE, DDCR/7/1/1/1

405. [p. 1] [291] [COMMISSION TO WALTER RUDSTON GRANTING HIM COMMAND OF ONE HUNDRED AND TWENTY FOOTSOLDIERS WITHIN THE EAST RIDING][292] **[7 JUNE 1634]**

Thomas, Viscount Wentworth, lord Wentworth, Newmarsh and Oversley, lord deputy of the realm of Ireland, lord president of his Majesty's right honourable council established in the north parts, lord lieutenant of the county of York, and one of the lords of his Majesty's most honourable privy council to whom these presents shall come, greeting. Know yee that for the good opinion I have received of the fidelity, care, sufficiency and diligence of Walter Rudstone, esquire, captain, I have given him the charge and reading of one hundred & twenty foot soldiers within the East Riding of the county of York to serve his Majesty under me within the said county or elsewhere by my directions, giving unto the said Captain Walter Rudstone full commission by virtue hereof to receive the said soldiers into his charge and to command and direct them as their captain and leader, willing and requiring his lieutenant and all other officers and soldiers of the said band and company to be obedient, dutiful and ready to receive and accomplish the directions and commandment of their said captain … that shall concern and be for the advancement of his Majesty's service in the premises. In witness whereof I have signed this commission and caused my seal of arms to be put thereunto. At the castle of Dublin the seventh day of June, *Anno Domini* 1634. Wentworth.

<Mr Walter Rudstone Captain>

Thomas Edmundes

406. [p. 2] <WARRANT FOR SEQUESTRATION OF THE CUSTOMS OF DUBLIN>

Whereas for divers good reasons as thereunto moving we hold it very requisite that the office or place of customs ~~of~~ in this port of D.[293] now held and enjoyed by Sir E.B., knight,[294] should be presently sequestered and reposing special trust in your integrity and judgment, we have thought fit to make choice of you two to be sequestrators thereof, and to that end we do hereby require and authorize you two jointly, not only forthwith to enter into and upon the said office ~~but~~ and to execute the same but also to demand and receive into ~~the same~~ your custodies all and every such book or books of entries as to the said office, do or ^ought^ properly to belong, and to keep due account of all goods and merchandize either inward or outward bound and to do and execute all and every thing and things that are fit and requisite to be done in and about the execution of the said office until you receive our directions to the

[291] The page is slightly torn where it has been folded. Endorsements read 'Mr Walter Rudstone, captain, East Riding' and, at the bottom of the page in small writing, 'Hayton, near Northlington'.

[292] This manuscript contains copies of original warrants, so the names of individuals have been inserted as initials. Individuals have been identified where possible (see editorial conventions for details).

[293] Dublin.

[294] Edward Bagshaw (see *Lib. mun. pub. Hib.*).

contrary. And in the meantime the said Sir E.B., his deputy and deputies, are required to forbear to take upon him and them or any of them the meddling with, or having to do with, the execution of the said office as he and they and every of them will answer the contrary at their peril. And for &c. Given &c.

To our well beloved C.M. and T.C., esquires.[295]

407. [p. 3] <WARRANT FOR THE PUNISHING SUCH AS REFUSE TO BRING TIMBER FOR HIS MAJESTY'S USE CONTRARY TO A FORMER DIRECTION TO ONE C.C.[296] TO THAT PURPOSE>

Whereas we have lately given several war[rants][297] and directions unto Mr C.C. of C.[298] for the sending and conveying hither of a certain proportion of timber which was ~~brought~~ bought in those parts towards the erecting of certain buildings to be speedily made and had in this his Majesty's Castle of D.,[299] he the said Mr C. hath complained unto us that notwithstanding the power so given him by our said warrant for the pressing as well of the shipping, boats, cots and other vessels for the transporting of the said timber as also for the taking up of boatmen and other labourers, ~~and~~ yet such is refractories and presumption of some and the dishonesty of others that they not only peremptorily refuse to obey the power and authority we gave him but also divers having received their monies aforehand ~~re~~ came away and leave the work undone, by which means the buildings are for the present at a stand and do likewise to be unless some speedy course be taken for the prevention thereof and the punishing of such dishonest and impudent persons as have already transgressed; to which end we do hereby straightly charge and command you and every of you wheresoever the bearer hereof shall require it that you do from time to time cause to be apprehended and punished according to their descents either by committing them to the gaol all and every such person and persons as either already have or hereafter shall offend in that kind, and you **[p. 4]** are likewise to be aiding and assisting as well unto the bearer as such as he shall employ under him in the management and following this business in the taking up and pressing from time to time all and every such kind of shipping, boats, cots, boat and men and all kind of labourers and workmen as shall be fit and requisite for that purpose; and if any shall refuse the service he or they being offered the usual hire and ~~accustomd~~ accustomed rates you are forthwith to commit to the gaol or otherwise to punish every such refuser or refractory person in such sort as you shall think fit to be inflicted for a contempt of this nature. And for &c. in the due execution whereof we require you and every of you not to fail as you tender the furtherance of his Majesty's service, and will answer the same at your uttermost perils. Given &c.

To all mayors, justices of the peace, sovereigns, portreeves within the several counties of C., W., &c.[300]

[295] Charles Monck and Thomas Cave (see *Lib. mun. pub. Hib.*).

[296] Calcott Chambré (d. 1635).

[297] Page cut off.

[298] Calcott Chambré of Carnew.

[299] Dublin.

[300] Carlow, Wicklow etc.

408. <WARRANT TO THE LORD CHANCELLOR CONCERNING THE ISSUING OF WRITS FOR THE PARLIAMENT> [14 MAY 1634]

Whereas the king's most excellent Majesty by his commission bearing date at W.[301] the – of – hath signified unto us his gracious pleasure concerning the summons of a parliament to be holden in this realm which is to be commenced the 14th day of July next, these are therefore to will and require you presently after **[p. 5]** receipt hereof to issue forth the usual writs of summons in that behalf to the lords of this realm, both spiritual and temporal, and the sheriffs of the several counties within this realm for choosing of knights, citizens and burgesses to be here in a readiness at the day aforesaid to give their help and attendance, and that generally you do and execute those and all other things which is in like cases is requisite and accustomed. And for so doing &c. Given the 14th of May 1634.

To our very good lord, the lord chancellor of Ireland.

409. <WARRANT CONCERNING THE ARCHBISHOP AND CLERGY>

These are to pray and require your lordship presently upon sight hereof to cause to issue forth under his Majesty's great seal several writs to the several archbishops of this kingdom hereby ~~req~~ requiring and authorizing them and every of them to call before them the several bishops, deans, archdeacons and clergy in these several provinces to appear before them in the convocation house to be holden in the cathedral church of St Patrick's in Dublin the 14th day of July next ~~ensuing~~ then and there to handle & conclude of such matters as shall be propounded on his Majesty's behalf. And for so doing &c. Given &c.

To our very good lord, the lord chancellor of Ireland.

410. [p. 6] <WARRANT TO BE CHIEF REMEMBRANCER>[302] [20 MAY 1634]

Whereas by reasons of the manifold misdemeanours and abuses committed by R.K.[303] in the execution of the place or office of chief remembrancer to his Majesty in his highness's Court of Exchequer, he the said K. being fairly proceeded against and questioned for the same was found and so ~~reduced~~ censured to be a man unworthy of the place and employment, by which means the said office being granted unto the said R.N.[304] and one J.K.[305] during good behaviour is now become void and in his Majesty's dispose. And forasmuch as we have been pleased to confer the same upon W.B.,[306] these are therefore to will and require you forthwith to draw up a fiant in due form of law containing a grant from his Majesty of the said office and place of chief remembrancer of the Court of Exchequer unto the said W.B., together with all such

301 Whitehall.

302 See warrant no. 8.

303 Robert Kennedy (see *Lib. mun. pub. Hib.*).

304 This may have been a mistake. It could be in a reference to Sir Dudley Norton, a former office holder.

305 John Kennedy (see *Lib. mun. pub. Hib.*).

306 William Bramhall (see *Lib. mun. pub. Hib.*).

fees, wages, perquisites, profits, emoluments, privileges and advantages whatsoever as the said R. & J.K., Henry Draicott, Roger Mainwaring, Richard C.[307] or J. C.,[308] or any other chief remembrancer of that court formerly had enjoyed or received by virtue ~~of~~ or reason, the said office or place are belonging any ways incident or appertaining to the same, to have, hold, exercise or enjoy the said office with all ~~fees~~ the said fees, profits, perquisites, allowances and premises during the good behaviour of the said W.B. in as large, ample and beneficial manner to all intents and purposes whatsoever as the said R. and J.K., [**p.** 7] H.D., R.M., R.C. & J.C. or any other chief remembrancer of that court formerly had ^and^ enjoyed or ~~received by virtue or reasons of the said office~~ of right ~~ou~~ ought to have held and enjoyed the same, to be executed and exercised by him the said B. or his sufficient deputy or deputies during ~~his~~ good behaviour as aforesaid, inserting therein all such clauses as in cases of like nature are usual. And the said fiant fairly engrossed in parchment under your hand to be sent us to be further passed as appertaineth. For doing whereof this shall be your sufficient warrant. Given &c. 20 May 1634.

To our ^trusty &^ well beloved, ~~and trusty~~ his Majesty's attorney and solicitor general, or either of them.

411. <A WARRANT FOR PRINTING OF A BOOK> [28 MARCH 1634]

Whereas C.S.[309] hath petitioned unto us setting forth that for these many years past [*sic*] he hath taken a great deal of pains in endeavouring to compose and reduce the manner and art of teaching children the Latin tongue to a brief way and method, and now having brought the same to perfection hath humbly besought us ~~that~~ to give way that the same being complied into a volume and entitled the art of teaching of the Latin ~~Tongue~~ speech may be permitted to pass the press, whose request therein we have thought fit to grant the rather in regard the work hath already [**p. 8**] been perused and approved by the reverend father in God, the lord archbishop of Armagh, primate and metropolitan of all Ireland, as a work that may much tend to the advancement of learning and produce a common ~~& future~~ benefit both to the present and future ages. These are therefore to will and require you forthwith to draw up a fiant in due form containing a grant, free leave, full power, licence and liberty from his Majesty, his heirs and successors, unto the said C.S. to have and cause to be printed the said intended book which is to be entitled the Art of teaching the Latin speech, and to teach and practice it and to sell or cause to be sold at reasonable rates in any part of this kingdom such and so many of the said books as he shall think convenient, or can be vended for and during the abode and residence of him the said S. in this kingdom, or till our pleasure therein shall be further known with an inhibition or commandment that none other person or persons within the said kingdom shall print or vend or cause to be printed & sold any of the same books without the consent and allowance of him the said S., who, together with his assigns, are solely to enjoy the benefit that may

307 Richard Colman (see *Lib. mun. pub. Hib.*).

308 James Carroll (d.1639), landowner and state offical (see *DIB*).

309 Christopher Syms.

redound thereby during his abode in this kingdom as aforesaid or during our pleasure *in lieu* and recompense of his pains and travail therein [**p. 9**] bestowed. And in case any shall print or cause ^the said book^ to be printed for sale during the time aforesaid that then and in such cases it shall and may be lawful to and for him, the said S. and his said assigns, to seize upon & to take up ^to^ his and to their proper use and uses all such book or books as shall be so printed or offered to sale aforesaid for and during the term aforesaid. And the same fairly engrossed in parchment under your hand to send unto us to be further passed as ~~appertanth~~ appertaineth. And for so doing this shall be a sufficient warrant given at his Majesty's Castle of D.[310] the 28th day of March 1634.

To our well beloved, his Majesty's attorney and solicitor general, or either of them.

412. <WARRANT FOR THE DISSOLUTION OF THE SEQUESTRATION OF SIR E.B.[311] OFFICE>

Whereas for divers good reasons us [*sic*] thereunto moving we gave you two jointly full power & authority by our warrant of the 22nd of this month to enter upon and by way of sequestration to keep and exercise the office or place of customer in this port of D.[312] held by Sir E.B., knight, until you should [**p. 10**] receive further directions ^to the contrary^; now upon the said Sir E.B. his humble submission and the hope we have of his ^future^ conformity in the execution of that his employment we are pleased and accordingly do hereby revoke and disannul the said sequestration, willing and hereby requiring you two not only to desist from any further ^inter^meddling with the execution of the said office but also to be accountable & responsible to him the said Sir E.B. for the mean profits thereof during such time as the same remained ~~are~~ sequestered into your hands as aforesaid. And for so doing &c. Given &c.

To our well beloved C.M. and T.C., esquires.[313]

413. <WARRANT TO ASSIST G.H. WITH MEN FROM ONE STAGE TO ANOTHER IN CASE HE SHALL SEE CAUSE TO ~~RE~~ REQUIRE IT> [2 JUNE 1634]

Whereas we have appointed G.H., gent, to convey his Majesty's treasure to the city of London for the payment of the shipping appointed to guard this coast of Ireland, these are ~~to therefore~~ therefore to will and require you and every of you to be aiding and assisting unto the said G.H. in conveying the said treasure and to furnish him with sufficient able men to convey and guard the same as occasion shall require from [**p. 11**] stage to stage until he come to London aforesaid where he is directed to pay the same, whereas you may not fail &c. Given &c. the 2nd day of June 1634.

To all mayors, sheriffs, bailiffs, constables and all other his Majesty's officers whom it may concern.

310 Dublin.

311 Edward Bagshaw (see *Lib. mun. pub. Hib.*).

312 Dublin.

313 Charles Monck and Thomas Cave (see *Lib. mun. pub. Hib.*).

414. <WARRANT FOR A GUIDE AND POST HORSES>

Whereas this bearer G.H., gent, is employed by us into England for his Majesty's special service we therefore require you and every of you whom it may concern to furnish the said G.H. with sufficient horses and a guide from place to place, he paying for the same according to his Majesty's usual and accustomed rates; whereof you may not fail. And for so doing this shall be your warrant. Given &c.

To all mayors &c. *ut supra.*

415. <LICENCE OF ABSENCE FOR 3 MONTHS>

Whereas upon humble suit made unto us by Thomas M., gent,[314] his Majesty's customs for the port of G.[315] we have [been] pleased to licence him to make his repair into England and there to remain about the dispatch of certain special affairs of his own for and during the space [**p. 12**] of three months next ensuing the date hereof. These are therefore to will and require all and every, his Majesty's officers, ~~and~~ minsters and loving subjects whom it may concern, not only to take due notice thereof but also to afford him the full benefit ^of this our^ licence without any prejudice be incurred by him in his said employment of customer by reason of his absence during the time aforesaid; whereof they and every of them are not to fail. And for so doing this shall be a sufficient warrant. Given &c.

416. <WARRANT FOR THE PRESSING OF THE POST BARQUE FOR THE E. OF C.[316] TO GO FOR ENGLAND>

Whereas our right trusty and ^right^ well beloved the E. of C. being now in this town of D.[317] is to make his present repair into England and inasmuch as there are no shipping in this port that are bound thither for the present with that speed as his lordship desires, we therefore upon his humble ~~request~~ suit have thought fit and do accordingly thereby require you forthwith to take his lordship aboard, you and him and his to transport waft and carry over, and his lordship having so wafted and landed there to return ~~hith~~ ^hether^ with all the speed and expedition you can; for doing whereof this shall be your warrant. Given &c.

417. [p. 13] <WARRANT TO EXAMINE WITNESSES BETWEEN PARTY AND PARTY>

Whereas there is a difference depending before us between H.B., plaintiff, and E.B., defendant, and inasmuch as the truth cannot ^certainly^ appear but by examination of witness upon oath, we therefore have thought fit and accordingly hereby require and authorize you to examine upon oath all such witnesses as shall be produced to be examined in this matter and upon such interrogatories as either party shall administer and present, and the depositions so taken, to return unto us with all convenient speed

314 Thomas Maynard (see *Lib. mun. pub. Hib.*).

315 Galway.

316 Richard Boyle (1566–1643), 1st earl of Cork (see *DIB*).

317 Dublin.

that we may thereupon proceed to a hearing of the cause; for doing whereof this &c. Given &c.

To our trusty and well beloved Sir William Ussher, knight, and P.D.,[318] esquire, clerks of the Council, or either of them.

418. <WARRANT FOR A COMMISSION BETWEEN PARTY & PARTY>

Whereas there is a difference depending before us between R.T., plaintiff, and C.E., defendant, and inasmuch as the truth therein cannot appear unto us without the examining of witness[es] upon each, we therefore have thought fit and do accordingly hereby pray and require your lordship forthwith to cause a commission to issue to that purpose under the great seal and the same to be **[p. 14]** unto our well beloved W.S., clerk, chancellor of Ferns,[319] G.G. & R.H., gent,[320] authorizing them or any two of them to examine upon oath all and every such witnesses as shall be produced by either party to be examined concerning this matter and upon such interrogatories as either party shall present or exhibit, the said commission to be returnable with all convenient speed and at the furthest by the 10th of the next month provided the plaintiff do give 15 days notice of the execution of the said commission unto the ~~said~~ defendant that he likewise may be prepared and ready against the time of the execution thereof. And for so doing &c. Given &c.

To our very good lord, the lord chancellor.

419. <WARRANT FOR A FALCONER>

Whereas our servant and falconer H.M. hath complained unto us that himself and such as he employeth already to kill hawk's meat are often times abused and threatened to have their pieces taken from them, of which disrepective usage & carriage towards our servants we cannot but take special notice, and therefore we require all and every, his Majesty's officers, ~~and~~ ministers & loving subjects whatsoever whom it may concern, not only to take due notice that the said M. is our servant **[p. 15]** but also to permit him and such as he shall from time to time employ under him to take and kill any kind of birds or fowl for hawk's meat as aforesaid without any manner their pelts or hindrances whatsoever; whereof they and every of them are not to fail at their perils. Given &c.

420. <WARRANT FOR PAYMENT OF 250*li.* OUT OF THE TREASURY UNTO SIR G.R.[321]>

Whereas his Majesty having thought fit to employ the service of our right trusty and well beloved Sir G.R., knight of his ~~Majesty's~~ learned Council in his Majesty's affairs of this kingdom, his highness was graciously pleased to allow unto him the said Sir G.R.

318 Paul Davies (Davis) (d. 1672), clerk of the privy council and secretary of state (see *DIB*).

319 Walter (or William) Stafford, appointed chancellor in 1610 (see Cotton, *Fasti*).

320 Possibly Robert Harpole (or Hartpole), MP for Carlow (see McGrath).

321 George Radcliffe (1593–1657), lawyer and politician (see *DIB*).

the sum of 500*li.* sterling yearly to be paid proportionally at M.[322] and Our Lady day during his employment in the said service here; and forasmuch as there is due unto the said Sir G.R. the sum of 250*li.* sterling at Our Lady day last as for his allowance for the half year then ending, these are therefore to pray and require your lordship to pray and require your lordship to make present ~~satisfaction~~ payment out of such his Majesty's monies as remain in your hands or which shall first come to your hands of the said sums of 250*li.* sterling unto the said Sir G.R. according to the purport of his Majesty's [**p. 16**] letters unto us of the 17th of May 1633, a copy whereof we have already sent you; hereof you may not fail &c. And for so doing &c. Given &c.

To our very good lord, the Lord Mountnorris, his Majesty's vice-treasurer and receiver-general of his Majesty's revenue in Ireland.

421. <WARRANT CONCERNING THE PURSUIVANTS FEES>

Whereas notwithstanding the late proclamation for timely payment to be made into his Majesty's Exchequer of his Majesty's rents and revenues due for the half year ending at Easter last, yet such is the backwardness of divers his Majesty's ~~Subjects~~ tenants therein as that many of them hitherto have failed and contemptuously neglected to bring in the same, by which means not only the army but all other his Majesty's officers and ministers for whose payments the same were to be designed have suffered in general; upon consideration whereof we have lately issued our warrants from the table for the attaching and bringing in of such defaulters the better to quicken them to hasten their payments. But the pursuivants, who were by us employed in that behalf, do complain that when they and their deputies have made long and tedious journeys into divers remote parts of the kingdom to their great travel & extraordinary charge, they are often bereaved of their [**p. 17**] fees by reason of the countless dealings of some of the said defaulters, who understanding of such ~~debeders~~ warrants to be issued against them, do repair hither in the pursuivants absence and pay their monies and so having received their [ ] acquaintance depart home again without once regarding the pursuivants fees to their, the said pursuivants, exceeding great loss and prejudice. We therefore, holding it not fit that they being employed by our special directions and in matters tending so much to the good of his Majesty's service should be deprived of their just and due reward, do hereby will and require you and every of you henceforth not to deliver and acquittance [*sic*] or other discharges unto any person or persons ~~as~~ as are indebted unto his Majesty and who have been or shall be sent for by our warrants for the rents aforesaid until every such person or persons shall first present him or themselves unto the proper pursuivant who hath been sent for by him or them, and that he the said pursuivant shall intimate & make known unto you that he is satisfied his due fees. Whereof you and every of you are not to fail. And for so doing this shall be your warrant. Given &c.

To our well beloved, the deputy receiver & to all other the officers of his Majesty's Court of Exchequer whom it doth or may concern and to every of them.

322 Michaelmas.

422. [p. 18] <WARRANT TO BIND ONE TO THE GOOD BEHAVIOUR>

Whereas we think it very fit that T.C., gent, should for his late irreverent and disrespective[323] carriages towards some persons of eminence and members of the state here be bound to the good behaviour, these are therefore to pray and require your lordship to give directions for his immediate ~~enlargement~~ apprehension and to cause him to be restrained of his liberty until he enter into good recognizance with sufficient sureties to be bound to the good behaviour for the space ^of one^ whole year next ensuing towards all his Majesty's liege, people and especially towards our trusty and well beloved Sir G.R., knight,[324] one of his Majesty's privy council in this kingdom. Whereof we pray your lordship not to fail &c. Given &c.

To our trusty and well beloved, the lord chief justice of the chief place.

423. <WARRANT FOR THE FERRIES>

These are to will and require you forthwith ~~to pay~~ upon sight hereof to draw up a fiant in due form of law containing a grant from his Majesty, R.H., H.M. & J.H. of the ferries in a schedule hereunto annexed, mentioned and of all other ferries within this kingdom not formerly granted away by his Majesty or any of his Majesty's predecessors, to have and to hold unto ~~the~~ them the said R.H., H.M. & J.H., **[p. 19]** their executors and assigns, ^for &^ during the term of 21 years next ensuing the date of the letters patents hereupon to be passed, reserving upon & out of all & every the said ~~passages and~~ ferries & passages the yearly rent in the said schedule annexed, mentioned & contained; and inserting a clause for the extinguishing of the rents of what they do not enjoy, the said R., H. & J., and taking upon every of the narrow passages for every man half penny, & for every horse a penny & for every loaded carre[325] a penny as hath been accustomed, and also for ^every^ bread passage for every man a penny, for every horse two pence, and for every loaded carre two pence, and that they may from time to time take for the commissions to enquire of all ferries that are withholden and detained from his Majesty within the kingdom; and inserting a clause in the said fiant to enable the said R., H. and J. to put down all cots and insufficient ferry boats in all such places as shall by inquisition be found to be inconvenient for his Majesty's subjects, taking such rates & paying such rents rateably and proportionally. As for the ferries before mentioned, and inserting therein all such clauses and conditions ~~therein~~ as in grants of like nature are usual, together with a power to be reserved unto us and the deputy or deputies or other chief governor or governors of this ~~kink~~ kingdom for the time being, to resume and revoke the said grant **[p. 20]** if it shall be thought fit to impose a ~~greatrent~~ greater rent hereafter then is now reserved. And the same fairly engrossed in parchment under your hand to send unto us to be further passed as appertaineth. And for so doing this shall be your warrant. Given &c.

To our trusty and well beloved his Majesty's attorney & solicitor general, ~~&~~ or either of them.

[323] i.e. disrespectful.

[324] Sir George Radcliffe (1593–1657), lawyer and politician (see *DIB*).

[325] i.e. cart.

424. <WARRANT FOR THE PAYMENT OF THE CIVIL LIST>

Although by our warrant of the 15th of the last month we did require your lordship not to make payment upon any warrants of full pay of any money of his Majesty's unto any person or persons whatsoever until you did receive our further directions in that behalf, yet we considering how his Majesty's rents and revenues have since that time been paid & bought in a good measure into the Exchequer, we think it fit and so do hereby pray and require your lordship out ^of such^ of his Majesty's monies aforesaid to make present payment as well unto the judges as all such others as are or do stand within the compass of the civil list of such entertainments as are severally due unto them for the ~~haf~~ half year ending at Easter last. And for so doing this shall be your lordship's warrant, any former directions notwithstanding. Given &c.

To our very good lord, the Lord Mountnorris, his Majesty's vice-treasurer and receiver-general at his ~~Majesty's~~ highness's revenues in Ireland.

425. [p. 21] <WARRANT FOR THE PAYMENT OF 1,002*li.* TO THE EARL OF CARLISLE[326] FOR THE IMPOST OF WINES>

Whereas his Majesty by his letters of the seventeenth of December 1633 hath authorized us to give order to your lordship to pay to our very good lord, James E. of C., or his assigns, all such sums of money and arrears as are either already accrued or hereafter shall grow due by the impost of wines according to the old rates paid ~~unto~~ ^before^ the surrender of his letters patents over and above the rent of 1,400*li. per annum* ~~formely~~ formerly reserved to his Majesty, now forasmuch as it appeareth by a certificate under Sir James Ware's[327] hand that the impost of wines according to the old rates for the year ending the 25th March last amounted to the sum of 2,402*li.* 7*s.* 10*d.* sterling, out of which the rent of 1,400*li.* being deducted there will remain due to the said earl the sum of 1,002*li.* 7*s.* 10*d.*, these are to will and require you, out of such his Majesty's revenues as now remain under your charge or shall next come to your hands, to pay to the said E. of C. or his assigns the said sum of 1,002*li.* 7*s.* 10*d.* sterling. And for so doing this, ~~shall be~~ together with his assign's acquaintance confessing the ~~same~~ receipt thereof, shall be to you and the commissioners of your accounts a sufficient warrant ^& discharge^ in that behalf. Given &c.

To our very good lord, the Lord Mountnorris, his Majesty's vice-treasurer and general-receiver.

426. [p. 22] <WARRANT FOR A FIANT FOR MAKING TOBACCO PIPES>

These are to will and require you forthwith to draw up a fiant in due form of law containing a grant from his Majesty, his heirs and successors, unto W.L., esquire, his heirs and assigns of licence, for the sole making and selling of tobacco pipes throughout all this kingdom of Ireland for the term of 31 years, to begin at the

326 James Hay (*c.* 1580–1636), 1st earl of Carlisle (see *ODNB*).

327 James Ware, auditor general, privy councillor and distinguished historian and antiquarian (see *DIB*).

determination of one J.C.,[328] patent of a licence for the sole making of the said pipes, the said L. or his assigns paying into his Majesty's Exchequer here the yearly rent of 10*li.* sterling during the said term of 31 years, inserting therein a clause of restraint to all others from the making [of] the said pipes in this realm and from the selling of them, whether made here or imported from other parts, to be sold without the licence of the said W.L. or his assigns by the forfeiture to him or them ~~to~~ together with all such other clauses of *non obstant* and otherwise as are beneficial and usual. And the same fairly engrossed in parchment under your hand to send ^unto^ ~~to~~ us to be further passed as appertaineth according to the purport of his Majesty's letters unto us of the 28th of April last, a copy whereof for your better information we have hereby sent you. For doing whereof this shall be your warrant. Given &c.

427. [p. 23] <WARRANT CONCERNING THE LICENCES OF ALEHOUSES' MONIES WHICH ARE ~~NOT~~ RECEIVED AND NOT PAID>

Whereas we are informed that divers of the commissioners and the receivers of the money to the money for the licensing of alehouses throughout this kingdom, as well in counties as within cities and towns corporal, having received of the said monies do not return the same into his Majesty's Court of Exchequer as by the commission & instructions they are directed, but do detain it contrary to their said directions and contrary to our said expectation, these are therefore to require all and every such person and persons of the said commissioners and receivers as have any ~~the~~ of the said monies in their hands forthwith upon sight hereof to appear before us to answer their said neglect and contempt in that behalf, hereby admonishing and requiring all others that shall receive any of the said money hereafter to be more careful in the due returning in of the same according to their directions as they will answer the contrary at their perils. Given &c.

428. <WARRANT TO TRANSPORT PLATE & MONIES>

Whereas J.G., esquire, hath made known unto us that he being to make his repair into England divers friends of his have desired him to carry over with him divers parcels of plate which are hereunder written to be exchanged for now, to which end, and for [**p. 24**] the transportation of 200*li.* in monies for his own use, he humbly beseecheth us to grant him our licence whose request therein we have thought fit to grant. And therefore we do hereby will and ~~re~~ require you and every of you to permit and suffer the said J.G. to put aboard & transport, as well the said money as the ~~same~~ parcels of plate undernamed, without any your lets or hindrances whatsoever, where you & every of you are not to fail. And for so doing &c. Given &c.

Four great white bowls &c.

To all and every, his Majesty's officers of the customs in the port of D.[329]

[328] Joshua Carpenter (1585–1656), MP for Carlingford (see McGrath).

[329] Dublin.

429. <WARRANT TO SEIZE ON HAWKS>

Whereas we are credibly informed that there are divers loose and idle persons who make it their trade of life to steal hawks and sometimes to buy them for a small value, which they commonly sell up & down to such as come out of England hither on purpose to bind & transport them for their own private gain, by which means the nobility & gentry of the kingdom cannot furnish themselves with hawks either for their own provision or to pleasure their friends in England, and inasmuch as we are informed that there are in any such persons which come from Connacht with **[p. 25]** hawks in that kind and being given to understand that you are to make your repair into that province we therefore have thought fit and do accordingly hereby authorize you where you shall meet any such persons in your journey as have hawks to sell, not only to seize upon them but also to bring and present the same unto us to be disposed of as we shall think fit. And for so doing this shall be your warrant in the due execution whereof we require all & every, his Majesty's officers, ministers and loving subjects whom it may concern to be aiding and assisting unto you as there shall be occasion, whereof they may not fail herein. Given &c.

To our well beloved Thomas Hill, gent.

430. <WARRANT FOR STAY OF ALL SHIPPING>

Whereas for reasons best known unto our self we have thought fit to restrain for the present setting forth or going of any ships, barques, vessels or boats out of this harbour either for England or elsewhere, these are therefore to require & authorize you forthwith to take such order as that neither ship, barque nor boat or vessel do depart or go to sea out of this port **[p. 26]** or harbour of Dublin without our ~~p~~ express ~~order~~ warrant or directions in that behalf; and for so doing this shall be your warrant, in the due execution whereof we require we require [*sic*] all and every, his Majesty's officers and ministers, owners and masters of all ships and vessel whatsoever, to be aiding and assisting unto you and your deputy and deputies as there shall be occasion; whereof you and they are not to fail at your and their perils. Given &c.

To our well beloved W.M., esquire,[330] his Majesty's searcher for the port of Dublin.

431. <~~WHEREAS THE PERSONS~~ WARRANT TO ATTACH FOR NOT BRINGING IN THEIR PORT AND TITHE CORN>

Whereas the persons undernamed stand severally indebted unto ~~divers~~ his Majesty in divers pecks of port and tithe corn which by his highness is assigned towards the provision of our household and should have been long since delivered by them into our granary, for which they have been called unto ~~for~~ by such as we entrusted in that behalf, but they have wilfully neglected the bringing in thereof, by which means we have been forced for the duly provision of our household and stables to send

330 William Scott (see *Lib. mun. pub. Hib.*).

from time to time to the market to our very great charge and trouble occasioned by their non payment and delivery of the corn so due by them, these are therefore to will and require you forthwith to repair to the several dwellings ~~houses~~ of the said persons undernamed and them there, or wheresoever they can be found, to attach and immediately to bring before the steward and comptroller of our house whom we hereby authorize to commit into prison [**p. 27**] such and so in any of the persons as shall not give sufficient assurance for the delivery present delivery [*sic*] of the corn so due, and them respectively or shall otherwise refuse to compound for the same by payment in ready money at such rates as are and have been of late given by our officers in the market for several sorts of grain which by them long since ought to have been long since brought in, [*sic*] whereof you may not fail. And for so &c. Given &c.

To any of his Majesty's pursuivants.

432. <WARRANT FOR THE TRANSPORTING OF 500*li.* IN MONEY & PLATE & HOUSEHOLD FURNITURE & 5 HORSES>

Whereas A.D., wife of J.D., esquire, having urgent occasion to make her present repair into England with her family hath humbly besought us to be pleased to grant her our licence for the transportation of 500*li.* in money, which without her very great prejudice she cannot want at her arrival in England nor can she by any means get returned over so soon as may serve her ^husband's^ occasions there, as also five horses or geldings for her and her family to ride on or such household plate and furniture as she ~~shall~~ hath occasion to make use of on the other side, whose requests therein we have thought fit to grant and therefore do hereby will and require you and every of you to permit & suffer the said A.D., herself or her servant, to put aboard [**p. 28**] and transport as well the said money and plate as the said horses or geldings and furniture aforesaid out of this port without any your lets or hindrances; for the doing whereof &c. Given &c.

To all and every, his Majesty's officers of the customs in the port of Dublin.

433. <A WARRANT UPON THE CONTRACT MADE WHICH SIR T.P.[331] IN THE SURRENDER OF HIS PENSION OF 6*li.* 8D. *PER DIEM* ~~FOR~~ TO THE LORD MOUNTNORRIS FOR THE PAYMENT OF 500*li.* TO THE LORD DEPUTY>

Whereas his Majesty by his letters of the 10th of July last hath ratified and confirmed a contract made by us (upon his Majesty's direction) with Sir T.P., knight, for the surrender of his pension of 6*li.* 8*d.* sterling, granted to him and his son during their lives for the sum of 500*li.* English which we paid unto him and hath likewise by the said letters authorized and required you to pay unto us the said sum of 500*li.* without any defalcation, these are to require your lordship out of such his Majesty's revenues as, nor are or shall, next come to your hands to satisfy and pay unto us the lord deputy the sum of 500*li.* And for so doing this, together without acquaintance confessing

[331] Possibly Sir Thomas Phillips (*c.* 1560–1636), soldier and planter (see *DIB*).

the receipt thereof, shall be ~~to~~ unto you and the commissioners of your accounts sufficient warrant and discharge in that behalf. Given &c.

To our very good lord, the Lord Mountnorris, his Majesty's vice-treasurer and general-receiver &c.

434. [p. 29] <WARRANT FOR THE PROROGUE [OF] THE PARLIAMENT>

Thomas Viscount Wentworth, baron of Wentworth Woodhouse, lord Newmarsh and Oversley, lord president of his Majesty's Council established in the north parts of England, lord lieutenant of Yorkshire, one of his Majesty's most honourable privy council, and lord deputy general of Ireland, to the lords spiritual and temporal and to the commons in this present parliament assembled, greeting. Forasmuch as the general assizes and the time and season ~~and~~ ^of^ harvest is like to continue until towards the latter end of ~~harvest~~ October, we have thought it fit and convenient, as well for his Majesty's service in the circuits of the justices of the assizes where the justices of ^the^ peace and divers others here employed are necessarily to attend as for the good of the subjects of this kingdom in general, to prorogue this present parliament and do by their present prorogue the same until the 4th day of November next ensuing the date hereof, on which day our purpose is to hold the same as this his Majesty's Castle of Dublin. Given under our seal at his Majesty's said castle &c.

By the lord deputy's commandment.

435. [p. 30] <WARRANT FOR A COMMISSION ABOUT THE CUSTOMS>

Whereas we are informed that there are divers foul and gross abuses ~~committed~~ frequently done and committed by divers persons, as well merchants as others, in all or the greatest part of the ports in this kingdom to the great prejudice and loss of his Majesty in the revenue of his ~~kingdom~~ customs, and so the damage likely to increase every day more & more unless some speedy course be taken, as well for the prevention thereof for the future as the punishment of such as have already transgressed to the terror of others, to which end we do hereby will and require you forthwith to draw up a commission to be directed to our ~~to us~~ right trusty and well beloved Sir G.R.,[332] knight, ~~of~~ one of his Majesty's privy council in this kingdom, thereby giving him the said Sir G. full power and authority to examine and find out as well by oath as otherwise who the said transgressors are, what their several offences and transgressions were, and when the same were done and acted. The said commission to be returnable by the latter end of ^the^ next Michaelmas term at the furthest or sooner if it may ^be^ conveniently ~~be~~ done. And the same fairly engrossed in parchment under your hand to send ~~to us~~ unto us to be further passed as ~~aforesaid~~ appertaineth; for doing whereof this shall be your warrant. Given &c.

To our trusty and well beloved, his Majesty's attorney and solicitor general, or either of them.

332 George Radcliffe (1593–1657), lawyer and politician (see *DIB*).

436. [p. 31] <WARRANT FOR PLATE>

Whereas our well beloved W.H., esquire, hath made known unto us that he hath 2 silver pots & 2 silver tankards to be brought out of England hither, for the better conveyance whereof he humbly besought our warrant which we have thought fit to grant. And therefore we do hereby require you and every of you to permit and suffer the said 2 silver pots & ~~2 si~~ 2 silver tankards to be put aboard and transported hither without any your lets or stays whatsoever. Whereof &c. Given &c.

To all and every, his Majesty's officers of the customs in the port of Chester and the creeks and members thereout belonging.

437. <WARRANT FOR A COMMISSION TO ISSUE FOR THE ENQUIRY OF CERTAIN LANDS IN THE COUNTY OF LIMERICK>

These are to pray and require your lordship to issue forth a commission ~~forth of this~~ under the great seal of this kingdom directed to the right reverend father in God, the lord bishop of Limerick, to our well beloved Sir T.S., Sir H.W.[333] and Sir P.S., knights,[334] and to the escheator and feodary of the province of Munster and their deputies or to any two or more of them, whereof the said escheator and feodary or their deputy or deputies to be always one, to ~~excell~~ enquire as well by the oaths of good and lawful men of the county of Limerick as by all other good ways and means whatsoever of his Majesty's right title and interest unto the town and lands of [**p. 32**] Rosmeane in the ^said^ county containing the 6th part of a plough land, which by letters patents of King James of happy memory were past [*sic*] unto one J.W., esquire, and by mean conveyance from him came and is now in the possession of Sir Thomas B., knight; and the same to be returnable with all convenient speed and at the furthest be the last of the next Michaelmas term; for doing &c.

To our &c., the lord chancellor.

438. <WARRANT TO SEIZE ON TOBACCO PIPES>

Whereas it pleased his Majesty of blessed memory with the advice and consent of the right honourable ~~the Lo.~~ Sir Oliver St John, knight,[335] then deputy general of his highness's realm of Ireland, by his letters patents dated the 30th day of October in the fifteenth year year [*sic*] of his Majesty's reign of England &c. for a good consideration therein, expressed to grant unto J.C.,[336] his executors, administrators and assigns, and to all and every such person and persons as he the said Coker ~~shoulde~~ ^should^ nominate and appoint special licence and ~~authority~~ full liberty, power and authority for and during a certain term therein limited by himself, his deputies, servants or assigns, to make tobacco pipes and the same so made to vend, utter and sell in and

333 Hardress Waller (1604?–1666), MP for Limerick county (see McGrath).

334 Percy Smith, later governor of Youghal (see *Lib. mun. pub. Hib.*).

335 Oliver St John (1559–1630), Viscount Grandison and Baron Tregoz, lord deputy of Ireland (see *DIB*).

336 John Coker.

through the ~~kingdom~~ whole kingdom of England with a clause of restitution to all and every other person and persons without the said C.['s] licence to make, vend & utter tobacco pipes within the said kingdom; as likewise reserving by the said letters patents a seizure of the [**p. 33**] forfeiture of the moiety of all such tobacco pipes as should be made by any such person or persons then such as were thereto authorized by the said C., to the furtherance whereof his Majesty was then graciously pleased to charge and command all mayors, justices of the peace, sovereigns, portreeves, sheriffs, bailiffs, constables and all other the officers and ministers or others his Majesty's loving subjects whatsoever, from time to time to be aiding and assisting unto the said John Coker, his executors, administrators, deputies, factors and assigns, in the seizing or taking of all such tobacco pipes, clay & other stuff & instruments as shall be forfeited or seized by virtue of the said grant. Now these are in his Majesty's name by virtue of the said letters patents to will and command all mayors, justices of the peace, sovereigns, portreeves, sheriffs, bailiffs, constables and all other his Majesty's loving subjects whatsoever to aid and assist P.K. who is lawfully deputated by John P. and assigned to A.L., widow, relict & executrix of the said J.C., and the due execution or seizure of all tobacco pipes, clay stuff & instruments of all such person & persons as shall attempt the making, sale or utterance of any tobacco pipes within the [ ] province of Leinster & [**p. 34**] all city, towns corporate, franchises & privileged places within the same contrary to the intent of his said Majesty's late letters patents granted as aforesaid. And for so doing this &c. Given &c.

439. <WARRANT FOR THE 2ND EXAMINATORS OFFICE IN THE CHANCERY>

These are to will and require you forthwith upon sight hereof to draw up a fiant in due form of law containing a grant from his Majesty unto W.R., esquire, & W.R.[337] of the office of the 2nd executor of the Court of Chancery with all fees, duties and perquisites thereunto belonging in as large and ample manner as the same was granted to Sir T.C., knight,[338] by letters patents of our sovereign lord the king as likewise a grant unto the said W.R. & C.R.[339] of the office of receiving, ~~and~~ filing & transcribing copies of all depositions taken by commission on the ^part &^ behalf of any party or parties in any cause or suit depending in the court of Chancery in this kingdom in as large and ample manner as the same were heretofore granted to Sir T.C., J.P. & N.C.,[340] or to any [or] either of them, unto the said W.R. during the term of his natural life, inserting therein all such other clauses as in grants of like nature are usual. And the same fairly engrossed in parchment [**p. 35**] under your hand to send to be further passed &c. Given &c.

To our well beloved, his Majesty's attorney & solicitor general, or either of them.

[337] William Ryves (d. 1648), judge (see *DIB*).

[338] Thomas Cary (Carry), master in chancery and prothonotary of court of common pleas 1627–34 (see Hughes, *Patentee officers*).

[339] William Ryves, see above note 337; Charles Ryves, see note 57.

[340] Thomas Cary, see above note 338, J.P. (unresolved), and Nathaniel Catelyn (see *Lib. mun. pub. Hib.*).

440. <WARRANT FOR THE TAKING OF PARTRIDGES &C.>

Whereas our very good lord the earl of C.[341] hath made known unto us that for his better recreation and pleasure in M.[342] in the county of K.[343] he is desirous to have his lands furnished with divers sorts of game we, upon his lordship's humble suit, have thought fit and do accordingly hereby give & grant free leave, licence and authority unto such person as ~~shall~~ his lordship shall nominate and appoint under his hand and seal in that behalf, not only to take with nets and other engines as well hares as partridges in any part of the province of Leinster (the lands of noblemen and such gent of quality as have manors and royalties of their own without their own consents and also 7 miles about this city of D.[344] only excepted) but also to carry the said hares & partridges unto his lordship's said lands to be disposed of as aforesaid, willing and hereby requiring as well the masters of the game as also others whom it may concern within the said province, not only to take due notice thereof but also to afford such as his lordship shall [**p. 36**] employ as aforesaid the full benefit of this our warrant without any their lets and hindrances whatsoever. And for so doing &c.

441. <LICENCE OF ABSENCE FOR 6 MONTHS>

Whereas upon humble suit made unto us by our well beloved Sir T.C., one of his Majesty's privy council &c., we have been pleased to licence him to make his repair into England and there to remain for the space of 6 months next ensuing the date hereof about the dispatch of certain special affairs of his own, these are therefore to pray and require your lordship to cause a licence of absence to be drawn up for him and to affix the great seal thereunto and thereby giving him leave to remain in England during the time aforesaid without any forfeiture to be made by him of any office or offices which he the said Sir T.C., either alone or joineth with any other, doth hold from his Majesty in this kingdom or any other prejudice to be incurred by him by reason of his absence during that time. And &c. Given &c.

To our very good lord, the lord chancellor.

442. <WARRANT FOR THE OFFICE OF THE HANAPER &C.>

These are to will and require you forthwith to [ ] draw up a grant for his Majesty, his heirs and successors, unto G.C. [345] and R.M.,[346] esquires, not only of the office of clerk of the Hanaper but also of the place or office of [**p. 37**] the clerk of the Crown in his Majesty's High Court of ~~Chancery the~~ Pleas or office of the Crown in his Majesty's High Court of Chancery of this kingdom, to have, hold, possess and enjoy

341 Earl of Cork: Richard Boyle (1566–1643), 1st earl of Cork (see *DIB*).

342 Maynooth.

343 Kildare.

344 Dublin.

345 George Carleton (see *Lib. mun. pub. Hib.*).

346 Robert Meredith (*c.* 1592–1668), clerk of the hanaper and later chancellor of the exchequer (see McGrath).

the said offices and places of the Hanaper and clerk of the Crown in his Majesty's said court of Chancery unto them the said G.C. and R.M., and either of them, upon and immediately after the decease, surrender, removal or other avoidance of Sir J.K., knight,[347] who holds the ~~said~~ same during the life or lives of them, the said G.C. and R.M., and the longest liver of them together with such yearly fees and stipend as are now allowed and given unto him the said Sir J.K. for the execution of the said several offices from his Majesty and also all such other fees, profits, perquisites and commodities whatsoever unto the said offices, or either of them, belonging and incident or anywise appertaining, and in as large, ~~and~~ ample and beneficial manner as N.S., T.A., L.A., W.A, W.P.,[348] and the said Sir J.K. or F.E.[349] or any other formerly held and enjoyed the same, to be exercised by them the said G.C. and R.M., or either of them, their deputy or deputies, or ^the^ deputy or deputies of one of them, inserting therein all such clauses as in like cases are usual. And the same fairly engrossed in parchment under your hand to send unto us to be further passed &c. Given &c.

To our &c. the attorney and solicitor, or either of them.

443. [p. 40][350] [WARRANT RELATING TO THE POST OF SECOND EXAMINATOR OF THE COURT OF CHANCERY]

office of second examinator of the Court of Chancery with all fees, duties and perquisites thereunto belonging in as large and ample manner as the same was granted unto Sir G.C., knight,[351] by letters patents of our sovereign lord the king, as likewise a grant unto the said C.R. & G.R.[352] of the office of receiving, filing and transcribing copies of all depositions taken by commission on the part and behalf of any party or parties in any suit or cause, depending or to be depending, in the Court of Chancery in this kingdom in as large and ample manner as the same were heretofore granted unto the said Sir G.C. & unto J.P. and N.N.,[353] or to any or either of them, to have and to hold the said several offices and either of them unto the said C.R. during the term of his natural life and after his decease to the said G.R. during the term of his natural life, inserting therein all such other clauses as in grants of like nature are usual. And the same fairly engrossed in parchment under your hand to send us &c. Given &c.

To our trusty and well beloved, his Majesty's attorney & solicitor general, or either of them.

347 John King (d. 1637), administrator and landowner (see *DIB*).

348 Nicholas Stanyhurst, Thomas Alen, Lancelot Alford, W.A. (unresolved), William Philips (see *Lib. mun. pub. Hib.*). The initials 'W.A.' must have been mistakenly noted. It was likely in reference to Lancelot Alford who was a previous office holder.

349 Francis Edgeworth (see *Lib. mun. pub. Hib.*).

350 Pages 38 and 39 are missing in the manuscript.

351 George Carre (d. *c.* 1663); possibly an error by the scribe for Sir Thomas Cary.

352 Christopher Ryves and George Ryves (see *Lib. mun. pub. Hib.*).

353 J.P. (unresolved) and Nathaniel Neave (see *Lib. mun. pub. Hib.*).

444. <WARRANT TO TAKE PARTRIDGES>

Whereas we have employed L.M. and R.D., our servants, to take partridges and enter some of our hawks the better to prepare them for our disport when we shall please to make use of them, and understanding that the parts of the counties of Kilkenny and Tipperary are stored with game of that kind, we have addressed [**p. 41**] them to repair thither for the purpose aforesaid. These are therefore to will and require you ~~forthwith~~ and every of you whom it may any ways concern not only to permit and suffer our said servants to hawk ~~att~~ at and take partridges as abovesaid within the limits of the said counties without any your lets and ~~hindrances~~ interruptions, but also to afford them meat for themselves & their horses at usual rates when they shall be occasioned to repair unto you for that purpose as you will &c. Given &c.

To all justices of the peace, mayors, sovereigns, portreeves, constables and all other his Majesty's officers and loving subjects to whom it may appertain.

445. <WARRANT FOR THE OFFICE OF A MASTER IN THE COURT OF CHANCERY>

These are to will and require you forthwith upon sight hereof to draw up a fiant in due form of law containing a grant from his Majesty ~~of~~ unto G.R., doctor in the civil laws,[354] of the office of one of the masters of the Chancery in this kingdom which is now void and in his Majesty's gift by the voluntary surrender & yielding up of the same by Sir T.C., knight,[355] who formerly held and enjoyed the said office with a grant unto the said G.R. of the annual [**p. 42**] fee or stipend of 20*s*. English for exercising the said office ~~with a grant unto the said~~ together [with] all other fees, wages, profits, salaries, advantages, commodities, pre-eminences and authorities to the said office belonging or appertaining, to have, hold, use, exercise and enjoy the said office and other the premises unto the said G.R. during his Majesty's will and pleasure in as large and ample manner and form as Sir A.F., Sir W.T., knights,[356] the said Sir T.C., or any of them or any other held and enjoyed the same, inserting therein all such ^other^ clauses as in grants of like nature are usual. And the same fairly engrossed in parchment under your hand to send unto us to be further passed as appertaineth. And for so doing &c. Given &c.

To our trusty and well beloved, his Majesty's attorney and solicitor general, or either of them.

446. <A WARRANT TO CONVEY ONE FROM T.[357] GAOL HITHER>

Whereas for reasons best known to ourself [*sic*] we think it fit that one H.M., who now remainth prisoner in Trim gaol upon suspicion of treason, should be forthwith to cause him to be conveyed hether. These are therefore to will and require you forthwith to

354 George Ryves, see note 57.

355 Thomas Cary, master in chancery and prothonotary of the court of common pleas (1627–34) (see Hughes, *Patentee officers*).

356 Ambrose Forthe, William Temple (see *Lib. mun. pub. Hib.*).

357 Trim.

cause him to be ~~deliv~~ delivered over to the sheriff~~s~~ of the county of Dublin [**p. 43**] who is likewise to deliver him to the sheriffs of the city, ~~of~~ and they to the gaoler of Newgate who is to keep him in sure and safe manner until he shall receive our further directions concerning him or that he be thence delivered by a due course of law, whereof you and the said sheriffs and gaoler are not to fail at your perils. And for &c. Given &c.

To our well beloved, the high sheriff of the county of Meath.

447. <WARRANT FOR A COMMISSION FOR THE COURT OF CASTLE CHAMBER>

According to his Majesty's letters dated the 24th of September last, a copy whereof we herewith send you, these are to will and require you to draw up a commission for the Court of Castle Chamber according to a former commission under the great seal of England date[d] the 8th day of October in the first year of his Majesty's reign directed to the same commissioners and with the same powers; and also authorizing them to sit & hold the said court not only on the ordinary days but any other days and times as well in term as out of term when they shall think meet and convenient; and to have all other the powers and jurisdiction to all purposes which are or may be exercised in his Majesty's High Court of Star Chamber in England according to the purport of his Majesty's [**p. 44**]...[358]

448. <WARRANT FOR THE OFFICE OR [PLACE OF MARSHAL] OF THE ARMY IN IRELA[ND] >

Th[ese]...upon...of law...the offic[e]...in this king...Viscount of...in reversion...Lord Viscount P.[359] by...lord King James unde[r]...bearing date the at Dub[lin]...in the 15th year of his reig[n]...fallen unto him by the death of the...Viscount Powerscourt, to have, hold, possess, occupy and enjoy the said office or place of Marshal of the Army here unto the said Lord Viscount Valencia for the term of his life together which all such commands, fees, profits, entertainments, commodities, privileges, pre-eminences and advantages whatsoever, incident to the said office in as large, ample ^& beneficial^ manner as the said Lord Viscount Powerscourt or any other formerly held and enjoyed the same to be exercised by himself or his [**p. 45**] ...during ...[V]iscount...[e]ntertainments...& in such...[Visc]ount Powerscourt...[ex]ercising the...[s]uch clauses as ...nal, and which are...[M]ajesty's letters unto us...[co]py whereof for...herewith sent you...[engro]ssed in parchment under...be further passed as...[d]oing &c. Given &c.

To &c.

449. <WARRANT [FOR] A PARDON FOR SIR ROGER JONES>

Whereas upon humble suit made unto us by Sir R.J. of S., knight,[360] and H.T. and J.D., yeomen, we have been pleased to grant unto them his Majesty's free and

[358] This page is badly torn.

[359] Richard Wingfield (1551?–1634), 1st Viscount Powerscourt and soldier (see *DIB*).

[360] Roger Jones of Sligo (d. 1644), 1st Viscount Ranelagh (see *DIB*).

gracious pardon for their offence committed in & by their undue transportation of certain quantities of wool out of this realm of Ireland ~~with~~ without licence in that behalf, these are therefore to will and require you forthwith [**p. 46**] to draw up a fiant in due form of law (of a pardon unto your said Sir R.J., H.T. & J.D., and to every and either of them[)] of any penalties or forfeitures unto his Majesty for the said offence, inserting therein all such clauses as in like cases is usual. And the same fairly engrossed in parchment ~~as~~ under your hand to send unto us to be further passed &c. Given &c.

To our trusty and well beloved, his Majesty's attorney and solicitor general, or either of them.

450. <WARRANT TO THE AUDITOR TO MAKE FORTH DEBENTURES FOR MR SECRETARY'S ENTERTAINMENT>

Whereas his Majesty by his letters patents dated the 12th of July last hath granted unto our right trusty and well beloved Sir P.M., knight,[361] the place of principal secretary of state here with the yearly ~~rente~~ fee of 200*li.* sterling *per annum*, and whereas likewise his Majesty by his letters of the 21st of October last hath granted and continued unto him the yearly allowance of 100*li.* for intelligences and such like services as was formerly allowed unto Sir Dudley Norton, knight, his predecessor in that place, and hath authorized ~~him~~ ^us^ to give warrant to the vice-treasurer and all other his Majesty's officers [**p. 47**] whom it may concern to make ~~present satisfaction~~ payment thereof unto him or his assigns, accordingly the first payment to be given from Easter last past [*sic*] and to be continued during such time as he shall enjoy the said place, these are to will and require you to make forth debenture unto him, both for the said allowance for intelligences and for his fee of 200*li.* sterling *per annum* for the half year ending at Michaelmas last and so half yearly hereafter as the same shall grow due unto him that payment may be made unto him accordingly by his Majesty's vice-treasurer. And for your so doing this shall be your ~~warrant~~ sufficient warrant. Given &c.

To our trusty and well beloved Sir James Ware, knight, his Majesty's auditor general.

451. <A WARRANT TO PAY THE LORD PRESIDENT OF CONNACHT HIS MICHAELMAS ENTERTAINMENT AS PRESIDENT AND CONSTABLE OF ATHLONE CASTLE>

These are to pray and require your lordship forthwith upon sight hereof to make out of such his Majesty's monies as remain in your hands unto our very good lord, the lord president of Connacht, of such fees or entertainment as are due unto his lordship as he is lord president of the said province and constable of his Majesty's Castle of Athlone for the half year ending at Michaelmas last, according to two several warrants of full pay signed by us and herewith sent you; for doing &c. Given &c.

To our &c., the Lord Mountnorris, &c.

361 Philip Mainwaring (1589–1661), secretary of state for Ireland (see *DIB*).

452. [p. 48] <WARRANT TO EXAMINE [A] WITNESS CONCERNING MURDER>

Whereas we are informed by James McTernon (whose son was ~~most~~ not long since most foully murdered within some 8 miles of Jamestown) that he is able to prove that there hath been some private proceedings and passages between W.H., now prisoner at Jamestown, and one Teige Ó Laughlan, who is now in this his Majesty's Castle as prisoner, being both of them suspected for the ^same^ murder, ~~and~~ ^we^ thereupon (as reposing special trust and confidence in your wisdom and integrities) have thought fit hereby to require you from time to time to take the examinations of all such witnesses as can give testimony for the further and better discovery of the said murder, and the examinations so taken by you jointly and severally to commit to writing & to return the same and to bind over the witnesses to appear and give evidence at the trial. Whereof we require you and every of you not to fail. And for so doing &c. Given &c.

To our trusty and well beloved Sir C.C., knight and baronet,[362] Sir George S., knight,[363] and H.C., esquire,[364] and to every of them, either jointly or severally, as occasion shall be offered.

453. <LICENCE OF ABSENCE>

These are to will and require you presently upon sight hereof to draw ^forth^ a fiant in due form of law containing a licence unto T.S., esquire,[365] clerk and writer of the tallies and counter tallies of bills whatsoever of the receipt of the Exchequer of the kingdom of Ireland and also clerk [**p. 49**] of his Majesty's Treasurer and clerk of the Pells & memorandums of the receipts and issues of the said Exchequer, that he the said T.S. for and during the space of 3 years next ensuing the date hereof may go and remain and absent himself in the kingdom of England or elsewhere for or about his affairs, and that in the mean the said T. may by his deputy or deputies, attorney or attorneys, collect, perceive, levy and receive all and singular the issues, profits, revenues, commodities and emoluments whatsoever which do belong or appertain to the said Thomas by reason of the said office or otherwise whatsoever in as large, ample and beneficial manner and form as the former licence was made unto the said T.S., and the same to send unto us fairly engrossed in parchment. And for so doing &c. Given &c.

454. <LICENCE OF ABSENCE>

Whereas upon humble suit made unto us by Sir R.H., knight & baronet and clerk of the Nichells in this kingdom of Ireland,[366] we have been pleased to ~~make~~ licence him to make his repair into England and there to remain for the space of six months

362 Sir Charles Coote (d. 1642), army officer (see *DIB*).

363 Sir George Shirley (Shurley), chief justice of the king's bench (1620–25) (see Hughes, *Patentee officers*).

364 Henry Crofton.

365 Thomas Stockdale (see *Lib. mun. pub. Hib.*).

366 Robery Hannay (see *Lib. mun. pub. Hib.*).

next ensuing the date hereof about the dispatch of certain special affairs of his own, these [**p. 50**] are therefore to will and require all and every, his Majesty's officers, ministers and loving subjects whom it may concern, not only to take due notice thereof but also to afford him the true benefit of this our licence with any prejudice to be incurred by him any way in ^the^ forfeiture of his said office of clerk of the Nichells, he leaving a sufficient deputy to execute the same in his absence during the time aforesaid; whereof they and every of them are not to fail. And for so doing this shall be a sufficient warrant. Given &c.

455. <JUDGE CRESSY, HIS WARRANT TO RECEIVE 200*li.* IRISH>

Whereas his Majesty hath been graciously pleased by his letters bearing date the 12th of April last to require and authorize us to give warrants for payment to be made unto H.C., esquire,[367] ~~of~~ one of the justice of ~~this~~ his highness's court of chief place, of the arrearages of the yearly wages of 200*li.* Irish belonging to the judges place as also of the usual allowance for robes from the time of the decease of Sir C.S., knight,[368] his predecessor; and whereas we are certified that the said Sir C. died the 16th of December, *anno domini* 1632, and for that it appeareth by his letters patents made of the said office as well unto the said C. as to the said H.C. that the said wages were payable ~~guarterly~~ quarterly *vizt* at midsummer, Michaelmas, Christmas and Easter, and that after the decease of the said Sir C. and before his Majesty's letters patents were passed unto the said Hugh C. of that place, which was not until the 21th of [**p. 51**] June then next ensuing, there happened to be due two quarter days of payment of the said wages, *vizt.* at Christmas and Easter next ensuing, the said Sir C., ~~death~~ decease[d], amounting both to 100*li.* Irish and for robes which grew due at the said feast of the Nativity of Our Lord, *anno domini* 1632, 20 marks sterling, these are therefore to pray and require your lordship, according to his Majesty's said command and directions forthwith, to pay unto the said H.C. out of such his Majesty's monies as now remain in your hands the said several sums of 100*li.* Irish & 20 marks sterling according to the purport of his Majesty's said letters, a copy whereof for your better information we have herewith sent. And this, together with the acquaintance of the said H.C. of the receipt thereof, shall be your lordship's sufficient warrant & discharge in that behalf. Given &c.

To our very good lord, the Lord Mountnorris, vice-treasurer and ^general^ receiver of his highness's revenues here in Ireland.

456. <WARRANT TO CARRY DIVERS BEFORE G.C., ESQUIRE>

These are to will and require you forthwith upon receipt hereof to cause diligent search and enquiry to be made throughout your county of Ca: for the several bodies of ~~your~~ the undernamed persons, and them wheresover they can ^be found to^ apprehend or cause[369]

367 Hugh Cressy, justice of the king's court of chief place (see *Lib. mun. pub. Hib.*).

368 Christopher Sibthorpe (d. 1632/3), judge and religious writer (see *DIB*).

369 Pages 52 and 53 are missing in the manuscript.

457. [p. 54] [WARRANT FORBIDDING THE TRANSPORTATION OF PIPESTAVES OR HOGSHEADSTAVES WITHOUT A SPECIAL LICENCE]

observance of our directions for the future, these are therefore straightly to charge and command you and every of you not to admit of any entries nor to permit any person or persons upon any pretence whatsoever to put aboard or transport any pipestaves or hogshead staves without our special licence granted in that behalf; whereof you may not fail as you will answer the contrary at your perils. Given &c.

To our trusty and well beloved, his Majesty's officers of the customs in the port of Wexford and the creeks and members thereunto belonging.

458. <WARRANT FOR THE APPREHENSION OF ONE FOR BREAKING PRISON AND STEALING GOODS>

Whereas Abraham Eastwood, keeper of the Marshalsea of the liberty of Thomascourt, Dublin, hath complained that unto us that one T.H. being not long since arrested was delivered to his custody where having remained some 16 weeks he not only found and apprehended the opportunity to break prison but also feloniously did steal and take away divers parcels of goods of the said E. We therefore, upon the said E.['s] humble ~~petition~~ suit & affidavit made of the truth of his complaint, have thought fit and do accordingly [**p. 55**] hereby straightly charge and command you and every of you not only to make diligent search and enquiry for the body of him the said T.H. but also to apprehend him wheresoever he shall be found, and him in sure and safe manner to convey from constable to constable unto us that we may give further directions concerning him as there shall be cause; whereof you and every of you are not to fail at your perils. And for so doing &c. Given &c.

To all mayors, sheriffs, justices of the peace, bailiffs, constables and to all ~~others~~ & every other his Majesty's officers, ministers and loving subjects whatsoever whom it may concern.

459. <WARRANT FOR MR SMITH TO PRESS MEN AND BOATS TO SET UP THE SEA MARKS &C.>

Whereas R.S., gent, being marshal and water-bailiff hath made known unto us that for the better guidance and direction of shipping into ~~England~~ this harbour of Dublin he is presently to set up certain perches, buoys and other sea marks, in the performance of which service he must of necessity make use of the advice and help of seamen and carpenters. And inasmuch as he cannot, as he affirmeth, procure any to assist him in that ~~be~~ behalf without our warrant we, upon his request and out of our care to have so good [**p. 56**] a work and speedily performed which may tend to their preservation of many, as well his Majesty's subjects as others bound for this port, have thought fit and do ^accordingly^ hereby authorize him the said R.S. not only to press such and so many seamen, carpenters and artificers for his assistance in the work as he shall think fit but also to take up such and so many cabbards, boats, ropes and anchors as shall be fitting for the service, he paying for the same such rates as shall be reasonable. And for so doing this shall be his warrant in the due execution whereof we require all owners and masters of shipping to be aiding and assisting unto him as there shall be occasion, and thereof not to fail at their perils. Given &c.

460. <WARRANT CONCERNING THE SUBSIDY FOR THE COUNTY OF D.[370]>

These are to pray and require your lordship upon receipt hereof to cause to issue two several commissions according to the usual and accustomed form for the levying of the two first payments of the four first subsidies granted unto his Majesty in the first session of the present parliament, and the same to be directed unto our trusty and well beloved Sir W.P., knight and baronet,[371] his Majesty's surveyor general and Master of the Wards, and Sir A.L.[372] and Sir S.M.,[373] knights, E.B., esquire, his Majesty's solicitor general,[374] Sir J.W., knight,[375] Ni. B.[376] and J.B.,[377] esquires, or unto any four or more of them as commissioners [**p. 57**] in that behalf for the county of D. The said commission to be returnable with all convenient expedition. And for so doing &c.

To our very good lord, the lord chancellor.

461. <WARRANT TO CERTIFY THE PROFITS OF ^THE^ CROWN SINCE 30 ELIZ.>

We require you upon sight or receipt ~~hereof~~ of this our warrant forthwith to make full and ample certificate unto us of all such debts, duties, fines, amercements, homage, respite of homage, sum and sums of money, which have grown due ~~du~~ to the Crown by any means whatsoever in the Courts of Chancery, Kings Bench, Common Pleas, Exchequer, and Court of Wards in this kingdom, or before the judges of assize and gaol delivery, justices of the peace, clerk of the market and before commission for ecclesiastical causes and other judges of record, or by reason of the goods and chattels, real or personal, of any person or persons attainted of felony or treason, or for the mean profits of their lands, tenements and hereditaments, or for arrearages of rents incurred from the 30th year of Queen Elizabeth until the beginning of his now Majesty's reign, and whereof no part hath been answered unto his highness since the belonging [*sic*] of the reign nor any legal grant or discharge [**p. 58**] thereof made, paid in and satisfied into his highness's receipt upon sheriffs' accounts, or otherwise, since or from the 14th of January in *anno domini* 1633. Whereof you may not fail as you shall answer the contrary at your perils. Given &c.

To the auditor of the Court of the Exchequer and all other [of] his highness's officers there and in the receipt, and every of them respectively whom it may concern.

[370] Dublin.
[371] William Parsons (see *DIB*).
[372] Adam Loftus (see *DIB*).
[373] Samuel Mayart (see *DIB*).
[374] Edward Bolton (see *DIB*).
[375] James Ware (see *DIB*).
[376] Nicholas Barnewall.
[377] John Bysse, MP for Dublin in 1634 (see Kearney, *Strafford in Ireland*, p. 260).

462. <WARRANT TO ENQUIRE OF, AND RESTORE, B. GOODS &C.>

Whereas W.B. and R.B., merchants and owners of the good ship called the *Sunne*, have humbly petitioned unto us setting forth that the said ship, by foul tempestuous weather, was upon Wednesday night last cast away upon the shore of Mirrian[378] within this harbour of D.,[379] where although (through God's providence and mercy) the lives of all that were in the said ship were saved yet divers of the country people thereabouts having intelligence thereof came and entered the said ship and took away a great part of the petitioners by force, for the re-having ~~th~~ whereof and in commiseration of ~~your~~ ^the^ poor petitioners' deplorable & distressed estate we have thought fit and accordingly we do hereby require and authorize you not only to make diligent search for such person or persons as have so taken away the said goods or any part thereof, and having so found them, [**p. 59**] or such of them as shall be so found, to require them to make present restitution thereof to the petitioners, which if they shall refuse to do then you are to attach their persons and them to keep in safe and sure manner until our further pleasure be known, but where you shall find any of the said goods you are to seize upon the same & to make present restitution thereof to the said proprietors, for doing whereof this shall be your warrant; in the due execution whereof we require all and every, his Majesty's officers, ministers and lo[ving] subjects whatsoever to be aiding and assisting unto you as there shall be occasion and as they will answer the contrary at your perils. Given &c.

To any of his Majesty's pursuivants.

463. <WARRANT FOR SIR R.F.[380] TO RECEIVE 100*li.* *PER ANNUM* AS A SERVITOR>

Whereas his Majesty hath been graciously pleased to enquire by his several letters, ~~enrolled~~ which are already enrolled ~~that the office~~ in your office, that the sum of 40*s.* 5*d.* ^*per diem*^ should be added to the present establishment of this kingdom to be paid unto servitors here as we, his Majesty's deputy, should [**p. 60**] ~~think fit~~ direct, and forasmuch as we have thought fit that 100*li.* sterling *per annum* thereof should be conferred upon our trusty and well beloved Sir Robert Farrer, knight, these are therefore to will and require you forthwith to make entry of him the said Sir R.F. as a servitor at that rate from the first day of April 1633 and so to make debenture for him for the three half years ending at Michaelmas last and likewise for every half year hereafter as the same shall grow due, that payment may be made ~~the~~ unto him accordingly by ~~Ma~~ ^his Majesty's^ vice-treasurer. And for &c. Given &c.

To our trusty and well beloved Sir James Ware, knight, his Majesty's auditor general.

464. <WARRANT FOR DIVERS PARTIES TO RECEIVE THE STIPENDS AS SERVITORS>

Whereas his Majesty hath been graciously pleased to require by his ~~letters patents~~ several letters, which are already enrolled in your office, that the sum of 40*s.* 5*d.* *per*

378 Merrion.

379 Dublin.

380 Robert Farrer.

diem should be added to the present establishment of this kingdom and to be paid unto servitors here as we, his Majesty's deputy, should direct, and inasmuch as we have thought fit in regard of the good and faithful services done to his Majesty by the persons undernamed to confer upon them thereout [**p. 61**] for their release and yearly allowance, the several sums at their names appearing, these are therefore to will and require you forthwith to make entry of the said persons undernamed as servitors in his Majesty's pay at the rates; and from the times, their said means respectively appearing, and to make out debenture for them for what is already due, or hereafter half yearly shall become due, that payment may be made accordingly by his Majesty's vice-treasurer unto them &c. Given &c.

G.P. *generosus* 66*li.* 13*s.* 4*d.* sterling *per annum* and to begin from Michaelmas 1634.

And others &c.

To our trusty and well beloved Sir J.W., knight,[381] his Majesty's auditor general.

465. <WARRANT TO FORBEAR THE EXECUTION OF ONE CONDEMNED>

Whereas there are remaining in your custodies or custody of some of you the bodies of J.S. and E.D. who were both condemned this term, these are to ~~to~~ will and require you and every of you, for [**p. 62**] the reasons best known unto us, to forbear and respite the execution of the said S. & D. until our further pleasure be known. Whereof &c.

To the sheriffs of the county ~~of~~ and city of Dublin and county at large.

466. <WARRANT FOR COMMITTAL OF SIR P.C.[382]>

Whereas for reasons best known to our self and others of his Majesty's honourable privy council we think it fit that Sir P.C., knight, J.C. and D.C., should be restrained and kept as close prisoners for a time. These are therefore ~~toh~~ to charge and command you forthwith to receive into your custody ~~the~~ and safe keeping the bodies of the said Sir P.C., J.C. & D.C., and them having so received to keep as close prisoners apart in several rooms, not permitting them to confer or discourse one with the other until our ~~further~~ pleasure be ^further^ known. And for so doing &c.

To Samuel Davis, esquire, constable of his Majesty's Castle aforesaid.

467. [p. 63] <WARRANT TO THE VICE-TREASURER FOR 1,200*li.* TO REPAIR THE CASTLE>

These are to pray and require your lord forthwith according to the purport of his Majesty's letters unto us of the 28th of October last, a copy whereof we have herewith sent you, to pay and deliver unto J.C., esquire,[383] 1,200*li.* sterling out of such his Majesty's treasurer as ~~is now~~ ^remain^ in your custody to be disposed of and employed

381 James Ware (see *DIB*).

382 Piers Crosby (1590–1646), courtier and army officer (see *DIB*).

383 Joshua Carpenter (see McGrath).

~~to towardes~~ in the repairing of the ruins of this his Majesty's Castle and, in addition, of stables and gardens thereunto, we having nominated ^& appointed^ the said Josua Carpenter to take care of that business and who shall be accountable upon oath for the monies so received by him and expended in the said works. And for so doing this shall be your ~~warrant~~ lordship's and the commissioners' ~~warrant~~ of your accounts sufficient warrant & discharge in that behalf. Given &c.

To our very good lord, the Lord Mountnorris, his Majesty's vice-treasurer and receiver-general of Ireland.

468. [p. 64] <MR BILLINGSLEY'S WARRANT FOR A FIANT>

These are to will and require you forthwith to draw up a fiant in due form of law containing a grant of a lease from his Majesty, his heirs and successors, unto W.B., esquire,[384] his executors, administrators and assigns of the above particulars, for and during the term of 31 years next ensuing the date of the said grant, for and at the yearly rent of 30*s.* harps, inserting therein all such beneficial clauses as in the like cases are usual. And the same fairly engrossed in parchment under your hand to send unto us to be further passed as appertaineth; for doing whereof &c. Given &c.

To &c., his Majesty's attorney & solicitor general, or either of them.

469. <A PASS FOR A TROOPER>

Thomas, Lord Viscount Wentworth, baron of Wentworth Woodhouse, Lord Newmarsh and Oversley, lord president of his Majesty's Council established in the north parts of England & lord lieutenant of the county and city of York, one of his Majesty's most honourable privy council, and lord deputy general of the kingdom of Ireland, do hereby make it known unto all those whom it may concern that the bearer hereof, C.F., esquire, a gent of our troop of horse, being desirous to travel into the Low Countries and there to remain **[p. 65]** for a time ~~to enrich~~ with an intent to enrich his knowledge in martial discipline, we upon his humble suit have been pleased to grant him these our letters of passport and licence in that behalf as being willing to give all fitting encouragement that way inclined, and more especially to him to whose ^good^ condition hath by his fair and civil ~~c~~ carriage under us fulue [*sic*] within our view. And therefore we do hereby will and require all & every, his Majesty's officers, ministers and loving subjects whatsoever, not only to take due notice thereof but also to permit & suffer him as well to ~~tk~~ take shipping in ~~a~~ ^any^ port in this kingdom & to pass & return without any their lets and molestations whatsoever, he behaving himself as becometh. And we likewise require all others who shall read or see this our passport to afford him such fair treaty and respective usage as agents of quality shall be thought fit to merit from the subjects of such princes as are in league and amity with our sovereign lord, the king's most excellent Majesty, and for which we shall not be wanting to afford to any of their subjects on the like occasion. Given &c.

[384] William Billingsley.

470. [p. 66] <WARRANT FOR THE PAYMENT OF MONIES>

Whereas J.B. hath petitioned unto us setting forth that there is ^yet^ due unto him and remaining unpaid the sum of 180*li.* 11*s.* 9*d.* sterling of those monies which by ~~him~~ his Majesty's special directions were designed to have been paid unto him out of the cheques, we therefore ^upon his humble petition^ have thought fit and accordingly we do hereby pray and require your lordship to make present payment unto him the said J.B. of the said sum of 180*li.* 11*s.* 9*d.* if upon his accounts made it shall appear there is so much due unto him; for so doing &c. Given.

To our very good lord, the Lord Mountnorris, his Majesty's vice-treasurer and receiver-general.

471. <WARRANT TO PASS THE CURSITORS OFFICE TO MR CARRE>

These are to will and require you forthwith to draw up a fiant in due form of law containing a grant from his Majesty unto G.C., esquire,[385] of the office and offices of cursitor or engrosser, of all ^& all^ manner of original writs issuing out of the High Court of Chancery in this kingdom being now void and in ~~the~~ our dispose by the death of J.B.[386] who lately held the same, to have and to hold, exercise and enjoy the said office and offices of cursitor, ~~and~~ clerk and engrosser as aforesaid unto the said G.C. together with all fees, duties, profits, perquisites, advantages and emoluments whatsoever thereunto belonging or in anywise appertaining, and in as large, ample & beneficial [**p. 67**] manner as C.B., G.P., P.H. and the said J.B.,[387] or any other formerly held and enjoyed or of right ought to have held and enjoyed the same, to be exercised by himself ^or^ his sufficient deputy during the good behaviour of him the said G.C., inserting therein all such behaviour as ~~of right ought~~ in grants of like nature are usual. And the same fairly engrossed in parchment under your hand to send us to be further passed as appertaineth; for doing whereof &c. Given &c.

To our trusty and well beloved, his Majesty's attorney and solicitor general, or either of them.

472. <WARRANT FOR A TRUNK TO PASS UNSEARCHED>

Whereas Francis W., esquire, who is lately gone into England, hath a trunk which contains his clothes and other necessaries to be speedily sent after him, these are to will and require you and every of you to permit and suffer the said trunk to be put aboard and transported without any manner of search or stage whatsoever. And for &c. Given &c.

To all and every, his Majesty's officers of the customs in the port of Dublin.

385 George Carre (d. *c.* 1663) (see *Lib. mun. pub. Hib.*).

386 James Browne (see *Lib. mun. pub. Hib.*).

387 Christopher Berford, Gyles Parker, Peter Harrison and James Browne (see *Lib. mun. pub. Hib.*).

473. [p. 68] <WARRANT TO BE PRONOTARY OF THE COMMON PLEAS>

These are to will and require you forthwith to draw up a fiant in due form of law containing a grant from his Majesty, his heirs & successors, of the ~~onel~~ chief and only pronotary, *alias* prothonotary, of his Majesty's Court of Common Bank in this kingdom with all and singular the rights, profits, duties and emoluments unto the said office or offices or any of them belonging or anyways appertaining, and also the *custos* of all bills, philes [*sic*], pleas, records, enrolments of deeds and evidences, remembrances, rules of court & rolls whatsoever of the same Court of Common Bank or Pleas, unto William Plunkett of Dublin, esquire, so belonging to the office of the pronatary, *alias* prothonotary, of the said court or to the said office of *custos* of all bills, philes [*sic*], pleas, records, enrolments of deeds and evidences, remembrances, rules of court and rolls whatsoever of the same court, except only the said W.P., his licence, to be held and enjoyed by the said W.P. or his sufficient deputy or deputies during his good behaviour in as large and ample manner as G.R., W.R., W.C. Sir T.C.[388] and the said W.P., or any ~~othe~~ other officer or officers or either of them heretofore held and enjoyed the said officers, together with ~~all the~~ a small stipend or fee of 10*s.* Irish to be paid out of his Majesty's revenue by the hands of the vice-treasurer at the feasts of St Michael the Archangel & of Easter by even portions, and all such other and the like fees, wages, rewards, commodities, profits, advantages and emoluments whatsoever as the said G.R., W.R., W.C., Sir T.C. and the said W.P., or any of them, did usually take or receive or ought to have had or received for the same offices or either of them, wherein [**p. 69**] you are to insert clauses as well for his indemnity for the time past [*sic*], for and from all and every act and acts, had committed, suffered or done by the said W.P., of, in, for or in any sort concerning the execution of the said offices or any of them, and also for his further and better security for the time to come as in grants of like nature are usual. And the same fairly engrossed in parchment under your hands to send unto us to be further passed as appertaineth &c. Given &c.

To our &c., his Majesty's attorney & solicitor general, or either of them.

474. <WARRANT FOR A COMMISSION ISSUED UNDER THE GREAT SEAL FOR THE APPREHENSION OF REBELS>

Whereas we have received information from our very good lord, Lawrence Lord Esmond,[389] that there are divers ill disposed persons in and about the counties of Wexford & Kilkenny and the parts thereto adjoining who having committed divers burglaries, felonies and other misdemeanours are now in open rebellion and upon their keeping, and because we, by the advice of his Majesty's privy council, do think [**p. 70**] it requisite that for the better apprehension and bringing of the said malefactors under the view of his Majesty's justice it were necessary his lordship's power should (for this present occasion) be strengthened by his Majesty's commission whereby he might be enabled to treat with some of the said rebels for the better

388 George Robinson, William Robinson, William Crowe and Sir Thomas Cary (Carry) (see *Lib. mun. pub. Hib.*).

389 Laurence Esmond (1565–1545), 1st Barond Esmond and soldier (see *DIB*).

cutting of, or arresting of, the rest in case any of them should voluntarily desire it and upon his word put themselves into his lordship's hands. These are therefore to will and require your lordship forthwith to issue a commission under the great seal of ~~England~~ this kingdom directed to the said Lord Esmond thereby authorizing and requiring him that (taking to his assistance such of the company under his lordship's command and such others as he shall think fit) he do effectually take course for prosecuting, arresting and apprehending the said rebels & every or any of them, and also their & every or any of their relievers or abettors, and them and every of them so apprehended forthwith to commit to the next gaol for the country ~~forthwith~~ where they shall be so apprehended there to remain without bail or main prize till they shall be proceeded against according to their several offences, and be afterwards delivered by due course of his Majesty's laws or by our ~~apprehension~~ ^censure^ in that behalf signified; thereby also further authorizing that if any ~~the~~ of the said rebels or malefactors shall voluntarily on [*sic*] themselves on his lordship's word for their safety coming unto him in such case as his lordship may parley with any [**p. 71**] of them for the better discovering, apprehending and cutting of[f] of the rest provided that he give an account unto us of this doing in execution thereof from time to time as the occasion thereof shall require, and inserting a clause that none of his lordship's said soldiers, or any others by him employed in this behalf, commit any waste or spoil in the country but content themselves with such meat, drink and lodging as the country affords them for which they are to pay ready money or leave ticket as in such cases hath been accustomed. Lastly your lordship is to insert in the said commission a clause of assistance thereby requiring all his Majesty's officers and subjects whatsoever being thereunto required to be from time to time aiding and assisting unto his lordship and such others as he shall appoint in the execution of this commission as they, and every of them, will answer the contrary at their perils.[390] Whereof &c.

To our very good lord, the lord chancellor.

475. <WARRANT TO THE SHERIFF FOR PROVISION OF HORSE AND VICTUAL FOR THE LORD DEPUTY HIS TROOP & FOOT COMPANY>

Whereas we have appointed the risings out for the province of Leinster to be at Kildare on the 23rd of June next and whereas also we have appointed to be at the Naas by the 22nd of the same month and on the 25th coming back, and to be at K. on the 23rd and 24th of the same [**p. 72**] month, and in regard we are to have soldiers, both horse and foot, to attend us in the journey, these are therefore to will and require you to make provision of 40 barrels of oats, according to the measure of Bristow bond barrel, to be laid up in the Naas against that time and 40 barrels likewise to be laid up at Kildare in like manner for provision of horse, and also you are required to be careful to make provision of bread, drink, ~~& meat~~ beef and mutton

[390] Esmond and others since reported rebellion in County Kilkenny in 1636; but these were ongoing troubles in Co. Wexford for several years previously. David Edwards, 'Out of the blue? Provincial unrest in ireland before 1641' in Jane Ohlmyer and Micheál Ó Siochrú (eds), *Ireland, 1641: Contexts and reactions* (Manchester, 2013), pp 95–114.

for 10 foot companies and 3 troops of horse with their officers against the same time at reasonable prizes for which you shall receive payment by such officers as ^we^ shall appoint for that purpose. Whereof &c. Given &c.

To our well beloved, the high sheriff of the county of Kildare.

476. <WARRANT FOR 3,000*li.* TO BE RETURNED INTO HIS MAJESTY'S EXCHEQUER IN ENGLAND>

These are to pray and require your lordship out of such his Majesty's revenues as are now remaining under your charge, or shall next come to your hands, to return into England and cause to be paid into his Majesty's Exchequer there the sum of 3,000*li.* English, which sum is to be there issued towards the defraying the charge of his Majesty's two ships, the *Bona Venture* and the *Ninth Whelp*, appointed for the guard of the coasts of this kingdom for this present year 1635 as the right honourable ~~the~~ our very good lord, the lord commissioners [**p. 73**] of the Admiralty shall direct. And for so doing this shall be, as well to you as the commissioners of your accounts, a sufficient warrant and discharge in that behalf. Given &c.

To our very good lord, the Lord ~~Mountnorris~~ Viscount Mountnorris, his Majesty's vice-treasurer and general-receiver of his highness's revenues in Ireland.

477. <WARRANT TO SIR P.P.[391] TO PRODUCE RECORDS TOUCHING THE TITLE OF THE CROWN>

Whereas we are informed that there remains in your custody amongst other the king's majesty's evidences and records in Birmingham Tower, the office or inquisition entitling his Majesty to certain lands, tenements and hereditaments in the barony or territory of Ossory, some parts ~~where~~of which inquisition by his Majesty's learned council is conceived necessarily to be made on his Majesty's behalf to the clearing of ~~his Majesty's~~ ^the Crown's^ title to the barony or cantred of Idough in the county of Kilkenny, wherefore these are to will, ~~and~~ require & authorize you upon receipt hereof to deliver unto the Master of the Rolls,[392] or to such as he shall appoint, a true copy of so much of that office or inquisition for the late inquisition for the [**p. 74**] late plantation of Ossory as will any way serve for furthering his Majesty's service at this present, for which &c. Given &c.

To our trusty and well beloved Sir P.P., keeper of his Majesty's records and evidences in Birmingham Tower.

478. <WARRANT FOR THE 2*d.* PAYMENT OF THE SUBSIDIES &C.>

These are to pray and require your lordship, upon receipt hereof, forthwith to cause to issue several commissions according to the usual and accustomed form, as well for the levying of the second payment of the four subsidies first granted is [*sic*] also

[391] Philip Perceval (see *DIB*).

[392] Christopher Wandesford (see *DIB*).

for the levying of the second payment of the two subsidies by a second act granted to his Majesty in the first session of the late and last parliament, to be directed unto the commissioners already named for each ~~pa~~ county throughout this kingdom in a book annexed to our warrant to your lordship of the eleventh of the last month for the applotting and levying of the first payment of the four subsidies &c. And this commission to issue to be ^now^ returnable with all convenient expedition, and for so doing this shall be ~~your~~ a ^sufficient^ warrant. Given &c.

To our very good lord, the lord chancellor.

479. [p. 75] <WARRANT FOR THE DELIVERY OF EVIDENCES FOR THE ENTITLING HIS MAJESTY TO THE BARONY OR CANTRED OF IDOUGH IN *COMITATU* K.[393]>

Whereas for the furtherance of his Majesty's service some use ~~is~~ is to be made of the charters and confirmations granted formerly of all or any liberties, jurisdictions, privileges, lands, tenements or hereditaments for incorporating or concerning the new corporations of K. and C.,[394] or either of them, as also of any other books, manuscripts or records remaining with the said corporations respectively as very useful for the furtherance of his Majesty's present service, as also of another book or manuscript written or compiled by Friar Clyn,[395] the which we are informed remains in the custody of R.S., esquire,[396] all which are to be produced at enquiry, to be taken by his Majesty's commissioners for his Majesty's right and title to the barony or cantred of Idough in the county of Kilkenny, which commission is to be expedited at Kilkenny. Wherefore these are to will and require, and in his Majesty's ~~name~~ behalf we do hereby straightly charge and command you, the mayor of K. and also you, the sovereign of Callan, that you and either of you respectively deliver and produce unto the Master of the Rolls,[397] one of his said commissioners, at such time as they shall be desired of you all ~~which you~~ charters, confirmations [**p. 76**][398]...Idough...attend...you...evide...nece... shal...[**p. 77**] your lordship...is to issue under...cted unto the sheriff...re by giving him...sumon all the tenants...or territory of...appear and...his Majesty in...here~~with~~ why a commission...urie and finding...the said...right...rne...ie

400. [p. 78] [WARRANT TO SIR WILLIAM RYVES, THE ATTORNEY GENERAL, RELATING TO A GRANT OF PARDON TO LADY DOCWRA[399] AND LORD DOCWRA[400]]

...good services as out of his royal bounty to give unto the said accountant the said lord's executrix for the use of herself and her son, the now Lord D. These are therefore

393 Kilkenny.

394 Kilkenny and Carlow.

395 John Clyn (d. 1349?), Franciscan friar and annalist (see *DIB*).

396 Robert Shee, alderman and mayor of Kilkenny in 1633 (see William Carrigan, *The history and antiquities of the diocese of Ossory* (4 vols, Dublin, 1905), iii, 61–62).

397 Christopher Wandesford (see *DIB*).

398 Pages 76 and 77 are badly torn.

399 Dorothy Docwra.

400 Henry Docwra (Dowkra or Dockwra) (1564–1631), 1st baron of Culmore, soldier and administrator (see *DIB*).

to will and require you forthwith to ~~req~~ draw up a fiant in due form of law containing a grant of his Majesty's free and gracious pardon unto the said Lady D. and the now Lord Dowcra ^in such manner reform as may acquit them, and either of them^, of the said sum upon ^the said^ account appearing to be due according to the purport of his Majesty's letters unto us of the 12th of March, a copy whereof for your better instruction we have herewith sent you. And the same fairly engrossed in parchment under your hand to send unto us ~~to~~ to be further passed as appertaineth; for doing whereof &c. Given &c.

To our trusty and well beloved Sir W.R., knight, his Majesty's knight, [*sic*] his Majesty's attorney general.

481. <WARRANT TO THE CLERK OF THE FIRST FRUIT & CLERK OF THE HANAPER TO PAY INTO THE RECEIPTS HIS MAJESTY'S MONIES> [15 MAY 1635]

These are to will and require you and every of you upon sight hereof not only to present ~~unto~~ us with an account in writing of such monies of his Majesty's as do at this instant remain in your hands, but also to make present ~~satisfaction~~ payment of the said money into the receipt office of his Majesty's Court of Exchequer and thereof not to fail. Given &c. the 15th of May 1635.

To our well beloved W.C., esquire,[401] clerk of the first fruits, & R.M., esquire,[402] deputy clerk of the Hanaper.

482. [p. 79] <WARRANT FOR PAYMENT OF THE CIVIL LIST>

Whereas by our directions of the 13th of this instant your lordship was required to make present unto our very good lord, the lord chancellor, to all and every the judges, the master and attorney of the Court of Wards, and those of his Majesty's Council learned, of their entertainment due unto them for the half year ending at ~~the~~ Easter last, and inasmuch as we likewise think fit that all those who are contained in the civil list and as yet unpaid should likewise receive payment ~~hereof~~ of their entertainment due for the half year ending at Easter last as aforesaid, we therefore pray and require your lordship out of such his Majesty's monies as are now remaining, or shall next come to your hands, to make payment unto them accordingly. And for &c. Given &c.

483. <A LICENCE FOR ONE E. A POOR MAN TO BEG>

Whereas one R.E. of K. in the county of K. hath petitioned unto us setting forth that upon Tuesday last at night by an unexpected fire, his house together with a child ~~and~~ of his and also what cows and sheep he had were most miserably consumed, and his wife thereupon fallen distracted and he and his family brought to that poverty and misery as that he and they are not able any longer to subsist without the **[p. 80]**

[401] William Crofton (see *Lib. mun. pub. Hib.*).

[402] Robert Meredith, see note 346.

charitable benevolence of good and ~~weld~~ well-disposed Christians, wherefore he humbly besought us to grant him our licence to ask and receive relief of such as in pity and commiseration of his distressed estate will be pleased to ~~off~~ afford the same unto him, whose request therein for the county of Kildare and the Queen's County we have thought fit to grant and the rather in regard we have received very good testimonies of his loss and misfortunes. These are therefore to pray and require all and every, his Majesty's officers, ministers and loving subjects whatsoever within the said county of Kildare and the Queen's County, not only to permit and suffer him the said R.E. to pass peaceably and quietly by them without any their lets, stays or molestations whatsoever he demeaning himself as becometh, but also to be aiding and assisting unto him herein that he may repair as well to churches, fairs, markets and other public places within the said counties to entreat the benevolence of all well~~beloved~~ disposed and charitable people whose pity & good consideration we do hereby recommend him. And we do hereby require all preachers and ministers within their several parishes in the said two counties upon the Sabbath and holy days to signify and read publicly the contents hereof unto their several congregations there gathered together provided that this our licence shall continue and be of force no longer then for the space of 6 months next ensuing the date [**p. 81**] hereof. And for so doing any ^former^ proclamation or general restriction to the contrary notwithstanding. Given &c.

484. <A WARRANT FOR COMMISSIONERS TO ISSUE ABOUT THE ALEHOUSES>

These are to pray and require your lordship forthwith upon receipt hereof to cause to issue several commissions under the great seal according to the form herewith sent you about the reducing of the needless multitude of alehouses ~~for~~ to a lesser number in this kingdom, the said commissions to be directed to the persons named in the schedule hereunto annexed as commissioners in that behalf, or to any two or more of them, whereof the *Custos Rotulorum* ~~to~~ in each county to be always one. And the said commissions so to issue, to continue and be of force during our pleasure; for doing &c.

To our very good lord, the lord chancellor.

485. <WARRANT TO APPOINT OVERSEERS OF THE WARDS IN IDOUGH>

Whereas his Majesty hath been found by a late inquisition taken by virtue of a commission under the great seal of this kingdom to be justly entitled to the [**p. 82**] territory of Idough in the county of Kilkenny, and forasmuch as we ~~do~~ out of our due care of his Majesty's just profits do think it fitting that a speedy course be taken for the preservation from waste and spoil of the wood and timber growing in and upon the lands of the said territory, these are therefore to require ~~and~~ and authorize you to nominate and appoint such and so many persons as you shall think fit to be overseers of the said woods who are hereby enabled and authorized to see and take a special care that the said woods and timber be not wasted, cut down, spoiled nor carried away by any person or persons whatsoever, and where they shall find any to transgress or offend in that kind then you or they are to certify us forthwith of the names and places of ~~habl~~ habitation of such transgressors or offenders that we may thereupon take a course for the punishing of them in that measure that the quality of their several offences shall be found to demerit. Hereof you are not to fail And for so doing &c. Given &c.

To our well beloved, the sheriff of the county of Kilkenny.

486. [p. 83] <WARRANT FOR THE COMMISSIONERS FOR THE PLANTATION IN CONNACHT>

These are to pray and require your lordship forthwith to cause a commission to issue under the great seal of this kingdom ~~accorning~~ according to the purport of his Majesty's letters ~~patens~~ unto us of the 16th of this month, a copy whereof for your better information we have herewith sent you. And for so doing this shall be you[r] lordship's sufficient warrant. Given &c.

To our very good lord, the lord chancellor.

487. <WARRANT FOR THE TRANSPORTING [OF] HORSES>

Whereas we have formerly directed our warrant for the restraining of the transportation of horses out of that port for that it was found to be a general hurt in regard that the best and most serviceable horses were too frequently carried away out of the kingdom, now forasmuch as we are given to understand that there be divers ~~persons~~ gent[s] and men of quality whose occasions do often draw them into England and Scotland do find great inconveniency for want of horses upon their arrival, they have therefore been humble suitors unto us to grant them licence to **[p. 84]** carry with them saddle naggs for themselves and servants for their necessary uses. We have therefore thought it meet to grant their requests and do authorize you, the officers of that port, to give leave to such ^as^ of your knowledge do not otherwise transport them but upon their necessary occasions as aforesaid provided the said nags exceed not the height of 14 handfuls, and that you keep a strict account of the names of all such as shall transport the same and the number of what you allow unto them, they paying all such duties as hath been usually paid in the like cases, for which &c. Given &c.

To the customer, surveyor, comptroller, collector and searcher of the port of Dublin.

488. <WARRANT FOR ONE TO BE CONVEYED TO THE MARSHALSEAS>

Whereas E.A. and R.A. of Dublin, merchants,[403] having lately petitioned unto us setting forth that one Cormac McDonnell being committed to the Marshalseas of the Four Courts upon an execution at common law at their suit for a debt of 80*li.*

[403] Edward Arthur and Robert Arthur (see J. T. Gilbert, *Calendar of ancient records of Dublin* (18 vols, Dublin, 1892), iii, 195).

14*s.* 6*d.* sterling, he the [**p. 85**] said Cormac, without satisfying ^of^ the debt made an escape and so left the marshal liable to the same. We therefore upon the humble suit of the said Arthurs and J.K., brother ~~to the~~ and executor unto the late marshal, deceased, did grant our warrant for the attaching of the said C. who, being thereupon taken, is now remaining in the gaol of this town from whence our pleasure is that you take him and in sure safe manner convey and deliver him over unto the sheriff of the next county in the way directly from hence to D.[404] that so he may be conveyed from sheriff to sheriff until he be delivered over to the now marshal of the Four Courts aforesaid, who is required not only to receive but also safely to detain him until our further pleasure be known. Whereof you and the said several sheriffs are not ~~fai~~ to fail at your and their perils. And for so &c.

To our well beloved, the sheriff of the county of Sligo.

489. [p. 86] <WARRANT FOR AUTHORIZING MR G.C.[405] TO ADMINISTER OATHS AS CLERK OF THE COUNCIL FOR CONNACHT>

These are to pray and require your lordship forthwith to cause a commission under the great seal and to be directed unto our trusty and well beloved G.C., esquire, clerk of the council for the province of Connacht, and unto his deputy W.S., gent, giving them and either of them according to the customs heretofore used and the general instructions of the said province, full power and authority from time to time and at all times to take all affidavit[s] and to administer oaths as well for the taking of answers to any bills of complaint as for the taking ~~from~~ the examinations of party or witnesses which shall from time ~~to~~ to time be needful to be examined in any cause, wherein the lord president and governor or council of the said province shall desire to be informed by oath; and also from time to time as occasion may require to minister supremacy according to the statute of *secondo Elizabetha* as they or either of them the said G.C. or W.S. shall ~~require~~ be directed by the council there established. And for so doing &c. Given &c.

To our very good lord, the lord chancellor.

490. [p. 87] <WARRANT FOR ~~AUTHORIZING~~ PASSING CERTAIN LIBERTIES TO THE LORD ARCHBISHOP OF DUBLIN[406]>

Whereas his Majesty by his letters bearing date at Westminster the 15th day of June last past [*sic*] hath required and authorized us to cause a grant to be passed under the great seal of this kingdom to the most reverend father in God, Lancelot, lord archbishop of Dublin, and his successors, of divers new liberties with a confirmation of the former liberty according to a bill prepared ready for his Majesty's signature by his highness's attorney general of England, saving only that the fair mentioned in the said bill to be held on the vigil and feast of the Invention of the Holy Cross and

404 Dublin.

405 George Carr (d. *c.* 1637) (see *Lib. mun. pub. Hib.*).

406 Lancelot Bulkeley, see note 232.

the market event in Sepulchres are to be omitted; and that market every Tuesday in St Kevin's Street with liberty to sell victuals in St Patrick's Street as hath been there used should be granted them; and that the fair mentioned in the said bill to be kept four days next after term and four days after *Chrastinum Aray* should be granted to be held at other days, (*vizt*) the one four days next after Michaelmas term and not at the four days mentioned in the said bill; and that the fair held ~~att~~ ^on^ the Vigil of St Benedict in the tholsel of the city of Dublin and all other the grants and confirmations contained in the said bill should pass without any alteration. These are therefore according to the tenor & effect[407]

491. [p. 90] <WARRANT TO PASS THE OFFICE OF FIRST FRUITS>

Whereas it pleased the late sovereign King James of famous memory by his highness's letters patents bearing date at Dublin the 9th of December in the 9th year of his highness's reign of England &c. to erect, constitute and ordain one office called the office of first fruits and of the twentieth part within this kingdom, and by the said letters patents did give and grant unto the[m], Francis E. & W.C.,[408] the foresaid office of first fruits & twentieth part and to the survivors of them with all fees, perquisites, profits and commodities ^to^ the said office or offices incident belonging or appertaining with the annual fee of thirty six pounds, thirteen shillings, four pence current money of Ireland, payable at the feast of Easter and St Michael the Archangel by equal portions as by the said letters patents amongst other things more at large it doth and may appear, we are pleased upon humble suit of H.S., esquire, and upon the surrender of W.C., the surviving patentee, to grant to the said office unto R.W., gent.[409] These are therefore to will and require you to draw up a fiant in due form of law of the said office of first fruits and 20th part the said R.W. during his good behaviour with a grant of all fees, perquisites, profits and commodities whatsoever due to the [**p. 91**] said office in as large and ample manner as the said F.E. and W.C. ~~enjoyed~~ or both, or either of them, enjoyed the same with the said fee of 36*li.* 13*s.* 4*d.* current money of Ireland, as fully and as amply and with all other clauses as are inserted in the said former letters patents which we herewith send you to peruse. And the same fairly engrossed to send us to be further passed as appertaineth. And for so doing this shall be your warrant. Given &c.

To our well beloved, his Majesty's attorney and solicitor general, or either of them.

492. <WARRANT TO BE CHANCELLOR OF THE EXCHEQUER>

These are to will and require you forthwith ~~upon~~ to draw up a fiant in due form of law containing a grant from his Majesty, his heirs and successors, unto R.M., esquire,[410] of the office of chancellor of his Majesty's Court of Exchequer within

407 Pages 88 and 89 are missing in the manuscript.

408 Francis Edgeworth and William Crofton (see *Lib. mun. pub. Hib.*).

409 Robert Wadding (see *Lib. mun. pub. Hib.*).

410 Robert Meredith, see note 346.

this kingdom, to have, hold, possess and enjoy the said office of chancellor of the Exchequer unto him the said R.M. during his good behaviour together with all fees, stipends, profits, perquisites, ~~and~~ commodities and emoluments whatsoever unto the said office belonging or in anywise appertaining and in as large ample and beneficial manner as Sir R.C., [**p. 92**] Sir D.N. or Sir T.H., knights,[411] deceased, or any of them or any other formerly held and enjoyed the same, inserting therein all such clauses as in like cases is usual. And the same fairly engrossed in parchment under your hand to send unto us to be further passed as appertaineth; for doing whereof this shall be your sufficient warrant. Given &c.

To our well beloved, his Majesty's attorney and solicitor general, or either of them.

493. <WARRANT TO STAY A SHIP>

Whereas one J.N. of D., merchant, hath petitioned unto us setting forth that he and one A.B. and P.R. of Dublin, likewise merchants, became partners of late in a voyage made into England and St Malo in France, he the said N. is clear out of purse (as he alleageth) the sum of 1,100*li.* at least being disbursed by him of his own monies by the said B. and R., directions for which he cannot get them to come to an account with him but as he feareth whereof he hath made faith before the clerk of the council they intend suddenly to depart for some ~~other~~ ^foreign^ parts beyond the seas in a ship now riding in that port of Wexford, [**p. 93**] which if they should, would tend to his utter undoing; upon consideration whereof we think it fit upon the petitioner's humble suit that a speedy course should be taken for his relief and that rather in regard he hath put in security to answer the defendants' damages if upon the examination of the cause their stay should appear to be causeless. These are therefore to require and authorize you and every of you forthwith to make stay of the said ship and having taken her sails ashore and secured ~~her~~ such goods as are aboard her, which you are to keep in safe custody until our pleasure be further known, you are to take the said R. (who is aboard the said ship) bound in bonds of 2,000*li.* to appear before us within 8 days after the taking of such bonds and then not to depart without our special licence that so the matter may be by us fully heard and such order given therein as we upon examination of the cause shall think fit. And for so doing &c.

To all and every, his Majesty's officers of the customs in the port of W.

494. [p. 94] <A PROTECTION>

Whereas his Majesty hath been graciously pleased by his letters of the 4th of June last to signify unto us that his royal pleasure is that one J.J. (who is employed in this kingdom about the prosecution of certain special services of his Majesty) should for his better safety ~~sho~~ be received ~~into his~~ for a time into his highness's ~~pleasure~~ protection, we therefore, in pursuance of his Majesty's pleasure signified in that behalf, have thought fit and do accordingly hereby straightly charge and command

411 Richard Cooke, Dudley Norton and Thomas Hibbotts (see *Lib. mun. pub. Hib.*).

you and every of you not only to take due notice thereof but also to be careful that no violence be done or offered to the person of him the said J.; and that you and every of you do likewise forbear arresting, imprisoning, troubling or any ways molesting him, either for debt or any other civil cause whatsoever during the space of one whole year next ensuing the date hereof he behaving himself as becometh; whereof you and every of you are not to fail as you will answer at your uttermost perils. And for so doing &c.

To all mayors, sheriffs, justices of the peace, sovereigns, portreeves, bailiffs, constables and sergeants and ^to^ all and every other his Majesty's officers, ministers and loving subjects whom it may concern.

495. [p. 95] <WARRANT FOR THE LORD MOUNTNORRIS TO PAY TO MR STEWARD 432*li.* 12S. HARPS OF SIR F. HAMILTON'S[412] ENTERTAINMENT>

Whereas not long before our coming forth of England, being willing to comply with Sir Frederick Hamilton's pressing opportunities, we did by the privity and direction of his Majesty enter into bond with him for the payment of the sum of 500*li.* sterling unto Alderman Gurney of London of whom the same was borrowed and taken up to supply his, the said Sir F.H., pressing and urgent occasions which sum, with interest, was to have been paid within half a year ~~alf~~ after but the payment thereof being by Sir Frederick neglected we our self are called upon by the said Alderman Gurney to see the debt discharged according to the condition of the bond entered unto by us jointly with the said Sir F.; whereof his Majesty having taken special notice, his highness hath been graciously pleased to give his princely directions that for our indemnity in that behalf and towards the satisfaction of the said debt, the entertainment due unto Sir F.H. and the foot company under his command, should be stopped and paid unto us until, as well the principal sum of 500*li.* as also the consideration thereof, for forbearance [*sic*] should be duly satisfied. These are therefore [**p. 96**] to will and require your lordship to pay unto our steward, Josua Carpenter, whom we have appointed to receive the same towards the payment of the said debt, in part payment the sum of 432*li.* 12*s.* harps which was due unto the said Sir F.H. and that the foot company under his command for the half year ending the last of March last as by the warrant of full pay herewith sent you appeareth, and this you are to pay out of any his Majesty's monies now remaining or which shall come first come [*sic*] to your hands. And your lordship is further required not to pay or impress unto the said Sir F. any monies out of his next growing entertainment until this debt and the consideration thereof be fully satisfied and that the same be fully signified by us unto you; and for what monies you shall so pay unto our said stewards upon that our warrant being grounded upon his Majesty's royal and gracious ~~pleasure~~ gracious [*sic*] signified as aforesaid, his acquaintance upon the warrant of full pay for the receipt thereof shall be, as well to your lordship as the commissioners of your accounts, sufficient warrant and discharge. Given &c.

To our very good lord, the Lord Mountnorris.

[412] Frederick Hamilton (*c.* 1590–1647), soldier (see *DIB*).

496. [p. 97] <WARRANT TO BE CONSTABLE OF THE CASTLE OF DUBLIN>

These are to will and require you forthwith to draw up a fiant in due form of law containing a grant for his Majesty, his heirs and successors, unto M.M., esquire, [413] of the office of constable of the castle of D. the same being now void by the voluntary surrender of R.D., esquire,[414] who lately held the same, to have and to hold the said office of constable of this Majesty's said castle unto him the said M.M., together with the yearly fee or stipend of 26*li.* 13*s.* 4*d.* harps from his Majesty for the execution of the said office belonging or in ~~as large~~ anywise appertaining, and in as large, ample and beneficial manner as R.B., H.P., T.H., R.D. or S.D.,[415] or any other formerly held and enjoyed the same, and the said office to be held by him the said M.M. during good behaviour, inserting therein all such clauses as in like cases are usual. And the same fairly engrossed in parchment under your hand to send us to be further passed as appertaineth; for doing &c. Given &c.

To our trusty and well beloved, his Majesty's attorney and solicitor general, or either of them.

497. [p. 98] <A WARRANT FOR B.C. TO PASS INTO HOLLAND>

Thomas, Lord Viscount Wentworth, baron of Wentworth Woodhouse, Lord Newmarsh and Oversley, lord president of his Majesty's Council established in the north parts of England, lord lieutenant of the county and city of York, one of his Majesty's most honourable privy council & lord ~~president~~ deputy general of the kingdom of Ireland, do hereby make it known unto all whom it may concern that the bearer hereof, B.C., gent and our servant, being to make his present repair into Holland and other places in the Low Countries and there to remain for a time about the dispatch of certain special and weighty affairs, we (for his better safety and accommodation) have thought fit to ~~accommodate~~ afford him these our letters of passport and by the same to pray and request ~~th~~ all and singular the officers, minsters and subjects of such ~~kingeslord~~ kings, princes, states and lords that are in league and amity with our sovereign lord, the king's majesty of great Britain, and through whose kingdoms, dominions, government or territories our said servant shall have occasion to take his journey, not only to permit him and such his servants as shall attend him to travail and to pass without any their lets and molestations but also to afford him that fair respect and treaty as is fit **[p. 99]** to be given to one that is a subject ~~to one~~ of our sovereign lord, the king's majesty of great Britain, and we on the other side will be ready and willing and ready to make the like due respects unto any the subjects or servants of the said kings, princes, states or lords that shall have occasion to come to these parts. Given under our hand and seal &c.

413 Mathew Mainwaring (see *Lib. mun. pub. Hib.*).

414 Roger Davis (see *Lib. mun. pub. Hib.*).

415 Robert Branthwaite, Henry Perse, T. H. (unresolved), Roger Davis and Samuel Davis (see *Lib. mun. pub. Hib.*). The initials 'T. H.' may have been mistakenly noted. It could be Tristram Eccleston who assumed the position of constable in 1600.

498. <WARRANT TO BE CHIEF CHAMBERLAIN OF THE EXCHEQUER>

These are to will and require you forthwith to draw up a fiant in due form of law containing a grant from his Majesty unto J.U., esquire,[416] of the office of chief chamberlain of his Majesty's Court of Exchequer in this kingdom of Ireland, to have and to hold the said office of chief chamberlain unto him the said J.U., together with the yearly fee or stipend of 13*li.* 6*s.* 8*d.* Irish from his Majesty for the execution of the said office and also all other fees, rewards, pensions, profits, duties, rights, perquisites and emoluments whatsoever to the said office belonging or in anywise appertaining, and in as large, ample and beneficial manner as P.D., esquire,[417] or any other formerly held & and [*sic*] enjoyed or of right ou[gh]t to have held and enjoyed the same, during his good [**p. 100**] behaviour in the execution thereof, and to be ~~exer~~ exercised by him of his sufficient deputy or deputies, inserting therein all such beneficial clauses as in grants of like nature are usual. And the same fairly engrossed in parchment under your hands to send unto us to be further passed ~~us~~ as appertaineth. And for so doing &c.

To our trusty and well beloved, his Majesty's attorney ~~general~~ and solicitor general, or either of them.

499. <WARRANT FOR A PARDON FOR TRANSPORTING WOOL>

Whereas upon humble suit made unto us by one E.M., merchant, we have been pleased to grant him his Majesty's ~~letters patent~~ free and gracious pardon for his offence committed in and by his undue transportation of a certain quantity of wool out of this realm of Ireland without licence in that behalf, these are therefore to require and authorize you forthwith to draw up a fiant in due form of law of a pardon from his Majesty unto the said E.M. for the said fact thereby acquitting ~~and~~ him for the said offence, inserting therein all such clauses as in cases of like nature are usual. And the same fairly ~~in g~~ engrossed in parchment under your hand to send unto us to be further passed as appertaineth; for so doing &c.

To our trusty and well beloved, his Majesty's attorney general.

500. [p. 101] <WARRANT FOR ONE NOT TO BE SET IN THE PILLORY TILL THE LORD DEPUTY'S PLEASURE IS KNOWN>

Whereas one W.L. was upon the eighteenth of this instant month censured in his Majesty's High Court of Castle Chamber for ~~use~~ making use of counterfeit begging passes to be set on the pillory the next market day in this city of Dublin and there to have one of his ears cut off, and that every ~~day~~ market day during this term he the said W. should be set on the pillory as the said decree and censure appears, but forasmuch as we are informed that the ballore[418] of this city, being the appointed officer for the

[416] John Ussher (see *Lib. mun. pub. Hib.*).

[417] Paul Davies (Davis) (d. 1672), clerk of the privy council and secretary of state (see *DIB*).

[418] i.e. bailor.

execution of the said decree, hath upon the last market day so wounded the said L. in the head and the face upon the cutting off of his ear that he the said L. is in some of his life [*sic*]. We, upon consideration thereof, have thought fit and accordingly hereby ~~require~~ will and require as well the constable of his Majesty's Castle as also the ~~C offic~~ sheriffs of this city of Dublin and all other officers whom it may concern, that they and every of them do forbear to cause the said L. to be carried unto or sett upon the pillory any more until our pleasure be further known; whereof they are not to fail &c. Giving &c.

501. [p. 102] <WARRANT FOR ONE R.L. HIS ENLARGEMENT>

Whereas one R.L. (besides the payment of a fine ~~was~~ to his Majesty) was lately censured in his highness's Court of Castle Chamber to remain in the prison during pleasure, we, upon humble suit made in his behalf, have thought fit that he should be enlarged for the present to which end you are hereby required and authorized to take him the said L., bound with 2 good sureties in a recognizance of 200*li.* sterling, with condition to render his body back again to the constable of this his Majesty's Castle upon ten days warning to be left at the of one M.S. &c. [*sic*], whensoever he shall be called upon. And for &c.

To our well beloved, the clerks of his Majesty's Court of Castle Chamber.

502. <WARRANT FOR ONE TO BE CLERK OF THE HIGH COMMISSION COURT>

These are to will and require you forthwith ~~upon~~ ^to^ draw up a fiant in due form of law containing a grant from his Majesty, his heirs and successors, unto M.S., esquire,[419] of the office of the registership and c[ontroller]ship of the acts and recognizances of the High [**p. 103**] Commission of causes ecclesiastical through the whole realm of Ireland to be held by him the said M. St., together with all and singular stipends, profits, commodities, advantages, wages, rewards, fees ^and^ perquisites whatsoever and howsoever thereunto belonging or in anywise appertaining to be exercised by himself or his sufficient deputy or deputies during good behaviour, and in as large and ample ^& beneficial^ manner as any other formerly held and enjoyed the same, inserting therein all such beneficial clauses as in like cases are usual. And the same fairly engrossed in parchment under your hand to send unto us to be further passed &c. Given &c.

503. <WARRANT OF ASSISTANCE FOR MR JOHNSON FOR DRAWING MAPS FOR THE COUNTIES OF ROSCOMMON AND MAYO>

Whereas we have thought fit to employ J.J., Master in Arts,[420] to describe and set out the scituation [*sic*] of the several quarters, cartrons, gueeves and other parcels of land, together with ~~any~~ their quality and present value they are now set at, and what they

[419] Michael Stanhope (see *Lib. mun. pub. Hib.*).

[420] John Johnson.

may at the best be worth and proprietors as they now are in the several counties of R. and M., and how they do [**p. 104**] but one upon another; and in regard the assistance of you the undernamed persons is conceived necessary for the better and speedier effecting hereof, these are therefore to will and require you and every of you to repair unto the said Mr Johnson at such times and places and so often as he shall appoint for that purpose and there to give your best furtherance and assistance unto him in that behalf. And hereof you nor any of you may fail &c. Given &c.

504. <WARRANT FOR ONE TO BE COMMITTED TO THE MARSHALSEAS>

Whereas one F.B. was lately attached by our directions and now remaineth in the custody of R.G.,[421] one of his Majesty's pursuivants, and forasmuch as the said G. informeth us that he feareth the said B. will make an escape from him in regard he hath no place of strength or safety to detain and keep him in, we therefore have thought fit and do ~~according~~ accordingly hereby require and authorize you to take and receive into your custody the body of the said Betson and him safely to detain until you receive our directions for his enlargement; whereof you may not fail &c. Given &c.

To John Dobbs [*sic*], marshal of the Four Courts.

505. [p. 105] <WARRANT FOR LEVYING OF ONE PENNY A SMOKE FOR L. IN *COMITATU* CATH.[422] FOR SERVICE>

Whereas we have received good testimony that one James and Edward Gormogan, two notorious malefactors and who for a long time had greatly disquieted divers parts of this kingdom and more especially the counties of Wicklow, Kildare and Catherlagh by the continual stealths and robberies committed by them and their associates to the great grievance and annoyance of the well affected subjects, were apprehended and brought to justice by the good endeavours of G.L., gent, which service of his being ^both^ acceptable to us and a great ease to many of his subjects well affected who are thereby freed from the continual danger and hazard of their lives and goods, we hold it very necessary that the said L. should receive some recompense as well *in lieu* of his service as the better to encourage him and others to perform the like good services hereafter, which recompense we think fit should be levied in part upon that county of Catherlagh where the said malefactors, as we are informed, were born, maintained and relieved. And where the inhabitants might have apprehended them if they had so pleased, these are therefore to will & [**p. 106**] require you forthwith to cause the high constable of the ~~high~~ several boroughs in that county to collect and levy, as well within liberties as without, the sum of one penny sterling out of every smoke within these several precincts upon such of the inhabitants as have either holding in lands or have any couples of corn, garrans, or any personal estate, and the same being so levied

421 Robert Gilbert, second pursuivant at arms (see *Lib. mun. pub. Hib*).

422 Catherlagh or Carlow.

to deliver over unto the said L. or his assigns as a reward for his good service; whereof you and the said constables are not to fail at your and their perils &c. Given &c.

To our well beloved, the high sheriff of Catherlagh.

506. <WARRANT FOR THE PAYMENT OF A DEBT OUT OF THE LORD LAMBERT'S[423] ENTERTAINMENT>

Whereas upon complaint made unto us by T.W. and R.H. about eighteenth months past [*sic*], W. against our very good lord, the Lord Lambert, for a debt of 88*li.* 14*s.* sterling appearing unto us by his lordship's bond exemplified under the hand of a Master of Chancery in England and ~~by the said~~ by the said bond appearing due to have been paid by his lordship the 17th [**p. 107**] of June 1624 to the plaintiffs, and by their petition alleged to be yet unsatisfied we were pleased by our letters missive to pray and require his lordship either either [*sic*] to take a course for the payment of the debt or by his answer in writing to show cause to the contrary; whereupon his lordship by his letters unto us assuming within a short time time [*sic*] thereafter to make it appear that he was not liable to the payment to the payment [*sic*] of the said debt, we were pleased in favour to him to forbear any further proceedings thereupon till we might understand his lordship's just defence (in case he could make any) in that behalf. But his lordship failing hitherto either in taking course for the plaintiff's satisfaction (of whose sufferance by these delays we cannot but be sensible) or to show us any satisfactory legal & equitable reason why the said debt should not be paid by his lordship against whom we have (in our respect to his person) forborne hitherto to proceed in any strict way as in equity and justice we might [*sic*]; we ^now^ ~~therefore~~ think fit without further [**p. 108**] delay and for avoiding of further ~~cly~~ clamours of the parties concerned, whom we conceive we ought in justice to afford relief answerable to the merit of this cause, and so do order that the plaintiff be paid as well the 88*li.* 14*s.* ~~princip~~ principal debt as also consideration for the forbearance thereof after the rates of 8*li. per centum, vizt.* from the 7th of June *anno domini* 1624 till the day of the date hereof, amounting to the sum of 81*li.* 11*s.* 6*d.* or making in the whole one hundred [and] ^seventy^ pounds, five shillings, six pence, half penny out of the entertainment due unto him, the said Lord Lambert and the foot company under his command for the half year ending at Michaelmas last, which being yet remaining in Mr Vice-Treasurer's hands he is required forthwith upon sight hereof and the receipt of the defendant's warrant of full pay ^of^ ~~for~~ the full ^pay [*sic*] for the said^ half year ending at Michaelmas last as aforesaid, to pay and satisfy unto the plaintiff's agent or attorney lawfully authorized in this behalf, provided that after such defalcation made the overplus of the [**p. 109**] entertainment due unto the said Lord Lambert and his ~~foot~~ company be paid unto his lordship's agent who shall have full power and authority to receive the same. And for so doing &c.

[423] Charles Lambert, 2nd Lord Lambert, 1st earl of Cavan.

507. <WARRANT TO BE COMPTROLLER OF THE CUSTOMS IN THE PORT OF WEXFORD>

Whereas the office or place of comptroller of the customs of the port of ~~Dublin~~ Wexford & Arklow in the county of Wicklow and of all other creeks, bays and members belonging to the said port of W. became lately void and in his Majesty's gift by the death of J.S., gent,[424] late comptroller there, and is now granted to J.P., esquire,[425] by letters patents under the great seal of this kingdom together with all fees, profits and perquisites, have since the death of the of the [*sic*] said J.S. been collected and received by J.F., customer,[426] & other officers of the said port, as also many of them due and yet detained by sundry merchants and masters of ships and barques who are ready [**p. 110**] to pay the same if they know truly to whom the said perquisites did belong as we are informed. We ~~are informed~~ therefore, at the humble request of the said J.P., the now patentee, and his assigns, with the said J.P. is to receive the same, who hath likewise besought us ~~further~~ for our further warrant to assist him for the receiving thereof, we do therefore hereby require the said ~~J.H.~~ J.F. and all and every other officer and officers of the said port, and all merchants, owners & others who have received any of the said fees or have entered any ships, wares, or merchandizes since the death of the said Smith, either outwards or inwards or along the coast by cocket let pass or otherwise, that upon sight hereof and notice of this our direction they pay unto the said J.P., or to his use by his direction, all such fees and perquisites which upon account or otherwise shall be found, due & payable since the death of the said J.S., and that from henceforth they permit and suffer the said J.P. by himself or his deputies to receive all and all manner of fees, profits, perquisites and advantages, [**p. 111**] incident or belonging to the office before mentioned; whereof they nor any of them may fail as they will answer the contrary at their perils. Given &c.

To our well beloved J.F., the customer of the port of W., and to all other officers there and to all owners, merchants and masters of ships, and to all other officers whatsoever whom this may concern and to every of them.

508. <WARRANT FOR ONE TO BE AN ENSIGN>

Whereas the place of ensign unto the foot company of Sir F.F., knight, is become void and in our dispose by the death of W.H., late ensign to the said foot company, we have thought fit to confer the same upon T.F. These are therefore to will and require you ~~foth~~ forthwith ~~upon~~ to make entry in the cheque rolls remaining in your custody (of the said T.F.) as ensign, bearer [**p. 112**] unto the said company, from the day of the death of the said H. at the usual fee or entertainment of an ensign in his Majesty's pay in this kingdom. And for so doing &c. Given &c.

To our trusty and well beloved Sir J.K., knight, muster master general & clerk of the cheque, and in his absence to his deputy.

424 John Smith (see *Lib. mun. pub. Hib.*).

425 John Perryn (see *Lib. mun. pub. Hib.*).

426 John Fowler (see *Lib. mun. pub. Hib.*).

509. <A LICENCE FOR THE STAGE PLAYERS TO TRAVEL THE COUNTRY>

Whereas R.D., H.H., W.J. and others for themselves and the rest of their company have made humble suit unto us to licence them and their said company to use and exercise their quality of stage playing in all cities, towns and corporations, or in any other sitting & convenient places within this kingdom, whose inquest therein we have thought fit to grant and do hereby licence and authorize the rest of the abovenamed persons and their fellows and company to use and exercise their said quality and acting of any tragedies, comedies or [**p. 113**] histories in any [of] the ~~town~~ cities, towns & corporations, or in any other fitting places within this his Majesty's realm, with music, drums and trumpets in meet and decent manner at all times for their best profits, Sabbath days, solemn feasts and times of divine service only excepted. And we do hereby likewise will and require all mayors, sheriffs, bailiffs, constables and all other his Majesty's officers, ministers and loving subjects to whom it doth or may appertain, to afford unto them the full benefit of this our licence and to take due notice thereof, and them nor any of them by any ways or means to trouble, molest or disturb in using or exercising their said quality of playing but to afford them the use of their town halls, tholsels and such like places sitting for the exercising and acting of their quality at ~~the~~ times when the same shall not be otherwise employed, they behaving and demeaning themselves as becometh. And this our licence [**p. 114**] to continue during our pleasure; whereof &c. Given &c.

510. <WARRANT FOR ONE TO EXECUTE THE OFFICE OF CLERK OF THE CROWN FOR W.[427] & LONGFORD>

Whereas R.G., gent, hath petitioned unto us setting forth that one W.B.,[428] who pretendeth to hold ~~from~~ as patentee from his Majesty the office ~~of~~ or offices of the clerk of the Crown of the counties of Westmeath and Longford, both (contrary to the ^duty of his^ place) committed many great and fowl abuses, offences and misdemeanours in the execution of that office whereby his estate ~~thes as~~ ^therein is^ determined and the office become forfeited, the benefit of which forfeiture the said R.G. ~~bes~~ humbly besought us to grant unto him according to the purport of certain letters patents under the great seal of this kingdom bearing date the 18th day of March in the 14th year of his ~~late~~ ^late^ Majesty's reign of famous memory, by which he had a grant made unto him in rendition of the office or offices of the clerk of the Crown of the counties of Meath and L. as the same should then [*sic*] after fall void either [**p. 115**] by death, ~~or otherwise~~ forfeiture, surrender or other~~wise~~ avoidance of any the estate or estates of the several officers, patente~~s~~ or patentees who then enjoyed the same. And forasmuch as the said B. upon his being questioned and examined by our direction could not clear himself of what was objected against him and for that it is apparent that the said office or offices are void, we therefore have thought fit for the present to cause the same to be sequestered into some ~~indiffr~~ indifferent hand and reposing trust and confidence in your integrity and abilities for that employment we do ^hereby^

[427] Westmeath.

[428] William Bradley (see *Lib. mun. pub. Hib.*).

give you full power and authority to take upon you to execute the said office or offices of clerk of the Crown for the said counties of Westmeath and Longford until the same shall be otherwise disposed of, and that our pleasure be further known. And in the meantime to take into your hands all the court books of entries and other things whatsoever belongeth unto the said office or offices, willing and surely requiring the said Bradley forthwith to deliver into ~~his~~ your hands all such books, writings, writs and records, and other things whatsoever belonging unto the said office or ~~of~~ offices and which he hath remaining in his custody; whereof &c. Given &c.

To our well beloved Terence Fury, gent.

511. [p. 116] <SEARCHER, GAWER[429] AND PACKERS PLACE TO BE SEQUESTERED INTO THE HANDS OF M.P.[430]>

Whereas the office or place of his Majesty's searcher, gawer and packer for the port of W.[431] and all creeks, bays and members thereunto belonging is now become void and in his Majesty's gift by the death of F.D.,[432] gent, late searcher there, and is not as yet by us disposed to be executed by any other in which vacancy some detriment may happen to his Majesty if the care thereof be not reposed in some trusty person to prevent the same, we therefore in confidence of the integrity of our well beloved J.P., esquire,[433] who is already an officer for his Majesty in the said port, have thought fit to commit and sequester the said office into his hand and custody together with the collecting and receiving unto or any way arising out of, or by virtue of, the said office, giving and granting unto the said J.P. full power and authority to depute and ~~authorize~~ appoint such person or persons as he the said J.P. shall think and will be responsible for, to execute the aforesaid office or place and to collect the fees, profits and perquisites thereof as aforesaid until the same shall be otherwise granted and settled by letters patents under his Majesty's great seal of this **[p. 117]** kingdom, of which our pleasure is all officers of the port before mentioned and all other whom it may concern are to take special notice as they, or either of them, will answer the contrary at their perils. Given &c.

512. <WARRANT FOR A COMMISSION TO BE RENEWED FOR THE CIVIL GOVERNMENT OF G.[434]>

These are to pray and require your lordship to cause this commission to be ^forthwith^ renewed and passed under the great seal of this kingdom and to be directed to our very good lord, Ulick, now earl of Clanricard and St Albans,[435] as his Majesty's lieutenant

429 i.e. gauger.

430 This must be an error as the warrant shows that the position was placed into the hands of John Perryn.

431 Wexford.

432 Francis Dixon (see *Lib. mun. pub. Hib.*).

433 John Perryn (see *Lib. mun. pub. Hib.*).

434 Galway.

435 Ulick Burke (1604–58), 5th earl of Clanricard and 2nd earl of St Albans (see *DIB*).

of the county of Galway and of the town of G. instead of the late ~~to~~ deceased earl of Clanricard,[436] and to insert therein our trusty and well beloved Sir T.R., knight,[437] and deputy lieutenant there as he hath formerly been; and in your now drawing up of this new commission you[r] lordship is to cause the Lord Mountnorris, Sir R.B. and the mayor of G. for the time being to be wholly left out and the most reverend father in God, Randall, lord archbishop of Tuam,[438] the reverend father in God, Thomas, lord bishop of Clonfert,[439] and our trusty and well beloved Sir Francis Willoughby, [**p. 118**] knight,[440] to be therein inserted amongst the rest of the commissioners: the said lord archbishop of Tuam, the said lord bishop of Clonfert, Sir Ch. Coote, within named Sir Francis W., Mr Justice Donellan[441] and W.H., esquire,[442] his Majesty's attorney there, and likewise within named or any two ~~are~~ or more of them to be of the quorum. And for so doing &c.

To our very good lord, the lord chancellor.

513. <WARRANT TO BE USHER OF THE EXCHEQUER>

Whereas the office of usher of ~~the~~ ^his Majesty's Court of^ Exchequer is now void and in our dispose by the late death of R.D.[443] who hold[s] the same, we have thought fit to confer the said ^office^ upon C.T., gent.[444] These are therefore to will and require you to draw up a fiant in due form of law ~~from his M~~ containing a grant from his his [*sic*] heirs and successors to the said C.T. of the said office of the said office [*sic*] of usher of his Majesty's Court of Exchequer, to have and to hold the said office to him the said T. together with all fees, profits, commodities, emoluments and advantages whatsoever to the said office belonging or in anywise appertaining in as large and ample manner as the [**p. 119**] said R.D.[445] ~~or~~ or R.D.,[446] or any other formerly held and enjoyed the same; the said office to be executed by himself, his sufficient deputy or deputies, & to be held and enjoyed during his good behaviour. And the same fairly engrossed in parchment under your hand to send unto us to be further passed &c. Given &c.

To our &c., his Majesty's attorney general.

514. <WARRANT TO DELIVER UP WRITING TO THE CLERK OF THE COUNCIL>

Whereas there is remaining in your custody certain bills of sale and other writings which you seized upon where ~~upon~~ by virtue of our warrant of the 30th of September

436 Richard Burke (*c.* 1569–1635), 4th earl of Clanricard (see *DIB*).
437 Thomas Rotherham (d. *c.* 1648), MP for Tuam (see McGrath).
438 Randall (or Randolf) Barlow (1572–1638), archbishop of Tuam (see *DIB*).
439 Robert Dawson, bishop of Clonfert, d. 1643.
440 Francis Willoughby (bap. 1614–66), 5th Baron Willoughby of Parham, governor of Galway (see *ODNB*).
441 James Donnellan (Donellan) (1588?–1665), lawyer and chief justice of Connacht (see *DIB*).
442 William Hilton, lawyer and judge of the prerogative court.
443 Richard Dutton (see *Lib. mun. pub. Hib.*).
444 Charles Topcliffe (see *Lib. mun. pub. Hib.*).
445 Richard Dutton, see above, note 429.
446 Robert Dutton (see *Lib. mun. pub. Hib.*).

last you made stay of P.R's ship in that port, we, for ~~best~~ reasons best known to our self, have thought fit and do accordingly hereby require you forthwith to cause all and every the said bills of sale & other writings whatsoever so seized upon to be forthwith safely conveyed and delivered and close scaled up unto the clerk of the Council here to be by him kept deposited until our further pleasure be known concerning the same; whereof &c.

To our well beloved J.F., esquire, his Majesty's customer of the port of W.[447]

515. [p. 120] <WARRANT FOR THE SEARCHER, GUAGER [*SIC*] & PACKER OF THE PORT OF W.[448]>

These are to will and require you forthwith to draw up a fiant in due form of law concerning a grant from his Majesty of the office and offices of searcher, guager [*sic*] and packer of the port of W. and the creeks and members thereunto belonging unto J.J., gent,[449] the same being now void ~~he~~ and in ~~the~~ our dispose by the late death of F.D.[450] who executed the said office, to have and to hold the said office and offices unto him the said Jackson, together with the yearly fee or stipend of 5*li.* English from his Majesty for the execution of the said office and offices and also all other fees, profits, perquisites and emoluments whatsoever thereunto belonging or in anywise appertaining, and in as large, ample and beneficial manner as the said F.D. or any other formerly held and enjoyed the same to be ~~further passed as appealleth~~ ^exercised by himself or his^ sufficient deputy or deputies and to be held during good behaviour, inserting therein &c. Given &c.

To our &c., his Majesty's attorney and solicitor general, or either of them.

516. <WARRANT FOR THE CLERK OF THE HANAPER OFFICE IN REVERSION>[451]

These are to will and require you forthwith to draw up a fiant in due form of law, his heirs and successors, unto G.C., esquire,[452] and Sir R.M., knight,[453] [**p. 121**] not only of the office of ~~clerk~~ ^clerk or^ keeper of Hanaper but also of the place or office of clerk of the Crown in his Majesty's High Court of Chancery in this kingdom, to have, hold, possess and enjoy the said offices and places of clerk of the Hanaper and clerk of the Crown in his Majesty's said Court of Chancery unto them the said G.C. and Sir R.M. and either of them immediately after the decease, surrender, removal or other avoidance of Sir J.K., knight,[454] who holds the same during the life or lives of them the said George C. and either of them, the said G.C. and Sir R.M., and the longest

447 John Fowler, customer of the port of Wexford (see *Lib. mun. pub. Hib.*).

448 Wexford.

449 John Jackson (see *Lib. mun. pub. Hib.*).

450 Francis Dixon (see *Lib. mun. pub. Hib.*).

451 See warrant no. 442.

452 George Carleton (see *Lib. mun. pub. Hib.*).

453 Robert Meredith, see note 346; Meredith was knighted on 6 September 1635.

454 John King (d. 1637), administrator and landowner (see *DIB*).

liver of them together with such yearly fees or stipend as are now allowed and given unto him the said Sir J.K. for the execution of the said several offices from his Majesty, and also all such other ~~fees~~ profits, perquisites &c. emoluments whatsoever unto the said offices and either of them belonging and incident or in anywise appertaining & in as large, ample and beneficial manner as N.S., T.A., L.A., W.P.[455] and the said ^Sir^ J.K. or F.E.[456] or any any [*sic*] other formerly held or enjoyed, or of right ought to have held and enjoyed the same, to be exhibited by them the said [**p. 122**] G.C. and Sir R.M. or either of them, their deputy or deputies or your deputy or deputies of the longer liver of them, ~~he~~ inserting therein all such clauses as in like cases are usual; and the same fairly engrossed &c. Given &c.

To our trusty and well beloved, his Majesty's attorney and solicitor general, or either of them.

517. <WARRANT FOR THE LORD ESMOND'S ARREARS>

These are to pray and require you according to the purport of his Majesty's letters unto us of the 7th of this month of M., a copy whereof we have herewith sent you, to make payment to our very good lord, the Lord Esmond, of ^the^ arrears due unto him from his Majesty upon the establishment which ended in the year 1623 after the proportion of a half without the deduction ~~of a~~ first of a third as is observed in the general of others whose particulars full[y] to be considered in that branch of the arrears. And for so doing this shall be you warrant. Given &c.

518. [p. 123] <WARRANT TO BE VICE-TREASURER>

These are to will and require you forthwith to draw up a fiant in due form of law containing a grant from his Majesty, his heirs and successors, unto our right trusty and well beloved Sir A.L., knight,[457] of the office and offices of vice-treasurer and general receiver of his highness's revenues and casualties and treasurer-at-wars in this kingdom of Ireland, to have and to hold the said office and offices unto him the said Sir A.L. together with all the fees, profits, rights, privileges, allowances and pre-eminences thereunto or therewith belonging, used or taken in as large and ample ~~manner~~ and beneficial manner as the Lord Mountnorris, Sir A.B. or Sir F.S.[458] or any other person or persons formerly enjoying the same offices, or any of them have formerly enjoyed or used the same, to be exercised by himself or his sufficient deputy or deputies during good behaviour, inserting *non obstantes* of any acts, statutes, provisions, instructions or restrictions or other things whatsoever in anywise to the contrary according to the purport of his Majesty's letters unto us of the 4th of this

455 Nicholas Stanyhurst, Thomas Alen, Lancelot Alford, William Philips (see *Lib. mun. pub. Hib.*).

456 Francis Edgeworth (see *Lib. mun. pub. Hib.*).

457 Adam Loftus (see *DIB*).

458 This may have been a mistake where the secretary got the initials mixed up. It could possibly be a reference to Mountnorris's predecessors Sir Arthur Savage and Sir Francis Blundell (see *Lib. mun. pub. Hib.*).

month of April, an abstract whereof for so much as concerns this particular we have herewith sent you. And you are likewise to insert therein all such beneficial clauses ~~therein~~ as in like cases are usual. And &c. Given &c.

To our &c., his Majesty's attorney & solicitor general.

519. [p. 124] <WARRANT FOR THE LORD DEPUTY'S TRUNKS TO PASS WITHOUT SEARCH AT CHESTER>

Whereas by his Majesty's order and directions we are presently to repair to the court and for that purpose have given ~~speedy~~ command for the speedy sending away of our trunks of our apparel and livings and those of our servants attending ~~on~~ us in that journey to the end they may be in a readiness against our coming thether, these are therefore to pray and require you to ~~require~~ suffer R.B., the bearer hereof to whom we have given the charge of conveying them to the city of London, to receive and put on shore the said trunks being ten in number directed to our agent W.R., esquire,[459] and having our seal of arms set upon them and the same to carry or send away as he hath been required by us without any your lets, search or other disturbance, for which we shall be ready to give ^such^ account to the farmers of his Majesty's customs if the same be required from us as may preserve you from prejudice. Given &c.

To all and every, the searchers and officers of the port of Chester.

520. <WARRANT FOR ONE TO BE SWORN BEFORE THE CLERK OF THE COUNCIL>

These are to require and authorize you to call before you one H.H., sometime servant unto Mr J.H.,[460] late archdeacon of Dublin and now deceased, and him the said H. to [**p. 125**] examine upon oath concerning his knowledge of what debts and demands were due from any person or persons unto him the said Mr H.[461] at the time of his death either by specialty or otherwise, and with all what other goods, monies or chattels the said H. did seized [*sic*] of either in his own possession or the possession or custody of any other to his use; and likewise to examine him in whose hands by special name the said goods, monies, chattels, lands or bills for any debts were at the time of [ ] ^the^ death of the said Mr H.,[462] or into whose hands the same or any part thereof have come since, and what shall be confessed by him the said H. to commit the same to writing and to send to us an authentic copy thereof under your hand. And for so doing &c.

To our trusty & well beloved Sir P.D., knight,[463] clerk of the Council.

459 William Raylton, agent to Wentworth at London.

460 John Haynes (see Cotton, *Fasti*).

461 Haynes.

462 Haynes.

463 Paul Davies (Davis) (d. 1672), clerk of the privy council and secretary of state (see *DIB*).

521. <WARRANT TO BE GENTLEMEN PORTER OF THE CASTLE OF DUBLIN>

These are to will and require you forthwith to draw up a fiant in due form of law containing a grant fro[m] his Majesty, his heirs and successors, unto T.M., esquire,[464] of the office of gentleman porter of this his Majesty's Castle of Dublin ~~of this his M~~ being now void by the death of G.H.[465] who lately held the same, to have and to hold the said office [**p. 126**] unto him the said Munday together with the yearly fee or stipend of 12*d.* Irish *per diem* and also all other fees, profits, perquisites and emoluments whatsoever to the said office belonging or in anywise appertaining, and in as large, ample and beneficial manner as the said G.H. or E.R.,[466] or any other formerly received or of right ought to have received the same, to be exercised by him the said T.M. himself or his sufficient deputy or deputies during good behaviour, inserting therein all such clauses as in like cases as are usual. And the same ~~faicl~~ fairly engrossed &c. Given &c.

To our ^trusty &^ well beloved, his Majesty's attorney & solicitor general, or either of them.

522. <WARRANT FOR M.C. TO OVERSEE THE TERRITORY OF THE FERTY>

Whereas his Majesty hath been found by a late inquisition, taken by virtue of a commission under the great seal, to be justly entitled to the territory of the F. in the county of W. and forasmuch as we, out of our due care of his Majesty's just profits, do think it fitting that a speedy course be taken for the preservation of the wood and timber growing in and upon the premises from waste and spoil, we therefore, out of the trust we repose in your honesty and care, have [**p. 127**] thought fit and do accordingly [ ] hereby nominate and appoint you to be overseer of the said territory giving you hereby full power and authority not only to look unto the towns and lands thereof but also to take a special care that the said woods and timber be not wasted, cut down, spoiled nor carried away, nor that the trees thereof be barqued[467] by any person or persons whatsoever. And where you shall find any ~~such~~ to transgress in that kind then you are to ~~hereby to testify~~ certify us, or the lords justices in our absence, forthwith of the names and places of habitation of such transgressors, offenders and barkers that we may thereupon take ~~of~~ a course for the punishment of them in that measure as the quality of their several offences shall ~~demerit~~ be found to demerit. And for so doing &c.

To our well beloved M.C., gent.

523. <WARRANT TO PAY THE FEES OF THE CLERK OF THE CROWN>

Whereas by our warrant of the last of February last [*sic*] we appointed you to be sequestrator of the office of clerk of the Crown of the county of M. until the same should be otherwise disposed of, or that our further pleasure ~~be~~ ^were^ known, and forasmuch as our then instruction [**p. 128**] was, and so now is, that you should be

[464] Thomas Munday (see *Lib. mun. pub. Hib.*).

[465] Griffin Hayes (see *Lib. mun. pub. Hib.*).

[466] Edward Roades (see *Lib. mun. pub. Hib.*).

[467] i.e. barked.

accountable for the fees and profits thereof unto J.C., esquire, these are therefore to will and require you to pay and deliver over unto the said J.C. all and singular the fees and profits which you have received by reason or virtue of the said office for the last assizes held for the said county and ~~for~~ so ~~doing~~ from time to time till you shall receive our order to the contrary; whereof you are not to fail. And for so doing &c. Given &c.

To our well beloved Thomas P., esquire.

524. <WARRANT FOR OWNERS TO BRING IN COALS>

Whereas we are informed that by reason of a late imposition set upon coals in England and Wales the owners and masters of ships come back hither empty and without any loading much more then hath formerly been accustomed, by means whereof this city and other places of this kingdom are like to be put to much scarcity and want of coals nor can they be ~~forthwith~~ therewith furnished duly and seasonably for their money. In regard whereof we have thought it fit and accordingly we do hereby require and authorize you ~~hereby~~ hence forward not to permit any m[aste]r or owner of any barque, ship or vessel within this port of D.,[468] or the creeks or members thereof, to put aboard and transport any ^manner of^ cattle [**p. 129**] before such owner or master hath entered into good bonds with sufficient security in the Custom House, to return his said ship, barque or vessel again laden with coals to some port in the kingdom. Whereof whosoever of them shall fail and so their bonds become forfeited, you are to certify us their names and not thenceforth to permit them to transport any cattle from hence, hereof [*sic*] you are not to fail. And for &c. Given &c.

To ~~our &~~ all & every, his Majesty's officers of the customs in the port of Dublin.

525. <WARRANT TO REPAIR THE FORT OF G.[469]>[470]

Whereas upon our being at G. we did observe that the old fort near that town wants many reparations and forasmuch as we think it very fit and requisite for his Majesty's service that the defects of the said fort to be speedily should be speedily [*sic*] repaired and so the ~~above~~ ^same to be^ made to be thoroughly tenable, these are therefore to pray and authorize you with all convenient speed to view, ~~speed~~ observe and thoroughly consider what what [*sic*] the said defects ~~were~~ are and, ~~so~~ having so done, to certify the same to us together with an estimate of the charge of the repairing of the said fort may amount unto; that upon our receipt thereof we may give such directions for the ~~assisting~~ issuing of money [**p. 130**] towards that service as there shall be cause. And for the better expediting of ~~the same~~ these our orders and directions o[u]r pleasure [is] that you, Captain Nicholas P.,[471] do make your present repair to G.; for doing whereof &c. Given &c.

To our &c., Th. R. & F.W., knights,[472] and Captain R.P, or to any two of them.

468 Dublin.

469 Galway.

470 See warrant no. 368.

471 Nicholas Pinner, naval officer.

472 Thomas Rotherham, former governor of St Augustine's fort (see McGrath); Francis Willoughby, governor of St Augustine's fort (see *ODNB*).

526. [INDENTURES TO BE MADE REGARDING MONIES RELATING TO THE OFFICE OF VICE-TREASURER AND GENERAL RECEIVER OF THE KING'S MONIES]

Let indentures be made in due form of law according to the tenor of words ensuing (*vizt*), this indenture tripartite made the eight and twentieth day of May 1636 between his Majesty's most excellent majesty [*sic*] on the first part, F.,[473] Lord Mountnorris, of the second part, and Lord Adam Loftus, knight, his Majesty's vice-treasurer or general receiver of Ireland, of the third part. Whereas there was remaining in the said Lord Mountnorris, his hands, at the time ^of his^ ~~of the~~ late discharge from his said office of vice-treasurer or general receiver of his Majesty's moni~~es~~, the sum of forty-three thousand, five hundred & fifty pounds, ten shillings and eleven pence sterling, being fifty-eight thousand, sixty and eight pounds, seven shillings, ten pence & demi[474] Irish, as by the certificate of the clerk of the Pells[475] bearing date the ninth day of February 1635[/6] ^appeareth^, witnesseth now these presents that the said sum of 43,550*li.* 10*s.* 11*d.* sterling is by special direction of his said Majesty delivered over into the hands of the said Sir A.L.;[476] and whereof his said ~~Majesty~~ most excellent Majesty doth hereby [**p. 131**] exonerate, acquit and discharge the said Lord Mountnorris, his executors and administrators, his and their goods & chattels and every of them by these presents, and the said Sir Adam L. for himself doth hereby acknowledge that he hath received the sum of 43,550*li.*, ten shillings & eleven pence sterling from the said Lord Mountnorris to his Majesty's use and to be disposed of at his Majesty's will and pleasure; in witness whereof the one part of these indentures to remain with the said Lord Mountnorris, the great seal and the seal of Sir A. L. ~~of~~ are affixed, and to the other part of those indentures to remain with the said ~~I~~ Sir A.L., ~~the said L~~ the great seal of Ireland and the said seal of the said Lord Mountnorris are affixed, and to the third ~~part~~ part of these indentures to remain in his Majesty's Court of Chancery, the said Lord Mountnorris & Sir A.L. have put to their hands and seals the date above written.

Signed William Ryves.

527. <WARRANT FOR THE LORD CHANCELLOR & THE MASTER OF THE ROLLS TO BE LORD JUSTICES IN THE ABSENCE OF THE LORD DEPUTY>

These are to will and require you forthwith to draw up a fiant in due form of law directed to our right trusty and right well beloved cousin and [**p. 132**] councillor Adam, Viscount Loftus of Ely, lord chancellor of Ireland, and to our right trusty and well beloved C.W., esquire,[477] Master of the Rolls of the Chancery of Ireland, thereby requiring and authorizing them to take upon them jointly the government of the kingdom as lords justices and to do all things accordingly to the tenor of the said commission and of such instructions as we shall leave with them signed under our hand, the said authority so to be ~~signed~~ committed unto them as subordinate to

473 Francis.

474 i.e. halfpenny.

475 Thomas Stockdale or Nicholas Loftus who held the office jointly (see *Lib. mun. pub. Hib.*).

476 Adam Loftus (see *DIB*).

477 Christopher Wandesford (see *DIB*).

his Majesty's deputy general without any revocation or diminution of the authority conferred upon us by his Majesty, and to continue only during our absence forth of this kingdom or until his Majesty's pleasure be signified to the contrary, according to the purport of his Majesty's letters of the 4th of April last to us directed, a true copy whereof forasmuch as concerns the said commission we herewith all send you. And the same fairly engrossed to send unto us under your hand to be further passed as appertaineth &c. Given &c.

To our trusty and well beloved, his Majesty's attorney general.

528. [p. 133] <TO BE CLERK OF THE COMMON PLEAS OF THE EXCHEQUER>

These are to will and require you to draw up a fiant in due form of law concerning a grant from his Majesty, his heirs and successors, unto J.D., gent,[478] of the office of clerk of the Common Pleas of his highness's Court of Exchequer in the kingdom the same being now void by the death of J.D., gent,[479] who lately held the same, to be held by him the said J.D.[480] together with all fees, profits, issues, rewards, advantages, privileges, perquisites, commodities ^and^ emoluments whatsoever to the said office to the said office [*sic*] belonging or in anywise appertaining, and in as large, ample and beneficial manner as the said J.D., E.D., J.D.,[481] or any other formerly held and enjoyed the same or of right ought to have held and enjoyed the the [*sic*] same, to be executed by him the said D.[482] or his sufficient deputy or deputies during good behaviour. And the same fairly engrossed in parchment under your hand to send unto us to be further passed &c. Given &c.

529. [p. 134] <WARRANT FOR THE MASTER OF THE ROLLS TO HEAR AND DETERMINING [*sic*] MATTERS BY CONSENT DURING THE LORD DEPUTY'S PLEASURE>

Whereas divers complaints have been preferred by petition unto us by sundry persons upon several occasions where~~upon~~ ^unto^ by reason of our departure for England we cannot give a hearing nor any final order, and by that means the suitors past prosecution is like to prove frivolous and the cost and travel they have been at in danger to be wholly lost and cast away, for prevention whereof and for the better deciding, accommodating and ending of such complaints and differences we, out of the confidence we repost in your good judgment and other abilities, have thought fit to refer the the [*sic*] hearing and ordering thereof wholly unto your self. And therefore in case any person or persons, plaintiff or defendant, whose business, cause, complaint or matter hath been in agitation or dependency before us as aforesaid, shall at any time until our return hether again apply themselves unto you in that behalf, we

478 John Domvill (see *Lib. mun. pub. Hib.*).

479 Joshua Downinge (see *Lib. mun. pub. Hib.*).

480 John Domvill.

481 Joshua Dowinge, E. D. (unresolved), J. D. (unresolved). It is quite possible that the initials were written in error. Previous office holders prior to Domvill's appointment were Edmund Midhopp and John Ferneley (see *Lib. mun. pub. Hib.*).

482 Domvill.

do hereby pray and authorize you not only to entertain and take cognizance of all and singular the said complaints and differences but also upon the hearing thereof to give such or do therein as you in your judgement shall think fit and as shall be agreeable to justice and equity provided that it be done by the consent of the several party's interests; otherwise you are to certify us the true state of the [**p. 135**] said several matters or differences together with your opinion ~~therof~~ thereupon at our return out of England to the end we may give such order as there shall be cause, and what order done or judgment you shall give by such consent as aforesaid, all and every, the person or persons whom the same may concern, are required duly and punctually to obey, fulfil and perform, & thereof not to fail as they and every of them will answer the contrary at their perils. And for so doing this shall be a sufficient warrant. Given &c.

To our trusty and well beloved Christopher Wandesford, esquire, Master of the Rolls, and one of the lords justices designed by his Majesty for the government of the kingdom of Ireland during absence.

530. <PASS FOR SUNDRY PERSONS INTO FLANDERS>

Thomas, Viscount Wentworth, baron of Wentworth &c. To all and singular, his ~~Maj~~ Majesty's officers, ministers and loving subjects whom it may concern, greeting. Whereas upon humble suit made unto us by the persons undernamed, we have been pleased to licence them to depart this kingdom and to make their repair into Flanders and the Low Countries about special affairs of their own[483]

531. [WARRANT RELATING TO THE APPOINTMENT OF SIR WILLIAM RYVES ON HIS MAJESTY'S BENCH]

[**p. 138**], knight, the same being now void by the death of Sir E.H., knight,[484] to have and to hold ~~one of the~~ the said place of one of the judges of his Majesty's Bench unto him the said Sir W.R.[485] together with all fees, profits, commodities, emoluments and privileges thereunto belonging in such ~~as~~ and as large and ample manner as the said Sir E.H. or any other formerly enjoyed ~~thatsplace~~ that place according to the purport of his Majesty's letters unto us of the 7th of A.[486] last, a copy whereof for your better instructions we have herewith sent you. And &c. Given &c.

Directed as aforesaid.

532. <WARRANT TO THE VICE-TREASURER TO REPAY 200*li.* IMPRESSED TO THE SURVEYOR BY THE COLLECTOR OF GALWAY>

Whereas during the time of our late being in England there was directions given by our very good lord, the lord chancellor, and the Master of the Rolls, the lord

483 Pages 136 and 137 are missing in the manuscript.

484 Edward Harris (see *Lib. mun. pub. Hib.*).

485 William Ryves (see *DIB*).

486 April.

justices [*sic*], unto the collector of the customs in the port of G. to impress unto the surveyors and measures employed in the surveying and setting forth of the lands in the several counties of R., S. & M.[487] the sum of 200*li.* sterling, the former sum of the former monies impressed them being exhausted. And forasmuch as it it [*sic*] is fit and requisite that the sum of 200*li.* be misreceived and disbursed for his **[p. 139]** Majesty's service should be repaid to the collector from when the same was received and who is accountable for the same to the farmer of the customs, these are therefore to pray and require you present[ly] forthwith to make present payment of the said 200*li.* unto the said collector of the customs in the port of G. and to charge the same upon your accounts as paid unto the said surveyors and measures; for doing whereof &c.

533. <WARRANT TO BE COMPTROLLER OF THE PIPE AND SECOND ENGROSSER OF THE GREAT ROLL>

Whereas his ~~May~~ Majesty by his letters of the 5th of July last hath been pleased to signify his pleasure to be that upon surrender to be made by E.K., g[ent],[488] of the office or offices of comptroller of the pipe and second engrosser of the great roll in his Majesty's Court of Exchequer here, which ~~he~~ the said K. now holds the same, should be repast [*sic*] by new letters patents unto him together with an augmentation of eight pounds sterling yearly fee (as of his Majesty's grace and bounty) to be added to the said Keating's annual fee of 12*li.* sterling, these are therefore to will and require you forthwith to draw up a fiant in due form of law containing a grant from his Majesty to the said E.K. of the said office or offices of clerk of the pipe and second engrosser of the great roll in the Exchequer and also of the said augmentation of eight pounds sterling yearly **[p. 140]** as aforesaid, the same to be ~~held~~ held and enjoyed by the said K. during his good behaviour and to be exercised by him or his sufficient deputy or deputies together with the ancient fee belonging to the said office or offices and all other fees, benefits, profits and emoluments incident thereunto as fully, amply and beneficially as the said E.K. or any other formerly held and enjoyed the same, inserting therein all such beneficial clauses as in like cases are usual. And the same fairly engrossed in parchment under your hand to send unto us to be further passed as appertaineth and according to the purport of his Majesty's said letters unto us, a copy whereof we have herewith sent you; for doing whereof &c.

To our trusty and well beloved, his Majesty's attorney and solicitor general.

534. <WARRANT TO THE VICE-TREASURER TO PAY THE COMPTROLLER OF THE PIPE 8*li.*, THE ARREARS OF HIS AUGMENTATION>

Whereas his Majesty by his letters ~~patents~~ bearing date at Westminster the 20th day of January in the second year of his reign hath been graciously pleased at the humble [petition?] of E.K., gent,[489] comptroller of the pipe and second engrosser of the great

[487] Roscommon, Sligo and Mayo.

[488] Edmond Keating (see *Lib. mun. pub. Hib.*).

[489] Edmond Keating, as above.

roll in the Court of Exchequer here, to grant ~~ut~~ unto the said E.K. as of his grace and bounty a yearly augmentation of eight pounds sterling to be added to his former annual fee of 12*li.* sterling from his Majesty. And forasmuch as his Majesty being given to understand that the said K. hath not partaken of his highness's said bounty as was intended, his ~~highness~~ Majesty hath been pleased by his letters unto us of the 5th day of July last to require and authorize us that payment be made unto him the said E.K. of the arrears [**p. 141**] of the said augmentation of 8*li.* sterling yearly since the date of the said letter of the 20th of January in the second year of his Majesty's reign. These are therefore to will and require you forthwith to make payment of the said arrears unto him the said K. according [to] the purport of his Majesty's said letters unto us, a copy whereof we have herewith sent you. And for so doing &c. Given &c.

To our &c. Sir Adam Loftus, knight, vice-treasurer and receiver-general.

535. <WARRANT AGAINST SPINNERS OF YARN CONTRARY TO THE STATUTE>

Whereas J.W., gent, being appointed and authorized by a proclamation lately issued to inform himself and to advertise the state of abuses and contempt committed and done against the said proclamation being made for reformation of spinners of linen yarn in this kingdom of Ireland, and the said W. being by the said proclamation likewise authorized to make stay of all such yarn as he should find to be made contrary to the said proclamation until our pleasure were further known, he the said White now informeth us that he cannot discharge and that good account of the trust reposed in him in that behalf and is expected at his hands in regard that divers persons transgressing do privately in their own houses and not in open markets make ~~saile~~ sale of their yarn. And although he hath often desired the assistance of their public magistrates yet they, at least [**p. 142**] many of them, have failed to afford ~~them~~ him the same in that measure as is fitting, ~~in that behalf~~ upon consideration whereof, and to the end so good a work as the reformation of so great and general abuses may not perish through ^want of^ the countenance of authority, our pleasure is, and accordingly we do hereby require and authorize you and every of you to be aiding and assisting unto the said J.W. and his deputies for whom he is to be answerable, to seize upon and make stay of all yarn found to be made contrary to the said proclamation and you & every of you are likewise to cause diligent search to be made in all and every house ~~and~~ ^or^ houses, sellers, chambers, shops, or other places ~~whatsoever~~ wheresoever and whatsoever, where you shall be informed by the said W. or his deputies that any such yarn remaineth hidden or concealed and the same to seize upon and forthwith to deliver over unto the said W. or some of his deputies, and likewise to furnish him or them with horses and other fitting carriages for the bringing up thereof to Dublin to be further disposed of as we shall direct, he or they giving or paying such hire for the same as shall be fit and reasonable. And we further require you and every of you whensoever you of [*sic*] yourselves shall find any such yarn made contrary to the said proclamation that you seize thereupon and send ~~same~~ the same with all convenient speed unto Dublin to be delivered unto the said W. or some of his said deputies, the parties so delivering the same taking the said W.

or his said deputies' hand for the receipt thereof, and for the charge of sending up of the yarn so seized [**p. 143**] upon a course shall be taken for good and reasonable satisfaction to be made. And therefore you and every of you are not to fail at your uttermost perils to ~~pmitt and~~ perform and execute with all rare and diligence which is hereby required. And for &c. Given &c.

To all mayors, sheriffs, justices of the peace, bailiffs, portreeves, burgomasters, sovereigns, provosts, constables and sergeants and to all and every other his Majesty's officers, ministers and loving subjects whom it may concern.

536. <WARRANT FOR A COMMISSION FOR ONE TO ENQUIRE THE LANDS AND ESTATE OF ONE THAT MURDERED HIMSELF>

Whereas W.R., esquire, hath petitioned unto us setting forth that one A.R.[490] of &c. hath lately killed himself being at the time of his death possessed of a good estate in goods, chattels, debts and credits which lie dispersed ^in private^ and unknown hands and several parts of this kingdom and in danger to be concealed from the knowledge of his Majesty's officers and ministers, and forasmuch as the said R. hath (as he saith by the help of some of his friends[)] discovered where a great part of the said goods, chattels, debts and credits are and hath voluntarily offered to prosecute the full discovery thereof upon his own charge, we upon consideration had of this offer of his, and with all duly weighing the just benefit ^& advantage^ that may accrue thereby unto his Majesty, have thought fit and do accordingly hereby ~~think fit~~ pray and require your lordship forthwith to ~~pray and require~~ cause a commission to issue under [**p. 144**] the seal of that court and to be directed unto our well beloved R.W. [&] H.C. of &c., esquires, R.W. & W.G., gent, giving them or any two of them, whereof R.W. or H.C. to be always one, full power and authority to enquire as well by the oaths of good and lawful men as by all other good ways and means whatsoever of which estate, ~~inlands~~ in lands, goods, chattels, debts and credits, the said Alan Rutledge or any other to his use was possessed of at the time of his death. The said commission to be returnable with all convenient speed and at the farthest in *crastino purificationis beate Marie Virginis proximo futuro*. And for so doing this shall be your lordship's sufficient warrant. Given &c.

To our very good lord, the lord chief baron of his Majesty's Court of Exchequer.

537. <WARRANT FOR J.H.[491] FOR THE KEEPING OF THE ROBES, CLERK &C. IN THE CASTLE OF D.[492]>

These are to will and require you forthwith to draw up a fiant in due form of law containing a grant from his Majesty unto J.H., gent, of the office or offices of keeping, cleaning, airing and dressing of the houses, rooms and buildings erected or to be erected within this his Majesty's Castle of Dublin, and of the charge of keeping,

490 Alan Rutledge.

491 James Horncastle (see *Lib. mun. pub. Hib.*).

492 Dublin.

cleaning and airing of all robes, hangings [*sic*] clothes of state, chairs, stools and other utensils usually kept and remaining within the said castle and likewise of the office of keeping and setting ^of^ the clerk within the said castle, the said offices being void by the death of one R.C.[493] who held the same, to have and to hold not only the said offices unto him the said **[p. 145]** J.H. from the time of the decease of the said C. together with two several fees for the execution thereof of 16 Irish *per diem* (*vizt.* eight pence by the day for keeping, cleaning and airing the houses and eight pence by the day for the keeping and setting the clerk[)], and also all such other fees, profits, commodities and emoluments whatsoever as to the said offices do anywise belong or appertain, and in as large, ample and beneficial manner as the said R.C., or any other formerly held and enjoyed or of right ought to have held & enjoyed the same, to be exercised by him the said H. or his sufficient deputy or deputies during his Majesty's ^good^ pleasure; but also to have and enjoy one meet and convenient lodging to dwell and lodge within the said castle of Dublin from time to time that he may more commodious give his attendance in the execution of the said offices from time to time and the same to be north east tower within the said castle [*sic*], inserting therein likewise all such beneficial clauses as in cases of like nature are usual. And the same fairly engrossed in parchment under your hand to send unto us to be further passed as appertaineth. And for so doing &c. Given &c.

To our trusty and well beloved, his Majesty's attorney and solicitor general.

538. <WARRANT FOR P. AND HIS WIFE TO EXERCISE DANCING UPON THE ROPES>

Thomas Viscount Wentworth, baron of Wentworth Woodhouse, Lord Newmarsh and Oversley, lord lieutenant of the county and city of York, lord president of his Majesty's most honourable privy council established in the north of England, **[p. 146]** lord deputy ~~of~~ general of the kingdom of Ireland and one of the lords of his Majesty's most honourable privy council, to all whom these presents ~~may concern~~ shall appertain, greeting. Whereas W.P. and C. his wife have humbly besought us that we would be pleased to grant unto them our licence of exercising their quality of dancing on the ropes and other feats of activity within this kingdom, whose request therein we have thought fit to grant and therefore do hereby licence and authorize the said W. and C. with their companies to use and exercise their said qualities in any of the cities, towns and corporations within this his Majesty's realm at all fitting times for their profit and the recreation of his Majesty's subjects, Sabbath days and solemn fasts and time of divine service on holy days only excepted, and we do will and require all justices of the peace, mayors, sovereigns, portreeves, bailiffs, constables and all other his Majesty's officers, ministers and loving subjects whom it doth or may concern to take due notice hereof and to afford them their townhall[s], motehalls, guildhalls or some other ~~convenie~~ convenient place for showing thereof when the same are not otherwise employed, and also not to molest or disturb or suffer them to be molested or disturbed in the showing and using of their said **[p. 147]** quality, they behaving themselves as becometh his Majesty's subjects. And this licence to continue only during our pleasure. Given &c.

493 Robert Cotterell (see *Lib. mun. pub. Hib.*).

539. <WARRANT TO THE AUDITOR TO MAKE OUT DEBENTURES OF MR N.[494] FEE OF 40*li. PER ANNUM*>

Whereas his Majesty by his letters of the 18th of July last hath signified unto us by his letters of the 7th of August in the second year of his reign had been graciously pleased to give order in the behalf of our well beloved T.N., esquire, clerk of the pipe in this kingdom, for enlarging the fee or stipend of 15*li.* English *per annum* belonging to the said office to 40*li. per annum* of like money, ~~with~~ which increase was accordingly enjoyed by the said T.N. until the same was omitted in the last establishment, and forasmuch as it is his Majesty's gracious pleasure that the same increase should be still continued, these are therefore to will and require you not only to take due notice thereof but also henceforth to make out debenture of the whole fee or stipend of 40*li. per annum* and half yearly as the same shall grow due that payment thereof may be made unto him the said T.N. according [to] the purport of his Majesty's letters unto us of the 18th of July last as aforesaid, a copy whereof we herewith send you. And for &c.

540. [p. 148] <WARRANT TO THE VICE-TREASURER SO TO PAY 2,461*li.* 8*s.* 3*d.* STERLING TO BE PAID TO J.H. OR TO SUCH AS SHALL BE AUTHORIZED HIS ASSIGNEE TO EARL OF CARLISLE>[495] [25 FEBRUARY 1636[/7]]

Whereas his Majesty by his letters patents under the great seal of England bearing date the 3rd day of A.[496] 1635 hath authorized us to give order unto you to pay unto our very good lord, James earl of C., his executors, administrators and assigns, all such sums of money which are or shall grow due by the impost of wines according [to] the old rates before the surrender of his former letters patents. Now forasmuch as it appearath by a certificate under Sir J.W.['s][497] hand for the impost of wines according ^to^ the old rates for the year ending the 25th of March last amounteth to 3,869*li.* 8*s.* 3*d.* sterling, out of which the rent of 1,400*li.* being deducted will remain due to the assign of the said earl: the sum of 2,461*li.* 8*s.* 3*d.* sterling, these are therefore to will and require you out of such his highness's revenues as now remain under your charge to pay unto Sir J.H., knight and baronet, assignee of the said earl or to such as are or shall be authorized by him to receive the same, the sum of 2,461*li.* 8*s.* 3*d.* sterling. And for so doing this ~~shall be~~ together with his acquaintance shall be to you and the commissioners of your accounts sufficient warrant and discharge in that behalf. Given at his Majesty's Castle of Dublin the 25th of February 1636[/7].

To our right trusty and well beloved Sir A.L., knight,[498] his Majesty's vice-treasurer and receiver-general.

494 Thomas Newcomen (see *Lib. mun. pub. Hib.*).

495 See warrant no. 425.

496 August.

497 James Ware (see *DIB*).

498 Adam Loftus (see *DIB*).

541. [p. 149] <WARRANT FOR THE PAYMENT OF 500*li.* UNTO W.C.[499] UPON SURRENDERING OF HIS OFFICE OF AUDITOR GENERAL UNTO J.W., KNIGHT[500]>

Whereas his Majesty hath been pleased to require (by his letters unto us of the 16th of the last month) that the sum of 500*li.* sterling should be paid unto W.C., esquire, upon surrender to be made by him of the office of auditor for the provinces of Connacht and Ulster, that the same might be past [*sic*] unto our trusty and well beloved Sir J.W., knight, his Majesty's auditor general. And forasmuch as the said W.C. hath surrendered the said office accordingly, these are therefore to pray and require you to make present payment unto the said W.C. of the sum of 500*li.* sterling according to the purport of his Majesty's letters unto us, a copy whereof we have herewith sent you. And for so doing &c. Given &c.

To our right trusty and well beloved Sir A.[501] Loftus, knight, his Majesty's vice-treasurer and receiver-~~general~~ general.

542. <WARRANT FOR SIR J.W.[502] TO BE AUDITOR GENERAL>

Whereas by the voluntary surrender of W.C., esquire,[503] the office of auditor for the provinces of Connacht and Ulster are become void and forasmuch as his Majesty by his letters of the 16th of January last (a copy whereof we have herewith sent you) hath signified ~~unto us~~ his pleasure unto us that upon such surrender made the said office should be ~~paid~~ passed unto our [**p. 150**] right trusty and well beloved Sir J.W., knight, his Majesty's auditor general here, to the end as that now he executes the said office of auditor for the province of Leinster and ~~Ulst~~ Munster so he may also therewith execute the said office of auditor for the provinces of Connacht and Ulster. These are therefore to will and require you forthwith to draw up a fiant in due form of law containing a grant from his Majesty, his heirs and successors, unto the said Sir J.W. of the office of auditor general of Ireland to be held by him the said Sir J.W. during his life together with such fees only from his Majesty as are allowed to the said office of auditor general by the last establishment and also all such other fees, duties, profits, perquisites and emoluments whatsoever as do otherwise belong or appertain unto the same, inserting therein all such beneficial clauses as in like cases ~~are~~ ^have been^ usual. And the same fairly engrossed in parchment under your hand to send unto us to be further passed as appertaineth. And for so &c.

To our &c., his Majesty's attorney and solicitor general.

543. <WARRANT TO THE VICE-TREASURER TO PAY TO M.A., BRICKLAYER, 35*li.* FOR WORK DONE IN THE CASTLE OF DUBLIN>

Whereas one J.A.[504] of this city of Dublin, bricklayer, hath lately petitioned unto us setting forth that there is due to him from his Majesty the sum of 35*li.* sterling for

499 William Crofton (see *Lib. mun. pub. Hib.*).

500 James Ware, auditor general, privy councillor and distinguished historian and antiquarian (see *DIB*).

501 Adam.

502 James Ware, see above.

503 William Crofton, see above.

504 James Acheson.

work done by him in erecting and ~~build~~ building a mint in his Majesty's Castle [in] the time of the late lord of Falkland's government, the examination of [**p. 151**] whose pretences in that behalf we referred unto Mr Vice-Treasurer and the Master of the Court of Wards who by their certificate of the 30th of April last have certified us that the said sum of 35*li.* is justly due unto him as appeared unto them by the oath as well of the said Allen himself as of one James Acheson who was overseer of the said work. We therefore have thought fit and accordingly ^we do^ hereby pray and require you out of such his Majesty's treasurer as remaineth in your hands forthwith to satisfy and pay unto the said J.A. the said sum of 35*li.* sterling; and for so doing this, together with his acquaintance acknowledging the ~~same~~ receipt thereof, shall be your sufficient warrant and discharge &c. Given &c.

To our &c. Sir A.L., knight,[505] his Majesty's vice-treasurer & receiver-general.

544. <WARRANT TO LAY SOLDIERS UPON SUCH DELINQUENTS AS THE SERGEANT AT ARMS CANNOT APPREHEND>

Whereas we are informed by the petition of Robert Savill, esquire, his Majesty's sergeant at arms for this kingdom, that he hath received several warrants directed unto him as well from us as of the late lords justices of this kingdom against divers persons who have by indirect ways concealed themselves from him and his deputies and so avoided the execution of the said warrants and others after they were [**p. 152**] attached have made escapes [*sic*] from the said sergeant and his deputies and have ~~contemned~~ often assaulted, beaten & abused them, by which means his Majesty's laws are not ^only^ violated and contemned but his good subjects frustrated of the fruits and benefit thereof by reason the said delinquents cannot be brought within the view of his Majesty's justice. Now forasmuch as it appeareth by several affidavits that his said information is true we are pleased, for the prevention of the like inconveniencies hereafter, hereby to require the said Sergeant R.S. and such his deputy and deputies, for whom from time to time he will be answerable, that when by reason of any the means aforesaid he or they shall not be able to ~~pr~~execute such process[es] as shall be directed unto him or them, either from us or any other lawful authority, he the said Sergeant Savill or his said deputies having first made affidavit of the truth thereof before the clerk of the Council shall forthwith thereupon repair to the captain or chief officer of the next company at the place where any such company shall be garrisoned, who upon sight of this our warrant is required to send such a number of ~~officers with a soldier~~ ^soldiers with an officer^ of the said company to lie on the lands or houses of every such delinquents as the several natures of the said offences respectively shall demerit, where they are to continue until such person or persons shall render their bodies to the custody of the said [**p. 153**] sergeant or his lawful deputy or deputies in that ~~behalf~~ obedience to such said warrants; and after such submission and not before the said soldiers so to be employed are required upon pain of their lives that neither in their marching forward or backward, or during their said lying on the delinquents,

[505] Adam Loftus (see *DIB*).

they commit any extortion or oppression on the country. In due execution whereof we require all and every, his Majesty's officers, ministers and loving subjects whatsoever being hereunto required to be aiding and assisting as there shall be cause and thereof not to fail at their perils. For all which this shall be a sufficient warrant. Given &c.

To our well beloved R.S., esquire, his Majesty's sergeant at arms or to his deputy or deputies.

545. <CERTIFICATE THAT 50 BARRELS OF WHEAT WAS BOUGHT OF D.[506] FOR THE USE OF HIS MAJESTY'S SHIPPING>

Whereas one R.D., merchant, being by port cocket licensed to carry in the good ship called the *Thomas of Chichester* in the county of Sussex a certain quantity of wheat for B. and other places in England, he the said D. and the said ship were by foul weather and contrary winds (as he allegeth) driven to this harbour ~~in Eng~~ of Dublin, whereupon his arrival we being given to understand that his ship was laden with wheat we gave directions that the ~~said~~ [**p. 154**] quantity of fifty barrels thereof should be taken up and bought for the use of his Majesty's shipping here for which he received good payment and satisfaction. Whereof we, upon the said Diggan's humble suit, have thought fit to give him this our certificate that as well his Majesty's officers of the customs in England as all others there whom it may concern may take due notice thereof. Given &c.

546. <A LICENCE TO BRING CORN HITHER FROM THE WEST>

Whereas one R.P. of this city of D.,[507] yeoman, hath petitioned unto us setting forth that having been of late in the western part of this kingdom he found so great store of corn there that the same may be well spared in a reasonable measure for the relief of this city as of other parts of this kingdom, they in the west having scarce vent[508] for their corn by reason of the great plenty thereof, and forasmuch as there is great scarcity of corn as well in this city as the country adjacent, we, upon the said R.P. his humble suit, have thought fit and do accordingly hereby give free leave and licence unto him the said P. to buy corn of all sorts within the province of Munster and the same to bring to this city for the use of the inhabitants thereof and [**p. 155**] the parts adjoining, he selling the same at fitting and reasonable rates. And of this one licence granted we require not only all mayors, sheriffs, justices of the peace and all other his Majesty's officers, ^ministers & subjects^ whom it may concern but also, more especially, the officers of the customs in any [of] the ports of the said province of Munster to take due notice and with all to give unto him the said P. or his assigns port cockets for the bringing of what corn he shall so buy unto this city, he or they putting in good security ~~for~~ to the officers of the customs of those ports respectively, from whence the said corn shall be shipped and brought not to transport into any

506 Dublin.
507 Dublin.
508 i.e. opportunity to sell.

other foreign parts or kingdom, any corn that shall be so bought but to being the same unto this city according to his undertaking, and thereof to return a certificate under ^the^ ~~your~~ hands of the officers here to the offices of the customs of those parts where the ~~parts~~ corn shall be shipped. And for so doing this shall be a sufficient warrant. Given &c.

547. <WARRANT FOR A MEDIUM FOR THE PAYMENT OF 3,000*li.* TO THE LORD CHANCELLOR AND OF THE TREASURY[509]>

Whereas his Majesty in regard of the good and faithful services done by our very good lord, the lord chancellor of this kingdom, as well unto his late Majesty of happy memory as unto his highness himself, hath [**p. 156**] been graciously pleased to bestow on his lordship the sum of 3,000*li.* sterling and to that purpose we were required by his Majesty's letters of the seventh of August last to cause a medium to be taken of what casual revenue of this kingdom hath come into the Exchequer for 7 years last past [*sic*] before our coming into this kingdom, and that being done, that all the ~~revenues~~ monies which that revenue shall arise unto above that medium should be paid unto his lordship till the said sum of 3,000*li.* were fully paid. And for that likewise we perceive by a certificate from yourself, Mr Chancellor of the Exchequer, and his Majesty's attorney general, that since our accession to the government that casual revenue of this kingdom hath arisen to a good and considerable sum, these are therefore to pray and require you (out of the monies so designed) to make payment unto your lordship of the said sum of 1,000*li.* sterling as parcel of the said sum of 3,000*li.* according to the purport of his Majesty's letters, a copy whereof we have herewith all sent you. And for so doing &c.

To our &c. Sir A.L., knight, his Majesty's vice-treasurer and receiver-general.

548. [p. 157] <WARRANT FOR THE PAYMENT OF 1,000*li.* TO THE LORD CHANCELLOR[510]>

Whereas his Majesty in regard of the good and faithful services done by our very good lord, the lord chancellor of this kingdom, as well unto his late Majesty of happy memory as unto his highness himself, hath been graciously pleased to bestow on his lordship the sum of 3,000*li.* sterling and to this purpose we were required by his Majesty's letters of the 7th of August last to cause a medium to be taken of what casual revenue of this kingdom hath come into the Exchequer of seven years last past [*sic*] before our coming into this kingdom, and that being done, that all the monies with that revenue shall arise unto above that medium should be paid unto his lordship till the said sum of 3,000*li.* were fully paid. And for that likewise we perceive by a certificate from yourself, Mr Chancellor of the Exchequer, and his Majesty's auditor general, that since our accession to the government the casual revenue of this kingdom over and above the medium hath arisen to a good and considerable sum and

[509] Adam Loftus (see *DIB*).

[510] As above.

forasmuch as in obedience to his Majesty's said letters we have given our warrants of the twelfth & thirteenth of February last for payment to be made unto his lordship of the sum of 2,000*li.* sterling so as there remains unpaid [**p. 158**] the sum of 1,000*li.* sterling. These are therefore to pray and require you (out of the monies so designed) to make payment unto his lordship of the sum of one thousand pounds sterling being the remain[der] of the said sum of ~~one~~ ^three^ thousand pounds ~~sterling being the remain~~ according [to] the purport of his Majesty's said letters. And for so doing &c. Given &c.

549. <A MEDIUM TO BE MADE OF THE CASUAL REVENUE IN THE EXCHEQUER>

These are to require and authorize you forthwith to take a medium of what his Majesty's casual revenue in the Exchequer here hath amounted unto for 7 years last past [*sic*] before our coming into this kingdom, as also what the same hath amounted unto upon a medium since our said accession to this government, and of the same to return us a certificate under your hands; for doing whereof &c.

To our ^right^ trusty and well beloved Sir A.L., knight,[511] his Majesty's vice-treasurer, Sir R.M., knight,[512] chancellor of the Exchequer & Sir J. W., knight,[513] his Majesty's auditor general.

550. [p. 159] <PROTECTION>

Whereas information is given unto us that one P.R., who was lately out upon his keeping, is able to do his Majesty acceptable service on the discovery and prosecution of other malefactors in & about the county of Cavan, and forasmuch as the said R. hath voluntarily submitted himself and for that purpose humbly prayed to be for some short time received into his Majesty's petition, whereby to be the better enabled to make the said discovery and prosecution we do hereby require you and every of ~~to~~ you to forbear either to apprehend or otherwise to trouble or molest the person of the said P.R. for and during the space of two whole months next ensuing ^the day of^ the date hereof, of which you nor any of you may fail. And for &c.

To all mayors, sheriffs &c.

551. <WARRANT TO BE HIS MAJESTY'S SECOND SERGEANT AT LAW>

Whereas the office of his Majesty's 2nd sergeant at law in this kingdom is now void and in ^our^ disposal by the death of Sir N.C., knight,[514] and forasmuch as we have received good testimony of the integrity, sufficiency[515]

511 Adam Loftus (see *DIB*).

512 Robert Meredith, see note 453.

513 James Ware (see *DIB*).

514 Nathaniel Catelyn (see *Lib. mun. pub. Hib.*).

515 Pages 160 to 165 are missing in the manuscript.

552. [p. 166] <WARRANT FOR A PARTICULAR OF THE RECTORY OF AGH[T]ERT>

Whereas E.W., clerk,[516] ^dean^ of Kilkenny, hath petitioned unto us setting forth that the rectory of A. in the county[517] &c. hath been for divers years together, and so still is, held by the lord barons of upper Ossory successively or by their assigns without any just right thereunto, or having no legal grant there~~of~~ from his Majesty, we upon the said Dean Warren's humble suit have been pleased to grant unto him a custodian of the said rectory until the same shall be by us otherwise disposed of. These are therefore to will and require you forthwith to draw up a particular of the rectory of Aghtert at the usual and accustomed rent to be reserved unto his Majesty thereout which is to be charged up and paid by the said E.W. during such time as he shall hold the same. And the said particular fairly engrossed in parchment to send unto us to be further passed as appertaineth; for doing &c.

To our trusty and well beloved, his Majesty's surveyor and auditor general and to either of them.

553. <WARRANT FOR A RECTORY FOR M.G.[518]>

These are to will and require you forthwith to draw up a fiant in due form containing his Majesty's donation of the rectory of Kilcormick in the diocese of Ferns unto M.G., clerk, the same being now **[p. 167]** void and in his Majesty's gift by the voluntary surrender of J.S., clerk, or by lapse or any other way whatsoever, to have, hold, possess and enjoy the said rectory unto him the said Goodhand together with all the rights, duties, tithes, members, profits and appurtenances whatsoever thereunto belonging or in anywise appertaining, and in as large, ample and beneficial manner as any other incumbent or incumbents ~~four~~ formerly held and enjoyed or of right ought to have held and enjoyed, ~~only~~ the same, directing his commission to the most reverend father in God, the lord archbishop of Dublin,[519] or to any other having lawful power and authority in that behalf in the now vacancy of the see of Ferns. And the same fairly engrossed in parchment under your hand to send unto us to be further passed as appertaineth; for doing &c.

554. <WARRANT TO D.A.[520] TO BE 2ND PREBEND *IN COMMENDAM*>

Whereas his Majesty hath been pleased to grant unto G. Andrews, dean, the two bishoprics of Ferns and Leighlin being now void and hath given power with all unto the said dean to hold some other livings *in commendam* together with the said bishoprics, these are **[p. 168]** therefore to will and require you forthwith to draw up a fiant in due form ~~of law~~ containing his Majesty's donation unto him the prebend

[516] Edmund Warren (see Cotton, *Fasti*).

[517] The rectory of Aghtert was in the barony of Upper Ossory, which was fomerly an administrative barony in the south and west of Queen's County (now Co. Laois).

[518] This is possibly a mistake by the scribe. According to J. B. Leslie, Valentine Goodhand was presented to the rectory of Kilcormick on 11 March 1634 (see Leslie, *Ferns clergy and parishes* (Dublin, 1936), p. 176).

[519] Lancelot Bulkeley (1568/9–1650), archbishop of Dublin (see *DIB*).

[520] Dean George Andrews (see *DIB*).

of S. in the diocese of Leighlin being both void and in his Majesty's gift *jure pleno*, to have, hold, possess and enjoy the said prebends unto him the said G.A. during his incumbency in the way of *condendam* [*sic*] together with all the right[s], duties, tithes, members, profits and appurtenances whatsoever thereunto belonging, and in as large, ample and beneficial manner as any other formerly held and enjoyed or of right ought to have held and enjoyed the same, directing his admission and instalment thereunto *cuicunque sufficientem in ea parte authoritatem habendi*. And the same fairly engrossed in parchment under your hand to send unto us to be further passed as appertaineth; for doing whereof &c. Given &c.

To our trusty and well beloved Sir W.U.[521] &c.

555. <WARRANT FOR A ~~*COMENDIU*~~ *COMMENDAM* FOR THE LORD ARCHBISHOP OF TUAM>

Whereas the most reverend father in God, R.,[522] lord archbishop of Tuam, having held *in commendam* together with the said archbishopric the deanery of the church of the Holy Trinity, his grace finding that they being so remote the one from the other could not be conveniently [**p. 169**] discharged by one man, wherefore he voluntarily surrendered the said deanery into his Majesty's hands who thereupon hath been graciously pleased towards the better support of that see to give way that his lordship should hold *in commendam* some other preferment answerable in value to the said deanery that should be nearer to the seat of his archbishopric. We therefore, in pursuance of his Majesty's gracious intention towards the said lord archbishop and expressed in his highness's letters of the 19th of November last, a copy whereof we have herewith sent you, have thought fit and accordingly we do hereby will and require you forthwith to draw up a fiant in due form of law containing a grant *in commendam* unto the said R., lord archbishop of Tuam, thereby giving his lordship full power and authority to have & to hold such and so many spiritual livings or benefits in this kingdom either with cure or without cure, compatible or not compatible, as shall amount to 70*li.* sterling by the year according as the same shall stand taxed in the first fruit office, always provided that the deanery of the said see of Tuam be not ~~out~~ ^one^ of the said livings or benefices so to be held by him and that the said benefices likewise shall not exceed in number, ^inserting^ therein [**p. 170**] all such clauses as in ^like^ cases are usual. And the same fairly engrossed &c.; for doing &c. Given &c.

To our trusty & well beloved Sir W. U., knight,[523] &c.

556. <WARRANT FOR THE MAKING OF A CUSTODIAN FOR A RECTORY FOR DEAN WARREN>[524]

These are to pray and require your lordship to cause a custodian to be granted under the seal of his Majesty's Court of Exchequer of the rectory within mentioned unto E.W., dean

[521] William Ussher (*c.* 1610–71), clerk of the privy council, MP for Co. Wicklow (see McGrath).

[522] Randall (or Randolf) Barlow, archbishop of Tuam (see *DIB*).

[523] William Ussher, see note 521 above.

[524] See warrant no. 552.

of K.,[525] within named at the yearly rent reserved unto his Majesty and within specified during such time as the said W. shall hold the the [*sic*] same. And for so doing &c.

To our right trusty and well beloved, the lord chief baron &c.

557. <WARRANT FOR JONATHAN HOYLE FOR THE RECTORIES OF DYSERT ENOS & KILTEALE[526]>

These are to will and require you ~~for~~ forthwith to draw up a fiant in due form containing his Majesty's presentation of J.H., clerk, to the rectories of D. & K. in the diocese of Leighlin being in his Majesty gift *pleno jure devoluto seu alio quocunque modo* ~~&c.~~, to have, hold, and possess the said rectories unto him the said H. together with all rights, duties, tithes, members, profits and appurtenances whatsoever thereunto belonging or in [**p. 171**] anywise appertaining, ~~to the same~~ and in as large, ample and beneficial manner as any other incumbent or incumbents formerly held and enjoyed the same, directing his admission to the most reverend father in God, the lord archbishop of Dublin, or to any other sufficiently authorized and qualified in that behalf, inserting therein a clause *pro hac vice tantum* which fiant being fairly engrossed in parchment under your hand you are to send unto us to be further passed as appertaineth; for doing &c. Given &c.

Directed as aforesaid.

558. <WARRANT FOR A PARTICULAR OF THE RECTORY OF A.[527]>[528]

Whereas E.W., clerk, dean of K.,[529] hath petitioned unto us setting forth that the rectory of A. being part in the Queen's County and part in the county of K.[530] hath been ^for^ divers years together, and so still is, held by the lord barons of upper Ossory respectively or by their assigns without any just right thereunto as having no legal grant thereof from his Majesty, we upon the said Dean Warren's humble petition have been pleased to grant unto him a custodian of the said rectory until the same shall be by us otherwise disposed of. These are therefore [**p. 172**] to will & require you forthwith to draw up a particular of the said rectory of Aghter[t] at the usual and accustomed rent to be reserved unto his Majesty thereout which is to be charged upon and paid by the said E.W. during such time as he shall hold the same, and the said particular fairly engrossed in parchment &c.

559. <WARRANT FOR 2 VICARAGES AND A RECTORY FOR MR INCE>

These are to will and require you forthwith to draw up a fiant in due form of law containing his Majesty's ~~gra~~ presentation of R.I., clerk, to the vicarages of K. & R. in

525 Edmund Warren, dean of Kilkenny (see Cotton, *Fasti*).

526 Jonathan Hoyle, rector of Dysert Enos and Kilteale (see Cotton, *Fasti*).

527 Aghtert.

528 See warrants no. 552 and 556.

529 Edmund Warren, dean of Kilkenny (see Cotton, *Fasti*).

530 Kilkenny.

the diocese of L.[531] being now void and in his Majesty's gift by the voluntary resignation of J.C.,[532] and also the rectory and vicarage of B. in the diocese of D. being in his Majesty's gift *pleno jure*, to have, hold, possess and enjoy the said vicarages and rectory unto him the said J. together with all the rights, duties, tithes, members, profits, and appurtenances whatsoever thereunto belonging or in anywise appertaining, and in as large, ample and beneficial manner as any other incumbent or incumbents formerly held and enjoyed the same, inserting therein a clause of union *pro hac vice tantum*, and directing his admission **[p. 173]** to the archbishop of Dublin or to whomsoever else that is sufficiently qualified and authorized in that behalf. And the same fairly engrossed &c. Given &c.

To our trusty and well beloved Sir W.U. & P.D., esquire,[533] clerks of the Council, or either of them.

560. <WARRANT TO A NOBLEMAN TO MAKE PAYMENT OF THE MEAN PROFITS OF CHURCH LIVINGS INTO THE EXCHEQUER OR APPEAR>

After our hearty commendation to your lordship we send you here enclosed a petition preferred unto us by Sir W.R., knight,[534] his Majesty's attorney general, on his Majesty's behalf concerning the mean profits of certain rectories and vicarages in the petition mentioned a long time detained by your lordship from the Crown. We pray your lordship either to make present satisfaction of the mean profits unto his Majesty's Exchequer or by the first day of the next term to appear before us in person or by ~~his~~ ^your^ lordship's agent sufficiently instructed and authorized in that behalf to answer the contrary; and so we bid your lordship very heartily farewell. From his Majesty's Castle of Dublin the 23rd of March 1634[/5].

Your lordship's very loving friend,

Wentworth.

561. [p. 174] <WARRANT FROM MR DEAN ANDREWS TO BE BISHOP OF F. & L.[535]>[536]

Whereas the two bishoprics of F. & L. in this kingdom are now void by the last bishop there and forasmuch as his Majesty hath graciously been pleased to confer the same upon our trusty and well beloved G.A., dean of L.,[537] these are therefore to will and require you forthwith to draw up a fiant in due form of law containing a donation from his Majesty as well of the said two bishoprics unto the said G.A. as also for his investiture, consecration and restitution of temporalities of both the said bishoprics

531 Randolph Ince, clerk, to the vicarages of Kelliestown and Rathmore in the diocese of Leighlin (see Cotton, *Fasti*).

532 John Cawne *alias* Johnson (see Cotton, *Fasti*).

533 William Ussher, see note 521; Paul Davies, see note 463.

534 William Ryves (d. 1648), judge (see *DIB*).

535 Ferns and Leighlin.

536 See also warrant no. 554.

537 George Andrews, dean of Limerick (see *DIB*).

and all jurisdictions, powers, authorities, privileges, pre-eminences, advowsons, tithes, profits, rents, benefits, immunities, emoluments, members and appurtenances whatsoever to the said two bishoprics belonging or in anywise appertaining, to have and to hold unto him the said G.A. during his natural life in as large, ample and beneficial manner and form to all intents and purposes whatsoever as any of his predecessors have heretofore had and enjoyed the same, according to the purport of his Majesty's letters unto us of the 23rd of March last, a copy whereof for your better instruction we have herewith sent you, any common constitution or law ecclesiastical or civil against the holding of two bishoprics by any incumbent to the contrary notwithstanding. And the same fairly [**p. 175**] engrossed in parchment ^under your hand^ to send unto us to be further passed as appertaineth; for doing &c. Given &c.

562. <THE BISHOP ELECT OF FERNS TO HOLD TWO PREBENDS>[538]

Whereas his Majesty having been pleased to confer upon our trusty and well beloved G.A., dean of L.,[539] the two bishoprics of Ferns and Leighlin being void by the ~~last~~ death of the last lord bishop there, his highness, for a further testimony of his grace and favour towards him the said G.A. the better to enable him to support the dignity of that place, hath been likewise pleased to require that a grant should be made and past [*sic*] unto him the said G.A. to enable him to hold *in commendam* as well the prebend of F. in the diocese of F. and also the prebend of Illand[540] in the diocese of Leighlin aforesaid. These are therefore to will and require you to draw up a fiant in due form of law containing a grant *in commendam* unto the said G.A. of the said 2 prebends being both void & in his Majesty's gift *pleno jure seu alio quocunque modo*, to have and to hold the said prebends unto him the said G.A. during his incumbency in the said bishoprics [**p. 176**] together with all rights, duties, members, profits and appurtenances whatsoever thereunto belonging, and in as large, ample and beneficial manner as any other incumbent or incumbents formerly held and enjoyed ^or of right ought to have held and enjoyed^ the same, inserting therein all such clauses as in like cases are usual together with a clause of permutation to the end the said G.A. may change them or either of them for others more convenient according to the purport of his Majesty's letters unto us of the 23rd of March last, the copy whereof for your better instruction we have herewith sent you. And for so doing &c. Given &c.

563. <DEAN T.[541] WARRANT ~~TO BE B~~ FOR THE PREBENDSHIP OF M.[542]>

These are to will and require you forthwith to draw up a fiant in due form containing his Majesty's presentation and grant of the prebendship of M. of the cathedral church of St Patrick's, Dublin, unto Henry Tilson, Master in the Arts and dean of Christ

538 See warrants no. 554 and 561.

539 George Andrews, dean of Limerick (see *DIB*).

540 Ullard.

541 Henry Tilson (d. 1655), chaplain of lord deputy Wentworth, dean of Christ Church cathedral, later bishop of Elphin (see Cotton, *Fasti*).

542 Monmohenock.

Church, being void and in his Majesty's gift *pleno jure caduco seu alio quocunque modo*, to have and to hold the said prebendship unto him the said H.T. together with all the rights, members, profits and appurtenances thereunto belonging or in anywise appertaining, [**p. 177**] and in as large, ample and beneficial manner as any other incumbent or incumbents formerly held and enjoyed or of right ought to have held ^& enjoyed^ the same, directing his admission to the archbishop of Dublin and his installation to the dean and chapter of the said church of St Patrick's or any other having lawful power and authority in that behalf, and inserting therein a clause of union *pro hac vice tantum* unto the said deanery of Christ Church which fiant being fairly engrossed in parchment under your hand you are to send unto us to be further passed as appertaineth &c.; for doing &c. Given &c.

564. <DEANE TILSON'S[543] WARRANT FOR THE DENARY OF CHRIST CHURCH>

These are to will and require you forthwith to draw up a fiant in due form containing his Majesty's donation of the denary of the Cathedral Church of the Holy Trinity in Dublin called Christ Church unto our well beloved H.T., priest, Master of Arts, being now void and in his Majesty's disposal, to have, hold, possess and enjoy the said deanery unto him the said T. together with all the rights, ~~tithes~~ duties, unions, annexations, jurisdictions and appurtenances whatsoever thereunto belonging in as large, ample & beneficial [**p. 178**] manner as the lord archbishop of Tuam or any other dean of the said church formerly held, possessed & enjoyed the same, requiring the chapter of the said church or any one or more of them to install the said H.T. as in like causes ~~are~~ ^is^ usual. And the same fairly engrossed in parchment under your hand to send unto us to be further passed as appertaineth. And for so doing &c. Given &c.

565. <WARRANT FOR THE PREBENDSHIP OF ELPHIN>

These are to will and require you forthwith to draw up a fiant in due form of law containing his Majesty's presentation of W.N., clerk,[544] not only to the vicarages of A.[545] & the vicarages of St John's of Sligo but also to the prebendship of K[546] of the prebend of the Cathedral Church of St Mary's, Elphin, and to the rectory of K. to the said prebendship belonging all in the diocese of Elphin being void and in his Majesty's gift *pleno iure sive alio quocunque modo*, to have and to hold all the same unto him the said N. together with all the rights, duties, tithes, members, profits and appurtenances whatsoever thereunto belonging or in anywise appertaining, and in as large, ample and beneficial manner as any other incumbent or incumbents formerly held and enjoyed or of right ought to have held and [**p. 179**] enjoyed the same, ~~inserting~~ inserting therein a clause of union *pro hac vice tantum* and directing his admission to the bishop of the diocese, and the same fairly engrossed in parchment

[543] Henry Tilson, see above note 526.

[544] William Norris (see Cotton, *Fasti*).

[545] Achonry.

[546] Killala.

under your hand to send unto us to be further passed as appertaineth; for doing &c. Given &c.

566. <WARRANT FOR THE CHANCELLORSHIP OF THE CATHEDRAL OF THE [HOLY] TRINITY DUBLIN TO DR A.[547]>

These are to will and require you forthwith to draw up a fiant in due form containing his Majesty's donation of the chancellorship of the Cathedral Church of the Holy Trinity Dublin unto ~~the~~ J.A., clerk, Doctor in Divinity, the same being now void by the voluntary surrender of J.B., clerk,[548] who lately held the same, to have and to hold the said chancellorship unto him the said John Adderton [*sic*] together with all rights, duties, unions, profits, perquisites and appurtenances whatsoever thereunto belonging or in anywise appertaining, and in as large, ample and beneficial manner as the said B. or any other chancellor formerly held or enjoyed or of right ought to have held & ~~and~~ enjoyed the same, requiring the dean and chapter of the said church or one or more of them to install the said J.A. as in like cases is usual. And the same fair[ly] engrossed in parchment under your hand to send unto us &c. Given &c.

567. [p. 180] <WARRANT FOR A COMMISSION BETWEEN DEAN CULLEN[549] AND THE LADY BLENERHASSETT>

Whereas there is a difference depending before us between Mr Benjamin Cullen, dean of St Patrick's, plaintiff, and the Lady Blenerhassett, defendant, concerning certain wastes pretended to have been committed by her ladyship upon the woods of a farm which her ladyship doth hold called D. and for permitting certain houses there to become ruinous we, for the better discovery of the truth therein, have thought fit that a commission should issue under the great seal therefore to pray and require your lordship to cause a commission to issue to that purpose and to be directed unto R.P. and W.R., esquires, thereby giving them full power and authority to enquire of the said decays and wastes ^and^ with all to estimate what will repair the houses that are ruinous & to certify the same unto us, the said commission to be returned with all convenient speed and at the furthest by the last of the next term, the plaintiff being to give the defendant 12 days notice of the time and place of the execution of the said commission. And for so doing &c. Given &c.

568. <WARRANT FOR MR B.[550] TO BE CHANTER OF KILLALA>

These are to will and require you forthwith to draw up a fiant in due form containing as well his Majesty's grant of [**p. 181**] the chantership of the cathedral church of Killala unto W.B., clerk & dean of Athenry,[551] as also his Majesty's presentation of him the said

[547] John Atherton (1598–1640), chancellor of Christ Church Cathedral, Dublin, and later bishop of Waterford and Lismore (see *DIB*).

[548] John Bradley (see Cotton, *Fasti*).

[549] Bejamin Cullen (Culme), dean of St Patrick's cathedral (see Cotton, *Fasti*).

[550] William Buchanan (see Cotton, *Fasti*).

[551] This should be Achonry.

B. unto the rectories of C. & K.[552] in the diocese of A. the said chantership being void and in his Majesty's gift *jure devoluto* and the said rectories in his highness's gift *pleno iure* the same being now likewise void, to have and to hold the said chantership and rectories unto him the said B. together with all the rights, duties, tithes, members, profits and appurtenances whatsoever to the same belonging or in anywise appertaining, and in as large, ample and beneficial manner as any other incumbents formerly held and enjoyed or of right ought to have held and enjoyed the same, directing his admission to the said chantership of K.[553] to the dean and chapter of the said rectories to be directed to the bishop of the diocese, inserting therein a clause of union of the said chantership and rectories~~hipp~~ unto the said deanery of Athenry[554] *pro hac vice tantum.* And the same fairly engrossed in parchment under your hand to send unto us to be further passed as appertaineth; for doing &c. Given &c.

569. [p. 182] <R.F.[555] TO BE DEAN OF KILLALA>

These are to will and ~~take~~ require you forthwith to draw up a fiant in due form ~~of law~~ containing as well his Majesty's ^grant &^ donation unto R.F., clerk of the deanery of K., as also of his highness's presentation of him the said F. to the vicarages of C.,[556] B.[557] & K.E.[558] in the diocese of K.[559] the said deanery being void and in his Majesty gift *jure pleno* and the said ~~vicard~~ vicarages in his ~~Majesty's~~ highness's gift as being void by lapse, to have and to hold the said ~~lease~~ deanery and vicarages unto him the said F. together with all the rights, duties, annexations, jurisdictions, tithes, members, profits and appurtenances whatsoever to the same belonging or in anywise appertaining, and in as large, ample and beneficial manner as any other incumbents formerly held and enjoyed or of right ought to have held and enjoyed the same, requiring the chapter of the cathedral church of Killala or any one or more of them to install the said F. as in such cases is usual. And as for his admission to the vicarages the same is to be directed to the judge of the faculties, inserting therein a clause of union of the said vicarages unto the said deanery *pro hac vice tantum.* And the same fairly engrossed &c. Given &c.

570. [p. 183] <MR BOSWELL'S WARRANT TO BE PREBEND OF [ST] AUDEONS>

These are to will and require you forthwith to draw up a fiant in due form containing his Majesty's ~~donation~~ presentation of Dudley Boswell, clerk & Master in Arts, to the prebend of St Audeons, St Patrick's, Dublin, the same being void and in his Majesty's

[552] Corren and Killoran.

[553] Killala.

[554] This should be Achonry.

[555] Robert Fargie (see Cotton, *Fasti*).

[556] Castlecomer.

[557] Ballysaskeery or possibly the modern day vicarage of Ballinglasse (see Leslie, *Clergy of Tuam, Killala and Achonry*, revised by D. W. T. Crooks (Belfast, 2008), p. 346).

[558] Kilmore Erris.

[559] Killala.

gift by the promotion of Dr Robert Ussher[560] to be bishop of Kildare, to have and to hold the said prebend unto him the said B. ~~together to have and~~ together with all the rights, duties, tithes, members, profits and appurtenances whatsoever thereunto belonging or in anywise appertaining, and in as large, ample and beneficial manner as any other incumbent or incumbents whatsoever formerly held ~~any~~ and enjoyed the same, directing his admission to the lord archbishop of D.[561] And the same fairly engrossed &c. Given &c.

571. <DR USSHER'S WARRANT TO BE BISHOP OF THE BISHOPRIC OF KILDARE>

Whereas the bishopric of K. is become void by the death of the late bishop there and forasmuch as ~~are~~ his Majesty hath been ~~pleased~~ graciously pleased to confer the same upon our trusty and well beloved Robert Ussher, Dr in Divinity, these are therefore to will and require you forthwith to draw upon a fiant in due form **[p. 184]** of law containing a donation from his Majesty as well of the said bishopric of Kildare unto him the said R.U. as for his investiture, consecration & and restitution to the temporalities of the said bishopric as also to all jurisdictions, powers, privileges, franchises, advowsons, tithes, rents and emoluments whatsoever to the said bishopric belonging or in anywise appertaining, to have and to hold unto him the said R.U. during his natural life in as large, ample and beneficial manner as the said late bishop enjoyed the same; and for the better support of him the said Dr Ussher in the dignity of that bishopric you are to insert a clause for the enabling of him to hold *in commendam* the archdeaconry of Meath so long time as he shall continue in the said bishopric of Kildare as likewise to have and receive all the rents grown due, for and in respect of the said bishopric since ~~the~~ since [*sic*] the decease of the late bishop according to the purport of his Majesty's letters unto us of the 19th of October last, a copy whereof for your better instruction we have herewith sent you, inserting therein all such **[p. 185]** clauses as in cases of like nature are usual. And the same fairly engrossed in parchment under your hand to send unto us to be further passed as appertaineth. And for so doing &c. Given &c.

572. <WARRANT FOR THE ARCHDEANERY OF OSSORY>

These are to will and require you forthwith to draw up a fiant in due form of law containing a grant and donation unto G.D., clerk of the archdeaconry [*sic*] of Ossory,[562] the same being now void and in his Majesty's gift by lapse, to be held by him the said G.D. together with all the rights, duties, unions, annexations, jurisdictions and appurtenances whatsoever thereunto belonging or in anywise appertaining, and in as large, ample and beneficial manner as any other incumbent held ^~~& enjoyed~~^ and enjoyed the same, directing his admission to the Chapter or any one or more of them to install him as in **[p. 186]** such cases ~~are~~ ^is^ usual. And the same fairly

[560] Robert Ussher (*c.* 1592–1642), provost of Trinity College Dublin and bishop of Kildare (see *DIB*).

[561] Archbishop of Dublin: Lancelot Bulkeley (see *DIB*).

[562] Gilbert Deane (see Cotton, *Fasti*).

engrossed in parchment under your hand to send unto us to be further passed as appertaineth; for doing whereof &c.

573. <WARRANT FOR THE RENTS OF THE BISHOPRIC OF K.[563] TO BE SEQUESTERED>[564]

Whereas his Majesty hath been graciously pleased to confer the bishopric of Kildare ~~upon~~ (which is become void by the death of the late bishop there) upon our trusty and well beloved Robert Ussher, Dr in Divinity, and forasmuch as the said Dr Ussher informeth us that he feareth he shall have just cause to commence some suits against divers of the tenants of the said bishopric by the receiving of whose rents now paid he may greatly prejudice himself, we therefore, ~~upon~~ according to his Majesty's pleasure signified unto us by his letters of the 19th of October last, have thought fit to sequester the rents of the said bishopric during the said suits and reposing special trust and confidence in your integrities we have made choice of you two to be sequestrators thereof; and accordingly we do hereby pray and authorize you by your~~self~~ selves, agents or ~~serg~~ servants, to ask, demand, levy and take up the rents, issues [**p. 187**] and profits of the said bishopric as well [as] what is in arrear during the vacancy of the see as for the time to come until our further pleasure be known, and the same having so received to pay over unto the said Dr Ussher. And for so doing &c. Given &c.

To our trusty and well beloved J.D., esquire,[565] chief justice of the province of Connacht and E.D., Dr in Divinity.[566]

574. <WARRANT FOR J.M. TO BE SCHOOLMASTER OF ELPHIN>

These are to will and require you forthwith to draw up a licence in the usual form containing a grant of the place of the schoolmaster of the free school of E. in the county of Roscommon unto J.M., Master in the Arts, the same being void and in his Majesty's gift, to have and to hold the said place of schoolmaster unto him the said M. together with all the rights, duties, fees, wages, stipends, perquisites and profits thereunto belonging or appertaining in as large, ample and beneficial manner as the same hath ^been^ heretofore enjoyed by any other during good behaviour, inserting therein all such clauses as in such like cases are usual. And in the same fairly engrossed &c. Given &c.

To our &c. Sir W.U., knight, & P.D.[567] or any of them.

575. [p. 188] <WARRANT FOR THE PASSING THE RECTORY OF D. TO THE ARCHBISHOP OF TUAM>

These are to will and require you forthwith to draw up a fiant in due form ~~of~~ containing his Majesty's presentation of the most reverend father in God, R., lord

[563] Kildare.

[564] See warrants no. 570 and 571.

[565] James Donnellan, see note 427.

[566] Edmund (or Edward) Donnellan (see Cotton, *Fasti*).

[567] William Ussher, see note 521; and Paul Davies, see note 463.

archbishop of Tuam,[568] unto the rectory of D. in the diocese of Clonfert the same being void and in his Majesty's gift *pleno iure devoluto seu alio quocunque modo*, to have and to hold the said rectory *in commendam* unto him the said lord archbishop during his incumbency in the said archbishopric together with all the rights, duties, tithes, members, profits and appurtenances whatsoever thereunto belonging or in anywise appertaining, and in as large, ample and beneficial manner as any other incumbent or incumbents formerly held & enjoyed the same, directing his admission to the bishop of ^the^ diocese. And the same fairly engrossed in parchment under your hand to send unto us to be further passed as appertaineth. For doing whereof &c. Given &c.

576. <WARRANT TO BE CHANCELLOR OF CHRIST CHURCH FOR DR A.[569]>[570]

These are to will and require you forthwith to draw up a fiant in due form containing his Majesty's donation of the chancellorship of the Cathedral Church of the Holy Trinity, Dublin, unto J.A., clerk, Dr in Divinity, the same being now void by the voluntary surrender of J.B., clerk,[571] who lately held the same, to have & to [**p. 189**] hold the said chancellorship unto him the same J.A. together with all rights, duties, unions, profits, perquisites and appurtenances whatsoever thereunto belonging or in anywise appertaining, and in as large, ample and beneficial manner as the said chancellor or any other chancellor formerly held and enjoyed or of right ought to have held and enjoyed the same, requiring the dean and Chapter of the church or one or more of them to install the said J.A. as in like cases are usual. And the same fairly in parchment under your hand to send unto us to be further passed as appertaineth. For doing &c. Given &c.

577. <WARRANT FOR T.M. TO BE SCHOOLMASTER OF B.[572]>

Whereas the place of schoolmaster of the free school at Birr in the King's County is now void and in our dispose and forasmuch as we have thought fit to appoint T.M., clerk, to be schoolmaster there for the present until we shall further dispose thereof, these are therefore to authorize and dispose of the said T.M. not only to teach in the said school but also [**p. 190**] in lieu of his pains to receive and to take up to his own use all the profits and perquisites thereunto belonging or in anywise appertaining during his execution of the said place of schoolmaster which, whereof, we require all whom it ^doth or^ may concern ^to take due notice and to permit and suffer him quietly^ to enjoy the full benefit of this our grant. Whereof &c. Given &c.

568 Randall (or Randolph) Barlow, arcbishop of Tuam (see *DIB*).

569 John Atherton, see note 547.

570 See also warrant no. 566.

571 John Bradley.

572 Birr.

578. <MR FORWARD'S LICENCE OF ABSENCE FOR THREE MONTHS>

Whereas upon humble suit made unto us by R.F., clerk,[573] Bachelor in Divinity and chancellor of St Patrick's, Dublin, we have been pleased to licence him to repair into England and there to remain during the space of 6 months next ensuing the date hereof about the dispatch of certain affairs of his own, these are therefore to will and require all and every, his Majesty's officers, ministers and loving subjects whatsoever whom it may concern, not only to take due notice thereof but also to afford him the full benefit of this our licence without any loss, prejudice or ~~hindrance whatsoever~~ forfeiture to be incurred ~~by~~ ^for^ any church living held by him in this kingdom by reason of his absence ~~use~~ during the time aforesaid. [**p. 191**] And for so doing this shall [be a sufficient][574] warrant. Given at his Majesty's Castle [of][575] Dublin.

579. <MR B.[576] WARRANT FOR INSTALMENT AND POSSESSION>

Whereas the deanery of C.[577] being void & in his Majesty's gift and donation we have been lately pleased to confer the same upon one W.B., clerk, and inasmuch as the said B. hath complained unto us that he is opposed in the quiet and peaceable possession thereof we, upon his humble suit and the rather in preservation of his Majesty's right, ~~thereby~~ hereby to [*sic*] require and authorize you two jointly or severally to admit, induct and install the said B. into the said deanery which, when you have done, the sheriffs of the county of Westmeath & the King's County as well, now being as to come, are hereby ^likewise^ required to keep and maintain him in possession of so many of the said deanery ~~of the said~~ as is clear and uncontroverted until the same be evicted from him by due cause of law; whereof you and the said sheriffs is [*sic*] not to fail at your and their perils. And for so doing &c. Given &c.

To T.A. & J.J. or either of their ministers &c.

580. [p. 192][578] [UNIDENTIFIABLE WARRANT]

...that so it...requisite a...of this our...out of this...wholly conv...And for &c.

581. [WARRANT RELATING TO BOOKS AND PAPER]

[**p. 194**] of consequence upon their examination or in the books or papers then to commit such person or persons to prison there to remain until our further pleasure be known & you are also required to bring safely unto us all such books and papers as shall be so found, and forasmuch as we hold it requisite in a matter of this importance and that you may rest inexcusable if you shall render yourself tardy in the execution

[573] Robert Forward (see Cotton, *Fasti*).

[574] Page is torn here.

[575] Page is torn here.

[576] William Burley (see Cotton, *Fasti*).

[577] Clonmacnoise.

[578] Pages 192 and 193 are for the most part torn.

of these your directions to strengthen you with sufficient power and authority in that behalf, we therefore have thought fit and do accordingly hereby charge and command all owners and masters of shipping and boats, or other vessel or vessels whatsoever, to be very careful at their uttermost perils that they do henceforward neither land nor take on shipboard any person or persons whatsoever but such as shall be first viewed and observed by you or your deputies, and have their names registered in your book and receive certificate thereof under your or their hands, and those also to be landed or carried on shipboard in such boat or boats as you or your deputies shall appoint, and by no other person or persons whatsoever that so you may be the better enabled to take notice of all comers and goers whatsoever provided always that these our directions and power hereby given shall be no impediment or hindrance to any passenger or passengers so to be landed or carried aboard after search made or view had of him or them by ~~your~~ you our deputy or deputies accordingly, excepting to such person or persons as shall be found suspicious as aforesaid & in regard your pains and charges in maintaining men and boats for these uses must needs be great, we have thought fit hereby to [**p. 195**] authorize you to take and receive of every passenger, who by your licence shall take shipping in this port or in the creeks and members thereof to depart the kingdom, such fees as are ~~use~~ usually taken and received in other ports of the kingdom being warranted by your letters patents and no more, whereof your [*sic*] are not to fail at your peril. And so doing these shall be your sufficient warrant in the execution whereof we require all and every, his Majesty's officers, ministers and loving subjects whatsoever, to be aiding and assisting unto you as there shall be occasion. And in case any of them shall appear negligent therein we require you to certify unto us their names that we may thereupon take such further order with them as we shall think fit. Given &c.

To our well beloved W.S., esquire,[579] his Majesty's searcher for the port of D.[580] or to his deputy or deputies there.

582. <WARRANT TO PRESS A SHIP OR BARQUE>

Whereas our right trusty and well beloved Sir J.J., knight,[581] one of his Majesty's privy council~~ors~~ in this kingdom, hath made known unto us that he is to make his speedy repair into England about certain important affairs of his own, and in regard there is no shipping in this harbour as he informeth us that are bound for England with that haste and celerity as the necessity of his said affairs ~~importth~~ do require, he made humble suit unto us that we would be pleased to grant our directions for the pressing of a ship or barque [**p. 196**] for the speedy wafting of himself, his goods and servants over, whose request therein we have thought fit to grant and the rather in regard he hath undertaken & engaged himself unto us that he will pay and give any reasonable consideration and rather more then ordinary for the freight of such ship or barque; wherefore we do hereby require and authorize you forthwith to press any

579 William Scott (see *Lib. mun. pub. Hib.*).

580 Dublin.

581 John Jephson of Froyle, Hampshire, and Irish privy councillor.

such ship, barque or vessel now riding in this harbour as the said Sir J.J. or such as he shall employ in that behalf shall desire for the transporting of himself, his goods and servants as aforesaid, he ~~giving~~ giving the owner or master of such ship, vessel or barque such reasonable content and satisfaction as shall be fitting. Whereof &c. And for so &c. Given &c.

To our well beloved W.S.,[582] his Majesty's searcher of the port of D.[583]

583. <WARRANT TO PRESS THE KING'S SHIP FOR ASSISTANCE>

Whereas Sir J.J., knight,[584] one of his Majesty's privy council within this kingdom, being occasioned to make his repair into the realm of England for dispatch of his necessary affairs and hath humbly desired our order and assistance for his safe transportation and convoy in respect of several pirates infesting these coasts, we have thought fit so far to condescend to his said request as hereby to pray & require you to take care he be by you safeguarded or wafted from this port along the channel to the bar of Chester where he intends, God willing, to go ashore. And [**p. 197**] hereof you may not fail. And for so &c. Given &c.

To our well beloved Captain T.J., captain of his Majesty's pinnace called the *9th Whelp*.

584. <WARRANT SPECIAL FOR THE ATTACHING ONE [*SIC*]>

These are to charge and command you forthwith upon receipt hereof to repair to the dwelling house of one J.D. of T. in the county of C., shoemaker, and him there or wheresoever he may be found to attach and take unto your custody and safe keeping till he shall have made answer to such matters as, on his Majesty's behalf, shall be objected against him and afterwards till you shall receive our warrant for his enlargement. And hereof fail not at your peril; for doing whereof this shall be your sufficient warrant in the execution whereof we require all justices of peace, mayors, sheriffs, portreeves, bailiffs, constables, governors and all other his Majesty's officers and ministers to be aiding and assisting unto you as they and every of them will answer the contrary. Given &c.

To R.G.,[585] one of his Majesty's pursuivants, and to all other whom it may concern.

585. [p. 198] <WARRANT FOR A PROTECTION>

Whereas we do employ J.C., esquire, in special service for his Majesty, know yee that we have therefore taken the said J.C., his servants and goods into his Majesty's special

582 William Scott (see *Lib. mun. pub. Hib.*)

583 Dublin.

584 John Jephson, see above note 581.

585 Robert Gilbert second pursuivant at at arms (see *Lib. mun. pub. Hib.*)

protection, willing and commanding you and every of you in his Majesty's name that you maintain, protect and defend him the said J.C., his servants and goods not doing or inferring or suffering to be done or inferred to them or any of them any injury, molestation, arrest, loss, violence, hindrance, ~~or~~ impediment or trouble as you will answer the contrary at your peril. Given &c.

To all and singular sheriffs, escheators, mayors, bailiffs, ministers and others his Majesty's liege people.

586. <WARRANT TO BE PACKER, WEIGHER AND GA[U]GER>

These are to will and require you forthwith to draw up a fiant in due form of law containing a grant of the office of packer, weigher and ga[u]ger of and in all his Majesty's port, and of and in all towns and places within this his kingdom of Ireland, unto G.C., esquire, together with all perquisites and commodities thereunto belonging and accustomable, the same to be held, ~~exe~~ used and exercised by himself, his deputy or deputies to his use and behoof with clause of creation to the said office and all such other clauses and conditions as are usual in grants of like nature or [**p. 199**] necessary hereunto. And the same fairly engrossed in parchment to send unto us to be further passed as appertaineth; whereof &c. And for &c. Given &c.

To our trusty and well beloved Sir W.R.,[586] his Majesty's attorney general.

587. <WARRANT FOR THE ENQUIRY OF THE OFFICE OF CHIEF REMEMBRANCER OF THE EXCHEQUER>

These are to will and require you forthwith to draw up a commission in due form of law and to be directed to &c. or any two of you for the enquiry of the avoidance and forfeiture of the office of chief remembrancer of the Exchequer ~~inserted~~ inserting thereunto all s[587]

588. [p. 200] <COMMISSION FOR MASTER OF THE GAME>

To all people ^to^ whom this present writing shall come, Thomas, Viscount Wentworth, Newmarsh and Oversley, lord deputy general of the realm of Ireland, lord lieutenant and lord president of his Majesty's right honourable Council established in the north of England and one of the lords of his Majesty's most honourable privy council sendeth greeting. Know yee that we his Majesty's said deputy perceiving the great abuses and enormities practised by sundry idle persons and men of loose life and mean quality in the unlawful destruction of all sorts and kind of game as dear, hares, conies, pheasant, partridges, quails and moor game with greyhounds, hounds, setting dogs, guives,[588] buck-stalls, hay-nets, ferrets, hare pipes, cords and other engines out

586 William Ryves (see *DIB*).

587 Text ends abruptly.

588 i.e. gyves (shackles).

of the limits of their own grounds, forests, chases and parks contrary to his Majesty's laws and sundry statutes made and provided in such cases for prevention of which inconveniencies and for divers other good causes and considerations as thereunto moving, have given and granted and by these presents do give and grant unto our well beloved servant T.J., esquire, full power, licence and authority by himself and his servants and all such other person or persons as he shall by warrant under his hand and seal authorize and appoint, that he or they or any of them do from henceforth restrain all persons, which by the laws are to be restrained from the unlawful hunting, killing, destroying or taking any manner of game, either of beast or fowl, other then noisome fowl and vermin which by law are to be destroyed out of their own grounds, forests, chases or parks within the county of D., the city of D.,[589] and liberties of the same. And if he or they or any of them find any offending therein contrary to his Majesty's laws then to seize and take from them their dogs, nets, guives, ferrets and other engine and keep the same till **[p. 201]** our further pleasure be therein known. And hereof &c. And for &c. Given &c.

Several other warrants in the like nature.

589. <WARRANT TO BE CLERK OF THE MARKET>

These are to will and require you forthwith upon sight hereof to draw up a fiant in due form of law containing a grant ~~form~~ ^from^ his Majesty unto R.H., esquire,[590] of the office of clerk of the market in, by and throughout his highness's kingdom ~~of Ireland~~ and in, ~~and~~ by and throughout all his highness's kingdom of Ireland & in, by and throughout all and every cities, boroughs, towns, villages, place and places of and within the said kingdom of Ireland, as well within liberties as without being, now void and in his highness's hands and gift together with the fee and yearly stipend of 5*li.* sterling *per annum* for the use and exercise of this said office as also all such other fees, perquisites, profits, commodities and emoluments whatsoever to the said office anywise belonging, incident or appertaining or at any time heretofore due and accustomed in as large and ample manner as any other person or persons whatsoever or any officer or officers in the said office hath or ought to have received, perceived, taken or enjoyed the same, to have and to hold the said office, fees, perquisites, profits, commodities & emoluments unto the said R.H. during our pleasure to be exercised by himself or his sufficient deputy or deputies, inserting therein **[p. 202]** likewise all such other beneficial clauses as are mentioned in any letters patents of the said office granted heretofore to any person or persons whatsoever and as in grants of like nature are usual. And the same fairly engrossed in parchment to send unto us under our hand to be further passed as appertaineth. And for &c. Given &c.

To our well beloved, his Majesty's attorney general.

589 County of Dublin, the city of Dublin.

590 Robert Harebred (see *Lib. mun. pub. Hib.*).

590. <WARRANT FOR THE PASSING OF A FERRY>

These are to will and require you forthwith upon sight hereof to draw up a fiant in due form of law containing the erection of a ferry over the river of A. from the Woodkey within the city of D.[591] unto the other side of the water, or at any other place or places from the bridge of D., to the Ringsend over the said river for the carrying and re-carrying of passengers over the said water ~~together~~ with a grant or demise of the said ferry unto W.B., gent, his executors, administrators and assigns, for the term of 21 years to commence at M.[592] next with power to keep one or more ferry boats to pass and re-pass over the said river, as also authorizing the said W.B., his executors, administrators and assigns, during that term to receive and take the benefit and profit thereof in such sort as hath been accustomed or taking a halfpenny for ~~every~~ passenger yielding and paying therefore yearly unto his Majesty, his heirs and successors, the rent of four pounds sterling with an express[ed] inhibition forbidding all others to keep any ferryboat between the said bridge of D. and the Ringsend, inserting therein all such other clauses as in grants of like nature are [**p. 203**] usual. And the same fairly engrossed in parchment to send to us under your hand to be further passed as appertaineth. And for &c. Given &c.

Directed as aforesaid.

591. <WARRANT FOR MY LORD DEPUTY'S BREWER TO TAKE UP MALT>

Whereas W.U. of this city, brewer, whom we have made choice of for the serving of our household with provision of beer, hath been and [*sic*] humble suitor unto us that for his better accommodation in that behalf he might have our warrant whereby to enable him to the making of provision of malt in such sort as might be for the bettering of our service and the discharge of his own duty which request we have thought fit to grant. And therefore we do hereby give licence and authority to our said servant W.U. that he doth from time to time (during his employment under us) buy and provide in any [of] the villages or towns within this kingdom or in any markets or fairs within the same, such proportion of malt as for the provision of our house and family shall be expedient, provided nevertheless that he the said W.U. by colour hereof do neither engross the same in any unnecessary quantities to the prejudice of others ~~or~~ nor go about to demand the same at lesser rates and prizes then the market shall yield or then other his Majesty's subjects are accustomed to do. And for &c. Given &c.

592. [p. 204] <WARRANT CONCERNING FARTHING TOKENS>

Whereas it hath pleased his Majesty, by his Majesty's letters patents, to authorize and appoint Sir R.N., knight, and Sir F.C., knight, and their deputies and assigns for the issuing, disbursing, uttering and re-changing his highness's farthing tokens within this realm of I.,[593] and also by his highness's proclamation to publish his royal pleasure to be

591 Wood Quay, within the city of Dublin.

592 Michaelmas.

593 Ireland.

that no person or persons whatsoever except the said patentees and assigns shall utter disperse or issue or re-change and the said farthing tokens or any other farthing tokens within this kingdom, and whereas the said Sir R.N. and Sir F.C. have deputed and authorized E.L. of the city of D.,[594] merchant, to utter, dispose, disperse and re-change the said farthing tokens and by all lawful means, according to the tenor of the said letters patents and proclamation, to scarch and make enquiry after all and every such lewd and ill-disposed person or persons within the said kingdom of Ireland which counterfeit to make, disperse or re-change any of his Majesty's farthing tokens in copper money or any engine or instrument whatsoever for the making or counterfeiting of the said farthing tokens, and them to present according to the ~~true~~ purport of the said letters patents and proclamation and law and justice. And whereas the said E.L. hath made known unto us of divers persons in several places in this kingdom which have and daily do make and counterfeit his Majesty's said farthing tokens in copper and utter, disperse, dispose and re-change the same contrary to the tenor of the said letters and proclamation, these are therefore to require and command you and every of you whom it may concern to be aiding and assisting to the said E.L. and his deputies [**p. 205**] and every of them in the searching after and discovering all and every the person and persons which contrary to the said letters patents and proclamation have done, do or shall make counterfeit, disperse or re-change any of the said farthing tokens or make any instrument or ~~any instrument~~ engine for the making or counterfeiting thereof to the end the delinquents may receive condign punishment. Given &c.

To all mayors, justices of the peace, sheriffs, portreeves, sovereigns, burgomasters, bailiffs, constables and other his Majesty's officers, ministers and loving subjects whom it may concern.

593. <WARRANT FOR THE LORD DEPUTY'S SERVANT TO TAKE PARTRIDGES>

Whereas we have thought fit to employ this bearer J.M. for the taking of such necessary quantities of partridges as may be for the provision of our household and the better storing of the parts about this city ~~for~~ with that kind of game for our recreation and disport, and because our said servant upon this occasion may have use of men or horse for conveying the same hither from the parts more remote, we do require you and every of you whom it may concern in case the said J.M. shall at any time ~~during~~ hereafter during this his employment desire the same, to furnish or cause him to be furnished with such men and horses as he shall stand in need of for the purpose aforesaid, as also that you or some of you furnish him from time to time with meat, drink [**p. 206**] and lodging convenient, he paying for the same according to the usual rates provided, nevertheless that the same partridges be had and taken in such places as shall be most unfit for hawking at them and to the least prejudice that may be of noblemen and gent qualified for that recreation. And for so &c. And hereof &c. Given &c.

To all mayors, sheriffs, justices of the peace, sovereigns, portreeves, constables & all others &c.

594 Dublin.

594. <WARRANT FOR A PASS FOR ONE OF HIS MAJESTY'S WARDERS>

Whereas the bearer hereof E.W., one of the warders of his Majesty's Castle of D.,[595] hath humbly craved our pass to travel into England about his Majesty's special affairs, we have thought fit and hereby do licence the said E.W. to have the benefit of one whole month from the day of the date hereof to go and return. These are therefore to will and require all and singular his Majesty's officers, ministers and loving subjects whom it may concern quietly to permit & suffer him to pass and re-pass without any your let, hindrance and molestation, he behaving himself as becometh. Whereof you may not fail as you will answer &c. Given &c.

Directed as aforesaid.

595. <WARRANT FOR BRINGING IN OF WRITINGS AND DEEDS AT A DAY OF ~~HEA~~ HEARING>

Whereas we are informed there are remaining in your hands and custody the deeds of mortgage made by G., late earl of K.,[596] great grandfather to the right honourable the Lord D.[597] of the manor of C., and divers other writings and records concerning that manor now in difference and competition between the right [**p. 207**] honourable our very good lord the now earl of K.[598] and the said Lord D., and whereas we have appointed Thursday next being the 20th of this instant October in the morning for accommodating of the same difference, according to his Majesty's letters to us directed in that behalf, we have thought fit hereby to will and require you to attend where at this house the day prefixed and to bring along with you the mortgage and writings abovementioned to the intent the same may be viewed and made use of as appertaineth. Whereof you may not &c. Given &c.

To our well beloved G.P., esquire.

596. <WARRANT TO TRANSPORT HORSES>

Whereas S.M. hath been an humble suitor unto us that for his better accommodation we would be pleased to give him our licence for transportation of 9 horses for the use of himself and servants into such parts beyond the seas (being in amity with his Majesty) as he hath occasion to arrive them at, we have thought fit to grant his said request and do hereby ^will &^ require you to take notice hereof and permit and suffer the said horses to be embarked accordingly without any your let, molestation or interruption whatsoever, any [of] your former warrant or directions whatsoever to the contrary notwithstanding, whereof you may not &c. And for &c. Given &c.

To our well beloved W.S., esquire,[599] searcher of his Majesty's port of D.[600] and to all others whom it may concern.

[595] Dublin.

[596] Gerald Fitzgerald (1525–85), 11th earl of Kildare (see *DIB*).

[597] John Digby (1580–1653), 1st earl of Bristol (see *ODNB*).

[598] George Fitzgerald (1612–60), 16th earl of Kildare, politician (see *DIB*).

[599] William Scott (see *Lib. mun. pub. Hib.*).

[600] Dublin.

597. [p. 208] <WARRANT FOR EXAMINING WITNESSES BETWEEN PARTY & PARTY BEFORE THE CLERK OF THE COUNCIL>

Whereas we are informed that you, whose names are subscribed, are material witnesses to be examined in a cause depending before us wherein J.W. is plaintiff against N.M., defendant, these are therefore to will and require you forthwith upon sight hereof to repair to this city and to attend the clerk of the Council who is also hereby required to take your several depositions in writing upon oath to such interr[ogation] as shall be exhibited to that purpose, and the same or true copies thereof under your hand to certify unto us, after publication thereof had to be made use of, as appertaineth provided that the parties on both sides have present notice hereof and that oath be made of such notice given before the clerk of the Council to the end they may all have the like liberty to examine their several witnesses or to examine each other witnesses on cross interr[ogation] if they shall see cause for the same. And hereof &c.
W.H. *et al.*

598. <WARRANT FOR TRANSPORTING OF PIPESTAVES>

Whereas humble suit hath been made unto us by C.C., esquire,[601] for our licence to transport out of this kingdom the number 160,000 pipestaves to be embarked at the port of W.[602] and arrived at that in London in England, which request we have thought fit to grant and do there^fore^ hereby will & require you and every of you to permit & suffer the said C., or his agents or servants, to put aboard and transport the same accordingly provided that you [**p. 209**] first make entry thereof in your customs books and receive his Majesty's due customs out of the same, and provided also that you take good bond of the said C. to return your certificate from the surveyor general of the said port of London under his hand and seal within 8 months after the embarking of the said pipestaves that the same are landed at the said port of London; lastly, you are to be very vigilant that no other number of pipestaves be under colour or pretence hereof embarked contrary to your former directions in that behalf, whereof you &c. And for &c. Given &c.

To all and every, the officers of his Majesty's customs of the port of W.

599. <WARRANT OF SUMMONS>

These shall be to require and command you forthwith upon the receipt of this one warrant to make our ~~warrant~~ repair hither to his Majesty's Castle of Dublin and here to make answer to such matters as shall be objected against you by M.C. And hereof fail not. Given &c.

To our well beloved R.L., gent.[603]

601 Calcott Chambré (d. 1635).

602 Wicklow.

603 Pages 210 and 211 are missing in the manuscript.

600. [WARRANT CONCERNING THE TRANSPORTATION OF TIMBER OUT OF THE KINGDOM]

that so it may not be done in any larger measure then is requisite and necessary and that others may not under colour of this our warrant transport for their own uses any timber out of this kingdom upon pretence of the same is [*sic*] to be wholly converted to his lordship's use. Whereof you are not &c. And for &c. Given &c.

601. <WARRANT FOR RESTORING OF A SHIP UNTO THE PROPRIETOR BEING TAKEN FROM THE PIRATE>

Whereas the ship called the *Spread Eagle of Amsterdam* about the 28th of July last, being taken and surprised in the bay of D.[604] by certain Spaniards and Biscayners, the same by the good endeavour of Sir R.P.,[605] captain and commander of his Majesty's good ship the *A.*[606], was regained and recovered and the goods therein saved which [the] said surprised ship, by our directions unto you, hath been ever since stayed in this port & the goods and merchandize therein found by our several warrants of the 3rd & 26th of August last, inventoried and appraised and such thereof as were *bona peritura* ordered to be ~~sold~~ sold at the best rates and the rest to be safely kept and put up in his Majesty's storehouse in this port of Dublin. Now inasmuch as for good reasons as thereunto moving, we think it fit that the said ship and goods be restored and delivered unto the owners and proprietors thereof, these are therefore to will and require you forthwith upon sight hereof not only to deliver up the said ship and all the goods and merchandizes which are yet unsold and remain in his Majesty's said store, together with all the tackles, sails, furniture and provision whatsoever to the said ship belonging, but also forthwith to pay and deliver over unto the said owners and proprietors all and every which sum [**p. 213**] and sums of money which have been received by you or either of you for any of the said goods so sold, and likewise all such bills, bonds ^and^ notes that have been taken for the payment of any ~~sucmhe~~ sum or sums of money which either now are or hereafter shall grow due and become payable either by the said owners and proprietors themselves or ^by^ any other person or persons whatsoever unto whom any part of the said goods were sold and delivered as aforesaid. And we likewise require you and all others in whose hands and custody any bills, bonds and other writing which concern the premises do remain to deliver the same over unto the said owners and proprietors who have entered already into good bonds, to stand to such order as we shall make concerning salvage and ~~other~~ ^such^ charges as you or any other person or persons have been put unto about and saving inventoring and appraising of the said goods. Whereof you and every of you are not to fail. And for &c. Given &c.

To our well beloved T.M. and T.C., esquires, and to all others who it may concern.

604 Dublin.

605 Richard Plumleigh, see note 84.

606 Amsterdam.

602. <ANOTHER WARRANT FOR A PROTECTION>

Whereas C.M., gent, hath petitioned unto us setting forth that (a little before the Lord F.[607] coming to this government) he was persuaded by the Lady F.[608] to become bound unto divers persons in several sums of money which her ladyship owed, but she failing hitherto to make payment and the said Lord Falkland lately dead, by whom the said M. rested confident he should have been freed of the said debts if his lordship **[p. 214]** had longer lived, the creditors prosecute him with all extremity and will be content as with no other satisfaction but present payment, which he being not able to give them humbly besought us to receive him into his Majesty's protection for a certain time to the end he may be thereby the better enabled to apply himself being at his liberty unto the now Lord F. for some course to be taken for his discharge and disengagement from the said debts, whose requests therein we have thought fit to grant and the rather in regard it is constantly affirmed that he is sued for no proper debt of his own. These are therefore to will and require you to take due notice thereof and to afford him the full benefit of this protection in all respects by forbearing to sue, arrest, impede or otherwise molest the said C.M. in his person or goods for and during the space of three months next ensuing the date hereof, provided that this protection now granted do not extend to protect or free him from any debt due to his Majesty nor from any former ~~answerable debt~~ imprisonment. Whereof &c. And for &c. Given &c.

To all mayors, sheriffs, justices of the peace, bailiffs, constables, portreeves, sovereigns and to all other his Majesty's officers, ministers and loving subjects whatsoever whom it may concern and to every of them.

603. <LICENCE OF ABSENCE FOR A CAPTAIN OF A TROOP & 3 OF HIS COMPANY>

Whereas our very good lord, the Viscount W. of A.[609] and one of ~~his~~ the lords of his Majesty's most honourable privy council in England, having licence from his Majesty to attend his service there hath made suit unto us that **[p. 215]** he may receive no prejudice in his entertainments during his absence and that three of his horse troop and 3 of ~~his~~ ^the foot^ company under his command may be licensed to attend him in England during his continuance there, we are pleased to condescend to his lordship's said suit. These are therefore to will and require you not only to take ^due^ notice thereof but also to forbear imposing any check either upon his lordship or on the three soldiers of his horse and three of his foot aforesaid for their said absence with him in England. And for &c. Given &c.

To our trusty and well beloved, the muster master general and clerk of the cheque and in his absence to his deputy.

604. <WARRANT FOR A GOLD OR SILVER MINE>

Whereas his Majesty hath been pleased by his letters patents under the great seal of ~~England~~ this kingdom to enable & authorize W.D. to search, dig for and discover

607 Falkland: Henry Cary, see p. xxx, note 4.

608 Elizabeth Falkland (1585–1639), Viscountess Falkland, writer and translator (see *DIB*).

609 Viscount [Charles] Wilmot of Athlone, see note 13.

royal mines of gold, silver and other minerals generally throughout this kingdom wheresoever the said W.D. might find or suspect the same to be, and forasmuch as it appeareth unto us by authority under the said W.D.['s] hand and seal that he hath entrusted and employed in that behalf one J.F., who became an humble suitor unto us for our warrants for his better assistance and countenance therein, whose request we have thought fit to grant. These are therefore to will and require all and every, his Majesty's subjects in this **[p. 216]** ...[610]

605. [UNIDENTIFIABLE WARRANT]

...ame...tatute...ewe...of...s...

606. [p. 218] [WARRANT RELATING TO SHIPPING OF GOODS]

...wool unto the port of L.[611] in England provided that you first make entry thereof in your custom books and receive his Majesty's due customs thereout and that with all you take bonds that the same be not transported to no other foreign parts but only in England as aforesaid. And thereof to return your certificate within six months next after entry made thereof. And &c.

To all and every, the officers of his Majesty's customs in the port of D.[612]

607. <WARRANT FOR MAKING OF A SHERIFF>

We greet your lordship well. Whereas we have nominated & appointed our well beloved T.C. to be high sheriff of the county of D.[613] for the year next ensuing, these are therefore to pray and require your lordship upon receipt hereof to make forth unto him letters patents under the great seal of this kingdom of the said office according to the usual and accustomed manner. And our pleasure is that before he do entertain the execution of the said office, besides the oath of sheriff, that he do take the corporal Oath of Supremacy unto his Majesty according to the statute in that case made and provided, and do likewise enter into sufficient ~~rec~~ recognizance to his Majesty to be truly accountable in his highness's Exchequer for the said office as in such cases is usual. And for &c. Given &c.

To our very good lord, the lord chancellor.

608. [p. 219] <WARRANT FOR AN ARREAR FOR PENSION>

These are to will and require you forthwith to draw up a ~~debt~~ debenture unto J.B., pensioner, of the arrears which are due unto him a year and a half ending at

610 Pages 216 and 217 are badly torn.

611 London.

612 Dublin.

613 Dublin.

Michaelmas last of the pension granted and allowed unto him from his Majesty, that payment thereof may be made unto him accordingly by his Majesty's vice-treasurer unto him. And for &c. Given &c.

To our trusty and well beloved Sir J.W., knight,[614] his Majesty's auditor general.

609. <WARRANT FOR THE ENLARGEMENT OF ONE COMMITTED FOR THE PEACE>

Whereas J.S., gent, was by our directions committed to your custody until he had put in security for the peace, which seeing he hath performed as appears by certificate unto us, our pleasure is that you forthwith upon sight hereof do enlarge and set ~~forth~~ at ~~large~~ liberty the body of the said S. paying his fees. And for &c. Given &c.

To our well beloved M.B.,[615] one of his Majesty's pursuivants.

610. <WARRANT FOR RESTORING OF A PIECE OF ORDNANCE>

These are to pray and require[616]

611. [p. 220] <WARRANT FOR RESTORING OF A PIECE OF ORDNANCE>

Whereas you have in your custody one brass base being a piece taken up and weighed out of the sea by one J.H., diver, from whom you unjustly detain the same, these are therefore to will and require you forthwith to deliver up & restore the said piece of ordnance unto the said J., his servant, or some such other person as he shall appoint to receive it that the same may be disposed of as his Majesty by commission unto the said J., hath directed. Whereof &c. And for &c. Given &c.

To M.C., gent, and to all other persons whatsoever whom it may concern.

612. <WARRANT FOR A COMMISSION TO TAKE THE ACCOUNT OF HIS MAJESTY'S TREASURER>

These are to pray and require your lordship forthwith to issue out a commission under the great seal to be directed unto such former general commissioners of accounts and in the form of a former commission to them directed to take the final account of the Lord D.,[617] deceased, his Majesty's treasurer at wars, either from the Lady Docwra, his executrix, or from other his executors, administrators or terr [*sic*] tenants or any other who ought to be accountable for the same according to the purport of his Majesty's letter unto us of the 4th of April, a copy whereof we have already sent you. And &c.

To our very good lord, the lord chancellor.

614 James Ware (see *DIB*).

615 Mathew Bentley, see note 171.

616 Text ends abruptly.

617 Henry Lord Docwra, see note 400 and *DIB*.

613. [p. 221] <WARRANT FOR TURNING OVER OF A PRISONER TO THE 4 COURTS BEING IN THE PURSUIVANT'S CUSTODY>

Whereas you have remaining in your custody one R.S. being attached upon our directions these are to will and require you to deliver the body of the said S. unto the marshal of the 4 Courts who is commanded not only to receive but also to detain him in safe custody until our further pleasure be known; whereof you are not to fail. And for &c. Given &c.

To R.G.,[618] one of his Majesty's pursuivants.

614. <WARRANT ~~FOR~~ ^TO^ A COLLECTOR TO BRING IN AN ACCOUNT CONCERNING HOMAGE MONEY>

Whereas we, having taken into our consideration the state of his Majesty's revenue in this kingdom and expecting that the fines in respect of homage should be a good branch thereof, did call before us the officer trusted therewith to give us an account therein and forasmuch as we are informed that the said homage is duly and legally brought in and accounted for throughout the whole kingdom except in the province of Connacht, wherein you have been employed as collector for the homage arising out of the late surrendered lands there for the space of 12 years ended at Easter 1632 for which time we see no certain nor exact account as yet made by you, of which allowance ought to be given and for that it may appear that every of his Majesty's tenants do yearly pay and for what lands and time the same is paid which hitherto hath not not [*sic*] been ~~paid~~ observed the which we take as a great neglect in you; we therefore hereby expressly require and command you that you do forthwith **[p. 222]** make us a just and perfect account and that at the furthest by the end of the next ^Hillary^ term of all such sum & sums of money as you or your substitutes have received in that kind since the said surrenders wherein you are to insert the name of the tenant, the quantity of the land, the barony and county, and the sum by you received respectively and for what time, with a perfect particular for the arrears of your collection & ~~for~~ ^by^ whom, and upon what lands, the same are due. Hereof (as being matters much importing the furtherance of his Majesty's service) you are not to fail, for if you do we will give our order for your impoverishment until you perform and effect the same. Given &c.

To our well beloved E.O., gent,[619] collector of the homage fines for the province of C.[620]

615. <WARRANT TO RIDE POST>

Whereas the bearer hereof H.H. is to make his present repair to the court about certain important affairs these are therefore to will and require you and every of

[618] Robert Gilbert, second pursuivant at arms (see *Lib. mun. pub. Hib.*).

[619] Possibly Edward Ormsby from Tobercurry in Sligo and later sheriff of Co. Galway, b. *c.* 1590–d. after 1664.

[620] Connacht.

you, wheresoever the said H.H. shall land, ^to be careful^ to see him provided from thence from stage to stage of 3 good and able post horses with a guide, he paying therefore according ~~his~~ to his Majesty's usual and accustomed rates; whereof &c. And for &c. Given &c.

To all mayors, sheriffs, justices of the peace, bailiffs, constables, postmasters and to all other his Majesty's officers, ministers and loving subjects whatsoever whom it may concern.

616. [p. 223] <WARRANT FOR ESTABLISHING THE POSSESSION OF A FERRY>

Whereas complaint is made unto us by the humble petition of W.P. that divers persons under colour of grants from the mayor and other officers of the city do still keep several ferryboats upon the river of A. and therein do carry and re-carry passengers occasioned that way and receive money for the same upon that part of the said river by his Majesty lately granted to the said P., notwithstanding our inhibition in that behalf to the contempt of us and the no small prejudice of him the said P.; and because we are credibly informed under the hand of Sir G.R.[621] and Sir W.R.,[622] knights, that the right of granting the said ferries is in his Majesty and that the mayor nor officers aforesaid have any power of right to make any grants thereof by any words in their charter, we do therefore hereby ^will and^ require all such parties as under the authority of the mayor and officers aforesaid, or any others except the said A., do keep the said ferryboats forthwith upon sight hereof to desist and forbear the keeping and usage ~~there~~ of the same at any time hereafter during the term by his Majesty granted to him the said A., and resign and give up the quiet possession thereof unto him to the end he may enjoy the fruits and benefit of our said grant and be enabled to pay his Majesty's rent thereupon reserved until he shall be evicted by due course of law. And hereof they nor any of them may fail. Given &c.

617. [p. 224] <A LICENCE TO DRESS AND KILL MEAT IN LENT>

Whereas we are informed that divers butchers in and about this city and the suburbs of the same and others in the country have heretofore used in the time of Lent to kill and dress beeves,[623] muttons, veals, lambs and kids, [*sic*] selling the same at unreasonable and excessive rates, although the same were ~~neither~~ for the most part neither sweet nor wholesome to the great prejudice of his Majesty's loving subjects and contrary to the law to the intent therefore there may be a prevention and reformation ~~thereof~~ of the like abuses hereafter, we have thought good and so do hereby charge and command all and every the said butchers, as well in the countries ~~as~~ as within this city and suburbs aforesaid, to forbear killing and dressing any beeves, muttons, veals, lambs or kids during the time of the next Lent except he or they so killing the same be licensed by us or some other lawful authority in that behalf. And

621 Sir George Radcliffe (1593–1657), lawyer and politician (see *DIB*).

622 William Ryves, see note 115 and *DIB*.

623 i.e. beef.

because we have given licence to our servant W.H. to kill, dress and sell meat of any the kinds aforesaid within this city and the suburbs thereof during the next Lent aforesaid, these are to will and require you and every of you whom it may concern to take notice hereof and to permit and suffer the said H. to enjoy the full benefit of this our licence without any your lets or molestations, provided that if any person so to be licensed shall sell or offer to make sale of any other meat then such as shall be wholesome, sweet and merchantable or at rates unreasonable upon complaints thereof made unto us, we will cause such exemplary punishment to be inflicted upon them as an offence so dangerous [**p. 225**] and obnoxious unto his Majesty's subjects shall demerit; whereof we hereby require and authorize the mayor and sheriffs and other officers and ministers of this city and suburbs aforesaid to have a special care and to be very diligent in viewing and examining thereof, as also that they or some of them do from time to time cause all such as shall be found killing or selling ~~the sa~~ meat contrary to the tenor hereof to be attached and apprehended and committed to some of his Majesty's pursuivants there to remain during our pleasure. And hereof &c. Given &c.

To our well beloved, the mayor and sheriffs of the city of D.[624] and to all other his Majesty's officers, ministers and loving subjects whom it may concern.

618. <WARRANT FOR A COMMISSION TO ISSUE CONCERNING THE EMBEZZLING OF GOODS>

Whereas C.B., merchant, hath humbly ~~petitioned~~ petitioned unto us setting forth that in N.[625] last a barque of his freighted with wines and other commodities was ~~left~~ cast away and splitted against the rocks near the harbour of Waterford and the most part of the goods contained therein that came on shore were with fraud and force conveyed and taken away by divers of the country people whose persons and names are yet unknown unto him, but for the better discovery thereof and to the end he may endeavour to procure some relief [**p. 226**] against such as have so unconscionably dealt with him he humbly prayed our direction for the issuing forth of a commission whose request therein we have thought fit to grant; and therefore we do hereby pray and require your lordship & forthwith to ~~give~~ cause a commission to issue under the great seal to be directed unto the mayor and recorder of W. thereby giving them full power and authority to enquire and examine, as well ~~at~~ as well [*sic*] by either as all other lawful ways and means whatsoever, who they were by name and where they live that did and have so embezzled ~~his~~ and taken away his the said B. goods, and what the said goods so taken away were, and what the same were worth or might see valued at the said commission, to be returnable with all convenient speed and at the furthest by the first return of the next Easter term. And for &c. Given &c.

To our very good lord, the lord chancellor.

624 Dublin.

625 November.

619. <A WARRANT TO KILL MEAT IN LENT>

Whereas we have thought fit to licence W.H., butcher, to kill, dress and sell meat in Lent as beeves, muttons, veals, lambs, kids within this city of Dublin and the suburbs thereof during the next Lent aforesaid, these are to will and require ~~yo~~ you and every of you whom it may concern to take notice thereof and to permit and suffer the said H. to enjoy the benefit of this our licence without any your lets or molestations, provided that neither he nor any other person under **[p. 227]** him so licensed do make sale of any other meat then such as shall be wholesome, sweet and merchantable, and at rates reasonable upon complaint whereof made unto us we shall cause such exemplary punishment to be inflicted upon them as an offence so dangerous and obnoxious to his Majesty's subjects shall demerit. Whereof ~~wh~~ we hereby require and authorize the mayors and sheriffs and other officers and ministers of this city and suburbs aforesaid to take special ~~notice~~ care and be very diligent in viewing and examining thereof, as also that they or some of them do from time to time cause all such persons as shall be found killing or selling meat without licence or contrary to the tenor hereof, to be attached and apprehended and committed to some of his Majesty's pursuivants there to remain during our pleasure and hereof you nor any of you may not fail. And for so doing this shall be a sufficient warrant. Given &c.

To our well beloved, the mayor and sheriffs of the city of Dublin and to all other his Majesty's officers, ministers and loving subjects whom it may concern.[626]

620. [p. 230] [WARRANT RELATING TO AN OFFICIAL APPOINTMENT]

...*per diem* and also all such other fees profits, perquisites and emoluments whatsoever as do any way appertain or belong unto the said office, and in as large, ample and beneficial manner as the said B. or any other formerly held and enjoyed or of right ought to have held and enjoyed the same, to be exercised by himself or his sufficient deputy or deputies during good behaviour, inserting therein all such clauses as in grants of like nature are usual, and the same fairly engrossed in parchment under your hand to send unto us to be further passed as appertaineth; for doing whereof this shall be your sufficient warrant. Given &c.

To our trusty and well beloved, his Majesty's attorney and solicitor general or either of them.

621. <WARRANT FOR THE CLERK OF THE COUNCIL TO ADMINISTER OATH TO WITNESS BETWEEN PARTY AND PARTY>

Whereas there is a difference depending before us between one G.T., plaintiff, and the lord of C., defendant, which we referred unto Sir W.H. who informeth that the truth of the matter cannot we [*sic*] appear unless the witnesses to ~~bee~~ examined [*sic*] on either side be examined upon oath, we therefore have thought fit and do accordingly hereby require and authorize you (whensoever the said Sir W.H. shall desire it) to repair unto him to administer the oath unto such witnesses as shall be

[626] Pages 228 and 229 are missing in the manuscript.

examined by the said Sir W.H. in this behalf. And for so doing this shall be your sufficient warrant. Given &c.

To our trusty and well beloved Sir P.D., knight,[627] one of the clerks of the Council.

622. [p. 231] <WARRANT FOR THE PLACE OF CHIEF JUSTICE OF THE PROVINCE OF CONNACHT>

These are to will and require you upon sight hereof to draw forth a fiant in due form of law containing a grant from his ~~Majesty's~~ royal Majesty, his heirs and successors, of the place or office of chief justice of the whole province of Connacht unto J.D.,[628] to have and ~~to~~ hold, occupy and enjoy the said office with the incidents and appurtenances thereof unto the said J.D. *quamdiu in executione officii praedicti se bene gesserit* together with a grant from his Majesty, his heirs and successors, unto the said J.D. and his assigns, of the annual fee or stipend of 100*li.* sterling current money of and in England so long as he shall continue in the said office at ~~two~~ the two usual feasts of St Michael the Archangel and Easter by equal portions by the hands of the treasurer, vice-treasurer or other general-receiver out of his Majesty's revenue of this kingdom, the first payment thereof to begin at Easter next, and of all other authorities, ~~pre~~ privileges, fees, allowances, perquisites, profits, advantages and benefits whatsoever at any time ~~her~~ heretofore any way ^belonging^, incident or appertaining, and in as ample ~~manner~~ and beneficial manner as G.U., T.D.[629] or any other who did exercise or enjoy the said office, did or ought to use ^or^ enjoy the same. And that for the better encouragement of the said J.D. in his Majesty's service or clause, to be inserted therein from his Majesty, his heirs and successors, to licence and authorize the said J.D. notwithstanding the said office to continue his practice as a pleader or **[p. 232]** councillor at law in all his Majesty's courts and in all causes, although it be against his Majesty, his heirs and successors, in any suit or cause in his highness's Court of Castle Chamber, nor in any suit or cause arising or growing with the five counties of Galway, Roscommon, Sligo, Mayo and Leitrim in the said province of Connacht together with such beneficial clauses as are usually contained in such grants. And the same to send ~~us~~ to us fairly engrossed in parchment &c. Given &c.

623. <WARRANT FOR A PARK>

These are to will and require you forthwith to draw up a fiant in due form of law containing a grant from his Majesty, ~~office~~ his heirs and successors, of free warren unto our right trusty & well beloved W. Lord B, earl of W,[630] his heirs & assigns, throughout the several towns and villages of F. &c. within the county of W.[631]; and

[627] Paul Davies (Davis) (d. 1672), clerk of the privy council and secretary of state (see *DIB*).

[628] James Donnellan, see note 441 and *DIB.*

[629] G. U. (unresolved), Thomas Dillon. It is possible that 'G.U' is an error and the srcibe meant to write 'G. O.' for Geffrey Osbaldeston who held the office prior to Donnellan (see *Lib. mun. pub. Hib.*).

[630] This is a mistake by the secretary who inserted 'W' for an 'M'. It is William Lord Brabazon, earl of Meath, *c.* 1580–1651.

[631] Westmeath.

the said fiant is likewise to contain his Majesty's free leave and licence unto him the said earl of M. to enclose with any materials fit for enclosure so much land with the said towns as may contain [blank] pearches[632] and to hold the same so enclosed as a park with all liberties pertaining to a park, and at his pleasure to store and keep the same replenished with deer so that none hunt or disturb any thing therein that to a park pertaineth under the pain ordained by his Majesty's laws in that behalf and of the forfeiture of ten pounds sterling, inserting therein also **[p. 233]** a grant of his Majesty's most gracious and free pardon unto him the said earl of M. made for an enclosure he hath made of ~~pear~~ [blank] pearches or thereabouts of land within the said towns or some of them. And the same fairly engrossed in parchment under your hands to send unto us to be further passed as appertaineth and according to his Majesty's gracious letters of the – last, a copy whereof we have herewith sent. And for &c. Given &c.

To our trusty and well beloved, his Majesty's attorney and solicitor general, or either of them.

624. <WARRANT TO BE LORD CHIEF JUSTICE OF THE COMMON PLEAS>

Whereas amongst other punishments inflicted lately in his Majesty's High Court of Star Chamber in England upon Sir D.S., Viscount Kilmallock,[633] he was censured to be deprived of the office ~~of~~ ^or^ place of chief justice of his Majesty's highness's Court of Common Pleas in this kingdom, which said office or place being so become void his Majesty hath been graciously pleased to grant unto our right trusty and well beloved Sir G.L., knight,[634] second baron of the Court of Exchequer there. These are therefore to will and require you forthwith to draw up a **[p. 234]** fiant in due form of law containing a grant from his Majesty of the said office or place of ~~just~~ chief justice of the Court of Common Pleas unto the said G.L. together with all such fees, wages, robes, stipends, jurisdictions, authorities, augmentations, allowances, entertainments, perquisites, profits, emoluments, pre-eminences, privileges and advantages whatsoever as the said Sir D.S. or Sir N.W. or Sir W.W., knights,[635] or any ~~of them~~ other chief justice of that court formerly had enjoyed or received by virtue or reason of the said office, or are belonging or anywise incident or appertaining to the same, to hold, exercise and enjoy the said office with all the said fees, profits, perquisites, allowances and pre-eminences during his Majesty's pleasure in as large, ample and beneficial manner to all intents and purposes ~~as~~ whatsoever as the said Sir D.S., Sir N.W., Sir W.W., or any other chief justice of that court formerly had and enjoyed the same, according to the purport of his Majesty's letters unto us in that behalf of the 13th of March last, a copy whereof for your better information we have hereby sent. And for &c. Given &c.

To our ^trusty &^ well beloved, his Majesty's attorney and solicitor general, or either of them.

632 i.e. purchase.

633 Dominick Sarsfield, see note 11.

634 Gerard Lowther, see note 17.

635 Sir Dominick Sarsfield or Sir Nicholas Walshe or Sir William Weston (see *Lib. mun. pub. Hib.*).

625. <WARRANT CONCERNING WINE AND AQUA VITA>

Whereas the sheriff of the county of L. hath upon our letters of the last of February made his return unto us under his hand that the several undernamed persons have utterly refused to tell him [**p. 235**] by what licence and authority they sell wine or aqua vita or what rent they pay, to whom, or what gales, in manifest contempt of our directions issued to the said sheriff, these are therefore to will and require you to attach the bodies of the undernamed persons wheresoever they shall be found and to bring them immediately before us to answer their contempts and them not to set at liberty or discharge without our special directions, hereof you are not to fail. And &c. dat. &c.

To any of his Majesty's pursuivants.

626. <WARRANT FOR FAIRS & MARKETS>

Whereas our right trusty and well beloved the earl of Clanricard and St Albans[636] hath petitioned unto us that we would be pleased to afford unto him the benefit of a weekly market and two fairs yearly to be kept at the town of A. in the county of R.,[637] whose request therein we did not think fit to grant until we were first assured that the granting thereof would not entrench upon any other neighbouring fairs or markets, wherein we have received lately full satisfaction from the last & late going judges of assizes for that circuit who caused it to be enquired of by the grand jury who found that the same would not be any [**p. 236**] prejudice to any other fairs or markets as aforesaid. These are therefore to will & require you forthwith to draw up a fiant in due form of law containing a grant from his Majesty unto the said e[arl] and his heirs of one weekly market to be kept on every Monday and of two fairs yearly, the one upon St Peter and Paul's day and the other upon the fourteenth of September being the Exaltation of the Cross, referring thereout the sum of 40*li.* sterling rent to be paid unto his Majesty, inserting therein all such clauses as in like grants are usual. And the same &c. And for &c. Given &c.

To our right trusty and well beloved, his Majesty's attorney & solicitor general, or either of them.

627. <A WARRANT AUTHORIZING THE COMMISSIONERS FOR ALE AND BEER LICENCES TO CALL ALL SUCH PERSONS BEFORE THEM WHO SELL ALE OR BEER WITHOUT LICENCE>

Whereas, as ~~welb~~ well by ~~the~~ his Majesty's commission under the great seal of this kingdom for licensing of alehouses as also by our letters pursuing the same, you and the rest of the commissioners therein named are authorized not only to execute all the power and authority thereby committed unto you but also such ~~further~~ further directions and instructions as from time [to] time shall be sent unto you, and whereas

636 Ulick Burke, earl of Clanricard and St Albans (see *DIB*).

637 Athlone in the county of Roscommon.

we are informed that notwithstanding the same many and the greater number of those that do sell [**p. 237**] ale and beer throughout the kingdom, and divers of them of the better sort do still ^sell^ without licence contrary to his Majesty's proclamation published in that behalf, to the evil example of others to do the like and the great discouragement of those few that have already conformed themselves to the said proclamations; seeing the said delinquents escape still unpunished and that no course is yet taken to reduce them to conformity & to recover the losses sustained thereby by his Majesty in his revenues, we therefore, taking the same into our consideration, have thought fit and do hereby require and authorize any of the commissioners as often as occasion shall require to call before you all and every such person or persons, as well soldiers or others, as you shall find to sell ale or beer without licence contrary to the said proclamations, either within liberties or without, and to take bonds of every such person or persons with one sufficient surety in 10*li.* sterling to his Majesty's use for the person appearance [*sic*] of the said delinquents in his Majesty's Court of Exchequer, and to certify his offence thither that he may be proceeded against in that kind as by the commission and proclamation is appointed, and upon refusal of any such delinquents to enter into bond as aforesaid then you to commit them to the next gaol there to remain until they shall become bound accordingly. And we likewise require every such gaoler to whom any such shall be committed from time to time to [**p. 238**] receive & safely to keep them, and if any constable shall refuse or delay to put any of your warrants in execution against any delinquents then you are likewise to bind over the said constable to appear before us to answer his contempt, or upon his refusal to become bound to commit him likewise as aforesaid, willing and requiring all mayors, sheriffs, portreeves, high sheriffs, petty constables, bailiffs & all other officers whatsoever to be aiding and assisting unto you in the due execution hereof as often as need shall require. Given &c.

To our trusty and well beloved, the commissioners for the ordering of alehouses and to all others whom it may concern.

628. <WARRANT FOR PASSING THE ILE P.[638] AND LONGER ILE TO BE HOLDEN BY THE NAME OF N.[639]>[640]

These are to will and require you forthwith to draw up a fiant in due form of law containing a grant from his Majesty, his heirs and successors, unto Sir J.L., knight, and others and their heirs forever, of the Ile called the Ile Plowden or Long Ile, between 39 & 40 degrees north latitude and of 40 leagues square of the adjoining continent, to be holden of his Majesty of his Crown of Ireland by the name of New Albion in the nature of a county palatine with such privileges, additions and dignities to the said Sir E.P.,[641] his deputies & [**p. 239**] assigns, as first governor of the premises and

638 Plowden.

639 New Albion.

640 See Edward C. Carter II and Clifford Lewis III, 'Sir Edmund Plowden and the New Albion Charter, 1632–1785' in *The Pennsylvania Magazine of History and Biography* (April, 1959), pp 150–79.

641 Edmund Plowden.

so successively to every governor as hereafter shall be or have been heretofore granted unto other governors of other colonies of the like nature, and by name unto that of Sir George C., late Lord Baltimore,[642] deceased, in Newfoundland together with other ^usual^ grants and privileges likewise accustomably given for the governing & ordering their planters and subordinates. And you are likewise to insert in the said fiant a grant of free leave and licence from his Majesty for the said colony inhabiting there to be upon the request of the governors and principals from time to time furnished and supplied out of this kingdom of Ireland with corn, cattle and ^such^ other necessaries as they shall have use of and also be furnished and have power to carry artificers & labourers hence into the said colony. And the same fairly engrossed in parchment under your hand to send us to be further passed as appertaineth and as his Majesty hath required by his letters of the 24th of July in the 8th year of his reign, a copy whereof together with ^that of^ the adventurer's petition unto his highness for your better instruction we have herewith sent you. And for &c. Given &c.

To our trusty and well beloved, his Majesty's attorney and solicitor general, or either of them.

[642] George Calvert, Lord Baltimore and former secretary of state to James VI and I (see *ODNB*).

WARRANT NO. 629

15 MAY 1639

MARSH'S LIBRARY, MS Z4.2.1

629. [f. 13] <WARRANT FOR APPREHENDING DANIEL HOWARD OF BANDONBRIDGE> [15 MAY 1639]

These are in his Majesty's name by virtue of his highness's commission for causes ecclesiastical under the great seal of Ireland to us and others directed to will and require you that forthwith upon receipt hereof you apprehend and attach, or cause to be apprehended and attached, the body of Daniel Howard of Bandonbridge within the county of Cork, tanner, wheresoever he may be found as well in places exempt as not exempt; and thereupon you detain and keep him under safe custody and bring him before us or others, our colleagues his Majesty's said commissioners, [or] any three or more of us in that behalf appointed in the cathedral church of St Patrick's, Dublin, the second session of the next Trinity term being on Friday, the one and twentieth day of June next ensuing, the date hereof to answer unto such matters (as on his Majesty's behalf shall be objected against him[)]. And for the better execution hereof we will and require, in his Majesty's name by the authority aforesaid, all justices of the peace, mayors, sheriffs, bailiffs, constables and all other his Majesty's officers and loving subjects, to be aiding and assisting unto you in and about the execution hereof as they tender his Majesty's service, and will answer the contrary at their perils. Given under our hands and the seal of the said court, the fifteenth of May, *anno domini* 1639.

Robertus Fenben
Benjamin Culme
Edward Parry[643]

<*Concordat cum decreto*: John Pilh.>

To John Mottershed, one of the messengers of his Majesty's High Commission Court, & to George Black, their deputy or deputies.

643 Edward Parry (d. 1650), dean of Waterford and later bishop of Killaloe; a member of the High Commission for Ecclesiastical Causes (see *DIB*).

INDEX

Note references are to warrant number. Place names have been modernised where possible, otherwise they are as they appear in the manuscript. Variants for personal and place names appear in parentheses after the principal or modern form. References to information contained in footnotes is indicated by n *after a warrant number.*